BIRTH COUNTS
statistics of pregnancy and childbirth

Volume 1, text

Alison Macfarlane

Miranda Mugford

with bibliographic assistance from Marie-Anne Martin

London: The Stationery Office

Applications for reproduction should be made in writing to The Stationery Office Limited, St Crispins, Duke Street, Norwich NR3 1PD.

The information contained in this publication is believed to be correct at the time of manufacture. Whilst care has been taken to ensure that the information is accurate, the publisher can accept no responsibility for any errors or omissions or for changes to the details given.

Alison Macfarlane, Miranda Mugford have asserted their moral rights under the Copyright, Designs and Patents Act 1988, to be identified as the authors of this work.

"Cover illustration supplied courtesy of The Stationery Office."

First published 1984

Second edition 2000

Volume 1: ISBN 0 11 621049 4

also available, Volume 2: ISBN 0 11 620917 8

Published by The Stationery Office and available from:

The Stationery Office
(mail, telephone and fax orders only)
PO Box 29, Norwich NR3 1GN
General enquiries/Telephone orders 0870 600 5522
Fax orders 0870 600 5533

www.the-stationery-office.co.uk

The Stationery Office Bookshops
123 Kingsway, London WC2B 6PQ
020 7242 6393 Fax 020 7242 6412
68–69 Bull Street, Birmingham B4 6AD
0121 236 9696 Fax 0121 236 9699
33 Wine Street, Bristol BS1 2BQ
0117 926 4306 Fax 0117 929 4515
9–21 Princess Street, Manchester M60 8AS
0161 834 7201 Fax 0161 833 0634
16 Arthur Street, Belfast BT1 4GD
028 9023 8451 Fax 028 9023 5401
The Stationery Office Oriel Bookshop
18–19 High Street, Cardiff CF1 2BZ
029 2039 5548 Fax 029 2038 4347
71 Lothian Road, Edinburgh EH3 9AZ
0870 606 5566 Fax 0870 606 5588

The Stationery Office's Accredited Agents
(*see* Yellow Pages)

and through good booksellers

Printed in the United Kingdom for The Stationery Office by Albert Gait Ltd.

TJ000110 C12 5/00 9385 12776

Preface

Amongst the most frequently used health statistics are those relating to childbirth and infancy. They include current and past trends in demography, survival and other measures of health and the availability, use and effectiveness of relevant medical and preventive services. Such information is required for population projections and the planning and monitoring of health and social services. Moreover, certain measures, such as levels of infant mortality have long been recognised as sensitive and important indicators of population health. This is because the wellbeing and growth rate of fetuses and infants reflect the preconceptional health and growth of their parents as well as predicting the likely quality of their own health as adults.

Such information is therefore much in demand but needs to be derived from a large variety of sources, most, but not all, being annual reviews of national statistics. The first edition of *Birth counts* demonstrated very quickly to NHS staff, voluntary organisations and teachers of many backgrounds, the value of having such data so easily accessible in one source. This new edition, as well as providing the updated information, also extends the availability of corresponding statistics from Scotland, Wales and Northern Ireland, a facility which will become increasingly important. The inclusion of detailed explanations of the effects of changes in methods of data collection and definitions are particularly valuable, and the clear illustrations and scholarly historical background make these potentially dry facts come to life in an eminently readable form.

Eva Alberman
Professor Emeritus, University of London

Foreword to the second edition

Birth counts is an attempt to review and bring together statistics collected by government departments and the National Health Service in England, Wales, Scotland and Northern Ireland about pregnancy, childbirth and newborn babies and the socio-economic circumstances in which they are born. This volume is a guide to the relevant data and the data themselves are brought together in the separate second volume.

Since the first edition was written in the early 1980s and published in 1984, many changes have taken place in the National Health Service and these have affected the scope and nature of the data collected. We have retained many but not all the data published in the first edition, while focussing on data for the 1990s. In addition, we have shifted our emphasis from cross-sectional data to time series. This edition of *Birth counts* was compiled at a time of continuing change in official statistics. The text was written in the first half of 1999 and revised early in 2000.

The moves towards devolution have been accompanied by a demand for 'national statistics' for all the four countries of the United Kingdom, so we have increased our coverage of data from Scotland and Northern Ireland, which were under-represented in the first edition. We have also included some data from the Irish Republic, as a reflection of the growing interest in 'cross border' statistics.

In producing *Birth counts* we have collaborated closely with statistical staff in the government statistical service, the Northern Ireland Statistics and Research Agency, the National Health Service and the Central Statistics Office of the Irish Republic. At the same time, *Birth counts* has formed part of the work programme of the National Perinatal Epidemiology Unit, an independent research unit funded by the Department of Health, as part of its policy research programme. We should like to stress that the responsibility for views expressed in *Birth counts* and any errors which may emerge are ours and that our views are not necessarily shared by the organisations which have provided the data or by the Department of Health, which has funded the work.

Alison Macfarlane
National Perinatal Epidemiology Unit
Oxford

Miranda Mugford
University of East Anglia
Norwich

March 2000

Acknowledgements

The data we have collated and presented in the two volumes of *Birth counts* come from a wide range of sources and many people took part in the process of compiling them. We should like to thank all the people involved and apologise to anyone whose name we have inadvertently omitted.

Our co-authors in Volume 2 worked in the National Perinatal Epidemiology Unit at various stages in the production of the book. Jane Henderson was responsible for most of the initial work of constructing and compiling the tables related to Chapters 7 and 11, with help from Sarah Howard, Toby Gosden and Richard Adams. Ann Furtado acted as administrator for the project as a whole, Joanne Stevens did the statistical programming needed for a considerable number of ad-hoc analyses and Alistair Dunn organised the structure for compiling and holding the tables on our computer network. Along with them, we should like to thank Ursula Bowler, who played an important part in preparing the tables for publication, Madalena Marques for help with data entry, Marie-Anne Martin for providing bibliographic assistance with Volume 1, Lesley Kumiega for seeking out and obtaining the various publications we required, Nadine Howard, Lynne Roberts and Lynda Pilcher for help with preparing the text and index for publication, Andy King for help with checking the proofs of the text and tables, Hazel Ashurst and Sarah Ayers for computing support and Jessica Wu for programming help during her short time in the Unit. Rona McCandlish, Sally Marchant, Jo Garcia, Anne Quinn, Ann Johnson, Valerie King, Simon Gates, Kirstie McKenzie-McHarg, Leslie Davidson and Peter Brocklehurst commented on drafts of the text, and Janet Keene and other people in the National Perinatal Epidemiology Unit helped in many ways.

Eva Alberman, Mildred Blaxter, Jean Chapple and Catherine Law formally reviewed the text for the Department of Health and Edward Higgs and Charles Webster reviewed it for historical accuracy. Beverley Botting, Susan Cole, Terry Falconer, Jenny Griffin, Meg Goodman, Douglas Harding, Lesz Lancucki, Margaret McGovern and Maureen Scott reviewed all or parts of the text. We should like to thank all the people involved in reviewing the text of *Birth counts* for their help and constructive criticism.

In addition, we have received a huge amount of help and advice from people working in the Government Statistical Service and the National Health Service who have sought out data for us and advised us about their interpretation.

In the Office for National Statistics, Penny Babb, Lois Cook, Nirupa Dattani, John Haskey, Deborah Lader, Kath Moser, Vera Ruddock, Lesley Sanders, Jeremy Schuman and Denis Till checked the sections of the text relevant to their area of work and the related tables. Nigel Physick used his extensive experience to check in meticulous detail the tables of data about infant mortality and abortion. Rosie McNiece and Jen Hollowell extracted data from the General Practice Research Database and helped us undertake the special analyses funded by the Department of Health. Jamie Knight and Seeromanie Harding produced tables from the ONS Longitudinal Study. Pat Broad and Paul Hyatt guided us through the maze of implications of changes in arrangements for publishing official data and gave us much valuable help and advice. Gaynor Tizzard of ONS Geography produced the maps in Appendix 5. Abigail Humber and Tom Gambrell helped find the publications we needed in ONS library. Many other people in ONS, including Anita Brock, Siobhan Carey, John Charlton, Nicola Cooper, Frances Drever, Ruth Edwards, Marion Fazackerley, Haroulla Filakti, Justine Fitzpatrick, Kate Foster, Linda Hart, Mike Hawkins, Simon Huxstep, Liz Kirby, Jenny Jones, Dave Lambert, Dami Lawal, Doug Newbiggin, Mike Quinn, Shiva Satkunam, Kay Sumpner and Rebecca Wood provided us with data and information.

Lesz Lancucki coordinated our requests for data from many different parts of the Department of Health and Georgina Baines did special tabulations of data from the Hospital Episode Statistics. Many other people in London and Leeds, including Mohammed Adrish, Suzanne Ainsworth, Clive Allanso, Roberts Baggs, Patsy Bailey, Jeanette Barrett, Imogen Briers, Marcus Calton, Russell Cavis, Helen Clark, Lou Coleman, Ann Custance, Karen Dooley, Simeon Duckworth, Malcolm Dudlyke, Judith Ellison, Norman Gallop, Graham Geddes, Stella Gondo, Gill Guzder, Irene Harmer, David Hewitt, David Hubbard, Craig Keenan, Mujaid Khan, Julie Lawlor, Gwyneth Lewis, Wincen Lowe, Rosemary Matheson, Corinne McDonald, Tracey Morton, Karen Nicolaysen, Susan O'Boyle, Damon Palmer, Noshad Qayyum, Richard Reed, Jim Rodger, Olu Sangowawa, Andy Savva, Mark Stephenson, Bhavi Surti, Emily Thrippleton, Yvonne Walton, Richard Winstanley and Robert Yates responded helpfully to our requests for their data.

Douglas Harding provided data from the Communicable Disease Surveillance Centre and Angus Nicoll advised us about the Centre's research on communicable disease in relation to pregnancy. Sue Ashbrook and Ian Simms provided us with data at an earlier stage. Pat Tookey from the Institute of Child Health provided data from the National Congenital Rubella Surveillance Programme.

Vivien Trew acted as a point of contact for data from all parts of the Welsh Office, now renamed the National Assembly for Wales. Michelle Davies of the Welsh Health Common Services Agency, now known as Health

Solutions, Wales did ad hoc tabulations of data from the Patient Episode Database Wales.

In Scotland, Caroline Capocci, Lynne Dalgleish, Roslyn Robertson and Carole Welch provided us with data in electronic and paper form from the General Register Office. Mark Hollinsworth and Beatrice Cant provided ad-hoc tabulations and comments on our use of data from the Information and Statistics Division of the Common Services Agency for the NHS in Scotland. Other ISD staff, including Jim Chalmers, Ross Elder, Susan Fraser, Conan Fyvie, Philip Johnston, Etta Shanks, Elaine Strange, Brian Whiteman, and Steven Williamson also provided data and advice. Carol Calvert, David Marr and Diane Stewart of the Scottish Executive Children's Social Work Statistics, formerly part of the Scottish Office Social Work Statistics Group, helped us to select data about services for children in Scotland.

John Gordon and Patricia Hamilton of the General Register Office Northern Ireland and Maire Rodgers and Jacqui Hyvart of the Northern Ireland Statistics Research Agency gave us help with vital statistics for Northern Ireland. In the Department of Health and Social Services, Jennifer Ball, Fergal Bradley, Karen Campbell, Michael Durkan, Owen Johnston, Sean McCann, Herbie McFarland, Pat McGlew, Richard McLardy, Jenny Orr, Stephen Sharp, Pauline Sheals and Caroline White provided data about health and social services and valuable insights into how they are collected.

Mary Heanue of the Central Statistics Office of the Republic of Ireland provided an extensive range of vital statistics and invaluable observations about how they are collected and compiled. Elaine Yeates and Paul Ell of the Database of Irish Historical Statistics at the Queen's University of Belfast gave us data for earlier years for both parts of Ireland. The Small Area Health Research Unit at Trinity College Dublin assembled the map of Ireland in Appendix 5.

Turning to smaller islands, Susan Cain and Peter McMahon gave us data from the Isle of Man. Yvonne Kaill and David Jeffs provided data for Guernsey, while John Harvey, Jill Birbeck and Richard Grainger gave us data for Jersey.

Jim Foley, Gary Watson, David Walton, Irene Jordan, Paul Lavery and Lisa Smith of the Department for Education and Employment provided and explained changes in data collected about education for children with special needs. Margaret Ayres, Jenny Ramsey, Dominic Asante and Vin Thakkar of the Home Office extracted data and documentation about trends in criminal offences in relation to children and illegal abortion.

For international data, we should like to thank Odile Frank and Georgina Kainer for data from the World Health Organisation's database and Jill Boreham and Elaine Campbell of the Clinical Trials Service Unit for help in manipulating the data. Michael Blakemore of the r-cade project at the University of Durham provided data from Eurostat and Godelieve Masuy-Stroobant of the Université Catholique de Louvain allowed us to reproduce data from her comparative European studies.

Turning to people outside realm of official statistics, we should like to thank Richard Baranowski of the Human Fertilisation and Embryology Authority, Liz McAnulty of the United Kingdom Council for Nursing, Midwifery and Health Visiting, Glynnis Mayes and Meryl Thomas of the English National Board, Sophie Robinson and Elaine Seth-Smith of the Maternity Alliance, Joanna Goodrich and Dave Leon of London School of Hygiene and Tropical Medicine and Brian Williams of the University of Nottingham.

Annelise Savill of the Stationery Office initiated the arrangements for publication and flattered us to write a new edition of Volume 1. Corinne Barker and Janine Eves dealt with the book at production stages and Sally Downes was responsible for graphic design.

In addition to the people we are able to name, these data could not have been compiled without the effort of large numbers of other people, most of whom we have never met. They include other people working in the Government Statistical Service, local registrars of births, marriages and deaths, people working in NHS medical records departments, other NHS staff whose work includes data collection on top of their normal duties and members of the public who fill in forms and provide information about their lives and circumstances.

We should like to thank the Controllers of Her Majesty's Stationery Office for permission to reproduce material from the text of the first edition of *Birth counts* and for permission to reproduce data from the Office for National Statistics, the Department of Health, the Department for Education and Employment, the Home Office, the Human Fertilisation and Embryology Authority, the General Practice Research Database, the Department of Social Security, the National Assembly for Wales, the General Register Office for Scotland, the Scottish Executive, the General Register Office Northern Ireland, the Northern Ireland Statistics and Research Agency and the Department of Health, Social Services and Public Safety of the Northern Ireland Executive. In addition, we should like to thank the Public Health Laboratory Service Communicable Disease Surveillance Centre for permission to reproduce data it collates, including data collected on behalf of the Registrar General and data collected by the Institute of Child Health London, the Scottish Centre for Infection and Environmental Health, the RCOG National Study of HIV in Pregnancy, the British Paediatric Surveillance Unit, the Oxford Haemophilia Centre and by the Public Health Laboratory Service itself. We should also like to thank the National Congenital Rubella Surveillance Programme, the Management Group of the Oxford Register of Early Childhood Impairment, the English National Board for Nursing, Midwifery and Health Visiting, the United Kingdom Central Council for Nursing, Midwifery and Health Visiting, the Information and Statistics Division of the Common Services Agency of the NHS in Scotland (ISD Scotland), the Central Statistics Office of the Irish Republic, the Civil Registry of the Isle of Man, the States of Guernsey Board of Health, the States of Jersey Health and Social Services, the World Health Organisation, and the United Nations Children's Fund (UNICEF) for permission to reproduce their data.

We should also like to thank the following for permission to reproduce data and literary material from other sources: Ann Oakley for an extract from *Birth, poverty and wealth* by her father, Richard Titmuss, Oxford University Press for material from *The Oxford dictionary of nursery rhymes* by Iona and Peter Opie, *Maternity in Great Britain* by the Joint Committee of the Royal College of Obstetricians and Gynaecologists and the Population Investigation Committee and from an article in *Health Education Research*, Janet Russell for permission to quote from her song *Breastfeeding baby in the park*, Fellsongs Music for permission to quote from *Childbirth shanty* by Sisters Unlimited, Lian Tanner for permission to quote from her song *The IPD*, the agent for Cecil Sharp's estate for verses from the manuscripts of Cecil Sharp, the Society of Authors for permission to quote from the preface to *The doctor's dilemma* by George Bernard Shaw, the English Folk Dance and Song Society for permission to quote from the journals of the Society, Leslie Shepard for a copy of *The baby farmer* from the Leslie Shepard Collection, Leon Rosselson for permission to quote from his songs *That's the way the wheels turn* and *Don't get married girls*, Harmony Music for permission to quote from *Palaces of gold* in *Look here* by Leon Rosselson, Lawrence and Wishart for permission to quote from *The long peggin' awl* in *Folk song in England* by AL Lloyd, Susan Macran and Dave Leon and for permission to quote from their analyses of data from the Office of Population Censuses and Surveys, Brian Williams for permission to quote his unpublished data, the Maternity Alliance for permission to quote extracts from *Mother courage: letters from mothers in poverty at the end of the century* edited by Christine Gowdridge, Susan Williams and Margaret Wynn, Godelieve Masuy-Stroobant for permission to quote data from her published work, the BMJ Publishing Group for permission to reproduce extracts from *Fifty years of progress as shown by vital statistics* by Percy Stocks in the *British Medical Journal* 1950; 1: 54-57 and *Reproductive mortality* by Valerie Beral in the *British Medical Journal*; 1979; 2: 632-634, the Confidential Enquiry into Stillbirths and Deaths in Infancy for permission to quote information from its fifth *Annual report*, Blackwell's Science for permission to quote data from *A thousand cases of abortion* by TN Parish in the *Journal of Obstetrics and Gynaecology of the British Empire* 1935; 42: 1107-1121, the Royal College of Obstetricians and Gynaecologists for permission to quote an extract from the *Report of the working party on unplanned pregnancy* and r-cade at the University of Durham for permission to reproduce data from Eurostat.

Contents

Text tables

Figures

Figure 1.1

Florence Nightingale's inscription in William Farr's copy of her book, *Introductory notes on lying-in institutions*

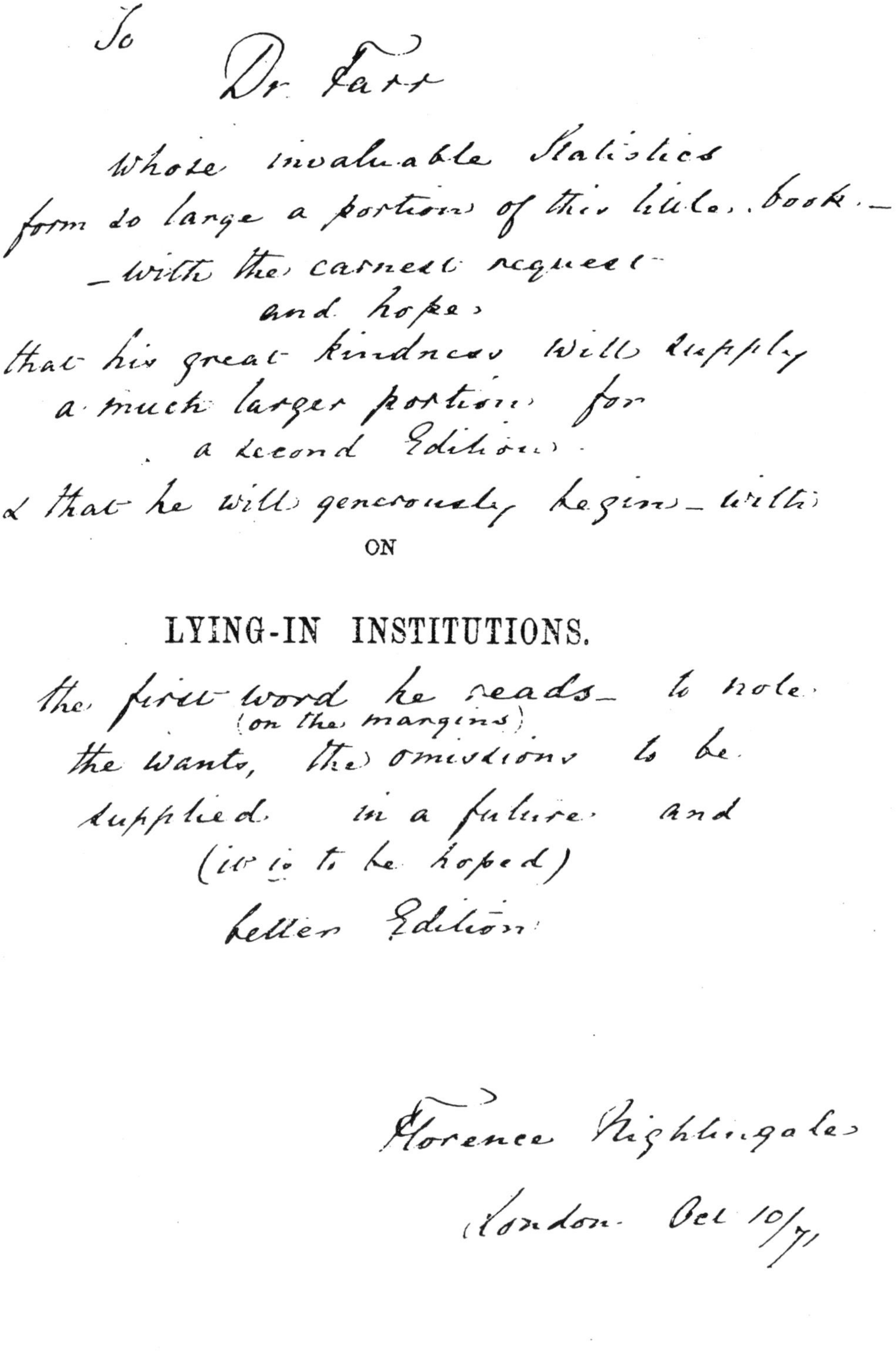

To

Dr Farr

whose invaluable Statistics
form so large a portion of this little book. —
— with the earnest request
and hope
that his great kindness will supply
a much larger portion for
a Second Edition.
& that he will generously begin — with

ON

LYING-IN INSTITUTIONS.

the first word he reads — to note
(on the margins)
the wants, the omissions to be
supplied in a future and
(it is to be hoped)
better Edition

Florence Nightingale
London Oct 10/71

1 Introduction

'The death rates of young children are, in my opinion, among the most important studies in sanitary science. In the first place, their tender young lives, as compared with the more hardened and acclimatised lives of the adult population, furnish a very sensitive test of sanitary circumstances; so that differences of infantile death rate are, under certain qualifications, the best proof of differences of household condition in any number of compared districts. And secondly, those places where infants are most apt to die are necessarily the places where survivors are most apt to be sickly; and where if they struggle through a scrofulous childhood to realise an abortive puberty, they beget a still sicklier brood than themselves, even less capable of labour and even less capable of education. It cannot be too distinctly recognised that a high local mortality of children must almost necessarily denote a high local prevalence of those causes which determine a degeneration of the race.'

John Simon, 1858[1]

The conditions in which most children in this country are born and grow up have changed beyond recognition since these words were written but infant mortality is still considered to be a sensitive indicator of the health of a population. Childbirth remains an emotive and controversial subject and although the issues at stake change, statistics continue to be quoted when they are discussed. All too often, however, they have been used, as a number of writers have put it, 'as a drunken man uses lamp-posts - for support rather than illumination.'[2,3]

Two areas in particular have been the subjects of heated debate over the past thirty years or so. Firstly, there has been controversy about the place of technological intervention in the management of pregnancy, childbirth and early infancy. Secondly, considerable attention has been focused on differences in stillbirth and infant mortality rates between countries and within the same country. Often these two themes have been interwoven and statistics have been used by some people to suggest that high rates are the result of too little technological intervention and by others to suggest that they result from too much.

Most people would now agree that there is insufficient evidence to support such simplistic explanations. They ignore both the impacts of social and economic factors on the outcome of pregnancy and the complexity of the processes involved in evaluating clinical effectiveness. Despite this, these controversies have undoubtedly contributed to the interest among midwives, obstetricians, paediatricians and people working in the community health services for collecting data to help them monitor and audit their own work.

1

An unfortunate side effect of this welcome trend has been a certain amount of duplication of effort. This has often arisen because the people involved have been unaware of the extent to which data are already being collected by others. The idea of compiling the first edition of *Birth counts* arose during discussions about the desirability of doing a fourth national birth survey in 1982 on the lines of those already done in 1946,[4] 1958,[5] and 1970.[6] It turned out that many of the data which people wanted to see derived from such a survey were already collected routinely by official bodies. Most people were unaware of this because the data are scattered in a variety of official publications and some are not published at all. The birth surveys gave an invaluable picture of birth at the time but were based on only a week's births. They are far more important for the longitudinal studies which have arisen out of them and have been a key tool in developing what has come to be called 'life course epidemiology.'[7] The people in the samples have been followed up in a series of surveys throughout the rest of their lives, so a wide range data about their health and social circumstances as children and adults can be related to the data about their birth.

Our first aim in compiling *Birth counts* was to bring together, in the second volume, data relevant to pregnancy, childbirth and newborn babies which are collected by or on behalf of central government and the National Health Service in the four countries of the United Kingdom. In doing this in our first edition, we followed the precedent set by the Committee on Child Health Services, which had brought together the available data on the subject in the second volume of its influential report published in 1976.[8]

Our second aim is to provide a guide to the data. This first volume is intended both to help readers find the data which we do not have room to include, and also to enable them to keep up to date with data for future years, as and when they are produced. To complement this, our third aim is to describe how the data are produced in order to help readers interpret them.

After outlining, in Chapter 2, the way data are defined, classified and collected, we go on, in Chapter 3, to show the variation in the outcome of pregnancy from time to time and place to place within Britain and Ireland. The next chapter describes the data collected about fertility control and fetal loss. This is followed by a discussion, in Chapters 5, 6, and 7, of measures of the characteristics and circumstances of parents and babies and the care they receive. In doing this we attempt to assess the extent to which these factors are associated with the outcome of pregnancy.

The principal measure of the outcome of pregnancy which can be derived from routinely collected data is mortality. This includes stillbirths, deaths at various stages of infancy and maternal deaths. Maternal deaths have fortunately now become so rare that statistics based on deaths occurring in a single year can no longer be subjected to a detailed breakdown, but as we show in Chapter 10, data for a number of years can be combined for analysis.

While statistics based on stillbirths and deaths in the first year of life are widely used, these deaths too are becoming increasingly rare. Even where it is possible to aggregate data for several years, the death rates for small populations, such as those served by district health authorities, are therefore based on small numbers of events. This makes it difficult to distinguish real differences from chance variation. Ideally, then, it would be preferable to use a measure which would be based on a larger proportion of the babies born. Measures of morbidity, that is of illness or disability, might satisfy this criterion. There are considerable problems both in agreeing on how to define such measures and in collecting suitable data. These problems are discussed in Chapters 8 and 9 and again in relation to morbidity in the parents, in Chapter 10. In our selection and discussion of data about impairment and illness in childhood we have focussed mainly on morbidity in children in the first year of life and morbidity in relation to circumstances at birth. We have not attempted more extensive reviews of routinely collected data on child health as they have been well covered in other publications.[9,10]

An item of data which is collected routinely and can also be considered in some senses to be a proxy measure of morbidity in a population is the incidence of low birthweight. Birthweight is certainly highly correlated with mortality, with the smallest babies carrying the highest risk of death, but it does have limitations as a measure of morbidity. Some small babies, in particular many of those whose weight is at the upper limit of the range defined as 'low birthweight', are perfectly healthy. The extent to which this happens varies between ethnic groups. Despite these reservations, the incidence of low birthweight is used extensively in this book as a measure of the outcome of pregnancy, as well as being discussed in its own right in Chapter 6.

A matter of concern both to parents and to people planning and providing services is the costs of having a baby, discussed in Chapter 11. Comparisons between the outcome of pregnancy and childbirth in different countries are a subject of continuing interest and feature in publications of organisations such as the World Health Organisation and UNICEF. We give a brief overview of these data and their interpretation in Chapter 12.

The first edition of *Birth counts* was compiled at a time when a number of groups, notably the Steering Group on Health Services Information, were making proposals for changes which they hoped would improve data collection in the National Health Service.[11,12] There were hopes that these, combined with developments in information technology, would lead to major advances in the quantity and quality of data available.

These changes, implemented in the late 1980s, were followed in April 1991 by the introduction of the NHS internal market. The impact of the internal market on data collection was to reinforce focus on quantity of NHS activity rather than its outcome. This meant that adequate data have not been available to monitor the impact of the rising interest in using research evidence to inform clinical practice. This has been generated by the Cochrane Collaboration in its work of reviewing the effects of health care interventions. Now, as we go to press in the summer of 1999, work is starting to implement ambitious new information strategies for the NHS.[13-15] These aim to bring together records of care a person receives from different NHS organisations and practitioners.

The need for a new edition of *Birth counts* has been apparent for some years, but we had decided to defer it until good quality data about inpatient maternity care in England became available from the Maternity Hospital Episode System. Data are still of poor quality, despite the increasing efforts being made to improve them. We hope this new edition will stimulate interest in routine data collection and draw attention to the need for better data to inform and monitor changes. These include both initiatives already under way, as well as the new policies, notably those aimed at tackling inequalities in health, being developed by the government elected in May 1997.

In this volume, we have attempted to describe how official statistics were collected at the end of the twentieth century and the changes made over the previous fifteen years or so. Once again, this has made us conscious of the way data collection systems have been shaped by the context in which they were set up and developed. We have therefore described these historical processes, because we believe this helps us to understand how data can be used today and how both the strengths and the limitations of the data have arisen. This is of crucial relevance to the third main aim of our book, to increase understanding about how the data can be interpreted. We hope this will increase the extent to which statistics can be used to illuminate the continuing debate about the work of the maternity services and their relationship with the other aspects of the circumstances in which children are born.

In doing this we are following in a long tradition which dates back at least to Florence Nightingale. In her book *Introductory notes on lying-in institutions*, published in 1871, she commented that 'It must be admitted, at the very outset of this enquiry that midwifery statistics are in an unsatisfactory condition' and that 'our information ... is by no means so full as we would wish.'[16] Her response to this was that 'Our only resource at present is to deal with such statistical information as we possess and to ascertain fairly what it tells us.'[16]

References

1   Simon J. *General Board of Health papers relating to the sanitary state of England.* London: HMSO, 1858.

2   Lang A. In: Mackay AL, ed. *The harvest of a quiet eye.* Bristol and London: The Institute of Physics, 1977.

3   Silverman W. Fetal heart-rate monitoring. *Lancet* 1979; ii: 908.

4   Joint Committee of the Royal College of Obstetricians and Gynaecologists and the Population Investigation Committee. *Maternity in Great Britain.* Oxford: Oxford University Press, 1948.

5   Butler NR, Bonham DG. *Perinatal mortality. The first report of the British Perinatal Mortality Survey.* Edinburgh and London: E&S Livingstone, 1963.

6   Chamberlain G, Philipp E, Howlett B, Masters K. *British births, 1970.* Vol. 2: Obstetric care. London: Heinemann Medical Books, 1978.

7   Kuh D, Ben-Shlomo Y, eds. *A life course approach to chronic disease epidemiology.* Oxford: Oxford University Press, 1997.

8   Committee on Child Health Services. *Report: fit for the future. [Chair: SDM Court].* Cmnd 6684. Vol. 2. London: HMSO, 1976.

9   Woodroffe C, Glickman M, Barker M, Power C. *Children, teenagers and health: the key data.* Buckingham: Open University Press, 1993.

10   Botting B, ed. *The health of our children.* OPCS Decennial Supplement Series DS No. 11. London: HMSO, 1995.

11   Steering Group on Health Services Information. *First report to the Secretary of State.* London: HMSO, 1982.

12   Steering Group on Health Services Information. *Supplement to the first and fourth reports to the Secretary of State.* London: HMSO, 1985.

13   Department of Health, NHS Executive. *Information for health.* Leeds: NHS Executive, 1998.

14   National Information Management and Technology Board. *Strategic programme for modernising information management and technology in the NHS in Scotland.* Edinburgh: Scottish Office, 1998.

15   Welsh Office. *Better information, better health: information management and technology for health care and health improvement in Wales. A strategic framework 1998 to 2005.* Cardiff: Welsh Office, 1998.

16   Nightingale F. *Introductory notes on lying-in institutions.* London: Longmans, Green, and Co, 1871.

2 Definitions, classifications and sources

'Fill in this application form in duplicate and do
Supply the information what and where and how and who,
We want your registration number, age and height and weight
So that we can keep the nation in a law-and-ordered state.
　　And that's the way the wheels turn,
　　Round and round the wheels turn,
　　That's the way the wheels turn
　　Round.'

Leon Rosselson, *That's the way the wheels turn.*[1]

Many of the statistics in *Birth counts* have been collected as a by-product either of legal processes or of the administration of health and social services. In this chapter we start by outlining how the statistics used most frequently in relation to pregnancy and childbirth are defined. Next we describe the main classifications of diseases and causes of death, and of procedures used in surgery and medicine. This is followed by a description of geographical and social classifications. Fuller details can be found in the publications listed in Appendices 1 and 2, while subsequent chapters discuss problems and dilemmas which can arise when using and interpreting these definitions and classifications. This chapter ends with brief descriptions of the most commonly used sources of data.

One of the many tasks undertaken by the World Health Organisation (WHO) is to try to co-ordinate the compilation of health statistics and to influence member countries to do so in a comparable way. To do this, it produces the *International classification of diseases* (ICD) which is revised by international agreement at approximately ten yearly intervals.

As well as being a classification of diseases and injuries, the ICD contains recommendations about how statistics should be compiled and tabulated. In practice, some countries' legal requirements conflict with these definitions. Even when this is not the case, the systems of registering births and deaths may not be organised in such a way that the statistics can be produced. We shall go into this in more detail in Chapter 12. Meanwhile, in this chapter we outline the World Health Organisation's definitions recommended in the ninth revision of the *International classification of diseases* and in the tenth revision, entitled the *International statistical classification of diseases and related health problems* and point out how what is done in the United Kingdom differs from WHO definitions.[2,3]

Definitions

The definitions of live birth and stillbirth in force in the United Kingdom are shown in Table 2.1. The WHO definitions of live birth and fetal death are given in Table 2.2 and its criteria for including live births and fetal deaths in published statistics are set out in Table 2.3. These rely on the definitions of birthweight and gestational age which are given in Table 2.4.

Statistics based on these definitions relate to the number of babies born. Some data relate to the numbers of women having babies. These are commonly described as 'maternities' or 'deliveries', but there is no statutory definition.

Under United Kingdom laws, all live births must be registered but fetal deaths are registered only from the twenty-fourth completed week of gestation onwards, in which case they are known as stillbirths. As there are some cases when fetal deaths occur before 24 weeks of gestation but the

Table 2.1

Definitions of live and stillbirths in force in the United Kingdom from October 1992 onwards

	England and Wales	Scotland	Northern Ireland
Name of act or order	Section 41 of the Births and Deaths Registration Act 1953 as amended by the Stillbirth (Definition) Act 1992	Section 56(1) of the Registration of Births, Deaths and Marriages (Scotland) Act 1965, as amended by the Stillbirth (Definition) Act 1992	Births and Deaths Registration Order 1976 as amended by the Stillbirth (Definition) (Northern Ireland) Order 1992
Definitions			
Birth	'Birth means a live birth or a stillbirth'.	'Birth includes a stillbirth'.	'Birth means a live birth or a stillbirth'.
Live birth	'Live birth means a child born alive'.	No explicit definition	'Live birth means a child born alive'.
Stillbirth	A stillborn child is 'A child which has issued forth from its mother after the 24th week of pregnancy and which did not at any time after being completely expelled from its mother breathe or show any other signs of life'.	A stillborn child is 'A child which has issued forth from its mother after the 24th week of pregnancy and which did not at any time after being completely expelled from its mother breathe or show any other signs of life'.	A stillbirth 'means the complete expulsion from its mother after the 24th week of pregnancy of a child which did not at any time after being completely expelled or extracted breathe or show any other evidence of life'.

Time within which event is required to be registered

	England and Wales	Scotland	Northern Ireland
Live birth	42 days	21 days	42 days
Death	5 days	8 days	5 days
Stillbirth	3 months	21 days	3 months

fetus weighs more than 500g, it is not possible for any of the countries of the United Kingdom to produce statistics which comply with WHO recommendations without a change in the laws. Before October 1 1992, fetal deaths before 28 completed weeks of gestation were not registrable as stillbirths in countries of the United Kingdom.

The criteria for inclusion in perinatal statistics shown in Table 2.3 represent a considerable change from recommendations made in the 1960s in the

Table 2.2

WHO recommended definitions of live birth and fetal death (stillbirth)

Live birth
Live birth is the complete expulsion or extraction from its mother of a product of conception, irrespective of the duration of pregnancy, which after such separation, breathes or shows any other evidence of life, such as the beating of the heart, pulsation of the umbilical cord, or definite movement of voluntary muscles, whether or not the umbilical cord has been cut or the placenta is attached; each product of such a birth is considered liveborn.

Fetal death
Fetal death is death prior to the complete expulsion or extraction from its mother of a product of conception, irrespective of the duration of pregnancy; the death is indicated by the fact that after such separation the fetus does not breathe or show any other evidence of life, such as beating of the heart, pulsation of the umbilical cord, or definite movement of voluntary muscles.

Source: *International statistical classification of diseases and related health problems, tenth revision*, 1992.[3]

Table 2.3

WHO recommended criteria for births to be included in perinatal mortality statistics

Minimum value for inclusion	Births to be included in national perinatal statistics	Births to be included in international perinatal statistics
Birthweight, if known, at least:	500g	1000g
Otherwise, gestational age, at least:	22 weeks	28 weeks
Or body length (crown/heel) at least:	25 cm	35 cm

Perinatal period
The perinatal period commences at 22 completed weeks (154 days) of gestation (the time when birth weight is normally 500 g), and ends seven completed days after birth.

Neonatal period
The neonatal period commences at birth and ends 28 completed days after birth. Neonatal deaths (deaths among live births during the first 28 completed days of life) may be subdivided into *early neonatal deaths*, occurring during the first seven days of life, and *late neonatal deaths*, occurring after the seventh day but before 28 completed days of life.

Source: *International classification of diseases, ninth revision*, 1977.[2]
International statistical classification of diseases and related health problems, tenth revision, 1992.[3]

Table 2.4

WHO definitions of birthweight and gestational age

Birthweight
The first weight of the fetus or newborn obtained after birth.

Low birthweight
Less than 2500 g (up to, and including 2499 g).

Very low birthweight
Less than 1500 g (up to, and including 1499 g).

Extremely low birthweight
Less than 1000 g (up to, and including 999 g).

Gestational age
The duration of gestation is measured from the first day of the last normal menstrual period. Gestational age is expressed in completed days or completed weeks (e.g. events occurring 280 to 286 completed days after the onset of the last normal menstrual period are considered to have occurred at 40 weeks of gestation).

Pre-term
Less than 37 completed weeks (less than 259 days) of gestation.

Term
From 37 completed weeks to less than 42 completed weeks (259 to 293 days) of gestation.

Post-term
42 completed weeks or more (294 days or more) of gestation.

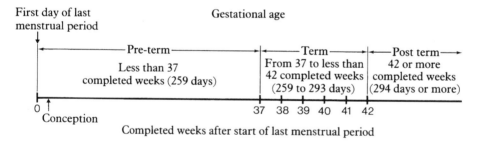

Source: *International statistical classification of diseases and related health problems, tenth revision,* 1992.[3]

eighth revision of the ICD. The eighth revision defined the 'perinatal period' as 'extending from the 28th week of gestation to the seventh day of life', but noted that some countries collected data down to the 20th week of gestation and up to the 28th day of life.[4] In the ninth revision the emphasis was shifted, making birthweight the primary criterion for inclusion in statistics, as estimates of gestational age are often unsatisfactory.[2] The tenth revision reverted to the principles used in the eighth revision, stating that 'The perinatal period commences at 22 completed weeks (154 days) of gestation (the time when the birthweight is usually 500g) and ends seven completed days after birth ...'[3] It also added the usual definition of the 'neonatal period' shown in Table 2.6.

Many birthweight statistics compiled in the past used the grouping 1,000g and under, 1,001–1,500g, 1,501–2,000g and so on. This grouping is different from the one defined by WHO in the ninth revision of the ICD, as can be seen in Table 2.4. The WHO grouping is now used almost universally. At a time before digital scales were common, problems could arise when comparing data classified in these two ways. Because of 'digit preference' a person reading a weight from a scale without a digital display was more likely to choose a round number such as multiples of 10 or 1,000 than a neighbouring unrounded one. Thus, for example, there were likely to be more babies recorded as weighing 1,500g than, say, 1,546g. Some effects of this are illustrated in Table 2.5, in which the same set of data from the transitional period are subdivided each way. It may be that the more widespread use of digital scales has resolved this problem.

The definitions of the various stillbirth and infant mortality rates to be found in this book are illustrated in Table 2.6. In general these are compatible with WHO's recommended age groupings for 'special statistics

Table 2.5

Comparison of birthweight groupings, England and Wales, 1980

Birthweight g	Percentage of total births with stated birthweight in groupings in left hand column	Percentage of total births with stated birthweight in groupings in right hand column	Birthweight g
All stated	100.00	100.00	All stated
Under 1,001	.31	.30	Under 1,000
1,001–1,500	.66	.65	1,000–1,499
1,501–2,000	1.41	1.36	1,500–1,999
2,001–2,500	5.13	4.85	2,000–2,499
Under 2,501	7.51	7.16	Under 2,500
2,501–3,000	19.99	19.21	2,500–2,999
3,001–3,500	38.98	38.90	3,000–3,499
3,501–4,000	25.99	26.70	3,500–3,999
4,001 and over	7.53	8.05	4,000 and over

Source: Derived from data in *OPCS Monitor DH3 81/4.*

Table 2.6

Definitions of stillbirth and infant mortality rates

Stillbirth rate $= \dfrac{\text{Stillbirths} \times 1000}{\text{Live births + stillbirths}}$

Perinatal mortality rate $= \dfrac{(\text{Stillbirths + deaths at 0–6 days after live birth}) \times 1000}{\text{Live births + stillbirths}}$

Early neonatal mortality rate $= \dfrac{\text{Deaths at 0–6 days after live birth} \times 1000}{\text{Live births}}$

Late neonatal mortality rate $= \dfrac{\text{Deaths at 7–27 days after live birth} \times 1000}{\text{Live births}}$

Neonatal mortality rate $= \dfrac{\text{Deaths at 0–27 days after live birth} \times 1000}{\text{Live births}}$

Postneonatal mortality rate $= \dfrac{\text{Deaths at 1–11 months after live birth} \times 1000}{\text{Live births}}$

Infant mortality rate $= \dfrac{\text{Deaths under the age of 1 year after live birth} \times 1000}{\text{Live births}}$

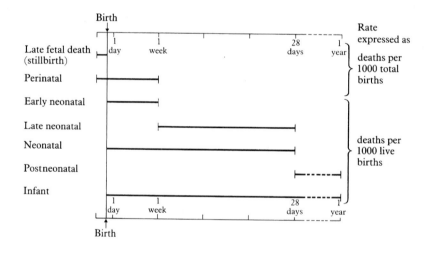

of infant mortality.' As the time of day of birth and death is not coded for analysis in England, Wales and Northern Ireland, it is not possible for these countries to produce the recommended statistics of early neonatal death which break the early neonatal period up into hours of life.

The definitions of maternal mortality set out by WHO in the tenth revision of the ICD are shown in Table 2.7. The expression 'termination of pregnancy' used there covers births and both miscarriages and induced abortions. In the eighth and earlier revisions, the term 'true maternal deaths' was used to describe all deaths attributed to causes classified in the chapter of the ICD entitled 'complications of pregnancy, stillbirth and the puerperium.' Deaths of women who were known to be pregnant at the time of death but which were attributed to any other cause, were described as 'associated deaths'. In the ninth and tenth revisions, however, some categories of what is now called 'indirect obstetric death' are included in the chapter of the ICD used to classify deaths attributed to conditions of pregnancy, childbirth and the puerperium. In the United Kingdom, the ninth revision definition was usually extended to cover deaths within a year of the end of the pregnancy. In the tenth revision of the ICD, WHO introduced two new definitions of 'late maternal death' and 'pregnancy-related death'. These are included in Table 2.7.

In clinical practice, parity is defined as the number of previous live and stillbirths. Hospital in-patient statistics in England use a definition based on

Table 2.7

WHO definitions of maternal mortality

Maternal death
A maternal death is the death of a woman while pregnant or within 42 days of termination of pregnancy, irrespective of the duration and the site of the pregnancy, from any cause related to or aggravated by the pregnancy or its management, but not from accidental or incidental causes.

Late maternal death
A late maternal death is the death of a woman from direct or indirect obstetric causes more than 42 days but less than one year after termination of pregnancy.

Pregnancy-related death
A pregnancy-related death is the death of a woman while pregnant or within 42 days of termination of pregnancy, irrespective of the cause of death.

Maternal deaths should be subdivided into two groups:

Direct obstetric deaths
Direct obstetric deaths are those resulting from obstetric complications of the pregnant state (pregnancy, labour and puerperium), from interventions, omissions, incorrect treatment, or from a chain of events resulting from any of the above.

Indirect obstetric deaths
Indirect obstetric deaths are those resulting from previous existing disease or disease that developed during pregnancy and which was not due to direct obstetric causes, but which was aggravated by physiologic effects of pregnancy.

Source: *International statistical classification of diseases and related health problems, tenth revision*, 1992.[3]

the number of previous pregnancies leading to one or more registrable births. In Scotland data are collected about the number of previous pregnancies 'irrespective of the outcome', usually known as gravidity.

Yet another definition is used in birth registration statistics. This is because at birth registration, under the terms of the Population Statistics Acts, information about previous live and stillbirths is collected only from women having children within marriage. In addition, informants are asked only about previous live and stillbirths to the woman by her current or any previous husband. The usual convention is for analyses of mortality to define 'parity' to include 'previous live and stillbirths by the current or any previous husband', while analyses of fertility confine the definition of parity to 'previous live births by the current or any previous husband'.

In 1990, in a white paper, *Registration: proposals for change*, the Office of Population Censuses and Surveys (OPCS) proposed recording the total number of previous live and stillbirths registered.[5] For many years, there was no legislation to implement the many proposals in the white paper, but in December 1998, the government announced a review of the registration service, to prepare for legislation to improve the services which register offices provide for the public.[6] It is hoped that this legislation will also provide an opportunity to bring about other long needed changes in the registration service, including those needed to improve data collection.[7]

WHO's suggested explanations of what is meant by impairment, disability and handicap are given in Table 2.8. They were set out in the *International classification of disabilities impairments and handicaps*, which was linked to the ninth revision of the ICD.[8] They are in some senses cumulative, in that impairment describes physical or psychological damage to a person, while disability describes how impairments limit the way the person functions and handicap disadvantage resulting from the impairment or disability. The interpretation of these definitions has been discussed widely both by professional organisations and by groups of people with disabilities. In particular, they have been heavily criticised by people with disabilities on

Table 2.8

Definitions of impairment, disability and handicap recommended by WHO in 1980

Impairment
In the context of health experience, an impairment is any loss or abnormality of psychological, physiological, or anatomical structure or function.

Disability
In the context of health experience, a disability is any restriction or lack (resulting from an impairment) of ability to perform an activity in the manner or within the range considered normal for a human being.

Handicap
In the context of health experience, a handicap is a disadvantage for a given individual, resulting from an impairment or a disability, that limits or prevents the fulfilment of a role that is normal (depending on age, sex and social and cultural factors) for that individual.

Source: WHO, *International classification of impairments, disabilities and handicaps*, 1980.[8]

the grounds that the distinction between the definitions of 'disability' and 'handicap' is not meaningful.

The tenth revision of the ICD commented that: 'The definition of impairment, an area where there was considerable overlap with the terms included in the ICD, had been widely accepted. The definition of disability broadly matched the field of action of rehabilitation professionals and groups, although there was felt to be a need for more attention in the associated code to the gradation of severity, which was often a predictor of handicap. There had also been increasing requests to revise the definition of handicap so as to put more emphasis on the effect of interaction with the environment.'[3]

In the late 1990s and early 2000s, a new classification was developed and tested. A beta-1 version was released in 1997 and a beta-2 version in 1999, based on the dimensions of body functions and structure, activity and participation shown in Table 2.9. After further testing and revision, the final version will be submitted to the World Health Assembly in 2001.[9]

Table 2.9

Definitions of dimensions recommended in ICIDH-2

In the context of a health condition:

Body functions are the physiological or psychological functions of body systems.

Body structures are anatomic parts of the body such as organs, limbs and their components.

Impairments are problems in body function or structure such as a significant deviation or loss.

Activity is the performance of a task or action by an individual.

Activity limitations are difficulties an individual may have in the performance of activities.

Participation is an individual's involvement in life situations in relation to health conditions, body functions and structure, activities and contextual factors.

Participation restrictions are problems an individual may have in the manner or extent of involvement in life situations.

Source: WHO, *ICIDH-2, International classification of functioning and disability, beta-2 draft*, 1999.[9]

Classifications

Diseases and causes of death

Most of the ICD consists, as its name suggests, of a classification of diseases and causes of death. The ninth revision of the classification has been used in England and Wales since 1979 and in Scotland and Northern Ireland since 1980, replacing the eighth revision. The tenth revision of the ICD is gradually being introduced in the countries of the United Kingdom. It has been used in most NHS systems in England since 1995 but is not due to be used for coding death certificates in Scotland until 2000 and in England

and Wales and in Northern Ireland until 2001. This is because the Office for National Statistics (ONS) and the General Register Offices for Scotland and Northern Ireland waited until they were able to obtain the necessary software for automatic coding of death certificates from the United States.

The Royal College of Paediatrics and Child Health, formerly the British Paediatric Association, publishes an expanded classification of conditions affecting children. This is linked to the ICD. It is revised each time the ICD is revised, and made compatible with it.[10] An *Obstetrics and gynaecology extract* which linked ninth revision ICD codes to definitions drawn up by the Fédération Internationale de Gynécologie et d'Obstetrique (FIGO) was published by the Information Services Division of the Scottish Health Services Common Services Agency, as it was then known. At the time of writing, a version has yet to be produced for the tenth revision. A list of these classifications, with publication details, is given in Appendix 2.

In the ninth revision of the ICD, WHO proposed that a separate certificate should be used to certify perinatal deaths, and that causes of death should be set out on it as follows:

a) main disease or condition in fetus or infant

b) other disease or conditions in fetus or infant

c) main maternal disease or condition affecting fetus

d) other maternal disease or condition affecting fetus or infant

e) other relevant circumstances.

A format based on this is used in England and Wales on the special medical certificates of stillbirth and neonatal death, which were introduced in 1986 and are reproduced in Appendix 6. This format was adopted in Scotland in 2000 and will be introduced in Northern Ireland in 2001.

In England and Wales, data collected at the registration of deaths of babies aged under one year have been linked routinely with those collected at birth registration since 1975, so it is unnecessary to include all the data items recommended by WHO on a single certificate. In 1982, OPCS did a pilot study of the new forms of stillbirth and neonatal death certificates. It then changed the format to allow more than one condition to be mentioned on each. It was not easy to determine how to use this information to classify causes of death. Groupings were subsequently devised[11,12] based on Jonathan Wigglesworth's 'Pathophysiological classification'.[13] These are described in ONS' annual volume of *Mortality statistics, Series DH3* as 'ONS cause groups'. This is discussed more fully in Chapter 3.

As mentioned earlier, an *International classification of impairments, disabilities and handicaps* was published in 1980 by the WHO for use in conjunction with the ninth revision of the ICD and was published 'for trial purposes'.[8] A new classification is being developed with the aim of replacing it in 2001.[9]

Clinical terms

Clinical terms were originally devised for use in general practice by James Read and known as 'Read codes'. They aimed to cover a wider range of conditions and procedures than the ICD.[14] Version 3 of *Clinical terms* is now a thesaurus of multi-disciplinary terms.[15] In the early 1990s, over 2,000 clinicians took part in its development for their specialties and disciplines. The terms are currently in a 'development in use' phase and are being used in clinical systems in many specialties. The aim is to provide feedback to ensure that coverage is appropriate and adequate for all areas of clinical use. The work was co-ordinated by the NHS Centre for Coding and Classification, which is now part of the NHS Information Authority. Contact details can be found in Appendix 1.

Operations and procedures

The need for a classification of surgical operations arose out of the establishment of the Hospital In-patient Enquiry in England and Wales from 1949 onwards. A classification developed in the early 1950s and published in 1956 built on an earlier classification published by the Medical Research Council in 1944. Further versions were published in the 1960s and early 1970s. A third version of this *Classification of surgical operations*, usually known as *OPCS-3*, was published in 1975,[16] and a fourth version, known as *OPCS-4*, was published in 1990.[17] Like its predecessors, *OPCS-4* grouped operations according to the part of the body or system to which they related. Operations can be coded in detail using four digit codes or grouped together using three digit codes.

While the classification at this level of detail is useful for people interested in particular procedures, broader groupings are needed for other purposes. In particular, for commissioning health care, groupings are needed which relate to the use of NHS resources. To meet this need, the National Casemix Office, now part of the NHS Information Authority, developed Healthcare Resource Groups (HRGs). These are groups of treatments which are expected to consume similar amounts of healthcare resources.[15,18] From 1998/99 onwards they have been used as a basis for costing in the NHS. Many HRGs were based on groups of codes in *OPCS-4* but they were then extended to types of care not included in *OPCS-4*.

To complement HRGs, Health Benefit Groups (HBGs) were developed to group populations of people by diagnosis into groups with similar needs for health care and, given appropriate treatment, similar likely benefit or outcome. The aim is to be able to link HRGs and HBGs for a given population in order to estimate the resources consumed or required, the implications of changes in patterns of care or delivery of care and expected outcomes.

By the late 1990s, *OPCS-4* had been in use for some years and had not been updated to keep pace with changes in health care. After a review, it was decided a new classification should be developed, using clinical terms as a basis.[19] Work to develop this new classification is known as the Healthcare Intervention Aggregation Project.[20]

Area of residence

Most official statistical publications contain data about births and mortality among residents of defined geographical areas rather than being based on the location of the hospitals to which people are admitted. The reasons for this are explained in Chapter 3. Maps of some of the areas can be found in Appendix 5. After two periods of relative stability these changed rapidly in the early and mid 1990s, with many districts merging and major changes of regional boundaries.

The areas used in this book are those used in the administration of the NHS. From April 1 1974 to March 31 1982, England was divided into 14 regional health authorities (RHAs). The English RHAs and Wales were subdivided into 98 area health authorities (AHAs) whose boundaries were drawn to coincide as far as possible with those used in the administration of local government. Many AHAs were then further subdivided into health districts. Sometimes these so-called 'statutory health districts' did not correspond very closely to the catchment areas of hospitals. In these cases different boundaries were drawn for 'management health districts' which included the areas for whose population the health district was responsible for providing services. This distinction between statutory and management authorities was largely removed in the 1982 reorganisation of the NHS in England and Wales in which AHAs were abolished, leaving only district health authorities. Apart from a handful of mergers, mainly in inner London, these continued in existence until 1991.

During the 1990s there were many changes and mergers at district level as a result of which many districts became coterminous with local authorities. On April 1 1999 primary care groups were set up to commission health care for populations within NHS districts. The districts and regions which existed from 1994 to 1996 and the changes made to regions in 1999 are described in Appendix 5. In 1994 the fourteen regional health authorities in England were reduced to eight and in 1996 they were replaced by regional offices of the NHS Executive. In 1999, further changes were made in south east England, to form a regional office for London.

Birth and death statistics are also published for local authority districts and counties in England and Wales and, in addition, for standard regions whose areas differed considerably from those of NHS regions. Standard regions were reconfigured on April 1 1996 to form government office regions. This book includes some data for standard regions and government office regions. Details of the regions are given in Appendix 5.

In Scotland, the NHS is administered by 15 health boards. The areas these health boards cover are not the same as those of the 29 single tier councils used in local government from April 1 1996. The relation between them is shown in Appendix 5. In Northern Ireland, health and social services are administered together, so common areas are used. The 26 district council areas are grouped within four health and social services boards, as shown in Appendix 5. When the Northern Ireland Assembly is re-established, new legislation is likely to change the structure of health and social services boards.

Many series of aggregated data are published separately for England, Wales, Scotland and Northern Ireland. Often, however, England and Wales are grouped together. Sometimes data are published for Great Britain, which is made up of England and Wales and Scotland, or the United Kingdom which includes Great Britain and Northern Ireland. Data for the Isle of Man and the Channel Islands, are collected separately, and are not usually included with those for the United Kingdom, but we have included some data for these islands. In addition, in response to the growing interest in 'All-Ireland' statistics, we have included some data for the Irish Republic.

Starting with the 1971 census, multivariate statistical techniques have been used to identify groups of geographical areas which are similar to each other. These have been used to construct groups of local authorities and health authorities and of the electoral wards which make them up.[21,22] Using data from the 1991 census, 'families' and 'clusters' of areas were identified. Data classified in this way are discussed in chapter 3. Because of the major changes in local government areas in 1996, this classification could no longer be used to group the areas which existed in the latter part of the 1990s so the classification was revised.[23]

Social class

Each time a census is taken, a classification has been drawn up in order to classify people according to their occupation. The publications containing the classifications for the 1971, 1981 and 1991 censuses are listed in Appendix 2 together with reports of work being done to develop a new classification for the 2001 census. Since 1911, occupations have been grouped into social classes. The way this developed is described in Chapter 5. The classification is also used in other official statistics. The classification used for the 1991 census did this on a basis of information about:

1 Occupation. The type of work the person does.

2 Industry. The type of industry the person works in.

3 Employment status. Self-employed or employed. Employed people are subdivided into managers, foremen, apprentices etc.

4 Economic position. Economically inactive or active. The latter includes people who are unemployed but seeking employment.

Up to the year 2000, the classification is being used to code economically active people into the Registrar General's social classes shown in Table 2.10.[24] Unemployed people are classified as occupied if they are seeking paid employment or are on various government training schemes.[25]

Although the way the social classes are described has remained the same since 1951, the way occupations have been classified has changed over this period. This arises because of changes in the nature of the occupations themselves. In particular, there were fairly radical changes between the 1970 classification used for the 1971 census and the 1980 classification used for the 1981 census. In England and Wales, the 1980 classification was used for most other data collected by government from 1979 to 1990. It was used from 1980 in Scotland. The classification used for the 1991 census has been used for coding occupational information recorded at birth and death registration since 1991.

Table 2.10

Registrar General's social class according to occupation

Group	Description	Example
I	Professional	Doctors, lawyers
II	Managerial and technical occupations	Teachers, most managerial and senior administrative occupations
IIIn	Skilled occupations non-manual	Clerks, shop assistants
IIIm	Skilled occupations manual	Bricklayers, coal miners below ground
IV	Partly skilled occupations	Bus conductors, traffic wardens
V	Unskilled occupations	General labourers
Others		
	Armed forces	
	Unclassified	People about whom there is no information or whose occupations do not fit into the classification; students
	Unoccupied	Unemployed people are only classified as unoccupied if they are not seeking paid employment, nor on a government employment or training scheme

Source: OPCS, *Standard occupational classification, Volume 3*, 1991.[24]

In 1991 following a proposal that social class coding should be discontinued, the classification was re-named 'Registrar General's social class based on occupation.' At the same time, the name of social class II was changed from 'Intermediate occupations' to 'Managerial and technical occupations'.

The *Classification of occupations* also contains another set of groupings, the 17 socio-economic groups shown in Table 2.11.[24] Social surveys done by and for government often use these groups rather than the social classes. This classification, introduced in 1951, aims to group together people with jobs of similar social and economic status, and is based on employment status and occupation. In many analyses, an abbreviated version of the socio-economic groups is used. This combines groups 1 and 2, groups 3 and 4, groups 8, 9 and 12, groups 7 and 10, groups 13, 14 and 15 and groups 16 and 17 to form nine larger groups.[26]

Following a review of social classifications, a new classification, the *National statistics socio-economic classification*, was developed for the 2001 census.[27] The categories used are listed in Table 2.12 and the ways in which it differs radically from the Registrar General's social class based on occupation is described in Chapter 5.

Ethnic origins

In the 1991 census of Great Britain, a question was asked about people's ethnic origins. This is shown in Table 2.13. This was the first time such a question was asked and the debate it provoked is described in Chapter 5. A revised question, shown in Table 2.14, will be asked in England and Wales in the 2001 census.[28] Scotland use a similar question or repeat that used in 1991. An ethnic question will be asked for the first time in Northern

Table 2.11

Socio-economic groups

1. Employers and managers in central and local government, industry, commerce, etc. – large establishments
2. Employers and managers in industry, commerce, etc. – small establishments
3. Professional workers – self-employed
4. Professional workers – employees
5. Intermediate non-manual workers
6. Junior non-manual workers
7. Personal service workers
8. Foremen and supervisors – manual
9. Skilled manual workers
10. Semi-skilled manual workers
11. Unskilled manual workers
12. Own account workers (other than professional)
13. Farmers – employers and managers
14. Farmers – own account
15. Agricultural workers
16. Members of armed forces
17. Inadequately described and non stated occupations

Source: OPCS, *Standard occupational classification, Volume 3,* 1991.[24]

Table 2.12

National Statistics Socio-economic Classification to be used from 2001 onwards

1. Higher managerial and professional occupations
   1A Employers and managers in large establishments
   1B Professionals
2. Lower managerial and professional occupations
3. Intermediate occupations
4. Small employers and own account workers
5. Lower supervisory, craft and related occupations
6. Employees in semi-routine occupations
7. Employees in routine occupations

8. Never worked and long-term unemployed
9. Unclassified

Source: *The ESRC review of government social classifications,* 1998.[27]

Table 2.13

The question asked about ethnic group in the census of population, Great Britain, 1991

Ethnic group	
Please tick the appropriate box.	White Black-Caribbean Black-African Black-Other *please describe*
	Indian Pakistani Bangladeshi Chinese Any other ethnic group *please describe*
If the person is descended from more than one ethnic or racial group, please tick the group to which the person considers he/she belongs, or tick 'Any other ethnic group' box and describe the person's ancestry in the space provided.	

Source: OPCS and GRO Scotland. *1991 census. Definitions, Great Britain*. 1992[25]

Ireland, where it will be similar to that used in Britain in 1991 with an additional category, 'Irish traveller'. The proposals to add questions on religion and income are discussed in Chapter 5.

Sources of statistics

In this section we give a brief outline of the way data are collected and where they are published. For fuller information we would refer readers to the various guides and the statistical publications listed in Appendices 1 and 2. At this stage, we confine our comments to the mechanics of data collection. We shall have more to say later about how the processes of collection affect the way the data can be interpreted and used.

The Government Statistical Service (GSS), which consists of the statistical divisions of government departments plus the specialised central government statistics departments, is responsible to a varying extent for most of the data in this book. Before April 1996, the Central Statistical Office was responsible for co-ordinating the work of the GSS. This is now part of the role of the Office for National Statistics. In addition, it publishes guides to statistics, and also compilations of data from a variety of government sources, the best known of which are *Social trends, Regional trends* and the *Annual abstract of statistics*.

Data derived from the civil registration of births, marriage and deaths are dealt with by the three general register offices which cover England and Wales, Scotland and Northern Ireland respectively. From 1970 until March 1996 the General Register Office for England and Wales formed part of the Office of Population Censuses and Surveys. On April 1 1996, the Central

Table 2.14

The ethnic group question to be asked in the census of population, England and Wales, 2001

What is your ethnic group?

♦   Choose one section from (a) to (e) then
tick the appropriate box to indicate
your cultural background

(a)   **White**
- ☐ British
- ☐ Irish
- ☐ Any other White background
please write in below

(b)   **Mixed**
- ☐ White and Black Caribbean
- ☐ White and Black African
- ☐ White and Asian
- ☐ Any other mixed background
please write in below

(c)   **Asian or Asian British**
- ☐ Indian
- ☐ Pakistani
- ☐ Bangladeshi
- ☐ Any other Asian background
please write in below

(d)   **Black or Black British**
- ☐ Caribbean
- ☐ African
- ☐ Any other Black background
please write in below

(e)   **Chinese or other ethnic group**
- ☐ Chinese
- ☐ Any other
please write in below

Source: *The 2001 census of population,* 1999[28]

Statistical Office merged with OPCS to form the Office for National Statistics. On the same day, the General Register Office for Northern Ireland became part of the Northern Ireland Statistics and Research Agency (NISRA). In 2000, the director of ONS took on the role of 'National statistician'.

While the general register offices supervise the work of local registrars, they do not employ them. Instead they are employed by local government.

Between May 1981 and July 1982, local registrars in England and Wales took industrial action against their local government employers. This affected the range and quality of data collected and published for 1981, and led to gaps which can be seen in the series in Volume 2 of *Birth counts*.

The four Chief Medical Officers (CMOs) for England, Wales, Scotland and Northern Ireland have statutory responsibility for data about the NHS. In principle, these are dealt with by the four central government health departments. Statistical staff in the Department of Health, the National Assembly for Wales, and the Scottish Executive Health Department are members of the Government Statistical Service. Staff in the Department of Health, Social Services and Public Safety of the Northern Ireland Executive, may be seconded from or associated with NISRA, which in turn has links with the GSS. In practice, ONS analyses some data on behalf of the CMOs for England and Wales. In Scotland, much of the work is done by NHS staff in the Information and Statistics Division (ISD), formerly known as the Information Services Division, of the Common Services Agency of the National Health Service in Scotland. Further changes are under way at the time of writing, following proposals for an independent national statistical service and also as a consequence of devolved government in Scotland, Wales and Northern Ireland.[29,30]

The principal statistical systems containing data about birth and infant mortality are summarised in Table 2.15.

Civil registration

By law, all live births and stillbirths and all deaths occurring in the United Kingdom must be registered with the local registrar within the times indicated in Table 2.1. Births and infant deaths are usually registered by the baby's parents. To register a stillbirth or a death, the informant normally produces a medical certificate, completed on evidence from the doctor or midwife who was present at the stillbirth or death or who examined the body. The certificates are shown in Appendix 6.

Information collected at birth registration includes the mother's area of usual residence, and her date and country of birth. For births within marriage only, the number of previous live and stillbirths within marriage by the woman's current or any previous husband is recorded. For births within marriage and those outside marriage registered jointly by both parents in England and Wales, the father's occupation and date of birth are recorded. For births outside marriage registered without the father's details, the mother's occupation is recorded. OPCS extended this in 1986 to give all mothers the option of recording their occupation, but was not able to provide a special place for this item on the birth certificate, in the absence of legislation on the white paper *Registration: proposals for change*.[5] In Scotland, the mother's occupation is coded for all births outside marriage, and the father's for births within marriages.

At death registration, the date of birth, date of death, place of death and place of usual residence of the dead person are recorded.[31] For a child aged under

Table 2.15

Statistical systems containing data about birth and infant mortality

System	Intended coverage	Primary function	England	Wales	Scotland	Northern Ireland
Live birth registration	All live births at any gestation	Required by law	ONS	ONS	GRO Scotland	GRO Northern Ireland
Stillbirth registration	All fetal deaths of at least 24 weeks' gestation	Required by law	ONS	ONS	GRO Scotland	GRO Northern Ireland
Death registration	All deaths	Required by law	ONS	ONS	GRO Scotland	GRO Northern Ireland
Birth notification	All live births and all stillbirths of at least 24 weeks' gestation	Required by law in order to inform health visitor of event	Health authorities	Health authorities	Health boards	Health and social services boards
Congenital anomaly notification	Congenital anomalies apparent at birth	Surveillance of congenital anomalies	ONS	ONS	Information and Statistics Division	Health and social services boards
Abortion notification	All terminations of pregnancy carried out under Abortion Act 1967	Required by law	Department of Health	National Assembly for Wales	Scottish Executive Health Department	None. Abortion Act does not apply.
NHS administrative returns	NHS hospital and community health services	To monitor activity and resources of NHS	Department of Health	National Assembly for Wales	Information and Statistics Division	Health and social services boards
Hospital inpatient statistics	Admissions to NHS hospitals	To collect information about use of beds, reasons for admissions and treatment given	Department of Health	National Assembly for Wales	Information and Statistics Division	Health and social services boards
Confidential enquiries into maternal deaths	Deaths during pregnancy or during labour or as a consequence of pregnancy within a year of delivery or abortion	To investigate causes of maternal mortality	Department of Health*	National Assembly for Wales	Scottish Executive Health Department	Department of Health, Social Services and Public Safety
Confidential Enquiry into Stillbirths and Deaths in Infancy (CESDI)	Fetal deaths at 20 or more weeks of gestation and deaths within a year of live birth	To identify deaths which can be attributed to suboptimal clinical care	CESDI secretariat	All Wales perinatal survey	Scottish stillbirth and infant death survey. No enquiry.	Department of Health, Social Services and Public Safety

* Since 1985 data for all four countries have been published in a single report

Before July 1 1999, the National Assembly for Wales was known as the Welsh Office and the Scottish Executive Health Department was known as the Scottish Office Department of Health. Before December 2 1999, the Department of Health, Social Services and Public Safety of the Northern Ireland Executive was known as the Department of Health and Social Services.

GRO, General Register Office
ONS, Office for National Statistics
NHS, National Health Service

16, the parents' occupations are recorded. Information about the cause of death is derived from the medical certificate, as is also done for stillbirths.

Local registrars in England and Wales forward the information collected at birth and death registration to ONS on the 'draft entry' forms shown in Appendix 6, although most register offices are now computerised and the information is therefore sent on disk. ONS processes the data and publishes them in annual volumes of statistics. Up to 1998 these were also published in the ONS *Monitor* series, but the tables from these were incorporated into ONS' quarterly journals *Population trends* and *Health statistics quarterly* in 1999. Birth statistics are published in *Series FM1*. Data about perinatal, infant and maternal mortality appear in *Series DH3*. Local registrars in Scotland and Northern Ireland forward similar information to their respective general register offices. The data are published in the *Annual report of the Registrar General for Scotland* and the *Annual report of the Registrar General for Northern Ireland*.

In England and Wales from 1975 to 1992, infant mortality 'linked files' brought together the data collected when the death of a child aged under one year was registered linked to the data collected when the child's birth was registered. This linkage was done as a special exercise in 1949–50[32] and again in 1964.[33] Since 1975 the linkage has been done routinely. Special volumes of data were published for 1975–77 and 1978–79.[34,35] Since 1980, data have been published annually in OPCS and ONS *Monitors* and annual volumes of data in the DH3 series. The system was redeveloped in the early 1990s and data about deaths of children of any age born from 1993 onwards are now linked to their birth registration.

In Scotland, there is no routine linkage of birth and infant death registration data, although this is possible using the very extensive facilities for record linkage which have been developed in Scotland.[36] Much fuller data are collated in the *Scottish stillbirth and infant death report*. In this, information collected about babies who die is linked to birth data from the SMR2 delivery record which is described later. The survey started as a research project, data from which were published in a series of reports.[37–39] Since March 1983, the survey has been run routinely by the Information and Statistics Division. There is no linkage of data from birth and infant death registration in Northern Ireland.

Notification of births

Under the National Health Service Act, 1977, all births, both live and still, must be notified to the local director of public health in England, Wales, Scotland and Northern Ireland within 36 hours of their occurrence. In practice, since the introduction of the internal market, notifications have been sent to community trusts. This enables a midwife and, later, a health visitor to visit the mother and baby. Notification is done by the professional attending the woman at birth. This is usually the midwife, but can also be an obstetrician, a general practitioner or, on rare occasions, the parents. The notification usually includes identifying details such as mother's name, place of birth, place of usual residence, and the birthweight and gestational age of the baby, but some districts collect more data than others. When the birth takes place outside the mother's usual district of residence, the notification is passed on to her home district.

In most districts in England and Wales, information from birth notifications is used to initiate the baby's record on a child health computer system. Amongst other things this system is used for organising the vaccination and immunisation programmes. Since 1991, these systems have been operated by community trusts.

In Northern Ireland, data from birth notifications are processed in the child health computer systems run by each of the four health and social services boards, then aggregated by the Department of Health, Social Services and Public Safety. Data are not published routinely.

Although the notification and registration systems work independently of each other in England and Wales, there is nevertheless some exchange of information between them. The health authority, or since 1991 the community trust, sends the local registrar lists of babies whose births have been notified together with their birthweights. The local registrar then returns the lists with the babies' National Health Service numbers, which it is currently his or her duty to allocate. The flows of information are shown in Figure 2.1. As parents have six weeks to register the birth, there can be a delay in allocating the baby's NHS number. A proposal for issuing the baby's NHS number at birth should be implemented by 2002. This will mean that the baby will immediately have a record in the National Health Service Central Register.[40] The registrar also provides the health authority with information about deaths. This usually includes their certified cause.

Notification of congenital anomalies

In 1964, local authorities in England and Wales were asked to notify all congenital anomalies found in stillbirths or within a week of live birth. Notification became the responsibility of health authorities in 1974. In some districts, the birth attendant completes the congenital malformation notification form (SD56) and forwards it to ONS while in many others the community trust completes it using the information on the birth notification. Where there is a local congenital anomaly register, the districts concerned have the option of forwarding data from this source to ONS. The data are published in an annual volume, in *Congenital anomaly statistics, Series MB3*. As the system is voluntary, there is likely to be considerable under-reporting, although this varies by condition. ONS has been attempting to tackle this problem by co-operating with local registers and has also extended the system to include anomalies diagnosed at any time. This is discussed in fuller detail in Chapter 8.

There are separate notification systems for Scotland and Northern Ireland. In Scotland, data on congenital anomalies come from the SMR11 baby record, raised at birth and, to a lesser extent, records of subsequent hospital in-patient stays by babies and the stillbirth and neonatal death

Figure 2.1

Flows of data about live births in England, 1999

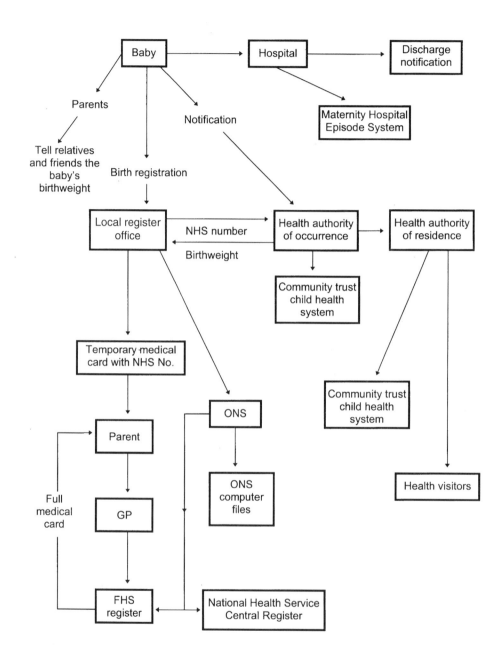

records. The data are published by ISD in *Congenital malformations in Scotland*. In Northern Ireland, congenital anomalies are monitored by the Regional Medical Genetics Centre at Belfast City Hospital and published in the *Annual report of the Chief Medical Officer for Northern Ireland*.

Abortion notification

Pregnancies terminated under the 1967 Abortion Act in England, Wales and Scotland must, by law, be notified to the respective Chief Medical Officer. There is no system of notification in Northern Ireland as the Abortion Act does not apply there. There are, however, a few legal terminations carried out in the province, under the same case law which applied in England and Wales prior to the 1967 Act. Abortion statistics for England and Wales are processed by ONS on behalf of the two CMOs. Data are published in an annual volume *Abortion statistics, Series AB*. Data previously published in ONS *Monitors, Series AB*, up to 1998 are now included in *Health statistics quarterly*. In Scotland, abortion statistics are processed by ISD on behalf of the CMO and published annually in *Scottish health statistics*, as well as in special *Health briefings*.

NHS administrative returns

Health authorities are required to compile a number of annual and quarterly data summaries or 'returns'. Some of these contain data about hospital services while others cover community health services, finance or staffing, referred to in the past as 'manpower' but now relabelled 'workforce'. In England, returns were formerly sent via regional health authorities. They are now sent direct to the Department of Health which issues a 'Health circular' each year setting out the data it requires. In Wales, they are sent to the Welsh Office, known as the National Assembly for Wales since July 1999, in Scotland to ISD and in Northern Ireland to the Department of Health and Social Services, known as the Department of Health, Social Services and Public Safety since December 2 1999. Over the years, the systems of paper forms have been computerised. Increasingly they are submitted on disk or through the NHS-wide Clearing Service, which uses the dedicated NHS computer network.

In England, data from many of the returns are published in *Health and personal social services statistics for England*. Data for Wales appear in *Health statistics Wales*, known as *Health and personal social services statistics for Wales* up to 1994. In Scotland the data are published in *Scottish health statistics* and in Northern Ireland they appear in separate volumes of *Hospital statistics* and *Community statistics*.

Hospital in-patient statistics

Summary returns of hospital activity contain very little indication about the diagnoses of, or treatments given to people admitted to hospitals. For information based on individual records, it is necessary to turn to the hospital in-patient statistics systems used in each of the four countries of the United Kingdom.

Hospital Activity Analysis (HAA), used up to the mid 1980s, was a computerised system run by each of the 14 regional health authorities in England, by the Welsh Office, and by the Department of Health and Social Services in Northern Ireland. These systems covered all patients in NHS hospitals, apart from women using maternity departments and residents in hospitals for people with mental illness or learning difficulties. Northern Ireland had a different form of HAA for maternity patients. These systems contained, for each person who died or was discharged from hospital after admission as an in-patient, information about conditions diagnosed, time spent in hospital and operations done, as well as the person's sex, age, and area of residence.

In England and Wales a ten per cent sample of HAA records was passed on to OPCS for analysis as the Hospital In-Patient Enquiry (HIPE). Up until 1980 data from HIPE were published jointly by OPCS, DHSS and the Welsh Office in an annual volume *Report on the Hospital In-patient Enquiry, Series MB4*. No HIPE data were published for 1981. From 1982 to 1985, when it was discontinued, HIPE was restricted to England. For many years, attempts were made to agree on a similar system to cover all stays in maternity departments in England and Wales. In the early 1980s an experimental Maternity Hospital Activity Analysis system was in operation in some areas, while local maternity computing systems were being developed in other places. Elsewhere, hospitals completed maternity HIPE forms manually for 10 per cent of in-patient stays in maternity departments.

It was problems such as these which prompted a review of all NHS data collected in England. The review committee, the Steering Group on Health Services Information, was chaired by Edith Körner. As a result, many of the datasets it recommended are known as Körner datasets.

The Steering Group recommended a new system, Hospital Episode Statistics (HES), for collecting data about hospital in-patient care. As its name suggests, it is based on episodes of care with a consultant. A set of data items, known as a minimum dataset, is recorded for each episode. Each in-patient stay can be made up of one or more 'finished consultant episodes', details of which are not routinely linked at national level. Rather than taking a sample, all records are intended to be included in the system at national level. Data are compiled on the basis of financial years. For specialities other than maternity, HES started in April 1987 and tabulated data are published in annual volumes and on a CD-ROM. Maternity HES, in which records have a 'maternity tail' containing data about episodes in which babies were born, was due to start in April 1988. It was delayed by six months because there was no pre-existing system covering all stays in maternity departments. The maternity data are still very incomplete[41-43]. Few were published until 1997 when the Department of Health started to publish a series of statistical bulletins containing maternity statistics.[43]

Wales and Northern Ireland introduced systems similar to HES, the Patient Episode Database Wales and the Hospital Inpatients System. Data in the 'maternity tail' are incomplete in both these systems and are not published. In both these countries, birth notification data obtained via child health systems are the main source of data about care given when a baby is born.

In Scotland, the Scottish Hospital In-Patient Statistics SMR1 scheme is a similar system run by the ISD. A separate record, SMR2, is completed for every hospital admission to a maternity unit, while a SMR11 neonatal record is used for all hospital treatment given to the baby during its stay, including transfers from department to department. It can be linked to the SMR2 delivery record and these can also be linked with SMR1 records about any previous in-patient stays by the mother.[36,44] The whole system was revised in the mid 1990s in preparation for the introduction of the tenth revision of the ICD in 1996. It is now known as the Core Patient Profile Information in Scottish Hospitals (COPPISH).

Except in Scotland, there has been until recently very little ability to link the records of a series of stays by the same person in different hospitals. The decision to re-issue NHS numbers and include them on every NHS record has increased the potential for linkage in England.

Confidential enquiries

Enquiries into maternal deaths cover deaths occurring during pregnancy and labour or within one year of delivery, miscarriage or induced abortion. Strict confidentiality is observed at all stages. Investigation into a given maternal death is co-ordinated locally by the director of public health or a member of his or her staff. Information about the circumstances of the death is collected locally from all staff involved in the care of the woman. Details of post-mortem investigations are also collected. In England, the information about the case is then passed on to the regional assessor, who is a senior consultant obstetrician in the same region. Where an anaesthetic is involved, the case is also referred to an anaesthetic assessor. When the assessors have added their comments about the case, the forms are sent to the Chief Medical Officer at the Department of Health. In Wales, Scotland and Northern Ireland, similar systems exist at a national level. Until 1984 reports covering deaths in England and Wales were published triennially, while reports for Scotland and Northern Ireland were published less frequently because of the smaller numbers of deaths involved. Starting with the triennium 1985–87, a single report covering all four countries is now published every three years. Maternal mortality enquiries are described in some detail in Chapter 10.

The Confidential Enquiry into Stillbirths and Deaths in Infancy (CESDI) was set up in 1992, for England, Wales and Northern Ireland to conduct their own enquiries on the same lines. The data for all three countries are then combined. As the name suggests, the Enquiry's brief was to collect information on all stillbirths and deaths in the first year of life, and to try to establish ways in which these deaths might be prevented. In addition, it collects data about all reported late fetal losses at 20–23 weeks of gestation. It established panels in each former NHS region of England and in Wales and Northern Ireland to perform enquiries into designated subsets of the deaths. A report covering the three countries is published annually and further information about these can be found in Chapter 3. Wales, Northern Ireland and many of the English regions also publish their own reports. Although it has conducted confidential enquiries in the past, Scotland does not have a continuous enquiry. Instead, each year it publishes data from SMR2 in the *Scottish stillbirth and infant death report.*

Censuses

A census has been taken every ten years since 1801, except 1941. A sample census was taken in 1966. The census includes questions about housing, employment, car ownership and household structure of the whole population. It is thus a source of data about the conditions of families with young children. In the 1951, 1961 and 1971 censuses questions were asked about fertility. A detailed analysis of the 1971 data was published in the *Fertility report from the 1971 census.*[45] Fertility data were not collected in the 1981 and 1991 censuses, so methods were developed to estimate fertility rates indirectly.[46] The 1991 census was the first to include a question on ethnic origin and the first since 1911 to include a question on morbidity.

Traditionally, the *Registrar General's decennial supplement on occupational mortality* is an analysis of deaths in the years surrounding each census in relation to the characteristics of people enumerated in the census. It relates the occupations of people who die to the occupations of people enumerated at the census and usually includes some analysis of perinatal and infant mortality by the babies' father's social class. For the 1971 census, separate occupational analyses were done for Scotland. The 1981 decennial supplement for Scotland was processed by OPCS along with that for England and Wales, and some aggregated analyses were also done for Great Britain.[47] A separate volume of data relating to babies and children was produced.[48] The decision to publish most of the tables in the main report on expensive and nearly illegible microfiches provoked widespread public criticism. Following this, in the late 1980s, a new broader approach was developed. Paper publication was reinstated, with additional data on disk or CD-ROM. Decennial supplements now include other related analyses of ONS data alongside the traditional analyses. For 1991, two separate volumes were published, one relating to occupational mortality and the other to analyses of health inequalities by social class.[49,50] A list of these decennial supplements can be found in Appendix 2.

The ONS Longitudinal Study, formerly known as the OPCS Longitudinal Study, links records of births, marriages, deaths and cancer registration occurring in a one per cent sample of the population of England and Wales with data collected about them at the census.[51,52] A number of volumes of analyses have been published and are listed in Appendix 2.

Surveys

ONS' Social Survey Division does both continuous and ad hoc surveys of the population. The General Household Survey, one of the continuous sample surveys, collects data about household structure, housing, education, employment and health and is thus a source of data about changes in the conditions of families with children. Successive cuts made in the Government Statistical Service have reduced the sample size of the General Household Survey.[53] It was suspended in 1997/98 and 1999/2000, but was reintroduced with a revised form and structure in 2000/01.

The Family Expenditure Survey collects data about spending patterns in families of different types, while the Family Resources Survey looks at resources within the family, social security benefits and housing costs. The Labour Force Survey, focussing on employment and unemployment, is done throughout the European Union.

The British Crime Survey is contracted out by the Home Office to the National Centre for Social Research, formerly known as Social and Community Planning Research (SCPR). The Health Survey for England, undertaken for the Department of Health by the National Centre for Social Research and University College London, looks at the health of children aged two years and over and of adults. A similar survey is done in Scotland. These and other regular surveys are described in annual reports on major regular social surveys published by ONS from 1996 onwards.

A number of ad hoc surveys done by ONS' Social Survey Division on subjects such as infant feeding and other surveys commissioned by government on subjects which are relevant to pregnancy and childbirth, are listed in Appendix 2. Some surveys formerly done by ONS and its predecessors have been contracted out elsewhere following market testing, while it has won contracts for other surveys.

Other sources of routine data

There are other sources of official statistics which contain data relevant to pregnancy and childbirth, although in some cases they do not deal with the subject explicitly. Some of them are mentioned in Table 2.16 which summarises the types of statistics which are collected, together with an assessment of some of their strengths and limitations.

Certain communicable diseases should, by law, be notified to the organisations responsible for monitoring them in each of the four countries of the United Kingdom. Further information, including details of their publications, are given in Chapters 9 and 10. A number of general practices also report them to the Royal College of General Practitioners' Research Unit.

Statistics on claims for National Insurance and social security benefits published in *Social security statistics* include claims for maternity allowances and maternity payments from the Social Fund. Details of these can be found in Chapter 11.

Data about consultations with general practitioners were collected in a series of studies at approximately ten yearly intervals. They therefore included some data about consultations during pregnancy. In the first three surveys, covering one year periods in 1955–56, 1970–71, and 1980–81, the general practitioners taking part undertook to keep an

Table 2.16

Types of official statistics relevant to health

Source of data	Examples	Characteristics
Civil registration	Births, stillbirths, marriages, deaths	Comprehensive coverage as documents required for legal purposes. Inflexible, as questions can only be changed by Act of Parliament.
Statutory notifications	Births, communicable diseases	Coverage should be complete as notification is required by law, but under-reporting does occur, especially with communicable diseases, which cannot be notified unless the person consults a doctor.
Voluntary notifications	Cancer registration, congenital anomalies	More under-reporting, but more opportunity to collect data than with statutory notifications and registrations.
Censuses of population	Census taken in 1961, 1966, 1971, 1981, 1991 and 2001	Statutory enumeration of whole population taken every ten years. Data become out of date, so demand for 'mid-term' census of a sample of the population arises, but the only one undertaken was in 1966.
Claims for National Insurance and Social Security benefits	Sickness absence, industrial injury and accidents	Sickness absence statistics confined to those paying full National Insurance contributions. Industrial illness and accident benefits can only be paid if it can be readily established that the condition was occupational in origin. This is difficult for some occupational diseases.
Administrative returns to central government health departments	Waiting list returns, bed availability and use	Emphasis on use and availability of services and facilities rather than on characteristics of people who use them.
Patients' contacts with the health service	Hospital Episode Statistics	Data concentrate on hospital in-patients with few data about outpatients and very unrepresentative data from general practice. Because record linkage is under-developed except in Scotland, data tend to deal with facilities and treatment rather than outcome.
Special analyses and record linkage	Registrar General's Decennial Supplement, ONS Longitudinal Study	Combined analyses of data from more than one source. Much more powerful than data from a single source but problems may arise when discrepancies arise in data, such as when different occupations are given at census and death registration. The ONS, formerly OPCS, Longitudinal Study overcomes this through record linkage, but has much smaller numbers in its one per cent sample.
Surveys, including 'one-off' surveys, surveys repeated at regular intervals and continuous surveys	Infant feeding, dental health, health surveys for England and Scotland, General Household Survey	Includes people who have not been in contact with the health services. Continuous surveys enable trends to be monitored over time. The General Household Survey is the only continuous government survey which relates people's perceptions of their health to a wide range of socio-economic factors. The health surveys for England and Scotland collect more detailed health data but their content changes from year to year.

age/sex register of their patients and to supply certain details about each consultation.[54-56] In the fourth survey in 1991–92, the general practitioners included had to have certain types of computer systems whose manufacturers wrote additional software for the survey.[57] Since participation involved a considerable amount of work, volunteer general practitioners had to be used instead of a random sample.

Other approaches are now being taken to collecting data from general practices by downloading them from their computer systems.[58] The General Practice Research Database consists of anonymised data on over two million patients from 288 general practices with the same type of computer system. Data from this are used for special projects and published routinely. Meanwhile the MIQUEST project is developing ways of downloading data from a wider range of systems. Further information can be found in Chapter 9.

This broad overview shows that a vast range of the data are collected by government and the NHS. In the chapters which follow we examine these in fuller detail and discuss how they may be interpreted and what they tell us about pregnancy and childbirth in its social and economic context.

References

1   Rosselson L. That's the way the wheels turn. In: *Bringing the news from nowhere: 125 songs by Leon Rosselson*. Wembley Park: Fuse Records, 1992.

2   World Health Organization. *International classification of diseases. Manual of the international statistical classification of diseases, injuries and causes of death. Ninth revision*. Vol. 1. Geneva: WHO, 1977.

3   World Health Organization. *International statistical classification of diseases and related health problems. Tenth revision*. Vol. 1. Geneva: WHO, 1992.

4   World Health Organization. *International classification of diseases. Manual of the international statistical classification of diseases, injuries and causes of death. Eighth revision*. Vol. 1. Geneva: WHO, 1967.

5   Office of Population Censuses and Surveys. *Registration: proposals for change*. Cm 939. London: HMSO, 1990.

6   Hewitt P. Written reply. *House of Commons Official Report (Hansard)*. 27–28. Dec 7 1998.

7   Office for National Statistics. *Registration: modernising a vital service*. London: Office for National Statistics, 1999.

8   World Health Organization. *International classification of impairments, disabilities and handicaps*. Geneva: WHO, 1980.

9   World Health Organization. *International classification of functioning and disability. Beta-2 draft*. On the Internet at http://www.who.int/msa/mnh/ems/icidh/. Geneva: WHO, 1999.

10   British Paediatric Association. *Classification of diseases: a paediatric adaptation of ICD-10*. London: Royal College of Paediatrics and Child Health, 1996.

11   Alberman E, Botting B, Blatchley N, Twidell A. A new hierarchical classification of causes of infant death in England and Wales. *Archives of Disease in Childhood* 1994; 70: 403–409.

12   Alberman E, Blatchley N, Botting B, Schuman J, Dunn A. Medical causes on stillbirth certificates in England and Wales: distribution and results of hierarchical classifications tested by the Office for National Statistics. *British Journal of Obstetrics and Gynaecology* 1997; 104(9): 1043–1049.

13   Wigglesworth JS. Monitoring perinatal mortality. A pathophysiological approach. *Lancet* 1980; ii(8196): 684–686.

14   O'Neil M, Payne C, Read J. Read codes, version 3: a user led terminology. *Methods of Information in Medicine* 1995; 34; 187–192.

15   NHS Centre for Coding and Classification. *Clinical terms, version 3. (Read codes.) Release overview*. Loughborough: NHSCC, 1994.

16   Office of Population Censuses and Surveys. *Classification of surgical operations*. London: OPCS, 1975.

17   Office of Population Censuses and Surveys. *Tabular list of the classification of surgical operations and procedures*. Fourth revision consolidated version. London: OPCS, 1990.

18   National Casemix Office. *Turning data into information*. Version 2. Winchester: National Casemix Office, 1998.

19   NHS Centre for Coding and Classification. *A strategic overview of OPCS-4*. Loughborough: NHS Executive, 1998.

20   Prentice T, Bentley T. Counting on clinical terms: the Healthcare Intervention Aggregation Project. *British Journal of Healthcare Computing* 1999; 16: 38–40.

21   Wallace M, Charlton J, Denham C. The new OPCS area classifications. *Population Trends* 1995; 79: 15–30.

22   Wallace M, Denham C. *The ONS classification of local and health authorities in Great Britain*. Studies on Medical and Population Subjects No. 59. London: HMSO, 1996.

23   *The ONS classification of local and health authorities of Great Britain: revised for authorities in 1999*. Studies on Medical and Population Subjects No. 63. London: ONS, 1999.

24   Office of Population Censuses and Surveys. *Standard occupational classification*. Vol. 3: Social classifications and coding methodology. London: HMSO, 1991.

25   Office of Population Censuses and Surveys and General Register Office for Scotland. *1991 Census. Definitions, Great Britain*. Series CEN91 DEF. London: HMSO, 1992.

26   Office for National Statistics. *Living in Britain: results from the 1996 General Household Survey*. London: The Stationery Office, 1998.

27   Rose D, O'Reilly, K. *The ESRC review of government social classifications*. London: Office for National Statistics and the Economic and Social Research Council, 1998.

28   Office for National Statistics. *The 2001 census of population*. London: The Stationery Office, 1999.

29   Office for National Statistics. *Statistics: a matter of trust. A consultation document*. Cm 3882. London: The Stationery Office, 1998.

30   *Building trust in statistics*. Cm 4412. London: TSO, 1999.

31   Devis T, Rooney C. Death certification and the epidemiologist. *Health Statistics Quarterly* 1999; 1: 21–33.

32   Heady JA, Heasman MA. *Social and biological factors in infant mortality*. Studies on Medical and Population Subjects No. 15. London: HMSO, 1959.

33   Spicer CC, Lipworth R. *Regional and social factors in infant mortality*. Studies on Medical and Population Subjects No. 19. London: HMSO, 1969.

34   Adelstein AM, Macdonald Davies I, Weatherall JA. *Perinatal and infant mortality: social and biological factors, 1975–1977*. Studies on Medical and Population Subjects No. 41. London: HMSO, 1980.

35   Office of Population Censuses and Surveys. *Mortality statistics, perinatal and infant: social and biological factors, 1978, 1979*. Series DH3 No. 7. London: HMSO, 1982.

36   Heasman MA, Clarke JA. Medical record linkage in Scotland. *Health Bulletin* 1979; 37(4): 97–103.

37   McIlwaine GM, Howat RC, Dunn F. *Perinatal mortality survey: Scotland, 1977*. Glasgow: University of Glasgow Department of Obstetrics and Gynaecology, 1977.

38   McIlwaine GM, Howat RC, Dunn F, Macnaughton MC. The Scottish perinatal mortality survey. *British Medical Journal* 1979; 2: 1103–1106.

39   McIlwaine GM, Howat RC, Dunn F, Macnaughton MC. Scottish perinatal mortality review 1979. *Health Bulletin* 1981; 39: 39–44.

40   Read A. The National Health Service Central Register. *Statistical News* 1998; 120: 8–12.

41   Middle C, Macfarlane AJ. Recorded delivery. *Health Service Journal* 1995; 105(5468): 27.

42   Macfarlane AJ. At last – maternity statistics for England [editorial]. *BMJ* 1998; 316(7131): 566–567.

43   Department of Health. NHS maternity statistics, England: 1989–90 to 1994–95. *Statistical Bulletin* 1997; 28: 1–44.

44   Smalls M, Pickering R, McKellar D. Linking maternity and neonatal discharge records. *Community Medicine* 1987; 9(2): 171–175.

45   Office of Population Censuses and Surveys. *Fertility report from the 1971 census*. OPCS Decennial Supplement Series DS No. 5. London: HMSO, 1983.

46   Brown A. Estimating fertility from household composition data in the census: the 'own-child' approach. *Population Trends* 1982; 29: 15–19.

47   Office of Population Censuses and Surveys. *Occupational mortality: decennial supplement 1979–80, 1982–83*. Part I: Commentary. OPCS Decennial Supplement Series DS No. 6. London: HMSO, 1986.

48   Office of Population Censuses and Surveys. *Occupational mortality 1979–80, 1982–83, England and Wales. Childhood supplement*. OPCS Decennial Supplement Series DS No. 8. London: HMSO, 1988.

49   Drever F, ed. *Occupational health*. OPCS Decennial Supplement Series DS No. 10. London: HMSO, 1995.

50   Drever F, Whitehead M, eds. *Health inequalities*. ONS Decennial Supplement Series DS No. 15. London: The Stationery Office, 1997.

51   Office of Population Censuses and Surveys. *Cohort studies: new developments*. Studies on Medical and Population Subjects No. 25. London: HMSO, 1973.

52   Hattersley L, Creeser R. *Longitudinal study 1971–1991: history, organisation and quality of data*. OPCS Longitudinal Study Series LS No. 7. London: HMSO, 1995.

53   Central Statistical Office. *Government statistical services*. Cmnd 8236. London: HMSO, 1981.

54   General Register Office. *Morbidity statistics from general practice, 1955–56*. Studies on Medical and Population Subjects No. 14. London: HMSO, 1958.

55   Royal College of General Practitioners, Office of Population Censuses and Surveys, Department of Health and Social Security. *Morbidity statistics from general practice, 1971–72: second national study*. Studies on Medical and Population Subjects No. 36. London: HMSO, 1979.

56   Royal College of General Practitioners, Office of Population Censuses and Surveys, and Department of Health and Social Security. *Morbidity statistics from general practice, 1981–82: third national study*. Series MB5 No. 1. London: HMSO, 1986.

57   Royal College of General Practitioners, Office of Population Censuses and Surveys, and Department of Health. *Morbidity statistics from general practice: fourth national study, 1991–1992*. Series MB5 No. 3. London: HMSO, 1995.

58   Hollowell J. The General Practice Research Database: quality of morbidity data. *Population Trends* 1997; 87: 36–40.

3 Variations in births and deaths

'How the people of England live is one of the most important questions that can be considered and how — of what causes and at what ages they die is scarcely of less account.'

William Farr, 1875[1]

The civil registration system is the main source of information about births and infant mortality and the way they vary from time to time and place to place. We start by outlining the data which are available for the periods before civil registration of births and deaths started and then go on to trace how the system developed. Next we describe trends in stillbirths, infant mortality and low birthweight during the twentieth century, including the way mortality varies by cause of death. Then we describe seasonal and day of the week variations before looking at differences between geographical areas. The chapter closes by discussing how trends and variations can be interpreted.

The development of birth and death statistics

Origins of birth and death registration

Although the practice of keeping records of births, marriages and deaths had already started by the sixteenth century, the earliest attempt to keep comprehensive records for the whole of England was made in 1538 when Thomas Cromwell, the Lord Chancellor, instructed parish churches to keep a weekly record of every baptism, wedding and burial in the parish.

The registers had a number of deficiencies which arose from their ecclesiastical basis.[2] They recorded baptisms not births, and burials not deaths. There was undoubtedly local variation in the extent to which they included private baptisms in places other than the parish church and burials of people who were not buried according to Anglican rites, or who were unbaptised. A fee was payable for a baptism but children of poor parents were supposed to be baptised free of charge, if their parents wanted an Anglican baptism. Even so, by custom, a celebration was expected when a child was baptised, so even churchgoers who were short of money may not have had all their children baptised.

Some efforts were made to centralise local registers. In 1590 Lord Burghley, the Lord Treasurer, tried unsuccessfully to centralise local parish registers for England and Wales in a single office and in 1597 and 1603 the Anglican Church issued orders requiring transcripts of the local records to be sent annually to the bishops' offices. Despite these attempts, it was never possible to analyse parish records for the whole country and derive national statistics from them until the nineteenth century, when summaries of data from parish registers were collected and published as part of the censuses of 1801 to 1831.[3]

During the seventeenth century, the numbers of 'dissenters' or 'non-conformists', as they were known after 1660, who belonged to churches other than the established Church of England, grew until in 1700 they made up about 10 per cent of the population. Dissenting congregations kept their own registers although some members had their children's baptisms either performed or recorded in Anglican churches.[4] This is because only the records of the Church of England could be presented in courts of law as legal records.

There were two periods during which parish registers were relatively complete. During the Commonwealth and Protectorate, from 1653 to 1660, Parliament set up a civil registration system under which births, marriages and burials were recorded in each parish by a secular elected official called a 'register' and marriages were conducted by Justices of the Peace. Although this system was not fully adopted everywhere, and ended at the Restoration, it is thought that its existence improved the completeness of recording of births and burials.[5,6]

Later in the seventeenth century, Acts of Parliament passed in 1666, 1678 and 1680 laid down that people should be buried in woollen cloth, to assist the wool trade. Compliance with the Acts had to be recorded for every burial, including those performed according to rites other than Anglican ones. From 1695 to 1705, a tax was placed on births, marriages and deaths and this payment had to be recorded, thus improving the completeness of registration.[3]

In general, parish registers were fairly complete in the early eighteenth century but had become less so by the 1780s, partly because of the continuing increase in membership of non-conformist churches and partly because of migration associated with the beginning of the industrial revolution. The system was in a state of virtual collapse between 1795 and 1820 but improved somewhat between 1821 and 1837.[4]

A number of historical studies using parish registers have developed ways of compensating for some of the deficiencies in the records in order to provide an overall picture of trends in mortality in the localities studied. Table 3.1 shows an example of such a study in which trends in infant and childhood mortality in Colyton, Devon over three centuries were documented.[7] The author pointed out that while infant mortality was at its highest in the early eighteenth century, mortality among children aged 1–14 years showed a different pattern, increasing during the seventeenth century and declining during the eighteenth. He also commented that infant mortality in Colyton which ranged from 120 to 158 per thousand births in the late sixteenth and early seventeenth century appeared to be low, compared with the rate of 235 per thousand observed from 1571 to 1586 in St Michael le Belfrey, York, 'a comparatively wealthy urban parish

Table 3.1

Estimated infant mortality rates, Colyton, Devon, 1538–1837

Period	Infant mortality rate/1,000 births	Mortality at ages 1–14 years (1,000q*)
1538–1599	120–140	124
1600–1649	126–158	176
1650–1699	118–147	200
1700–1749	162–203	124
1750–1837	122–153	119

*These are life table death rates, calculated by following a cohort of births through the relevant ages. See the original text for explanations of methods used and adjustments made.

Source: E A Wrigley. *Mortality in pre-industrial England: the example of Colyton, Devon over three centuries.*[7]

with thorough registration', and the rate of 240 per thousand in Wrangle, 'a tiny marsh parish', in Lincolnshire. Subsequent analysis of data for 1550–1649 covered a larger number of parishes and was followed by further detailed local analyses.[8,9]

The other major source of vital statistics in several English cities before the nineteenth century was the 'bills of mortality'. These were published weekly by local companies, and contained entries for cause of death. As this information was supplied to the parish clerk for a fee by local untrained informers, it cannot have been very exact. The 'bills of mortality' for London were published for plague deaths in epidemic years from the mid-sixteenth century onwards and were then published continuously from 1603 onwards. When civil registration was established in 1837, data from it were used to continue the London bill of mortality which was published in the Registrar General's weekly return. Similar data could still be found in the 'weekly return' in the *OPCS Monitor, Series WR* until the analysis was discontinued in May 1981. A number of detailed accounts of sources of historical data have been published.[10-13]

By the eighteenth century, the inadequacies of the bills of mortality and the declining parish register system were recognised and widely criticised. Various attempts were made to persuade Parliament to set up a system for compulsory registration of births, marriages and deaths and for setting up a special office to collect vital statistics. These were not successful until 1836.

The introduction of civil registration

Pressure to collect statistics was not the prime motive for setting up the registration system. Members of non-conformist churches wanted to have a civil registration system, because their own church records lacked legal status. Support also came from the legal profession, the medical profession and the British Association for Advancement of Science. The Poor Law Reform Act of 1834, and the debate about poor relief which surrounded it, raised questions about the size of the poor population. The strongest driving force for setting up a civil registration system, however, was the need for legal documents to establish people's rights to property.[14]

Two acts of parliament, 'An act for marriages in England' and 'An act for registering births, deaths and marriages in England', were passed in 1836. They established the basic registration procedure and a General Register Office to oversee it.[15] As a result of two further Acts of Parliament, a registration system was set up in Scotland in 1855 and a system for registering births and deaths in Ireland was set up in 1864. After the partition of Ireland under the Government of Ireland Act 1920, separate General Register Offices were set up in 1922 in Belfast and Dublin.[16]

In England, the registration system was based on the administrative divisions known as 'poor law unions' created by grouping parishes together to implement the 1834 Poor Law. In England and Wales two thousand local registrars recorded the births and deaths in their sub-districts. Each quarter they prepared a copy of the entries in their books and sent it to their superintendent registrar who then forwarded the copies to the General Register Office at Somerset House, where the Poor Law Commission also had offices. Similar procedures were set up in Scotland and Ireland.

The birth register included entries for the date of birth, the child's and the parents' names and the occupation of the father. Civil registration of births was not compulsory in England and Wales until 1875. Stillbirths did not have to be registered until 1927 in England, 1939 in Scotland and 1961 in Northern Ireland. At death registration, the name, age, occupation and sex of the deceased person was recorded together with the date and cause of the death. The person officiating at the burial was subject to a £10 fine if he or she did not report the death to the registrar within seven days.

The person who was responsible for setting up the system for analysing these data was William Farr who from 1837 to 1880 held the post of 'Compiler of Abstracts' in the General Register Office. To his intense disappointment, he never held the post of Registrar General. While today, the position is held by a senior civil servant, usually but not inevitably a statistician, in the nineteenth century it was a political appointment. The first Registrar General, Thomas Lister, was the brother-in-law of two leading Whig politicians, Lord Clarendon and Lord John Russell. He was described by Charles Babbage, inventor of the forerunner of the computer, as 'a flatulent young novelist' and the 'decorative headpiece' of the office.[17] When Thomas Lister died in 1842, he was replaced by Major George Graham, who was the brother-in-law of the Home Secretary and held the post until 1879, when he was replaced by Brydges Henneker, an ex-captain of the Royal Horse Guards. Whatever the reasons behind their appointments, Thomas Lister ensured that the General Register Office had a medical section and appointed William Farr, and George Graham ensured that he had the resources to do his work. When George Graham retired in 1879, William Farr made a bid for the post of Registrar General, but his failing health would have ruled him out in any case and he retired in 1880.[3] In fact, William Farr is much better remembered than the Registrars General under whom he served, both for his development of systems of data analysis and the distinctive style in which he presented the data and his interpretation of them.[3,15,18-20]

Figure 3.1

Infant mortality, Britain and Ireland, 1846–1997

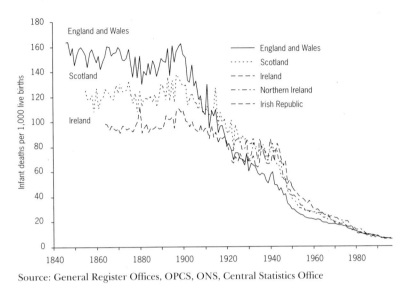

Source: General Register Offices, OPCS, ONS, Central Statistics Office

Infant mortality in the nineteenth and early twentieth century

Infant mortality rates for England and Wales, Scotland and Ireland for the years from 1846 to 1997 are shown in Figure 3.1. The data can be found in Tables A3.1.1 to A3.1.5 and similar data for the Channel Islands and the Isle of Man are in Tables A3.1.6 to A3.1.8. They show that infant mortality stayed at about the same level during the nineteenth century with a small downward trend in the 1870s and 1880s, followed by an increase in the 1890s. Since 1900, the rate has continued to decline, apart from a brief increase at the beginning of the second world war.

As these tables show, it is possible to construct infant mortality rates from 1846 for England and Wales, from 1855 for Scotland and from 1864 for Ireland. This can be misleading, as the concept of infant mortality did not emerge until later in the century, and reflected changes in perception of childhood.[21] When John Simon, Medical Officer to the General Board of Health, used the term infantile mortality in 1858, he was referring to the deaths of children under five.[22] William Farr first used the current definition indirectly to report deaths in 1875, when he wrote 'I show that in 1,000 infants born in 1875 no less than 158 died in the first year of life ...'[23] Even then he did not explicitly use the term 'infant' or 'infantile' mortality rate.

A factor which should not be ignored when interpreting trends in infant mortality in the nineteenth century, is that not all births were registered. The numbers which had not been registered were estimated after each census by cross-checking enumerated populations with numbers of registrations of births and deaths. As Table 3.2 shows, the deficit in birth registration became smaller between 1840 and 1870.[24,25] William Farr

Table 3.2

Estimated deficiency in birth registration in England and Wales in the mid-nineteenth century

Years	Estimated numbers of births not registered	Deficiency per 1,000 births
1841–50	38,036	65
1851–60	19,323	29
1861–70	13,614	18

Source: General Register Office, *Thirty fifth annual report of the Registrar General for the year 1872.*[26]

commented on this, 'I have reason to believe that a certain number of children born alive are buried as stillborn and that of deaths buried without a Registrar's certificate, a few are never registered.'[26]

If birth registration gradually became more complete, therefore, the same was probably true of infant death registration. There is good reason to assume that the infant mortality rates for the 1840s and 1850s were higher than registration data imply. Estimates which assume that half of unregistered babies died in infancy suggest that, had registration been complete throughout the nineteenth century, a very modest decline would have been observed in the rate.[25] Published infant mortality rates for Scotland and Ireland were lower than those for England and Wales, but showed similar fluctuations, as Figure 3.1 shows. The differences might suggest under-registration in Scotland and Ireland, but it has been suggested that the higher rates in England, especially in industrialised areas, were a consequence of poverty and poor housing.[27,28]

Even after birth registration became compulsory in 1875, under the Births and Deaths Registration Act of 1874, it is likely that some infant deaths escaped registration. From the 1860s onwards, a number of scandals emerged about the system of 'baby farming' or unpaid fostering. A contemporary broadsheet deploring 'baby farming' is shown in Figure 3.2. 'Baby farmers' took in and looked after babies, in particular babies born to unmarried women, including women working as wet nurses for wealthy families. Some of the 'baby farmers' neglected the babies they took in so that they died, while others disposed of them more quickly.[29,30] 'An act for better protection of infant life', passed in 1872, required 'baby farmers' to register and keep records, but it had many loopholes and children were still dying in this way in the 1890s.[29]

George Newman, Medical Officer of Health for Finsbury and later to become the first Chief Medical Officer of the Ministry of Health, commented on trends in the late nineteenth century in his book, *Infant mortality*, published in 1906:

> '... though the general death rate is decreasing the infant mortality rate is not declining. This means that whilst during the last half-century, a time of marvellous growth of science and of preventive medicine, human life has been saved and prolonged, and death made more remote for the general population, infants still die every year much as they did in former times.

Figure 3.2

A nineteenth century broadsheet about 'baby farming'

Source: Leslie Shepard Collection

Indeed, in many places it appears that they die in greater numbers, and more readily than in the past.'[27]

Although the infant mortality rate had started to fall during the first decade of the twentieth century, its high level was a major public issue at the time, partly because of the extent of the unfitness of recruits for the Boer War and the work of the committee investigating the reasons for this.[31,32] One view, held by followers of the eugenics movement, was that rising infant mortality at a time of falling childhood mortality was evidence of the survival of the fittest.[32-34] Others took the view that mothers were ignorant and needed to be educated to look after their babies while yet others saw the deaths of young babies as a consequence of poor housing, food and environmental conditions.[32,35]

These questions were aired at conferences on child welfare held by the Local Government Board in 1906 and 1908. To inform the debate, starting with the *Annual report of the Registrar General for 1904*, published in 1906, increasingly detailed tabulations of infant mortality were published. George Newman's book and a series of four reports on infant and childhood mortality produced by Arthur Newsholme for the Local Government Board investigated the possible contribution to infant mortality of such factors as 'antenatal influences', the employment of women, 'domestic and social conditions' and bottle feeding.[36-40] Many of the same questions are still being asked today and will be discussed in later chapters.

Registration of stillbirths

Under the Births and Deaths Registration Act of 1874, stillbirths did not have to be registered, but the stillbirth had to be certified and the certificate had to be produced when the body was buried. Anyone present at a stillbirth could certify the baby as stillborn. This was open to abuse. Sometimes as many as three or four children were buried with one stillbirth certificate.[41] The 1874 Act carried penalties for anyone burying a liveborn child as if it were stillborn, or burying a stillborn baby without a certificate.

Pressure for stillbirth registration in the 1890s led to parliamentary investigations. In 1893, the Select Committee on Stillbirth Registration published the results of an international survey.[42] This showed that Britain and Ireland lagged behind many other comparable countries in not having a system of stillbirth registration.

Arthur Newsholme, Medical Officer of Health for Brighton, who went on to become the Chief Medical Officer of the Local Government Board, commented on loopholes in the Act in the 1899 edition of his book *Vital statistics*:

> 'The Report of the Committee of the House of Commons on Death Certification says: "There is reason to think that if the statistics on the subject could be obtained, it would be found that the number of children buried in the United Kingdom annually as stillborn is enormous"; and the Committee are further convinced that "the absence of legal requirement that such births should be registered prior to disposal of the bodies is fraught with a very serious danger to child life". This is especially so in the case of illegitimate children.'[43]

The Select Committee's international survey confirmed that countries varied widely in their definition of stillbirth. The Royal Statistical Society's 'Special committee on infantile mortality' did a second survey and tried to establish criteria for registration of stillbirth. In a report published in 1912,

Figure 3.3

General fertility rate, England and Wales, 1838–1997

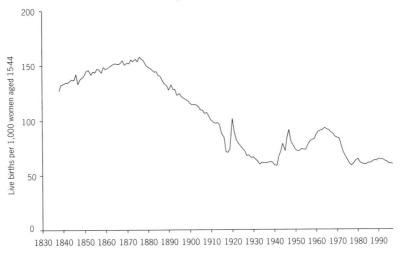

Source: General Register Office, OPCS, Office for National Statistics, *Birth statistics, Series FM1*

it identified two sets of issues, the gestational age after which a fetal death should be registered as a stillbirth and what constituted 'signs of life.'[44,45]

Stillbirth registration was finally introduced in England and Wales in July 1927, under the Births and Deaths Registration Act of 1926. It started in Scotland in 1939, Northern Ireland in 1961 and the Irish Republic in 1995.

Trends during the twentieth century

The fall in birth rates

The declining birth rate, shown in Tables A3.1.1 to A3.1.5 and in Figure 3.3 and the decrease in family size shown in Table 3.3 were a matter of public concern from the beginning of the twentieth century onwards. The data for the nineteenth century come from the 1911 census, the first in which information was recorded about fertility.[46–48] This was not repeated until the censuses of 1951, 1961 and 1971.

After many younger men died in the first world war, the decline continued and anxieties rose during the 1930s. This gave rise to a desire to increase the amount of information collected on the subject. Under the Population (Statistics) Act of 1938, additional data including the parents' ages and, for births within marriage, the mother's number of previous live and stillbirths by the current or any former husband were collected at birth registration in England and Wales from July 1938 onwards and in Northern Ireland and Scotland from the beginning of 1939. Age-specific fertility rates for England and Wales from 1939 onwards are shown in Table A3.2.1 and data

Table 3.3

Trends in family size

(a) Average size of completed family of women born in each five year period, 1841–65, and recorded as married in 1911, England and Wales, based on 1911 census.

Period of birth	Average number of live births
1841–45	5.71
1846–50	5.63
1851–55	5.40
1856–60	5.08
1861–65	4.66

The data for Scotland were analysed separately. It is considered that they showed a similar trend.

(b) Estimated average size of completed family of women married 1900–1929, Great Britain, based on Family Census 1946, provisional figures.

Period of marriage	Average number of live births
1900–09	3.37
1910–14	2.90
1915–19	2.53
1920–24	2.38
1925–29	2.19

Women who married for the first time when they were over 45 or whose first marriage had been dissolved when they were under 45 were excluded. Further details are given in the report of the Family Census.[50] The data for 1920–24 and 1925–29 were adjusted to allow for the fact that some of these women might not have completed their families by 1946.

Source: Royal Commission on Population. *Report.*[49] (Tables XV and XVI)

(c) Average achieved family size by the age of 45 by year of birth, England and Wales, 1924–1949.

Year of birth	Average number of live-born children by the age of 45
1924	2.11
1929	2.26
1934	2.42
1939	2.36
1944	2.21
1949	2.08

Note: Includes births at ages 45 and over which occurred up to the end of 1994
Source: Armitage B, Babb P. *Population review: (4) Trends in fertility.*[52]

for other countries are in Tables A3.2.2 to A3.2.5. Stillbirth registration came into force in Scotland under the same Act of Parliament.

The Royal Commission on Population, set up in 1943, decided that it needed further data to aid its deliberations. As no comprehensive fertility data had been collected since the 1911 census, it commissioned the Family

Figure 3.4

Total period fertility rates, England and Wales, Scotland, Northern Ireland, Irish Republic

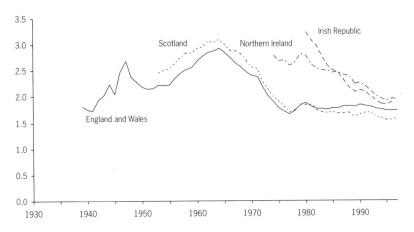

Source: General Register Offices, OPCS, ONS, Central Statistics Office

Census which was done in 1946. This was actually a survey of a 10 per cent sample of married women, with the sample being drawn using the 'reference leaves' of food ration books. The Royal Commission used many of the data from this survey.[49] A fuller report on the survey was published in 1954.[50] The data in Table 3.3 come from the Royal Commission's report and show a continuing decline in family size. The report on the Family Census attempted to estimate family sizes for the years between those covered by the two series.[50]

Birth rates declined overall from the mid 1960s reaching a low point in 1977. Age-specific fertility rates, shown in Tables A3.2.1 to A3.2.4, also declined in each age group, apart from women aged 15–19, among whom the decline did not start until 1972. The rates then increased sharply between 1977 and 1979, apart from those for women aged 15–19, among whom there was only a small increase.[51]

After a smaller increase early in the 1980s, fertility rates started to fall again overall in the 1980s and 1990s. In all the countries there were marked differences between age groups. While fertility rates fell among women aged under 25, they rose among older women, suggesting that women were continuing to postpone childbirth into their thirties and even into their forties.[52,53]

Tables A3.3.1 to A3.3.4 also show total period fertility rates (TPFRs) which are now commonly used to summarise age-specific fertility rates. The TPFR is a standardised measure which gives the total number of children who would be born to each woman if she experienced the age-specific fertility rates for the year in question throughout her child-bearing life. As Figure 3.4 shows, TPFRs are higher in Ireland than in Britain, but are declining in all the countries. To investigate these trends more fully needs

Figure 3.5

Stillbirth rates, England and Wales, 1928–97

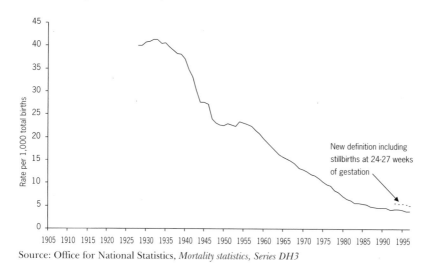

Source: Office for National Statistics, *Mortality statistics, Series DH3*

a variety of approaches and data from other sources, notably surveys.[54] Fuller data for England and Wales are published annually in *Birth statistics, Series FM1* and quarterly in *Population trends* and *Health statistics quarterly.* Data for the other countries are published in the *Registrar General's annual reports* for Scotland and Northern Ireland and in the Central Statistics Office for Ireland's *Vital statistics.*

Stillbirth and infant mortality rates

Stillbirth rates, and neonatal and postneonatal mortality rates for England and Wales are shown in Figures 3.5 and 3.6. The data are in Table A3.3.1 and the corresponding data for the other countries are in Tables A3.3.2 and A3.3.7. Although series can be constructed for earlier years, the term 'neonatal' did not come into official use until the mid 1930s.[55–57] The rates show very different temporal variations.

The stillbirth rate for England and Wales remained relatively constant through the 1930s but fell very rapidly during the second world war. It then remained fairly constant from 1949 to 1958 after which it fell steadily. Infant mortality rates for England and Wales for 1905 onwards are subdivided into neonatal and postneonatal in Figure 3.6. This shows a steady decline in neonatal mortality, with small fluctuations. Postneonatal mortality has fallen much more dramatically with much wider fluctuations in mortality, mainly due to infection. The peaks in the early years of the century coincided with hot Edwardian summers when diarrhoeal disease was a major killer. It is generally considered that improvements in housing, diet and sanitation made a major contribution to the decline in mortality

Figure 3.6

Infant mortality, England and Wales, 1905–97

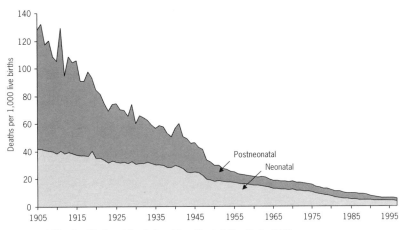

Source: Office for National Statistics, *Mortality statistics, Series DH3*

among babies and more widely.[58-60] It has also been argued that the decline in fertility played an important role.[61]

It is far from clear why there was a dramatic fall in the stillbirth rate and a decrease in the early neonatal mortality rate during the early years of the second world war, but there was a coincident increase in late neonatal and postneonatal mortality and also in death rates among children. It has been suggested that although the maternity services had fewer resources in wartime than in the preceding years, they were better organised and more equitably distributed and this may have influenced the stillbirth and early neonatal mortality rates.[62] Others have suggested that the improvements in organisation would have been unlikely to have come about before 1941. Indeed, one theory attributes the decline in rates to a decreased involvement in childbirth on the part of doctors who were redeployed in other areas, and a resulting increase in the responsibility taken by midwives. The increased mortality from pneumonia and bronchitis later in infancy may have been a consequence of fuel shortages during the exceptionally cold winters of 1940 and 1941,[63] and the disorganisation caused by evacuation of civilians to the countryside early in the war.

A factor which is thought likely to have helped reduce mortality in the later years of the war was the national food policy, one of whose aims was 'to pay special attention to those on whom the future depended.'[64] The Chief Medical Officer of the Ministry of Health expressed the view that:

'The national provision of milk and vitamin supplements to the priority groups has probably done more than any other single factor to promote the health of expectant mothers and young children during the war, and this

51

Figure 3.7

Stillbirth and perinatal mortality rates, England and Wales, 1960–97

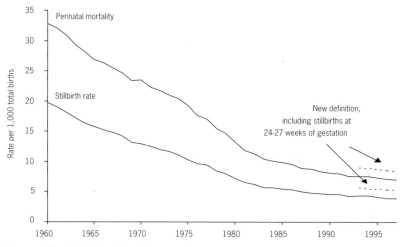

Source: Office for National Statistics. *Mortality statistics, Series DH3*

scheme together with rationing and the greatly improved nutritional qualities of the national loaf has contributed to the gradual decline in the maternal, neonatal, and infant mortality and stillbirth rates, so noteworthy in the last five years.'[64]

It has been suggested that similar influences during the first world war may have contributed to the decline in early neonatal mortality at that period.[65]

Although the series of perinatal mortality rates now published go back to 1928 and can be found in Tables A3.3.1 to A3.3.7, data were not presented in this way in the Registrar General's Statistical Review until 1950. The idea of combining stillbirth and early neonatal mortality rates to form a perinatal mortality rate was first proposed in an article published in 1948 in *Population Studies*.[66] The author, Sigismund Peller, supported his suggestion with the observation that, at that time, trends in first week deaths had more in common with those in stillbirths than they did with mortality in the rest of the first year of life. More recently, this practice is being questioned, in the light of differences between stillbirth and live birth registration. There is an increasing tendency to show stillbirths and an overall neonatal mortality rate separately, as we have done in Figures 3.5 and 3.6.

In general, during the second half of the twentieth century, there was an overall decline in stillbirth and infant mortality rates. Stillbirth and neonatal mortality rates fell particularly rapidly in the late 1970s and early 1980s. In England and Wales, perinatal mortality fell by 48 per cent from 19.3 per thousand in 1975 to 10.1 per thousand in 1985, as Figure 3.7 shows.

Figure 3.8

Infant mortality rates, England and Wales, 1960–97

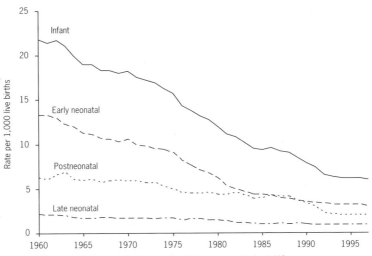

Source: Office for National Statistics. *Mortality statistics, Series DH3*

Despite this, there were exceptions to the overall decline. The early neonatal mortality rate rose slightly in 1970, but fell again in 1971, as Figure 3.8 shows. This increase was most marked in the second quarter of 1970. Babies who were born during this quarter are likely to have been in the first three months of gestation during the severe influenza epidemic which occurred during late December 1969 and early January 1970.[67] Other influenza epidemics in this period did not appear to be accompanied by increases in mortality, but there may have been short term fluctuations which were too small to affect the aggregated annual rates. For example, a local analysis in France showed a fall in average birthweight in babies born in the aftermath of the same epidemic.[68]

The second exception to the overall decline in mortality was the flattening off of the late neonatal and postneonatal mortality rates between 1976 and the late 1980s in England and Wales and Northern Ireland, and also, since 1978, in Scotland. These rates are usually calculated by dividing the numbers of deaths registered in a given year by the numbers of live births which occurred in the same year and were registered in that year or January of the following year. As it is possible that the considerable fluctuations in numbers of births during the 1970s could distort postneonatal mortality rates, 'birth cohort' rates were calculated. These relate deaths to the years in which the babies were born and are given in Table A3.6.1. They show a pattern which is similar but more marked than that in Figure 3.8. Since 1993, such 'birth cohort' mortality rates have been used routinely in OPCS and ONS publications in Series DH3.

Although conclusions were never established, possible explanations were advanced for the lack of any further decline in late neonatal and postneonatal mortality from the late 1970s to the early 1980s.[69,70] The first was that, as in the past, the postneonatal mortality rate was a sensitive indicator of socio-economic conditions, and these were not improving in England and Wales in the late 1970s and 1980s. A second suggested interpretation of the static rates was that developments in neonatal special and intensive care may delay, but not finally prevent, the death of very ill small babies.[71,72] Table A3.6.2 shows that in the mid 1960s the proportion of infant deaths which occurred in the postneonatal period started to increase. Furthermore, the number of postneonatal deaths certified as being due to conditions originating in the perinatal period was already rising steadily from the late 1970s onwards. A third suggestion was that while neonatal intensive care may prevent the death of babies who might otherwise have died, these babies may be particularly susceptible to any adverse conditions with which they are confronted later in infancy. These issues were never resolved before trends in mortality changed in the mid to late 1980s.

A small rise in the infant mortality rate for England and Wales from 9.4 per thousand in 1985 to 9.6 in 1986 influenced public perceptions about infant mortality and led to major developments in data collection. After the rise was featured in press reports on Christmas Eve, 1987, the Prime Minister, Margaret Thatcher, responded to questions in parliament with the suggestion that 'it may well be that it is a statistical error'.[73] Figure 3.8 shows that the rise was actually a continuation of previous trends towards a flattening off of neonatal mortality and a slight rise in postneonatal mortality.[74] A much more detailed analysis showed that the increase was largely in deaths attributed to the sudden infant death syndrome. This rise started in February and continued to May 1986, and was associated with exceptionally cold weather in February 1986.[75]

The rise in infant mortality prompted the House of Commons back-bench Social Services Committee to undertake another enquiry into the subject. In its report, it called for 'a targeted programme to reduce perinatal and infant mortality rates, particularly in poorer families ...'[76] The government, in its reply, announced it would set up a national confidential enquiry into stillbirths and infant death. English regions were asked to set up regional epidemiological surveys and ensure that they had a paediatric pathologist in post. The government also announced it would set targets for perinatal and infant mortality and ask the Medical Research Council to undertake a major review of research on cot death.[77] In response to the great interest in sudden infant deaths, OPCS and subsequently ONS devoted a special annual *Monitor* in the DH3 series to the subject. In 1999, this was incorporated into *Health statistics quarterly*.

The Confidential Enquiry into Stillbirths and Deaths in Infancy (CESDI), which is described later, was established in 1992. By this time, infant mortality trends had changed markedly. The postneonatal mortality rate for England and Wales had fallen from 4.1 per thousand live births in 1989 to 2.3 per thousand in 1992, as Table A3.3.1 and Figure 3.8 show. Tables A3.3.2 to A3.3.4 show that similar falls occurred slightly later in Scotland

and Ireland. The decrease was largely attributed to the government's 'Back to sleep' campaign, launched in December 1991, despite the fact that mortality had started to fall earlier. The campaign encouraged parents to avoid placing their babies to sleep on their fronts, over-wrapping them and covering their heads and exposing them to cigarette smoke. The extent to which these practices are adopted cannot be monitored through routine data collection systems, so local surveys are needed.[78] A second campaign launched in the summer of 1996 was not followed by a further fall in mortality.[79]

The lowering in October 1992 of the gestational age limit for registering a fetal death as a stillbirth from 28 to 24 completed weeks of pregnancy has made it difficult to monitor trends in stillbirth and perinatal mortality, as Figure 3.7 shows. For this reason, tables in this book show stillbirth rates according to both old and new definitions, wherever possible. This suggests that the decline in stillbirth and perinatal mortality rates slackened off in England and Wales in the 1990s.

Birthweight

It might be expected that trends in the incidence of low birthweight would shed some light on trends in mortality, but these data were not collected on a national scale until 1953 for live births and 1955 for stillbirths. The data in Tables A3.4.1 and A3.5.1 were collected up to 1986 using LHS 27/1 low birthweight returns derived from birth notification data and aggregated nationally first by the Ministry of Health and later by the Department of Health and Social Security. Birthweight data are now added to birth registration details and are shown in Tables A3.4.2 and A3.5.2.

Despite the strong correlation between stillbirth and infant mortality rates and the incidence of low birthweight, it is difficult to establish direct associations over time between mortality and the incidence of low birthweight. Perhaps one exception is the small peak in low birthweight in 1970, shown in Figure 3.9, coinciding with the rise in mortality described earlier.

A notable feature in Figure 3.9 is the continuing rise in the percentage of low weight births in the late 1980s and the 1990s. This can be attributed to the rise in the multiple birth rate and in the numbers of babies weighing under 1,000g. In the past, many of these babies would not have survived and would have been regarded as miscarriages. Increasingly they receive intensive care and many more survive. As a result, they are registered as live births. This is discussed more fully in Chapter 6. Similar trends can be seen in Table A3.4.4 which shows trends in Scotland and is derived from SMR2 data provided to the Scottish stillbirth and infant death survey.

In England and Wales, the neonatal mortality rate for low birthweight babies, shown in Figure 3.10, decreased considerably between 1963 and the late 1980s, but subsequently levelled off during the 1990s. These data are difficult to interpret because of missing birthweights in the early 1990s, the reasons for which are described in Chapter 6. Similar trends for Scotland can be seen in Table A3.5.3.

Figure 3.9

Incidence of low birthweight, England and Wales, 1953–97

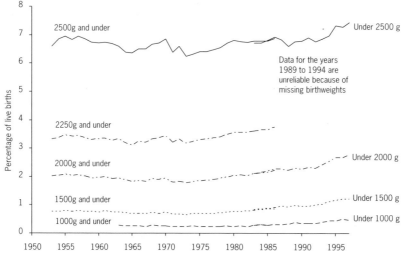

Source: LHS 27/1 low birthweight returns and ONS *mortality statistics*

Figure 3.10

Neonatal mortality among low birthweight babies, England and Wales, 1963–97

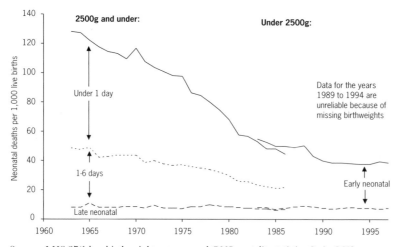

Source: LHS 27/1 low birthweight returns and ONS *mortality statistics, Series DH3*

Gestational age

In England and Wales, gestational age is recorded at the registration of stillbirths, but is not collected for live births, meaning that gestation-specific stillbirth rates cannot be calculated from registration data, although it would be feasible to derive them from the Hospital Episode Statistics. Numbers of stillbirths are shown in Table A3.4.3.

The lack of data also means that trends in preterm birth cannot be monitored until either a change is made in data collection or data from the Hospital Episode Statistics become more complete. Trends in preterm birth in Scotland are shown in Table A3.4.4, while mortality rates by gestational age are in Tables A3.5.4 and A3.5.5.

The change in definition of stillbirth has probably reinforced the tendency to register very preterm babies who die as live births and neonatal deaths, instead of regarding them as miscarriages. This, added to the increasing survival rate of very preterm babies, has contributed to the continuing rise in the reported incidence of very low birthweight, shown in Figure 3.9, and the incidence of preterm birth in Scotland, shown in Table A3.4.4.

Causes of death

It might be expected that trends in stillbirth and infant mortality rates, tabulated by cause, which are summarised in Tables A3.7.1 to A3.9.4, would shed further light on these changes in mortality, but it is often difficult to distinguish changes in diagnostic fashion from real changes.[80] Added to this is the impact of changes in the way causes of death are recorded and in the way they are classified. First, there was the change in 1979 to the ninth revision of the International Classification of Diseases (ICD). Then, in 1986, new forms were introduced for certifying stillbirths and neonatal deaths in England and Wales, but not Scotland and Ireland. The forms are shown in Appendix 6.

The classification of deaths attributed to perinatal causes in the ninth revision of the ICD differs considerably from that used in the eighth revision. A sample of deaths registered in 1978 was coded according to both revisions and the two codes were compared. This is usually called 'bridge coding'. Comparisons of codes used for infant deaths are shown in Tables A3.10.1 and A3.10.2.

The chapters of the ICD which are used to classify postneonatal deaths changed less between the eighth and ninth revision than did the chapter dealing with perinatal causes, but a change of a different sort had already taken place during the 1970s. This was the increasing use of the term 'sudden death, cause unknown' (ICD 795 eighth revision, 798 ninth revision) to classify 'cot deaths', which are a major cause of postneonatal death. This is illustrated in Figure 3.11, which shows the impact of this practice and then the decline in 'cot deaths' or deaths attributed to the sudden infant death syndrome in the late 1980s and early 1990s in England and Wales.

There is a continuing debate about the meaning of the term 'sudden infant death syndrome'.[81] A particular question is whether such deaths all occur spontaneously. Table A4.19.2, based on Home Office data, shows a slight rise in reports of violent deaths of babies, but that the numbers are still low. Data from ONS published in *Mortality statistics, injury and poisoning, Series DH4* show only 49 deaths due to homicide among children aged under 16 in 1996 and 30 open verdicts. A study of 456 sudden unexpected deaths in

Figure 3.11

Postneonatal mortality by cause, England and Wales, 1963–97

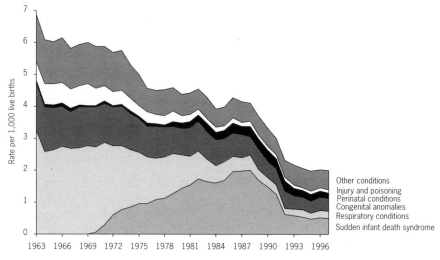

Source: ONS, *mortality statistics, Series DH3*

infancy in the years 1993 to 1996, undertaken as part of the Confidential Enquiry into Stillbirths and Deaths in Infancy, categorised 363 of them as 'sudden infant death syndrome'. Of the remaining 93, only 21 were attributed to 'suspected maltreatment'.[82]

The data in Tables A3.7.1 to A3.8.4 were derived using the time-honoured method of coding the underlying cause, grouped into chapters of the ICD. In 1993, OPCS introduced software which read all the conditions on death certificates and derived the underlying cause automatically. As it used different algorithms from the preceding manual methods, discontinuities arose in the data and methods had to be found to allow for these.[83] Scotland and Northern Ireland did not make this change but are doing so when moving to the tenth revision of the ICD.

Stillbirths and neonatal deaths could not be processed by this software as the new form of certificate introduced in 1986 in England and Wales has a different structure, with separate spaces for conditions originating in the mother, in the baby and for other factors related to the death. Although the form of certificate piloted had room for only one condition in each box, the version adopted allows for more than one.[84]

In developing ways of classifying stillbirths and neonatal deaths, OPCS started from a classification designed by a pathologist, Jonathan Wigglesworth.[85–87] It is based on features which can be observed without a post-mortem, supplemented by information from the mother and baby's clinical history, but was designed to be used by people who had access to case notes. It was adapted by the *International collaborating effort on birthweight, plurality, perinatal and infant mortality* to group underlying causes of death coded from death certificates.[88] This group also extended it to causes of postneonatal death. OPCS developed this further to take account of all the conditions mentioned on the certificate.[89,90] Trends in deaths classified in this way into what are described as 'ONS cause groups' are shown in Tables A3.9.1 to A3.9.4 and published annually by ONS in *Mortality statistics, Series DH3*. These will be revised for use with the tenth revision of the ICD.

The accuracy of clinical information on stillbirth and death certificates has long been a matter of concern and led to studies which found disparities between causes of death described in case notes and those recorded on the death certificate.[91,92] Similar discrepancies have been recorded in certifying deaths in adults.[93] In 1982 the Royal College of Physicians and Royal College of Pathologists published a joint report drawing attention to the need to improve the quality of death certification.[94] They suggested that medical students and junior doctors should be given formal training in the completion of death certificates, and that more post-mortems should be done. ONS has produced a video entitled *Death counts* to assist with this teaching.[95]

These discrepancies make it difficult to compare mortality rates within the same country. Even greater differences are possible internationally. In order to try and avoid this problem, the 'Nordic-Baltic' classification groups deaths according to the gestational age at birth and the timing of death in relation to labour.[96] This information is not available for deaths in England and Wales.

Confidential enquiries into stillbirths and deaths in infancy

The limitations of data on death certificates and the high profile given to perinatal mortality from the late 1970s onwards led to many local surveys and enquiries into perinatal deaths. Some were relatively shortlived, while others, such as the surveys in the Northern and South East Thames regions, became firmly established.[97–102] The possibility of national surveys and enquiries was discussed and surveys became established in Scotland and later in Wales.

As part of its response to the report from the House of Commons Social Services Committee about the rise in infant mortality, the Department of Health set up a working group in May 1989. Its terms of reference were: 'to consider and report on the issues raised by the proposal to make confidential enquiries into stillbirths and deaths in infancy, and to make recommendations.'[103] The working party recommended that confidential enquiries should be co-ordinated at regional level and should cover samples of late fetal losses, stillbirths and infant deaths.[103]

The Confidential Enquiry into Stillbirth and Deaths in Infancy (CESDI) was set up in 1992. It was based on the 14 regional health authorities in England. At the time of writing, it still uses the same geographical areas, although regional staff are now based either in a 'lead' district or employed by universities. Enquiries were also set up in Northern Ireland and in Wales where it was added to the pre-existing survey.

Initially CESDI in England was funded directly by the Department of Health. Since April 1996 it has been contracted to the Maternal and Child Health Research Consortium. This was formed by the Royal College of

Table 3.4

Subjects chosen for confidential enquiry, 1993–2000

Year of enquiry	Subject	Geographical coverage	Findings reported
1993	Intrapartum related deaths weighing 2.5kg or more	England, Wales, Northern Ireland	Second annual report[106]
1993–4	Sudden unexpected deaths in infancy	South Western Yorkshire, Trent regions	Third annual report[107]
1994–5	Intrapartum-related deaths weighing 1.5 kg or more	England, Wales, Northern Ireland	Fourth annual report[108]
1993–6	'Explained' sudden unexpected deaths in infancy	South Western Yorkshire, Trent, Northern, Wessex regions	Fifth annual report[82]
1995–7	Antepartum term stillbirths	West Midlands region	Fifth annual report[82]
1996–7	1 in 10 sample of deaths of babies weighing 1 kg or more excluding postneonatal deaths and congenital anomalies	England, Wales, Northern Ireland	
1997	All deaths of babies weighing over 4 kg	England, Wales, Northern Ireland	
1998–2000	Babies born at 27 or 28 weeks of gestation	England, Wales, Northern Ireland	

Source: Confidential Enquiry into Stillbirths and Deaths in Infancy. *Fifth annual report*[82]

Obstetricians and Gynaecologists, the Royal College of Paediatric and Child Health, the Royal College of Pathologists and the Royal College of Midwives. In 1999, CESDI became part of the work of the National Institute of Clinical Excellence (NICE).

CESDI has two main streams of activity. The first is to gather basic data on every stillbirth and infant death and every fetal loss from 20 weeks of pregnancy. This is done on a 'rapid report form'. Rapid report forms are collated at regional level. They are forwarded to the central secretariat and also used as a basis for regional reports. In contrast to death registration, their focus is on clinical information.

The second activity is confidential enquiry into subsets of events. Subjects of enquiries are listed in Table 3.4. In the confidential enquiry process, members of multidisciplinary regional panels are sent sets of anonymised case notes and then meet to review them. At the meeting they produce a summary of the case and complete a standard CESDI form. This includes comments on the standard of care, which is graded as follows:

0   No suboptimal care.

1   Suboptimal care but different management would have made no difference to the outcome.

2   Suboptimal care. Different management might have made a difference to the outcome.

3   Suboptimal care. Different management would reasonably have been expected to have made a difference to the outcome.

The results of the enquiries are collated at national level and have been published in a series of reports.[82,104–108] These are listed in Appendix 2.

Like other confidential enquiries, CESDI did not initially compare babies who died with control groups of babies who did not die. This made its findings difficult to interpret, as it was not known to what extent surviving babies had also received suboptimal care. In its studies of sudden unexpected deaths in infancy and later in its study of births at 26 or 27 weeks of gestation, CESDI has used control groups for comparison purposes. This, together with validation studies, should strengthen the conclusions it draws from its work.

Short term variations in births and infant mortality

Seasonal variation

> 'A child born in January will be laborious,
>
> In February, will love money much but women more.
>
> The person born in March will be honest and rather handsome.
>
> The person born in April will be subject to maladies and will travel to his disadvantage.
>
> A person born in May will be handsome and amiable,
>
> In June, will be small of stature and very fond of children,
>
> In July will be fat and constant,
>
> In August, ambitious and courageous,
>
> In September, strong and prudent,
>
> In October, will be wicked and inconstant and will have a florid complexion,
>
> In November, will be a gay deceiver,
>
> In December, will be of passionate disposition and will devote himself to public affairs.'

Quoted in the *Encyclopaedia of superstitions, folklore and the occult sciences of the world*, 1903.[109]

Astrology and our folklore bear testimony to widespread and deeply held beliefs that the time of year people are born has a profound effect on their personalities and the course of their lives. While it is unclear whether these beliefs still persist, statistics do reveal marked seasonal variation in both the numbers of babies born and in the mortality rates among them.

The *Registrar General's statistical review for 1967*[110] commented that, apart from the years of the two world wars, the seasonal pattern of births had remained unchanged since 1870, with the highest birth rate in the March quarter of the year from January to March and the lowest in the December quarter from October to December. It made the rather more mundane suggestion that income tax concessions might have some influence over the pattern. A maximum in the March quarter was, however, seen many centuries earlier, in an analysis of baptisms in Ludlow between 1577 and 1619, but in these data the minimum occurred in the summer months.[8]

In the 1970s, the birth rate tended to be highest in the March quarter and lowest in the December quarter, but in some years the birth rate was higher in the June and September quarters. It is notable that the years between 1975 and 1980 when the peak in births did not occur in the spring, were those in which the overall trend was changing. The changes in longer term trends are likely to have interacted with the seasonal pattern, so it was unclear whether a change in seasonality occurred. In the 1990s, in England and Wales, the numbers of births peaked in summer, as Figure 3.12 shows. An analysis of monthly births in Scotland over the year 1938–87 found two peaks during each year, a wide peak in spring and early summer and a narrow peak in October.[111] Over the 48 years, the main peak declined in importance and moved forward by two months, while the October peak became more prominent in the last decade. It was suggested that this might

Figure 3.12

Live births by month of birth, England and Wales, 1975–97

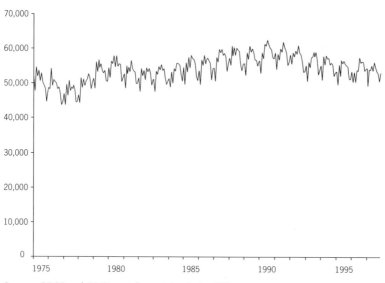

Source: OPCS and ONS, *mortality statistics, Series DH3*

have resulted from social changes, for example in the pattern of holidays, or in the environment or the climate.

Short term fluctuations in the numbers of births were examined in greater detail in an analysis of the total number of live and stillbirths in England and Wales each day from April 1 1969 to December 31 1980.[112] Each year there was a distinct peak in the numbers of births at the end of September, irrespective of whether the yearly maximum occurred in the spring or the autumn. The autumn peak is also apparent in some Nordic countries and has been attributed to the effects of Christmas and New Year festivities.[113]

Seasonal variation in births among the population as a whole can differ from that of specially selected groups. For example, the OPCS Longitudinal Study was used to estimate the seasonal distribution of births of the population as a whole, and the same data for people admitted to psychiatric hospitals during the years 1970 to 1976 was derived from the Mental Health Enquiry.[114] It was found that people diagnosed as having schizophrenia were more likely than the population as a whole to have been born during the March quarter, but no such difference was found for people with a diagnosis of neurosis. Studies elsewhere have shown a preponderance of births of schizophrenics in the latter part of the coldest period of the year,[115] both in countries where the peak in total births is in the coldest months, and also in the United States, where the peak is in the late summer. An analysis of data from the Mental Health Enquiry for England and Wales suggested that the increased rate of schizophrenia among winter births was also associated with being born in cities.[116] A study in Denmark reached similar conclusions.[117] This suggests that the influences behind the seasonality in schizophrenic births are different from those which cause seasonality in births in general.[118]

This may apply to other conditions. For example, compared with the general population, people with diabetes appear to be more likely to be born during the winter months than during the summer months.[119] Higher rates of birth after artificial insemination by donor were found in winter months in Sheffield and a subarctic region of Finland but not in a very much larger number of artificial inseminations in France.[120-122] Multiple birth rates can vary seasonally in some populations.[123-125]

Infant mortality rates by month of birth, published by ONS in its DH3 series, are shown in Figure 3.13. This uses 'birth cohort' rates with numbers of births each month as a denominator and the numbers of deaths at each stage of the first year of life as a numerator. A similar approach was used in two studies of seasonal variation in infant mortality in the 1970s.[126,127] They showed no sign of seasonal variation in stillbirths or neonatal deaths, but that postneonatal death rates were highest among babies born in the latter half of the year. Much of this was due to deaths attributed to the sudden infant death syndrome. Seasonal variation in these deaths was greatest at the age of three months.[128] This contrasted with a study of childhood mortality which showed that mortality peaked during the summer months, because of deaths from accidents during school holidays.[129]

Figure 3.13

Infant mortality by month of birth, England and Wales, 1975–96

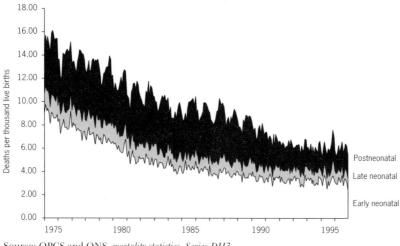

Source: OPCS and ONS, *mortality statistics, Series DH3*

As it happens, these seasonal patterns in mortality are very similar to those seen in burials recorded in the parish register of Ludlow between 1577–1619[8] and in aggregated data from five other parishes between 1550 and 1649. This does not mean that the pattern has remained unchanged since then, as the reason for the summer peak was different. The high death rate in summer amongst children in Ludlow was attributed to infectious diseases and these diseases, particularly diarrhoeal diseases, inflated infant mortality rates in the summer during the eighteenth and nineteenth centuries.

During the nineteenth century, the seasonal pattern in infant mortality varied over time from country to country.[130] In years with hot summers in England and Wales, mortality was highest in the summer. Furthermore, the level of infant mortality in summer influenced the annual rate, as was shown for example, in an analysis in the *Registrar General's Statistical Report for 1906*.[131] While such analyses tended to concentrate on the associations between high temperature, low rainfall and high mortality in summer, it was not meteorological conditions alone, but their interaction with poor housing and sanitary conditions which inflated mortality rates.[27,132]

Mortality from diarrhoea and communicable diseases declined rapidly between 1900 and the mid 1920s and the summer peaks disappeared.133 Although still high in less developed countries, infant mortality from these conditions is now extremely low in England and Wales as can be seen in Tables A3.7.1 to A3.9.4 and more detailed analyses in *Mortality statistics, cause, Series DH2*. There was no increase in mortality at any age in infancy during the heat waves in the 1970s, 1980s or 1990s. A review of seasonal variation in rates of infant mortality from 1912–1978 and stillbirth rates from 1928–1978 showed that in the 1930s and 1940s all the rates were higher in winter than summer. Seasonal variations disappeared from the stillbirth rate in about 1950 and from the neonatal mortality rate in about 1965.[134]

In England and Wales, seasonal variation in postneonatal mortality diminished over the years 1988 to 1992 when mortality attributed to the sudden infant death syndrome declined. Deaths by year and month of occurrence published in OPCS and ONS annual sudden infant death *Monitors* suggested a reduction in its seasonality.[135] Closer inspection showed, however, that while the absolute differences between seasons had declined along with the rate as a whole, the relative differences in mortality persisted.[136] These patterns need further investigation using a birth cohort approach.

Day of the week variations

'Born of a Monday, fair in face,
Born of a Tuesday, full of God's grace
Born of a Wednesday, merry and glad
Born of a Thursday, sour and sad
Born of a Friday, godly given
Born of a Saturday, work for your living
Born of a Sunday, never shall want
So there ends the week and there's an end on it.'

'The child of Sunday and Christmas day
Is good and wise and fair and gay.'

Traditional, quoted in *The Oxford dictionary of nursery rhymes*[137]

While our folklore has it that children born on Sunday or Christmas day are likely to have good fortune in life, the proportion of children who might be favoured in this way is considerably smaller than it was thirty years ago.

Since April 1 1969, the date of birth has been recorded and coded for analysis on all birth registrations in England and Wales. This made it possible to derive the numbers of births each day, and analyse them by day of the week of birth. When the daily births are plotted on a larger scale, as they are in Figure 3.14, a distinct seven day cycle can be seen. Within each week, the smallest numbers of births occurs on a Sunday and the maximum falls on Tuesday, Wednesday, Thursday or Friday. The main interruption of this seven day pattern occurs at public holidays.

In the 1970s, there were fewer births on Christmas day and Boxing Day than on any other day of the year.[112] This deficit was much less marked in the 1990s in England and Wales, but was still apparent in Denmark.[138] The numbers of births on other public holidays are also lower than on the corresponding days of the weeks before and after the holiday. During the

Figure 3.14

Total number of births each day, England and Wales, 1996

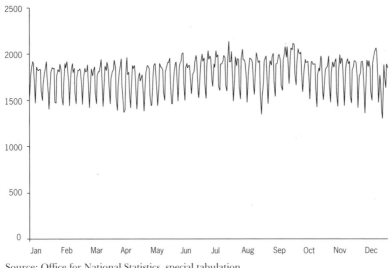

Source: Office for National Statistics, special tabulation

1980s and early 1990s, the differences became marginally smaller. The establishment of the weekly variation coincided with the greater use of induction in England and Wales, but persisted while induction rates fell in the late 1970s and 1980s. Similar cycles have been observed in patterns of birth in a number of other countries.[139-144] Births in Israel were found to have a Saturday deficit.[145] Day of the week variations in both inductions and elective caesarean sections make a major contribution.[139,142,146,147]

The ratios of the average numbers of births on each day of the week to the overall daily average for each year can be found in Table A3.11.1. Data from several developed countries suggest that this pattern became established during the 1960s.[148-150] It became more pronounced during the early 1970s in England and Wales and North America[148,150,151] and remained stable from the late 1970s onwards in England and Wales.[112,151]

Whatever the nature of the good fortune in store for babies born on Sunday may be, it was not necessarily reflected in their perinatal mortality rate. Table A3.11.2 gives perinatal mortality rates among babies born on each day of the week for the years 1970 to 1995. For most years in the early 1970s, the mortality rates among babies born at the weekend were higher than those among babies born on weekdays. The difference was wider and more consistent from 1976 onwards but seems to have declined during the 1980s and early 1990s. Elevated death rates at the weekend were also observed in Arkansas, USA[152] and Tayside, Scotland,[153] but no weekend excess was seen in studies in Osaka, Japan[154] and Norway.[155] Data from Scotland show raised intrapartum death rates from Saturday to Monday compared with the rest of the week in the mid 1990s.[156]

In the early 1980s there also appears to have been a higher incidence of low weight births at weekends than on weekdays in England and Wales, as can be seen in Table A3.11.3 in which births are tabulated by weight and day of the week. This pattern had changed by the mid 1990s. Now that birthweight data are almost complete in birth registration records for England and Wales, these patterns can be investigated more fully to establish reasons for the change.

Geographical differences

'Suffolk gives a baby a better start in life.'[157]

'Why do so many Rochdale babies die?'[158]

In the late 1970s, public attention was focused on the geographical variations in perinatal mortality, as a result of a campaign in the media and parliament. The low perinatal mortality rates in places such as Suffolk, Oxfordshire and Kingston upon Thames were contrasted with the relatively high rates in places such as Rochdale, Dudley, Wolverhampton and Walsall. In the early 1990s, comparisons between the low rate in Prime Minister John Major's Huntingdon constituency and the high rate in Bradford, attracted similar high profile comment.[159]

These geographical differences are no new phenomenon and they can also be seen in the mortality rates for adults. They were already recognised in the mid-nineteenth century and although the infant mortality rates for England and Wales for the early years of the twentieth century were about 25 times higher than those for the 1990s, the geographical patterns in Figures 3.15 and 3.16 have much in common.

The differentials have been more in the public eye in some periods of history than in others. They received considerable attention in the first decade of the twentieth century and some of the issues discussed were similar to those which re-emerged in the last quarter of the century. The same parts of the country also found themselves offered advice by those who considered themselves to have superior knowledge. At the Second National Conference on Infant Mortality, held in 1908, a clergyman from Rochdale reported that 'when he had endeavoured to tell the members of his mother's meeting how to bring up their babies, those Lancashire women had told him to go and play at marbles.'[160] Two decades after being targeted in the late 1970s, Rochdale was included in a Health Action Zone in 1998.[161]

The question of area variations in mortality has always been considered important and many analyses have been done, both in annual reports of the Registrar General, and in decennial supplements. Comparisons between 'healthy' and 'unhealthy' towns date back to the 1830s. In the mid-nineteenth century, William Farr grouped registration districts according to their overall mortality. He then used the group of 51 districts which had the lowest overall mortality, which he labelled 'the healthy districts', as a yardstick with which to compare the rest. In the decennial supplement for

Figure 3.15

Infant mortality, health authorities, England and Wales, 1997

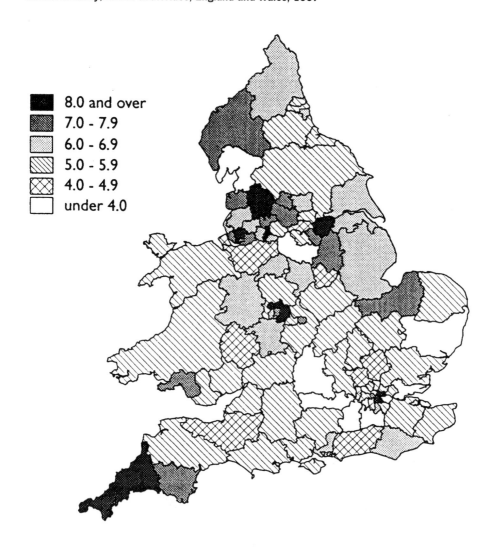

Legend:
- 8.0 and over
- 7.0 - 7.9
- 6.0 - 6.9
- 5.0 - 5.9
- 4.0 - 4.9
- under 4.0

Source: Office for National Statistics, *Mortality statistics, Series DH3*

Figure 3.16

Infant mortality, registration counties, England and Wales, 1907–1910

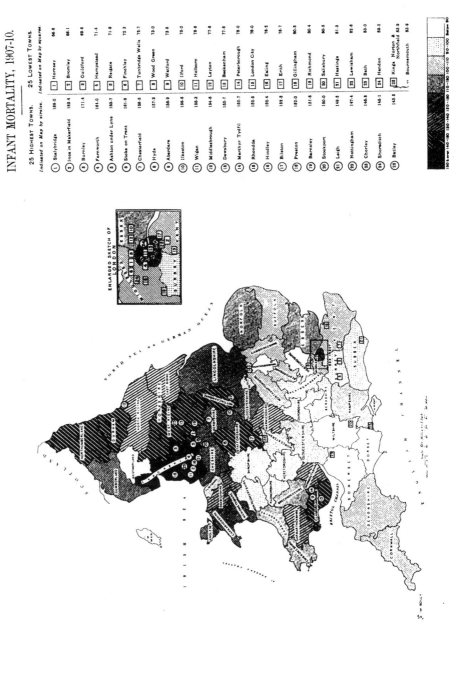

INFANT MORTALITY, 1907-10.

25 HIGHEST TOWNS.		25 LOWEST TOWNS.	
Indicated on Map by circles.		Indicated on Map by squares.	
① Stalybridge	189.0	① Hornsey	64.6
② Ince in Makerfield	185.4	② Bromley	66.1
③ Burnley	171.4	③ Guildford	69.6
④ Farnworth	164.0	④ Hampstead	71.4
⑤ Ashton under Lyne	163.7	⑤ Reigate	71.9
⑥ Stoke on Trent	161.9	⑥ Finchley	72.3
⑦ Chesterfield	158.5	⑦ Tunbridge Wells	72.7
⑧ Hyde	157.3	⑧ Wood Green	73.0
⑨ Aberdare	156.9	⑨ Watford	73.8
⑩ Ilkeston	156.6	⑩ Ilford	75.0
⑪ Wigan	156.3	⑪ Holborn	76.6
⑫ Middlesbrough	154.6	⑫ Leyton	77.8
⑬ Dewsbury	153.7	⑬ Beckenham	77.8
⑭ Merthyr Tydfil	153.7	⑭ Peterborough	78.0
⑮ Rhondda	152.8	⑮ London City	78.0
⑯ Hindley	152.4	⑯ Ealing	78.6
⑰ Bilston	152.3	⑰ Erith	78.7
⑱ Preston	152.0	⑱ Gillingham	80.3
⑲ Barnsley	151.6	⑲ Richmond	80.4
⑳ Stockport	150.0	⑳ Salisbury	80.5
㉑ Leigh	149.5	㉑ Hastings	81.3
㉒ Nottingham	147.4	㉒ Lewisham	82.8
㉓ Chorley	146.8	㉓ Bath	83.0
㉔ Shoreditch	146.1	㉔ Hendon	83.2
㉕ Batley	145.6	㉕ Kings Norton & Northfield	83.9
		⑳ Bournemouth	83.9

150 & over	140–150	130–140	120–130	110–120	100–110	90–100	Below 90

Source: Local Government Board, *Second report on infant and child mortality.*[37]

69

1871 he noted that the aggregated mortality rate for 1861–70 for all children aged under five in the Liverpool registration district was more than three times higher than the corresponding rate for the 'healthy districts'.[1] He commented, 'This procreation of children to perish so soon the sufferings of the little victims — the sorrows and expenses of their parents — are as deplorable as they are wasteful.'[1]

As well as doing these more detailed analyses, the General Register Office played a key role in the public health movement in the mid and late nineteenth century. Its weekly and quarterly publications provided local medical officers of health with comparative mortality statistics.[19] While Figure 3.15 shows mortality rates for district health authorities for 1997, Figure 3.16 shows infant mortality rates for 1907–10 for 'registration counties'.[37] These were groupings of registration districts which covered roughly the same areas as administrative counties. From 1911 onwards, new computing technology, in the form of machines for sorting and counting punched cards, made it feasible to analyse births and deaths according to the people's administrative area of usual residence as is done today.[14,162]

Interpretation of geographical differences in infant mortality has played an important part in the controversies about infant mortality referred to earlier. Analyses produced by the General Register Office for its own reports and for those of the Local Government Board tended to lend support to the view that high infant mortality was a consequence of adverse environmental conditions.[19,38,39]

Given the persistence of the differences, it is not surprising that, despite the fall in mortality, differences in stillbirths and mortality in infancy still existed in the 1990s, but local mortality rates for individual years are now based on small numbers of events. Because of this, tables for local areas in the first edition of *Birth counts* and in some analyses by OPCS in the 1980s, contained data aggregated over three year periods. The many changes made to administrative areas used in the National Health Service in the 1990s, has made it impossible to do this in this second edition. Therefore, instead of including data for areas as small as districts, this edition guides readers to the source documents, while giving data at regional level in Tables A3.12.1 to A3.16.2. The NHS regions and districts as they existed over the period 1994 to 1999 are listed in Appendix 5.

Data for England and Wales for the years up to and including 1973 can be found in the annual volumes of the *Registrar General's statistical review*. Since 1974 they have been published in *Local authority vital statistics, Series VS* now known as *Key population and vital statistics, Series VS and PP1*. This publication usually appears about 18 months after the end of the year to which it refers. Provisional data for health authority areas are usually published much sooner, about six months after the end of the year. Up to 1998, OPCS and subsequently ONS published these in a *Monitor* in the DH3 series, but in 1999 they were transferred to *Health statistics quarterly*. From 1993 onwards, the corresponding DVS5 tables have been released on

70

paper and disk at about the same time. These also contain local data about low birthweight, as do the DVS2 birth data. These tabulations have a long history and are the modern equivalents of the SD25 and SD52 tabulations provided by the General Register Officer to 'sanitary districts'. Similar data for Scotland and Northern Ireland can be found in the *Annual reports* of the respective registrars general.

Key population and vital statistics also includes tabulations of stillbirths and infant mortality rates for areas grouped according to the OPCS/ONS area classification described in Chapter 2.[163–164] It stopped doing so temporarily from 1996 onwards while it revised the classification.[165] This means that the data for 1995 shown in Figures 3.17 and 3.18 were the most recent available at the time of writing. Both show considerable variation between different types of area in their mortality and low birthweight.

Differences between urban and rural areas

In the early years of the twentieth century, one of William Farr's successors, John Tatham, compared infant mortality in the years 1873–77 and 1898–1902 in a group of urban counties and a group of rural counties.[166] While the mortality rates of the urban counties had increased, that of the rural counties had not. Infant mortality from diarrhoeal diseases increased over the period, especially in the urban counties where it was already twice as high as in the rural counties and was attributed to a decline in breastfeeding. In contrast to this, mortality from other infectious diseases declined. Tatham commented that death certification had become more complete during the last quarter of the nineteenth century and this was

Figure 3.17

Infant mortality, area aggregates, England and Wales, 1995

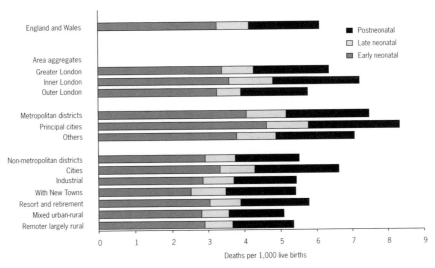

Source: Office for National Statistics, *Birth statistics, Series FM1*

71

Figure 3.18

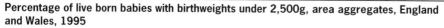

Percentage of live born babies with birthweights under 2,500g, area aggregates, England and Wales, 1995

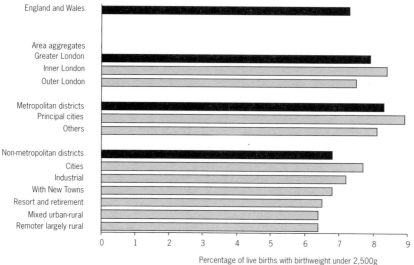

Percentage of live births with birthweight under 2,500g

Source: Office for National Statistics, *Birth Statistics, Series FM1*

likely to account for some, but certainly not all, of the changes in infant mortality. It could account for the increase in mortality attributed to premature birth. Despite the public concern about the subject there were still large differences over the years 1906–10 between the mortality of urban and rural counties.[167]

In 1875, the Public Health Act had formally subdivided England and Wales into urban and rural districts. County boroughs were created in 1888. These groupings were also used for analysis of the mortality rates which were produced for local government areas from 1911 onwards. An analysis of infant mortality rates from 1911–14 and 1931–45 showed that the rates aggregated for county boroughs remained about 30 per cent higher than those for rural districts, with those for London Administrative County and the group of urban districts lying somewhere in between.[168]

From 1950 to 1973, mortality rates were produced for 'conurbations', urban districts and rural districts. The urban areas were subdivided into categories according to whether the population was 100,000 and over, 50,000 to 99,999 or under 50,000. This grouping was intended to provide an improved measure of urban/rural differences, but there were no differences in the infant mortality of urban and rural districts in 1950. The differences reappeared and there was a marked urban/rural gradient in 1973. This was perhaps unexpected, as by 1973 a number of large new housing estates and some new towns had been built in the rural districts.

In the reorganisation of local government in 1974, the distinctions between urban and rural districts and county boroughs were abolished. It was explicitly intended to create local government districts which amalgamated urban areas with their rural hinterland. The only distinction was between the metropolitan counties which are within the major conurbations, and the non-metropolitan counties. This obscures some important differences compared with the tabulations classified into aggregated areas included in *Key population and vital statistics*. Figure 3.17, derived from this, shows clearly that inner city areas have higher rates of infant mortality than suburban and rural areas, while Figure 3.18 shows differences in low birthweight.

Data published in *Birth statistics, Series FM1* show the percentage of births to women born outside the United Kingdom by local authority district. It shows how births to women from the 'New Commonwealth' tend to be concentrated in the inner city districts with the highest mortality rates. The factors associated with these differences are discussed in Chapter 5.

Regional variations

Regional analyses of mortality have been done since 1838 using aggregates of registration districts. At that time, none of the regional groupings related to areas used to administer local or central government. Major changes in the regional boundaries were made in 1911, and 1965 and 1974, with smaller changes at other times. These changes are discussed in detail in Chapter 8 of the *Longitudinal study, Series LS No.1*[169] and changes from 1994 to 1999 are shown in Appendix 5. In April 1997, standard regions were replaced by government office regions. Trends in perinatal and infant mortality for standard regions are shown in Table A3.13.3.

The 14 regional hospital boards, used to administer the hospital service in England from 1948 to 1973 were replaced in 1974 by regional health authorities (RHAs) covering broadly similar areas. These continued with minor boundary changes until April 1994 when they were reduced to eight before being replaced in 1996 by regional offices of the NHS Executive. Changes took place in Scotland at the same time. In April 1999, further changes took place in south east England to form a Regional Office for London, a South Eastern Region which incorporated parts of the former Wessex Region and an Eastern Region. Tables A3.12.2, A3.13.2 and A3.13.4 to A3.16.2 show births and infant deaths in these regions which existed before 1999. Included in these are Tables A3.14.2 and A3.14.3 containing estimated conception rates which are explained in Chapter 4.

All these changes make it difficult to monitor trends even at regional level, particularly as some statistical systems made the changes earlier than others. Tables A3.13.1 to A3.16.2 attempt to chart trends at regional level within England. Despite the problems, they show that the less affluent regions have higher rates of stillbirth, infant mortality and low birthweight than the more affluent regions.

Interpreting trends and variations

Most analyses of time trends and geographical variations in stillbirth and infant mortality rates have included discussions of possible reasons why rates have tended to be higher in the northern and western parts of England and the western side of Scotland than in the south and east of England. These have ranged from nineteenth century speculation about unsanitary conditions in the more densely populated urban areas,[1] to George Newman's designation of infant mortality as 'a social problem',[27] to the claim that some areas have lower mortality rates 'simply because they have better maternity services'.[157] These reflect differences in opinion about the relative importance of 'nature, nurture or quality of assistance' as they would be described at the beginning of the twentieth century.[170] Similarly, there has been considerable speculation as to why mortality rates have or have not decreased over time.

There are many available data which can be used to try to answer these questions and these are discussed in the chapters which follow. Before doing so, two other sources of variation need to be considered. These are, firstly, the differences in the way the data are collected and, secondly, the part played by random variation.

Variations in the way data are collected

While the large discrepancies which occurred in the nineteenth century are unlikely to happen today, it is still possible that statistics may not have been compiled in a strictly comparable way in different places and at different points in time. This could happen even in the absence of changes in definitions and legislation.

It is not unlikely that decisions about whether to classify a very pre term delivery as a spontaneous abortion, or as a live birth which must be registered, may be affected by the circumstances in which the birth occurred and by the cultural and religious background of the people making the decisions. Similar considerations could affect decisions as to whether a fetal death occurred after 24 completed weeks of gestation and must therefore be registered as a stillbirth, or whether it occurred earlier when, by definition, it is not a stillbirth and does not have to be registered.

Furthermore, as the data in Figure 3.9 suggest, it seems very likely that the continuous extension of neonatal intensive care to smaller and iller babies has increased the tendency to register these very small babies as live births. These trends are likely to have been reinforced by the lowering of the limit for registering stillbirths from 28 to 24 completed weeks of gestational age. Because they are at such high risk of death, increasing the numbers of birth registrations of these very small babies would result in an underestimate of the extent to which the rate of neonatal death has fallen during recent years.

For obvious reasons, it is difficult to assess whether or not these differences do occur, let alone estimate the extent to which they affect published mortality rates. This is the reason why WHO recommended in the ninth revision of the ICD that birthweight should be used as a criterion for including a baby in the statistics. It was believed that this would make the data less sensitive to the effects of such differences.

Given these variations in recording the fact of death, it is not surprising that there are even greater variations in the way in which causes of stillbirths and infant deaths are recorded.[171] Interest in improving the quality of the clinical diagnoses recorded on stillbirth and death certificates is, however, growing among obstetricians, paediatricians and pathologists.[81,172–174]

We have already referred to some of the ways data collection has changed over time. This is affected by changes in the way society considers babies and children and in the nature of the illnesses and other conditions which affect them. These changes affect not only the way diseases are classified but the way mortality rates are defined.[21]

Variations due to chance

The stillbirth and infant mortality rates for England are based on relatively large numbers and thus random variation is unlikely to be a significant component of any change in the rates. It is likely to play a larger part in the changes in the rates for regions within England or for Wales, Scotland or Northern Ireland as they are based on fewer births. At the other extreme, in any small area such as a district health authority, stillbirth and infant mortality rates are likely to fluctuate quite widely from year to year. The rates may appear to be much higher or lower than the rates for the United Kingdom as a whole, but the differences may be no greater than would be expected by chance.

This is illustrated in Figure 3.19, in which the infant mortality rate for each district health authority in England and Wales for 1997 is plotted against the total number of births to residents of the district in the same year. The horizontal line is the infant mortality rate for England and Wales as a whole. The two curved lines are the upper and lower limits within which the rates for 95 per cent of the districts would fall if the differences from the England and Wales rate were attributable to chance. It can be seen that, for the districts with relatively few births, the limits are quite wide, but the limits are much narrower for districts with larger numbers of births.[175]

Returning to Figure 3.19, it is clear that the infant mortality rates for more than five per cent of the 100 districts lie outside the 95 per cent limits. Furthermore, if boundaries have not changed, and data for preceding years can be examined it will be found that some districts persistently have relatively high or relatively low mortality rates, while most others stay close to the national average. This suggests that it is not helpful to include all districts in ranked 'league tables' as the differences between most rankings are spurious. Although infant mortality has yet to be analysed in that way, Bayesian analyses of teenage conceptions leading to birth or induced abortion in different populations and of birth rates after in-vitro fertilisation in different clinics have reached similar conclusions.[176,177]

Figure 3.19

Infant mortality rates for NHS districts, together with confidence limits for overall rate, based on numbers of live births, England and Wales, 1997

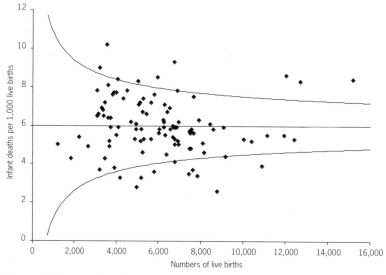

Source: Office for National Statistics, *Monitor DH3 98/1*

Births and infant mortality at the end of the twentieth century

By the late 1990s, infant mortality in the countries of the United Kingdom had fallen to six per thousand or below. The decline in stillbirth and infant death rates had slowed considerably, however. The percentage of low weight births rose slightly because of the increasing tendency to register the smallest babies. Seasonal variations in births and postneonatal mortality were still apparent. Although numbers of births were higher on weekdays than at weekends, there was no longer a difference in mortality. Geographical areas varied in their rates of mortality and low birthweight. In general this was highest in the more deprived areas and lowest in more affluent areas.

We can conclude from these observations that the differences between some stillbirth and infant mortality rates are greater and more persistent than would be expected by chance. In later chapters we discuss the possible association between stillbirth and infant mortality rates and the social, demographic and economic circumstances of parents of newborn babies and of the care which parents and babies receive. Another major consideration is the selection process by which babies come to be born, so we first consider in the next chapter the available data about contraception, sterilisation, abortion and fetal loss in late pregnancy.

References

1   Farr W. Letter to the Registrar General. In: *Supplement to the 35th annual report of the Registrar General on births, deaths and marriages in England, 1861–1870*. London: HMSO, 1875.

2   Wrigley EA. Births and baptisms: the use of Anglican baptism registers as a source of information about the numbers of births in England before the beginning of civil registration. *Population Studies* 1977; 31(2): 281–312.

3   Eyler JM. *Victorian social medicine: the ideas and methods of William Farr*. London and Baltimore: Johns Hopkins University Press, 1979.

4   Krause JT. The changing accuracy of English registration, 1690–1837. In: Glass DV, Eversley DEC, eds. *Population in history*. London: Edwin Arnold, 1965.

5   McLaren D. The Marriage Act of 1653: its influence on the parish registers. *Population Studies* 1974; 28: 319–327.

6   Drake M. An elementary exercise in parish register democracy. *Economic History Review* 1962; 14: 427–445.

7   Wrigley EA. Mortality in pre-industrial England: the example of Colyton, Devon, over three centuries. In: Glass DV, Revelle R, eds. *Population and social change*. London: Edwin Arnold, 1972.

8   Schofield R, Wrigley EA. Infant and child mortality in England and in the late Tudor and early Stuart period. In: Webster C, ed. *Health, medicine and mortality in the sixteenth century*. Cambridge: Cambridge University Press, 1979.

9   Wrigley EA, Schofield RS. English population history from family reconstitution: summary results, 1600–1799. *Population Studies* 1983; 37: 157–184.

10   Wrigley EA, Schofield RS. *The population history of England, 1541–1871*. London: Edwin Arnold, 1981.

11   Flinn M, ed. *Scottish population history from the seventeenth century to the 1930s*. Cambridge: Cambridge University Press, 1977.

12   Wrigley EA, Schofield RS. *The population history of England, 1541–1871: a reconstruction*. Cambridge: Cambridge University Press, 1989.

13   Bideau A, Desjardins B, Brignoli HP, eds. *Infant mortality in the past*. Oxford: Clarendon Press, 1997.

14   Higgs E. A cuckoo in the nest? The origins of civil registration and state medical statistics in England and Wales. *Continuity and Change* 1996; 11(1): 115–134.

15   Nissel M. *People count: a history of the General Register Office*. London: HMSO, 1987.

16   General Register Office for Northern Ireland. *Registering the people: 150 years of civil registration*. Belfast: General Register Office, 1995.

17   Moseley M. *Irascible genius: the life of Charles Babbage, inventor.* London: Hutchinson, 1964.

18   Farr W. Report to the Registrar General. In: *Fortieth report of the Registrar General for the year 1877.* London: HMSO, 1879.

19   Szreter S. The GRO and the public health movement in Britain, 1837–1914. *Social History of Medicine* 1991; 4(3): 435–463.

20   Humphreys N, ed. *Vital statistics: a memorial volume of selections from the reports and writings of William Farr.* London: Sanitary Institute, 1885.

21   Armstrong D. The invention of infant mortality. *Sociology of Health and Illness* 1986; 8(3): 211–223.

22   Simon J. *General Board of Health papers relating to the sanitary state of England.* London: HMSO, 1858.

23   Farr W. Letter to the Registrar General. In: *Thirty-eighth annual report of the Registrar General of Births, Deaths and Marriages in England. Abstracts of 1875.* Cd 1786. London: HMSO, 1877.

24   Glass DV. A note on the under-registration of births in Britain in the nineteenth century. *Population Studies* 1951; 5: 70–88.

25   Woods R. Infant mortality in Britain: a survey of current knowledge on historical trends and variations. In: Bideau A, Desjardins B, Brignoli HP, eds. *Infant mortality in the past.* Oxford: Clarendon Press, 1997.

26   General Register Office. *Thirty-fifth annual report of the Registrar General, for the year 1872.* London: HMSO, 1874.

27   Newman G. *Infant mortality.* London: Methuen and Co., 1906.

28   Aykroyd WR, Kevany JP. Mortality in infancy and early childhood in Ireland, Scotland and England and Wales 1871 to 1970. *Ecology of Food and Nutrition* 1973; 2: 11–19.

29   Smith FB. *The people's health, 1830–1910.* London: Croom Helm, 1979.

30   Rollet C. The fight against infant mortality in the past: an international comparison. In: Bideau A, Desjardins B, Brignoli HP, eds. *Infant mortality in the past.* Oxford: Clarendon Press, 1997.

31   Interdepartmental Committee on Physical Deterioration. *Report.* Cd 2175. London: HMSO, 1904.

32   Dwork D. *War is good for babies and other young children: a history of the infant and child welfare movement in England, 1898–1918.* London and New York: Tavistock, 1987.

33   Pearson K. The intensity of natural selection in man. *Proceedings of the Royal Society of London.* Series B. 1912; 85: 469–476.

34   MacKenzie DA. *Statistics in Britain, 1865–1930: the social construction of scientific knowledge.* Edinburgh: Edinburgh University, 1981.

35   Lewis J. *The politics of motherhood: child and maternal welfare in England, 1900–1939.* London: Croom Helm, 1980.

36   Local Government Board. *Third report by the Medical Officer on infant mortality in Lancashire. Supplement to the forty-third annual report of the Local Government Board*, 1913–14. Cd 7511. London: HMSO, 1914.

37   Local Government Board. *Second report by the Medical Officer on infant and child mortality. Supplement to the forty-second annual report of the Local Government Board, 1912–1913*. Cd 6909. London: HMSO, 1913.

38   Local Government Board. *Report by the Medical Officer on infant and child mortality. Supplement to the thirty-ninth annual report of the Local Government Board, 1909–1910*. Cd 5312. London: HMSO, 1910.

39   Eyler JM. *Sir Arthur Newsholme and state medicine, 1885–1935*. Cambridge: Cambridge University Press, 1997.

40   Local Government Board. *Report on child mortality at ages 0–5. Forty-fifth annual report of the Local Government Board, 1915–16*. Cd 8496. London: HMSO, 1916.

41   Donnison J. *Midwives and medical men*. New York: Schocken Books, 1977.

42   House of Commons. *Still-births in England and other countries*. Return to the House of Commons No. 279. London: HMSO, 1893.

43   Newsholme A. *The elements of vital statistics*. 3rd edition. London: S Sonnenschein and Co., 1899.

44   Report of the special committee on infantile mortality. *Journal of the Royal Statistical Society* 1912; 76: 27–87.

45   Dudfield R. Stillbirths in relation to infant mortality. *Journal of the Royal Statistical Society* 1912; 76: 1–26.

46   General Register Office. *Census of England and Wales, 1911*. Cd 8678. Vol. XIII: Fertility of marriage. Part I. London: HMSO, 1917.

47   General Register Office. *Census of England and Wales, 1911*. Vol. XIII: Fertility of marriage. Part II. London: HMSO, 1923.

48   Szreter S. *Fertility, class and gender in Britain, 1860–1940*. Cambridge Studies in Population, Economy and Society in Past Time No. 27. Cambridge: Cambridge University Press, 1996.

49   Royal Commission on Population. *Report*. Cmd 7695. London: HMSO, 1949.

50   Glass DV, Grebenik E. *The trend and pattern of fertility in Great Britain: a report on the family census of 1946*. Vol. I: Report. Vol. II: Tables. London: HMSO, 1954.

51   Britton M. Recent trends in births. *Population Trends* 1980; 20: 4–8.

52   Armitage B, Babb P. Population review: (4). Trends in fertility. *Population Trends* 1996; 84: 7–13.

53   Ruddock V, Wood R, Quinn M. Birth statistics: recent trends in England and Wales. *Population Trends* 1998; 94: 12–18.

54   Ni Bhrolcháin M. *New perspectives on fertility in Britain*. Studies on Medical and Population Subjects No. 55. London: HMSO, 1993.

55   General Register Office. *The Registrar General's statistical review for England and Wales for the year 1951*. Text. London: HMSO, 1954.

56   McKinlay PL. Some statistical aspects of infant mortality. *Journal of Hygiene* 1929; 28: 394–417.

57   Stouman K. The perilous threshold of life. *League of Nations Quarterly Bulletin of the Health Organisation* 1934; 3: 531–612.

58   Blane D. Real wages, the economic cycle, and mortality in England and Wales, 1870–1914. *International Journal of Health Services* 1990; 20(1): 43–52.

59   McKeown T, Record RG. Reasons for the decline of mortality in England and Wales during the nineteenth century. *Population Studies* 1962; 16: 94–122.

60   McKeown T, Record RG. An interpretation of the decline of mortality in England and Wales during the twentieth century. *Population Studies* 1975; 29: 391–422.

61   Reves R. Declining fertility in England and Wales as a major cause of the twentieth century decline in mortality. The role of changing family size and age structure in infectious disease mortality in infancy. *American Journal of Epidemiology* 1985; 122(1): 112–126.

62   Titmuss R. *History of the Second World War: problems of social policy*. London: HMSO and Longmans, Green and Co., 1950.

63   Winter JM. Economic instability and infant mortality in England and Wales, 1920–1950. In: Winter JM, ed. *The working class in modern British history*. Cambridge: Cambridge University Press, 1983.

64   Ministry of Health. *On the state of the public health during six years of war. Report of the Chief Medical Officer, 1939–1945*. London: HMSO, 1946.

65   Winter JM. The impact of the first world war on civilian health in Britain. *Economic History Review* 1977; 30: 487–507.

66   Peller S. Mortality past and future. *Population Studies* 1948; 1: 405–456.

67   Griffith GW, Adelstein AM, Lambert PM, Weatherall JA. Influenza and infant mortality. *British Medical Journal* 1972; 3(826): 553–536.

68   Hemon D, Berger C, Dreyfus J, Lazar P. Distribution des poids de naissance et épidemies de grippe. *Revue D' Epidémiologie Et De Santé Publique* 1977; 25(1): 33–39.

69   Macfarlane AJ. Infant deaths after four weeks [letter]. *Lancet* 1982; ii(8304): 929–930.

70   Pharoah POD, Macfarlane AJ. Recent trends in postneonatal mortality. In: Office of Population Censuses and Surveys and London School of Hygiene and Tropical Medicine. *Studies in sudden infant deaths*. Studies on Medical and Population Subjects No. 45. London: HMSO, 1982:1–8.

71 Hack M, Merkatz IR, Jones PK, Fanaroff AA. Changing trends of neonatal and postneonatal deaths in very low birthweight infants. *American Journal of Obstetrics and Gynecology* 1980; 137(7): 797–800.

72 Arneil GC, Brooke H, Gibson AA, Harvie A, McIntosh H, Patrick WJ. Post-perinatal infant mortality in Glasgow 1979–81. *Lancet* 1982; ii(8299): 649–651.

73 Thatcher M. Oral reply. *House of Commons Official Report (Hansard)*. 125. cols 141–4 (No. 70). Jan 12 1988.

74 Macfarlane AJ. The downs and ups of infant mortality. *British Medical Journal* 1988; 296: 230–231.

75 Campbell MJ, Rodrigues L, Macfarlane AJ, Murphy MF. Sudden infant deaths and cold weather: was the rise in infant mortality in 1986 in England and Wales due to the weather? *Paediatric and Perinatal Epidemiology* 1991; 5(1): 93–100.

76 House of Commons Social Services Committee. *First report: perinatal, neonatal and infant mortality*. Session 1988–1989. HC 54. London: HMSO, 1988.

77 Department of Health. *Government's reply to the House of Commons Social Services Committee's first report on perinatal and neonatal mortality*. Cm 741. Session 1988–89. London: HMSO, 1989.

78 Esmail A, Lambert PC, Jones DR, Mitchell EA. Prevalence of risk factors for sudden infant death syndrome in south east England before the 1991 national 'Back to sleep' health education campaign. *Journal of Public Health Medicine* 1995; 17(3): 282–289.

79 Office for National Statistics. *Sudden infant deaths, 1993–1997*. ONS Monitor Population and Health DH3 98/2. London: ONS, 1998.

80 Edouard L, Alberman E. National trends in the certified causes of perinatal mortality, 1968 to 1978. *British Journal of Obstetrics and Gynaecology* 1980; 87(10): 833–838.

81 Meadow R. Unnatural sudden infant death. *Archives of Disease In Childhood* 1999; 80: 7–14.

82 Confidential Enquiry into Stillbirths and Deaths in Infancy. *5th annual report*. London: Maternal and Child Health Consortium, 1998.

83 Rooney C, Devis T. Mortality trends by cause of death in England and Wales 1980–94: the impact of introducing automated cause coding and related changes in 1993. *Population Trends* 1996; 86: 29–35.

84 Gedalla B, Alderson MR. Pilot study of revised stillbirth and neonatal death certificates. *Archives of Disease In Childhood* 1984; 59(10): 976–982.

85 Cole SK, Hey EN, Thomson AM. Classifying perinatal death: an obstetric approach. *British Journal of Obstetrics and Gynaecology* 1986; 93(12): 1204–1212.

86   Hey EN, Lloyd DJ, Wigglesworth JS. Classifying perinatal death: fetal and neonatal factors. *British Journal of Obstetrics and Gynaecology* 1986; 93(12): 1213–1223.

87   Wigglesworth JS. Monitoring perinatal mortality. A pathophysiological approach. *Lancet* 1980; ii(8196): 684–686.

88   Alberman E, Bergsjo P, Cole S, Evans S, Hartford R, Hoffman H, McCarthy B, Pashley J, Hampton B. International Collaborative Effort (ICE) on birthweight; plurality; and perinatal and infant mortality. I: Methods of data collection and analysis. *Acta Obstetrica Et Gynecologica Scandinavica* 1989; 68(1): 5–10.

89   Alberman E, Botting B, Blatchley N, Twidell A. A new hierarchical classification of causes of infant death in England and Wales. *Archives of Disease in Childhood* 1994; 70: 403–409.

90   Alberman E, Blatchley N, Botting B, Schuman J, Dunn A. Medical causes on stillbirth certificates in England and Wales: distribution and results of hierarchical classifications tested by the Office for National Statistics. *British Journal of Obstetrics and Gynaecology* 1997; 104(9): 1043–1049.

91   Fedrick J, Butler NR. Accuracy of registered causes of neonatal deaths in 1958. *British Journal of Preventive and Social Medicine* 1972; 26(2): 101–105.

92   Edouard L. Validation of the registered underlying causes of stillbirth. *Journal of Epidemiology and Community Health* 1982; 36(3): 231–234.

93   Alderson MR, Meade TW. Accuracy of diagnosis on death certificates compared with that in hospital records. *British Journal of Preventive and Social Medicine* 1967; 21(1): 22–29.

94   Medical aspects of death certification. A joint report of the Royal College of Physicians and the Royal College of Pathologists. *Journal of the Royal College of Physicians of London* 1982; 16(4): 206–218.

95   Office for National Statistics. *Death counts*. Video. London: ONS, 1996.

96   Langhoff-Roos J, Larsen S, Basys V, Landmark G, Badokynote M. Potentially avoidable deaths in Denmark, Sweden, and Lithuania as classified by the Nordic-Baltic classification. *British Journal of Obstetrics and Gynaecology* 1998; 105: 1189–1194.

97   Chalmers I. *Enquiry into perinatal death: a report on national perinatal surveillance prepared for the Department of Health and Social Security*. Oxford: National Perinatal Epidemiology Unit, 1984.

98   Elbourne DR, Mutch LM. *Archive of locally based perinatal surveys*. Oxford: National Perinatal Epidemiology Unit, 1981.

99   Elbourne DR, Mutch LM. *Archive of locally based perinatal surveys*. Oxford: National Perinatal Epidemiology Unit, 1984.

100 Mutch LM. *Archive of locally based perinatal surveys.* Oxford: National Perinatal Epidemiology Unit, 1986.

101 Mutch LM, Elbourne DR. *Archive of locally based perinatal surveys.* Oxford: National Perinatal Epidemiology Unit, 1983.

102 Mutch LM, Elbourne DR. *Locally based perinatal surveys.* Report submitted to DHSS. Oxford: National Perinatal Epidemiology Unit, 1985.

103 Department of Health. *Confidential Enquiry into Stillbirths and Deaths in Infancy: Report of a Working Group set up by the Chief Medical Officer.* London: Department of Health, 1990.

104 National Advisory Body. *Confidential Enquiry into Stillbirths and Deaths in Infancy: report, March 1992–July 1993.* London: Department of Health, 1994.

105 Confidential Enquiry into Stillbirths and Deaths in Infancy. *Annual report for 1 January to 31 December 1993.* Part 1: Summary of methods and main results. London: Department of Health, 1995.

106 Confidential Enquiry into Stillbirths and Deaths in Infancy. *Annual report for 1 January to 31 December 1993.* Part 2: Additional results and tables. London: Department of Health, 1995.

107 Confidential Enquiry into Stillbirths and Deaths in Infancy. *3rd annual report for 1 January to 31 December 1994.* London: Department of Health, 1996.

108 Confidential Enquiry into Stillbirths and Deaths in Infancy. *4th annual report for 1 January to 31 December 1995.* London: Maternal and Child Health Consortium, 1997.

109 *Encyclopaedia of superstition, folklore and the occult sciences of the world.* Chicago: J H Yewdale, 1903.

110 General Register Office. *The Registrar General's statistical review of England and Wales for the year 1967.* Vol. III: Commentary. London: HMSO, 1971.

111 Russell D, Douglas AS, Allan TM. Changing seasonality of birth – a possible environmental effect. *Journal of Epidemiology and Community Health* 1993; 47(5): 362–367.

112 Macfarlane AJ, Thew P. Births: the weekly cycle. *Population Trends* 1978; 13: 23–24.

113 Ødegard O. Season of birth in the population of Norway, with particular reference to the September birth maximum. *British Journal of Psychiatry* 1977; 131: 339–344.

114 Hare EH, Bulusu L, Adelstein AM. Schizophrenia and season of birth. *Population Trends* 1979; 17: 9–11.

115 Birth season and schizophrenia [editorial]. *British Medical Journal* 1978; 1(6112): 527–528.

116 Takei N, Sham PC, O'Callaghan E, Glover G, Murray RM. Schizophrenia: increased risk associated with winter and city birth – a case-control study in 12 regions within England and Wales. *Journal of Epidemiology and Community Health* 1995; 49(1): 106–107.

117 Mortensen PB, Pedersen CB, Westergaard T, Wohlfahrt J, Ewald H, Mors O, Andersen PK, Melbye M. Effects of family history and place and season of birth on the risk of schizophrenia. *New England Journal of Medicine* 1999; 340(8): 603–608.

118 Torrey EF. Schizophrenic births [letter]. *Lancet* 1978; i(8069): 882.

119 Rothwell PM, Staines A, Smail P, Wadsworth E, McKinney P. Seasonality of birth of patients with childhood diabetes in Britain. *BMJ* 1996; 312(7044): 1456–1457.

120 Paraskevaides EC, Pennington GW, Naik S. Seasonal distribution in conceptions achieved by artificial insemination by donor. *BMJ* 1988; 297(6659): 1309–1310.

121 Rönnberg L. Seasonal distribution in conceptions achieved by artificial insemination by donor [letter]. *BMJ* 1989; 298(6659): 187.

122 Mayaux MJ, Spira A. Seasonal distribution in conceptions achieved by artificial insemination by donor [letter]. *BMJ* 1989; 298(6659): 187.

123 James WH. Seasonality in twin and triplet births. *Annals of Human Biology* 1980; 7(2): 163–175.

124 James WH. Seasonality in twin births. *Annals of Human Biology* 1976; 3(2): 193–195.

125 MacGillivray J, Samphier M, Little J. Factors affecting twinning. In: MacGillivray J, Campbell DM, Thompson B, eds. *Twinning and twins*. Chichester: John Wiley, 1988.

126 Weatherall R. Recent seasonal patterns of infant mortality in England and Wales. In: *Child health: a collection of studies*. Studies on Medical and Population Subjects No. 31. London: HMSO, 1976.

127 Macfarlane, AJ. Seasonal variations in postneonatal mortality. In: Office of Population Censuses and Surveys and London School of Hygiene and Tropical Medicine. *Studies in sudden infant deaths*. Studies on Medical and Population Subjects No. 45. London: HMSO, 1982:9–17.

128 Carpenter RG, Gardner A. Variations in unexpected infant death rates relating to age, sex and season. In: Office of Population Censuses and Surveys and London School of Hygiene and Tropical Medicine. *Studies in sudden infant deaths*. Studies on Medical and Population Subjects No. 45. London: HMSO, 1982.

129 Macfarlane AJ, Fox AJ. Child deaths from accidents and violence. *Population Trends* 1978; 12: 22–27.

130   Breschi M, Bocci ML. Month of birth as a factor in children's survival. In: Bideau A, Desjardins B, Brignoli HP, eds. *Infant mortality in the past*. Oxford: Clarendon Press, 1997.

131   General Register Office. *Sixty-ninth report of the Registrar General, for the year 1906*. London: HMSO, 1908.

132   Gale AH. *Epidemic diseases*. London: Penguin, 1959.

133   Gale AH. A century of changes in the mortality and incidence of the principal infections of childhood. *Archives of Disease In Childhood* 1945; 20: 2–21.

134   Hare EH, Moran PA, Macfarlane AJ. The changing seasonality of infant deaths in England and Wales 1912–78 and its relation to seasonal temperature. *Journal of Epidemiology and Community Health* 1981; 35(2): 77–82.

135   Gilman EA, Cheng KK, Winter HR, Scragg R. Trends in rates and seasonal distribution of sudden infant deaths in England and Wales, 1988–92. *BMJ* 1995; 310: 631–632.

136   Julious SA. There is still seasonality in sudden infant death syndrome in England and Wales. *Journal of Epidemiology and Community Health* 1997; 51(1): 101–102.

137   Opie I, Opie P, eds. *Oxford dictionary of nursery rhymes*. Oxford: Oxford University Press, 1951.

138   Melbye M, Wohlfahrt J, Westergaard T, Jensen AK, Koch A, Hjalgrim H, Kristensen A, Aaby P, Christmas Paper Study Group. Births at Christmas are different: population based survey of 2 million deliveries. *BMJ* 1997; 315(7123): 1654–1655.

139   Chan A, Keane RJ, Scott J. Elective caesarean section and child deprivation [letter]. *Lancet* 1996; 347(9009): 1196.

140   Cole S. Weekend births [letter]. *Lancet* 1984; ii(8396): 222.

141   Paccaud F, Neury J-J, Ackermann-Liebrich U. Weekend births [letter]. *Lancet* 1984; ii(8400): 470.

142   Rindfuss RR, Ladinsky JL. Patterns of births: implications for the incidence of elective induction. *Medical Care* 1976; 14(8): 685–693.

143   Mathers CD. Births and perinatal deaths in Australia: variations by day of week. *Journal of Epidemiology and Community Health* 1983; 37(1): 57–62.

144   Wells R. Still never on Sundays. *Medical Journal of Australia* 1980; 2: 160.

145   Cohen A. Seasonal daily effect on the numbers of births in Israel. *Applied Statistics* 1983; 32: 228–235.

146   Department of Health. NHS maternity statistics, England: 1989–90 to 1994–95. *Statistical Bulletin* 1997/28: 1–44.

147 Macfarlane, AJ. Trends in maternity care. In: Office of Population Censuses and Surveys, Department of Health and Social Security, and Welsh Office. *Hospital in-patient enquiry maternity tables 1977–1981*. MB4 No. 19. London: HMSO, 1986:9–25.

148 Rindfuss RR, Ladinsky JL, Coppock E, Marshall VW, Macpherson AS. Convenience and the occurrence of births: induction of labor in the United States and Canada. *International Journal of Health Services* 1979; 9(3): 439–460.

149 Martin JM. Never on Sundays. *Medical Journal of Australia* 1972; 1: 487–488.

150 Calot G. Le mouvement journalier des naissances à l'intérieur de la semaine. *Population* 1981; 1: 9–40.

151 Macfarlane AJ. Variations in number of births and perinatal mortality by day of week in England and Wales. *British Medical Journal* 1978; 2(6153): 1670–1673.

152 Mangold WD. Neonatal mortality by the day of the week in the 1974–75 Arkansas live birth cohort. *American Journal of Public Health* 1981; 71(6): 601–605.

153 Hendry RA. The weekend — a dangerous time to be born. *British Journal of Obstetrics and Gynaecology* 1981; 88: 1200–1203.

154 Fujimura M. *Personal communication*.

155 Bjerkdal T, Bakketeig LS. *Medical registration of births in Norway during the 5 year period, 1967–1971*. Norway: Institute of Hygiene and Social Medicine, University of Bergen, 1975.

156 Chalmers JW, Shanks E, Paterson S, McInneny K, Baird D, Penney G. Scottish data on intrapartum related deaths are in same direction as Welsh data. *BMJ* 1998; 317(7157): 539–540.

157 Spastics Society. *Advertisements*. 1978.

158 Gillie O. *Observer* 1978; 28th October.

159 National Audit Office. *Maternity services: report by the Comptroller and Auditor General*. London: HMSO, 1990.

160 Dyhouse C. Working-class mothers and infant mortality in England, 1895–1914. *Journal of Social History* 1978; 12(2): 248–267.

161 Department of Health. *Fifteen new health action zones to tackle health inequalities*. Press release 98/329. London: Department of Health, 1998.

162 Stevenson THC. Suggested lines of advance in English vital statistics. *Journal of the Royal Statistical Society* 1910; 73: 685–702.

163 Charlton J. Which areas are healthiest? *Population Trends* 1996; 83: 17–24.

164 Wallace M, Denham C. *The ONS classification of local and health authorities in Great Britain*. Studies on Medical and Population Subjects No. 59. London: HMSO, 1996.

165 *The ONS classification of health authorities in Great Britain: revised for authorities in 1999*. Studies on Medical and Population Subjects No. 63, London: ONS, 1999.

166 Tatham, J. English mortality among infants under one year of age. In: Interdepartmental Committee on Physical Deterioration. *Report*. Cd 2175. Vol. I. London: HMSO, 1904.

167 General Register Office. *The Registrar General's decennial supplement for the years 1901–1910*. Vol. II. London: HMSO, 1918.

168 General Register Office. *The Registrar General's statistical review for the six years, 1940–1945*. Vol. I: Medical. London: HMSO, 1949.

169 Fox AJ, Goldblatt PO. *Longitudinal study: socio-demographic mortality differentials, 1971–1975*. OPCS Longitudinal Study Series LS No. 1. London: HMSO, 1982.

170 Macfarlane AJ, Elbourne DR. Midwifery, obstetrics and neonatology. In: Armitage P, Colton T, eds. *Encyclopedia of biostatistics*. Chichester: Wiley, 1998.

171 Alberman E. The scope of perinatal statistics and the usefulness of comparisons. In: Chester R, Diggory P, Sutherland M, eds. *Changing patterns of childbearing and child rearing*. London: Academic Press, 1981:96–138.

172 Scott MJ, Ritchie JW, McClure BG, Reid MM, Halliday HL. Perinatal death recording: time for a change? *British Medical Journal* 1981; 282(6265): 707–710.

173 Uncertain certificates [editorial]. *Lancet* 1981; ii(8236): 22–23.

174 Busuttil A, Kemp IW, Heasman MA. The accuracy of medical certificates of cause of death. *Health Bulletin* 1981; 39(3): 146–152.

175 Macfarlane AJ. Some statistical approaches to comparisons between perinatal mortality rates for small areas. In: Chalmers I, McIlwaine G, eds. *Perinatal audit and surveillance*. London: Royal College of Obstetricians and Gynaecologists, 1980.

176 Goldstein H, Spiegelhalter DJ. League tables and their limitations: statistical issues of institutional performance. *Journal of the Royal Statistical Society, Series A* 1996; 335: 231–236.

177 Marshall EC, Spiegelhalter DJ. Reliability of league tables of in vitro fertilisation clinics: retrospective analysis of live births. *BMJ* 1998; 316: 1701–1705.

4 Fertility control and fetal loss in early pregnancy

'I wish, I wish, but it's all in vain,
I wish I were a maid again;
But a maid again I never shall be
Till apples grow on an orange tree.'

Traditional[1]

'The desperate anxiety of many women to get rid of an unwanted pregnancy is illustrated by their readiness to employ almost any method however distasteful, which holds out some hope that it may be effective for the purpose.'

Interdepartmental Committee on Abortion, 1939[2]

'We consider that legal abortion should be an option for women stressed by unwanted pregnancy. Current attitudes to sexuality and the current unavailability and effectiveness of contraception make the occurrence of some unwanted pregnancies inevitable. Restriction of legal abortion would cause hardship to women and children and could result in the reappearance of illegal abortion.'

Royal College of Obstetricians and Gynaecologists, 1991[3]

Women's desire to avoid unwanted pregnancy has been expressed in many different ways over the centuries. Knowledge about how to do so has existed for longer than is commonly thought, but services to make contraceptives available were first set up in the 1920s and 1930s and were not widely available until the last quarter of the twentieth century. The collection of statistics on this subject was motivated originally by requests to interpret demographic trends, and subsequently by the need to monitor the development of services set up to provide contraception, sterilisation and termination of pregnancy. This chapter starts by describing what we know about contraception and abortion in the era before we had statistics on the subject. It then goes on to describe the data now collected about contraception and sterilisation and discusses the problems in obtaining data about involuntary infertility and the menopause. A description of data on induced abortion is followed by a discussion of the dearth of data on miscarriage. As a result, estimated conception rates exclude conceptions leading to pregnancies which miscarried. The chapter ends by discussing problems involved in interpreting trends in abortion.

History and long term trends in fertility control

Most of the data we describe in this chapter have been collected only since the 1970s as a consequence of facilities becoming available under the NHS. This may make it easy to forget that forms of fertility control have been practised in this country for far longer, although data about their use are sparse.

Demographic analyses of the spacing of births or baptisms suggest that fertility control was practised in some places several centuries ago, especially in times of economic difficulty.[4] For example, analyses of data from the parish registers of Colyton, Devon, which we mentioned in Chapter 3, suggest that birth control was practised there in the seventeenth and the early eighteenth centuries.[5] The authors of the Colyton analysis suggested that withdrawal was the main method used, although abortion and infanticide may have played some part there and a larger part in other places and at other times.

While there is a dearth of data on the incidence of abortion in past centuries, there is plenty of evidence to suggest that it was attempted. Versions of the ballad Tam Lin, recorded from the sixteenth century onwards, contain verses such as:

> 'Up starts Lady Margaret's sister
>   An angry woman was she
> "If there ever was a woman with child
>   Margaret you are wi".
>
> Up starts Lady Margaret's mother
>   An angry woman was she
> "There grows a herb in yon kirk-yard
>   That will scathe the babe away" '.[6]

Herbals, such as Nicholas Culpeper's work *The complete herbal* published in the seventeenth century, recommended substances such as savin the oil of juniper, rue and pennyroyal be used to 'relieve obstructions' or as 'correctives' for 'female irregularities'.[7-10] Use of these remedies was mentioned in Edmund Spenser's *The faerie queene*,[11] Dryden's *Juvenal*[12] and in the oral tradition, often allegorically in verses such as this, in which thyme symbolises virginity:

> 'My old thyme it is all gone,
> And I can't get any new,
> But in the place where my old thyme stood
> It is all overrun with rue.'[13]

Many of the remedies were, in fact, ineffective, or effective only at lethal doses. It is probably as a consequence of this that infanticide, which is still used for fertility limitation in some parts of the world, played a considerable role in Britain up to the latter half of the nineteenth century.[14-16] The most common means of infanticide was 'overlaying' or suffocation in bed, something which could also happen by accident. Other means were drowning and strangulation, while some babies were neglected or abandoned as foundlings. Although deaths from these causes were mentioned in tabulations of death registration data, the under-registration of births and infant deaths, referred to in Chapter 3, means that the numbers of infanticides are likely to have been far greater than official statistics suggest. Criminal statistics are no more helpful. Although 'concealment of birth' was made a criminal offence in 1803,[17] there was a reluctance to commit people for trial and a further reluctance on the part of juries to find those who were tried guilty. Thus the data on the subject published in the Home Office's *Crime statistics* and shown in Table A4.19.1 probably represent only a very small proportion of the events which occurred.

Two practices commonly believed to be associated with infanticide were 'baby farming', which was mentioned in Chapter 3, and 'burial clubs'.[18] The clubs paid insured people benefits on the death of their child. Although the purpose of the insurance was to pay funeral expenses, the benefits are thought to have been higher than the cost of a funeral. Some people have thought that the extent to which 'burial clubs' encouraged infanticide had been exaggerated, however.[19,20]

In response to public pressure and extensive press coverage in the 1860s, when infanticide was referred to as 'the national stigma of an age' and 'par excellence the great social evil of our day', the government carried out an investigation into infant mortality and introduced new legislation. The provisions of the 1872 'Act for the better protection of infant life' included the licensing of baby farms while an Act of 1875 required that all infant insurance claims be reported to the government. Either as a result of this, or for other reasons, infanticide seems to have declined during the closing years of the nineteenth century.[15,16,21]

One of the possible reasons may have been the availability of contraceptives. While women had used substances which they thought to have spermicidal properties and primitive diaphragms as contraceptives for thousands of years, contraceptives do not appear to have been used very extensively in this country before the nineteenth century.[22-24] Despite official opposition to the idea of birth control, by the 1890s all the barrier methods of contraception in use today were on sale openly,[24-26] and intrauterine devices had been developed. As Figure 4.1 demonstrates, however, the successful use of contraception was unlikely to have been widespread until well into the twentieth century.[24,27] In the interwar years, the availability of contraceptives depended on the attitudes of local doctors.[21,26,28,29] Although research on sterilisation techniques started in the mid-nineteenth century, it was not until the development of more sophisticated surgical techniques in the twentieth century that it became an acceptable method of fertility control.

It is more likely that induced abortion had become the most widely used method of fertility control by the late nineteenth century,[7,8,15,18,21,29,30] although few data exist on the subject. In 1859, Charles Clay of St Mary's Hospital, Manchester, reported that 430 out of 790 women in his hospital and private practice who were over childbearing age had had abortions induced. Out of 6,970 pregnancies, 1,000 had been terminated.[31] Abortifacient substances were widely advertised in newspapers and magazines including the religious press.[7,8,18] The Local Government Board's enquiry into infant mortality in Lancashire reported in 1914 that abortifacients, including herbs and lead-based drugs, were readily available in all the towns visited[32] and that women who failed to abort themselves by taking these or pushing objects such as knitting needles into their wombs were known to go to illegal abortionists.[7,8,18] In the 1930s, abortionists were local women who were seen as helpful friends and valued members of many working class communities.[29] Abortion was, of course, illegal under Acts of Parliament passed in 1803, 1828, 1837 and in 1861, when the Offences Against the Person Act made both abortionists and the women who chose to have abortions liable to life imprisonment.[17]

Concern about the rising maternal mortality rate in the 1920s and 1930s directed official attention to induced abortion. The Ministry of Health's *Report on an investigation into maternal mortality*, published in 1937, concluded that there did not appear to be any reliable means of estimating the incidence of abortion, but evidence suggested that it was not restricted to any one class, that it was higher in some districts than others, and that it was frequent and appeared to be increasing.[33]

The British Medical Association's investigation into abortion, published in 1936, estimated that between 16 to 20 per cent of pregnancies in this country ended in abortion or miscarriage, but stated that it was impossible to assess what proportion were induced.[34] It quoted data from a survey by Beckwith Whitehouse of 3,000 of his patients in Birmingham, 17.2 per cent of whose 11,430 pregnancies ended in either induced abortion or miscarriage.[35] Also quoted were the data shown in Table 4.1 on 1,000 women admitted after abortion to St Giles Hospital, Camberwell between 1930 and 1934.[36] Concern about the subject led the government to set up the Interdepartmental Committee on Abortion. Its report, published in 1939, pointed once again to the problem of estimating the incidence of abortion. It suggested that between 110,000 and 150,000 abortions took place each year in England and Wales and that 'perhaps 40 per cent are criminal'.[2] In a minority report, one member of the committee, Dorothy Thurtle, suggested the proportion was higher than this. Although contraception became more widely available in the post war era, the evidence suggests that illegal abortion persisted until abortion was legalised under the 1967 Act.[37]

As we mentioned in the previous chapter, the decline in the population was a subject of much concern in the 1930s and 1940s, as it had been at the beginning of the century. A particular issue was the extent to which the decline reflected the use of abortion and birth control and the extent to which genetic and environmental factors were adversely affecting fertility.[21,26,29,30,38]

To inform its work of investigating possible reasons for decline, the Royal Commission on Population commissioned a survey of the use of birth

Table 4.1

Reported causes of 1,000 cases of abortion admitted to St Giles Hospital, Camberwell, 1930–34

Causes of abortion:	Number admitted	Number 'febrile'	Number of deaths
Reported induced abortion	485	387	15
Drugs only:	111	57	1
'Female pills'	27	14	0
Castor oil	21	11	0
Pills and purges	19	77	1
Miscellaneous	44	25	0
Instruments:	374	330	14
Syringe	135	116	3
Syringe and drugs	201	176	7
Catheter	8	8	0
Slippery elm bark	16	16	0
Knitting needle	5	5	0
Abortionist	9	9	4
Pathological factors consistent with spontaneous abortion	246	14	0
Aetiology unknown	269	81*	3
Total	1,000	482	18

Source: Parish TN. *A thousand cases of abortion.*[36]

*Estimated from statement in text.

control. This was done in 1946–7 by Ernest Lewis-Faning.[39] His sample was 3,281 women who were in general wards of selected hospitals and who at the time of the survey were in their first marriage. Paradoxically, when a second study, *Family intentions*, was done 20 years later, the prevailing worries were about the increasing population.[40] Fertility had, in fact, begun to decline from the peak reached in 1964, and the study was focused on child bearing intentions.

The 1967 study was followed up in 1972 by a study, *Families five years on*, which placed less emphasis on the subject of contraception and more on subsequent child bearing.[41] The *Family formation survey* was done in 1976 as a successor to the 1967 survey. It covered a sample of 6,589 women aged 16 to 49 living in England, Wales and Scotland and formed the United Kingdom's contribution to the World Fertility Survey. Unlike its predecessors, it included single women in the sample.[42] Although data on the use of contraception have been collected in other surveys, there has been no subsequent survey of family formation in the United Kingdom, although twenty other European countries did surveys on similar lines in the late 1980s and early 1990s.[43]

A major national survey of sexual attitudes and lifestyles gained a high public profile because public funding for the proposal was refused due, it was thought, to pressure from the Prime Minister, Margaret Thatcher. Among a wide range of questions on heterosexual and homosexual lifestyles, it included questions on the use of birth control in 1990 and 1991.[44,45] A further survey, covering people aged 16–44, was done in 1999.

Over these years, new birth control services were being developed and systems of data collection were set up to monitor their coverage and activities.

Contraception

'I'll sing you a song about a wondrous new device
The nation's latest contraceptive plan.
That funny little object they call the IPD
Has recently been changed to fit a man.

It's the IPD, the IPD
It may not feel too good for you
But it's not hurting me.
So every time the pain begins to fill your eyes with tears
Remember I put up with it for years.

It was proven to be safe for the average human male.
Though testing showed some minor side effects
There were two died of infection and six were sterilised
But only ten per cent were too depressed.'

Lian Tanner, *The IPD*.[46]

This satirical song about a mythical intrapenile device and the parody of the development of the intrauterine device on which it was based[47] remind us that the perfect contraceptive, devoid of side effects, has yet to be developed. This makes it important to monitor trends and variations in the use of the various methods of fertility control.

In general, routine collection of data about contraception started when birth control advice became available under the National Health Service. Until 1968, NHS services were theoretically restricted to women who had a medical need to avoid pregnancy, although some local authorities interpreted the restriction very liberally. The Family Planning Act of 1967, which came into effect in 1968 in England and Wales and separate legislation which came into effect in Scotland in 1970, enabled local authorities to provide contraceptive advice to all who asked for it regardless of marital status or medical need. This confirmed arrangements which had existed since 1931 and meant that local authorities chose whether to supply contraceptives in non-medical cases. Most of the authorities who used their powers under this Act did so by giving financial support to a voluntary organisation, the Family Planning Association (FPA), which had set up a number of clinics over the years since 1931.

At the time of the 1974 reorganisation of the NHS and local government, the clinics were transferred to health authorities and the services they provided became available free of charge. Contraceptive supplies dispensed and prescribed through clinics, have been available free of charge since April 1 1974. Since July 1 1975, those prescribed by general practitioners have been free of charge and they have been paid an 'item of service' fee for each woman registered with them for contraceptive services.

Data derived from community health returns about the activities of family planning clinics and general practitioners' claims for item of service payments for providing contraceptive services are published annually in *Health and personal social services statistics for England, Health statistics Wales* and in *Scottish health statistics*. More detailed data for England are published by the Department of Health in a statistical bulletin entitled *NHS contraceptive services*. Data are collected in Northern Ireland, but are no longer published.

Data about women's use of birth control services from 1975 onwards can be found in Tables A4.1.1 to A4.1.4. Not all the data found in these tables are published routinely. Tables A4.2.1 to A4.2.3 contain the only data collected routinely through the NHS about methods of contraception. They are confined to women and the small number of men attending clinics. Some clinics include data about small numbers of domiciliary visits. The data relate to the method of contraception in use or chosen at the individual's first visit to the clinic in each year. Subsequent changes of method are not recorded. The central government health departments also prepare annual summaries of numbers of clinic patients, subdivided into age groups.

Women receiving contraceptive advice from their general practitioners are subdivided only into those using intrauterine devices and those using all other methods of contraception. Even this distinction is made only because data in Tables A4.3.1 to A4.3.4 are derived from general practitioners' claims for payment and they are paid a higher fee for inserting an intrauterine device than for prescribing other contraceptives. This is a good example of the limitations of data derived from claims for item of service payments.

The volumes of health statistics also contain estimates of numbers and costs of prescriptions written by general practitioners for pharmaceuticals and appliances. These are derived from a sample of claims made by retail pharmacists for payments from the NHS. Time trends in prescriptions for oral contraceptives and contraceptive appliances from 1975 onwards are shown in Tables A4.4.1 to A4.4.5. Data are not usually published at this level of detail, so need to be obtained by making a special request.

Contraceptive appliances prescribed by general practitioners include intrauterine devices and diaphragms, but not contraceptive sheaths, now usually known as condoms. Condoms cannot be prescribed by general practitioners under the NHS, although family planning clinics provide them free of charge. The numbers of people who attend clinics and use condoms as their main method of contraception are shown in Tables A4.2.1 to A4.2.3. Obviously many more condoms are bought from shops and vending machines.

There is no precise way of estimating how many men use condoms and sales figures are subject to commercial confidentiality. In 1982, the Monopolies and Mergers Commission estimated that the London Rubber Company had between 90 and 95 per cent of the market for condoms in the United Kingdom.[48] Its sales in the year ending March 31 1982 amounted to over a hundred million condoms. Data about condoms imported were even more unreliable. The Customs and Excise quoted the weights of condoms and packaging combined rather than the numbers of condoms imported each year. Data from the Commission's report[48] are shown in Table A4.5.1.

The picture became no clearer in the late 1980s and early 1990s, despite the greater need to monitor condom use, to monitor the impact of campaigns to promote the use of condoms to prevent the transmission of HIV/AIDS. The second part of Table A4.5.1 shows data compiled from the London Rubber Company and market research surveys. This suggests increasing sales of condoms but it is difficult to relate it to the numbers of condoms used, let alone the numbers of men using them or the extent to which they are used for contraception.[49]

Although the general picture is of increasing numbers of prescriptions for oral contraceptives, it is not easy to draw together the trends in Tables A4.4.1 to A4.4.5. It is impossible to do so in Wales where there are major gaps in the data and in Northern Ireland, where data collection ceased in the early 1980s. In England and Scotland, there are discontinuities in the data about prescribing by general practitioners. Table A4.4.1 includes prescriptions for 'oestrogen-progestogen combinations', a marginally different category from oral contraceptives, between 1967 and 1975. The upsurge between 1972 and 1975 suggests that oral contraceptives became increasingly available under the NHS, rather than privately, in the period immediately before those prescribed by general practitioners were made free of charge on July 1 1975. In both England and Scotland, methods of data collection changed, as described in the footnotes to Tables A4.4.2 to A4.4.4.

There are two further problems with these data. Firstly, as prescriptions are written for varying numbers of cycles, it is difficult to relate them to the numbers of women taking oral contraceptives, and secondly, they do not include oral contraceptives dispensed in family planning clinics.

Data for 1975 onwards, shown in Tables A4.1.1 to A4.1.4 suggest that about a third of women aged 15–44 in Scotland and Northern Ireland and nearly two fifths of those in England used contraceptive services provided either by general practitioners or by clinics. There appeared to be a small rise in the 1990s. These figures may be a slight overestimate as some women are thought to use both clinic and general practice services.

In general, there was a decline in the use of clinics and an increase in the use of services provided by general practitioners. This may reflect women's choice or could be a consequence of cuts and closures of clinic services. The exception to these trends can be seen in an analysis of clinic use by age published in *Health and personal social services statistics for England* and in the Statistical bulletin *NHS contraceptive services*. This shows an increasing rate of use of clinics by women under the age of 20 and could reflect the provision of special clinics geared to the needs of women in this age group.

The proportion of pill users among women going to clinics has decreased, as can be seen in Tables A4.2.1 and A4.2.3. This may mean that women who want to change from oral contraceptives to other methods of contraception are selectively referred by general practitioners to clinics where the full range of methods are available, and that women who want to use oral contraceptives tend to go to general practitioners.

Tables A4.3.1 to A4.3.3 show an increase in the numbers of women registered with general practitioners for contraceptive services other than intrauterine devices. In practice this is likely to mean use of oral contraceptives.[50,51] In contrast, the fitting of intrauterine devices declined from the mid 1980s onwards in both clinics and general practice.

It can be seen that routinely collected data give us only very basic information on the use of contraceptives and tell us little about the people who use them. For this we have to turn to the series of surveys of birth control practices. Those studies we have already mentioned were concerned above all with interpreting trends in birth rates so their main interest in contraception was as an influence on the structure of the population.[39–42] In contrast to this, the two surveys in 1970[52] and 1975[53] were specifically concerned with the birth control services in England and Wales and the way women used them. The samples included single as well as married women. There was a further survey of birth control services in Scotland in 1982[54] but no further surveys were done in England and Wales.

Instead, some questions on the subject were included in the General Household Survey in 1983, 1986, 1989, 1991, 1993, 1995 and 1998. There are plans to include such questions again when the survey is relaunched in 2000. Meanwhile, similar questions were asked in 1997 in the ONS' Omnibus Survey.[55] In addition, a series of Health Education Monitoring Surveys, undertaken annually from 1995 onwards, ask more wide ranging questions about sexual behaviour and concern about HIV.[56,57]

The increasing use of contraception during the twentieth century is shown in Table 4.2 and the extent to which it has been used in the earliest stage of marriage is illustrated in Figure 4.1, data for which are given in Table A4.6.1. Contraceptive use may have been under-reported.[53] The 1946/7 sample contained a disproportionately high percentage of women from social groups with low income, who, in the past, made a lower than average use of contraception. In addition, older women may not have admitted to having used birth control.[39] There was also some evidence that women who married between 1946 and 1955, and were interviewed in the 1975 survey under-reported their use of birth control.[53]

Table 4.2

Percentage of women using birth control at some time during their married life

(a) Women married up to 1947

Date of marriage	Number of women	Percentage who used birth control
Before 1910	161	15
1910–19	361	40
1920–24	342	58
1925–29	339	61
1930–34	440	63
1935–39	617	66
1940–47	974	55
Omitted	47	
Total	3,281	

The report comments 'It should be noted that these percentages underestimate the percentage of women who will eventually use birth control in later marriage cohorts, since some of those not using it up to the time of the survey will subsequently adopt it. This accounts for the lower percentage in the last cohort'.

Source: Lewis-Faning E. *Family limitation*.[39] (Table 2)

(b) Women married 1951-70

Date of marriage	Number of women	Percentage who used birth control
Before 1951	87	83
1951–55	423	88
1956–60	707	92
1961–65	670	95
1966–70	588	93
Not known	45	
Total	2,520	

The data for the years 1966-70 are likely to be subject to a similar degree of underestimation as those for 1940-47, for the same reasons.

Source: Bone M. *The Family Planning Services: England and Wales*.[52] (Table R3.14)

It was concluded that a more accurate picture of the trends would show that the 'use was higher at the beginning of the period, rose rather less steeply between then and 1950–55 and then remained unchanged or even declined during 1956–60. As a result the steep increase from 1961–65 onwards would appear more abrupt than in the diagram.'[53] This coincided with the time when oral contraceptives became generally available. There was a temporary increase in the use of condoms during the same period. This suggests that the introduction of the pill may have coincided with, rather than caused, an increase in married couples' motivation to control their fertility.

Figure 4.1

Trends in use of contraception by married/cohabiting couples

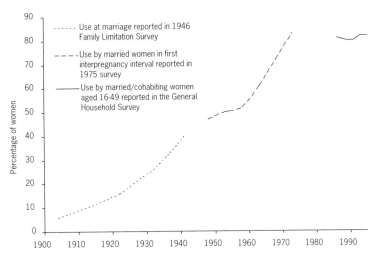

Source: Table A4.6.1 and *General Household Survey*

As these surveys did not include older single women, the Family Formation Survey, which did so, is used as a baseline for the trends in the 1980s and 1990s shown in Table A4.6.2. This is based on data from the General Household Survey and the ONS Omnibus Survey and shows a move from contraception to sterilisation over the period 1976–97. Among contraceptives, use of the pill and the intrauterine device declined and condom use became more common, as the AIDS epidemic got under way.

Not surprisingly, younger women were most likely to use the pill with just over half of women in their early twenties using it in 1997.[55] Sterilisation was more common among older women and their partners. Despite this, in 1997 four per cent of women aged 25–29 were sterilised and two per cent had partners with vasectomies, as Table A4.6.3 shows. In the 1980s, condom use was uncommon among partners of younger women, but Table A4.6.4 shows its use had spread down the age groups by 1997 and it was used by over a quarter of younger couples. The *Sex and lifestyle* survey showed a significant increase from the mid 1980s onwards in the proportions of men using condoms at first intercourse.[44,45]

Only six per cent of women aged 16–49 had used emergency contraception once in 1995, and two per cent more than once, but usage was very much more common among women under 30, as Table A4.6.6 shows. Figure 4.2 shows the rise in prescriptions for emergency contraception, both by clinics and by general practitioners.[51]

A special analysis of General Household Survey data for 1991, 1993 and 1995 in Table A4.6.7 showed that African-Caribbean and Indian women were less likely to use contraception than white women and their partners were much less likely to be sterilised.[58]

Figure 4.2

Numbers of prescriptions for emergency contraception, England, 1988–97

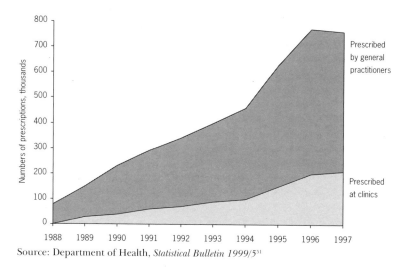

Prescribed by general practitioners

Prescribed at clinics

Source: Department of Health, *Statistical Bulletin 1999/5*[51]

Taken together, data from clinics and from general practitioners' prescriptions show a decline in the use of oral contraceptives in the late 1970s. Sales of oral contraceptives showed a similar decline between 1976 and 1979[59] and prescriptions for combined oral contraceptives fell in England in 1996. A major contributing factor to both short term and long term declines in use of oral contraceptives is publicity given, first in the medical press and subsequently in the national press, to research about their side effects.[60,61] These are discussed in Chapter 10.

Sterilisation

Female sterilisation has been available under the NHS on medical grounds since the Service started. It became explicitly available on request in 1974. The National Health Services (Family Planning) Amendment Act gave local authorities the power to provide vasectomy services from November 1972, on the same basis as those for contraception, but some vasectomies had been done under the NHS before this date.

Sterilisation can be performed at the time of, or a few days after delivery, in association with induced abortion or on its own, as what is sometimes called an 'interval procedure'. Data about sterilisations of hospital in-patients under the NHS in England are collected through the Hospital Episode Statistics (HES) and data about those in Wales are collected through the Patient Episode Database Wales (PEDW). In Scotland, data about sterilisations in association with abortion or delivery are collected through the SMR2 system. Interval sterilisations are included in the SMR1 system. In Northern Ireland, data are collected through the Hospital In patients System. Data from these sources are shown in Tables A4.7.1 to A4.10.1.

Routinely collected data about sterilisation in women up to the mid 1970s were reviewed in 1978.[62,63] Changes in data collection methods and in the ways operations are coded make it difficult to follow trends since then with any precision. The overall picture is of increasing numbers of operations, a change over time to endoscopic methods of sterilisation and a shift from in-patient to day case care.

Up to the early 1970s, the numbers of day case sterilisations in England and Wales could not be derived from the Hospital In-patient Enquiry but they were produced from 1979.[64] The data are now collected through the Hospital Episode Statistics. The number of sterilisations at the time of both NHS and non-NHS abortions can be derived from abortion notifications. As can be seen in Table A4.8.2, sterilisation is done at the same time as a substantial but declining percentage of NHS abortions. The small percentage of terminations of pregnancy on non-NHS premises which were accompanied by sterilisation rose up to the mid 1980s and declined afterwards.

No information is collected routinely about sterilisations done in the private sector as 'interval procedures', but a series of surveys in 1981, 1986 and 1992–93 tried to fill the gap in information about the activities of private hospitals.[65–67] Results of a further survey have not yet been published at the time of writing. Sterilisations at the time of the admittedly very small numbers of private deliveries should be included in HES, but have been excluded because of incompleteness of data. The data in Table A4.11.1 shows about 1,800 sterilisations in private hospitals in 1992–93. This does not include operations in NHS pay beds.[68]

Even less information is available about vasectomy. Only a small proportion of men who undergo it are admitted to hospital. The estimated numbers of vasectomies in NHS hospitals and family planning clinics are shown in Table A4.9.1 to A4.9.3, while data from private hospitals are shown in Table A4.11.1. Data from family planning clinics give separate estimates of the number of individuals adopting it as their method of contraception, the numbers of men counselled, and the numbers of operations performed. Data about hospital day cases are collected through HES in England, PEDW in Wales, SMR1 in Scotland and hospital statistics in Northern Ireland. No data are collected routinely about vasectomies performed in general practitioner's surgeries.

There are other operations and procedures which, while they are not done for contraceptive purposes, result in sterility. The most common of these are hysterectomy, the removal of the womb and/or bilateral oophorectomy, the removal of both ovaries. Trends in hysterectomy and oophorectomy in the NHS in England the Wales are shown in Table A4.10.1. These are taken from HIPE and HES. No data are routinely collected about operations in private hospitals but survey data are shown in Table A4.11.1.

Even if data about sterilisation procedures and other operations resulting in sterility were complete they would not tell us about the prevalence of sterility and subfertility in the population. The data from the surveys done

Figure 4.3

Female sterilisation by age, Great Britain, 1997

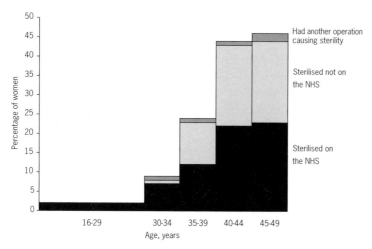

Source: ONS Omnibus Survey[55]

in the 1970s showed that sterilisation played a major part in birth control in women over 30.[42,53] The more recent data from the General Household Survey and the ONS Omnibus Survey in Table A4.12.1 and Figure 4.3 show that this is still the case. The dearth of more recent detailed data about the prevalence of sterility makes it very difficult to interpret changes since 1976 in the numbers of women using different forms of contraception.

Involuntary infertility and the menopause

Included in Table A4.6.2 are estimates of sterility from 'other causes' which are, in practice, natural causes, from 1986 onwards. Four per cent of ever-married women aged from 35 to 54 interviewed in the 1975 survey[53] were in this category, implying that either they or their partners were infertile. Table A4.6.3 shows that one per cent of all women and about two per cent of women aged 35 and over described themselves as 'possibly infertile'. The prevalence of infertility appears to be even lower in women under 30. This is probably because most couples in this age group who are unable to conceive will not have yet established conclusively, or indeed suspect, that they cannot do so.

The Royal Commission on Population attempted to estimate the incidence of involuntary childlessness and put it at between five and eight per cent of couples. Ernest Lewis-Faning attempted to collect data about the subject in his survey, but found it difficult as he felt that some women who had used birth control denied having done so.[39]

The early surveys also included women who had passed the menopause. These accounted for ten per cent of married women aged 16–55 in the case

Figure 4.4

Percentage of women who had passed the menopause, by age, England and Wales, 1975

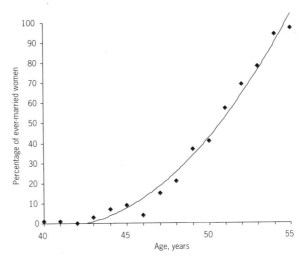

Source: *The family planning services: changes and effects*[53]

of Margaret Bone's 1975 sample. She estimated that the median age at menopause, that is the age at which half the women who reach that age will have had their last period, to be 49 years and 9 months.[53] Having done so, she commented that some women interviewed may have not recalled the date of their last period accurately, and that the use of oral contraceptives can mask the onset of symptoms of the menopause. In Figure 4.4 and Table A4.12.3, the women in her sample are tabulated according to whether or not they had reached the menopause at the time of interview.

More recent data are not available as the question of the menopause was not discussed in *Family formation, 1976*.[42] It does not feature among the questions asked in the General Household Survey over the subsequent twenty years nor was it covered in the *Sex and lifestyle* survey.[44,45] Studies of the women in the cohort of births in a week in March 1946 are following them through the menopause and should yield more up to date information.[69] The picture in the 1990s was likely to be more complex than in the 1970s, with fewer women having a 'natural' menopause and more of them starting hormone replacement therapy or having a hysterectomy before the onset of the menopause.[70,71]

Induced abortion

The 1967 Abortion Act came into force on April 27 1968 in England, Wales and Scotland. Under it, medical practitioners who terminate pregnancies are obliged to notify the fact to the Chief Medical Officer of the respective country.

Data derived from notifications of abortions in Scotland are published in *Scottish health statistics* along with data about Scottish residents who had abortions in England and Wales. In England and Wales, the data are processed and published on behalf of the Chief Medical Officers by ONS in its *Series AB*. A volume of *Abortion statistics* is published annually in *Series AB*. Up to 1981, *OPCS monitors* were published monthly and contained analyses of the notification forms received during the month. The numbers of forms received were not usually the same as the numbers of terminations performed. In 1981 the system was changed, and until 1998, *Abortion monitors* were published quarterly and contained data about the terminations performed during the quarter. In 1999, these data were transferred to *Health statistics quarterly*.

The Lane Committee, which reviewed the working of the Act up to 1971 included much information about the subject in its report.[72] Subsequent articles reviewed the first ten years of the working of the Abortion Act.[73,74] Trends in legal abortion from 1976 to 1989 and from 1990 to 1995 were reviewed in the 1990s.[75,76] Commentaries on trends in England and Wales are published annually in *Abortion statistics, Series AB*, while trends in Scotland are reviewed in the relevant *Health briefings*.

Trends in legal termination of pregnancy from 1968 to 1997 among women living or giving addresses in England and Wales, Scotland or Ireland are illustrated in Figure 4.5. The data for England and Wales and Scotland are shown in Tables A4.13.1 and A4.13.2. Very few private abortions take place in Scotland but some women who live in Scotland have private terminations in England and Wales, and these are included in the Scottish totals. Both sets of data show an increase in numbers of legal abortions up to 1973 as the services developed, then a decrease in the mid 1970s, followed by another increase with a levelling off in the late 1980s

Figure 4.5

Induced abortion rates, Great Britain and Ireland, 1969–97

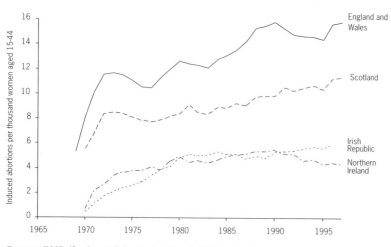

Source: ONS *Abortion statistics, Series AB* and ISD, Scotland

and 1990s. In England and Wales, the numbers of non-NHS abortions declined in the 1990s while the numbers done in non-NHS premises but paid for by the NHS increased.

The numbers of abortions in England and Wales for women known to be living elsewhere are given in Table A4.13.3. The fluctuations largely reflect changes in abortion legislation in the countries concerned and the overall decrease reflects the legalisation of abortion in most of Europe. In Northern Ireland, a small number of terminations are done on medical grounds under the case law which applied in England, Wales and Scotland before the 1967 Act. Considerably larger numbers of women from Northern Ireland and the Irish Republic travel to England for private sector abortions, as can be seen in Table A4.13.3. This also includes women from the Isle of Man and the Channel Islands, where the Abortion Act did not apply, although abortion was legalised in Guernsey in 1997 and in Jersey in 1998.

Increasing proportions of women are having abortions early in pregnancy, before 10 weeks of gestational age, as Tables A4.14.1 and A4.14.2 show. Less than two per cent of abortions to residents of Great Britain take place at 20 or more weeks gestation.

Numbers of terminations tabulated according to the woman's stated country of residence within the United Kingdom and region within England are given in Tables A15.1.1 and A15.1.2. Data for England and Wales are published by NHS district in *Abortion statistics, Series AB*, while those for Scotland are tabulated by health board in *Scottish health statistics*. It is noticeable that in the Thames Regions in general and in a number of London districts in particular, the numbers of abortions are relatively high in relation both to the numbers of births and to the numbers of women aged 15–44. This may reflect an increased incidence of abortion among women living in that area. It may also mean, however, that women from other parts of the United Kingdom and abroad give local accommodation addresses when having their pregnancies terminated in the areas where the rates appear to be high. Account is not always taken of this when advocating use of abortion rates as measures of NHS performance.[77]

Data for areas outside London are less likely to include women living elsewhere but giving addresses in the area, and can be more readily used to monitor the way services work.[78,79] Analyses for small areas can reveal marked differences in abortion rates within NHS districts.[80]

A selection of the data for England and Wales are summarised in Tables A4.16.1 to A4.16.5. Revised notification forms were introduced on March 1 1981 and April 1 1991. The second revision was to take account of changes to the Abortion Act under the Human Fertilisation and Embryology Act of 1990. Both these revisions caused some discontinuities in the data. Nevertheless Table A4.16.1 shows a move away from abortions using vacuum aspiration with combined dilation and evacuation to use of just one procedure, usually vacuum aspiration. It also shows that by 1997, prostaglandin was used in fewer than two per cent of terminations. A higher proportion of first trimester abortions in non-NHS premises compared to NHS premises can be seen in Table A4.16.5.

Abortions on grounds of fetal abnormality are shown in Table A4.17.1. Over the period 1979 to 1994, abortions because of central nervous system anomalies or chromosomal abnormalities in the fetus increased while those where the fetus had been damaged by viral disease in the mother, drugs or radiation fell to a very low level. Data about congenital anomalies are discussed in Chapter 8.

In the relatively small number of cases where women died during legal termination of pregnancy, death certification data and other relevant information are analysed as part of the Confidential Enquiries into Maternal Deaths. The question of maternal mortality from both legally and illegally induced abortion is discussed in Chapter 10.

Miscarriage

There is no comprehensive source of routinely collected data about miscarriages or spontaneous abortions, as they are sometimes known. It was suggested by some witnesses who gave evidence in the late 1930s to the Interdepartmental Committee on Abortion that a notification system should be set up. The idea was rejected as unrealistic then,[2] and has never been implemented.

Miscarriages are included in official statistics only if they result in a claim being made by a general practitioner for attending a miscarriage, or if they lead to admission to hospital or death. The minute numbers of deaths are included in the Confidential Enquiries into Maternal Deaths and are discussed in Chapter 10.

Numbers of general practitioners' claims for attending miscarriages are given in Table A7.10.2. Data collection at national level stopped in April 1997. It was not recorded whether the women involved are then admitted to hospital but a study in 1989 and 1990 in Alton, Hampshire found that bleeding occurred before the 20th week in 117 of 550 ongoing pregnancies and 12 per cent of them ended in miscarriage. Of the 67 miscarriages, 19 occurred at home.[81] Thus some of them may be included among admissions to NHS hospitals with miscarriage. Data about these are collected through the Hospital Episode Statistics in England, the Patient Episode Database Wales and SMR1 and SMR2 in Scotland, where they are tabulated by age of mother and health board in *Scottish health statistics*.

Most of the information recorded when general practitioners claim for payments for giving care to women who miscarry is discarded without being analysed. As the numbers of women are likely to be more complete than the numbers going to hospital, this is wasteful.

Miscarriage rates from Alton are lower than those cited in research studies but they relate to pregnancies known to general practitioners. Two studies suggested that 40 per cent of pregnancies which survive to the time of implantation are spontaneously aborted[82,83] although another study suggests that 15 per cent of all clinically recognised pregnancies miscarry.[84,85] Additional problems arise when comparing miscarriage rates from populations with different induced abortion rates and allowance should be made for this.[86]

Estimated conception rates

In order to try to compare the outcome of pregnancies which started at a similar time, an analysis of trends in induced abortion from 1968–80 analysed fertility rates in combination with data about abortions which had taken place six months earlier.[87] This did not fully take into account the distribution of gestational age at termination. OPCS subsequently started to publish statistics of conceptions leading to legal abortion or registered maternities. These are now published routinely in *Birth statistics, Series FM1*. Although it is possible to adjust abortion rates to allow for gestational age, this cannot be done for maternities as gestational age is not recorded for live birth registrations. Trends in these estimated conception rates are shown in Table A4.18.1 and conception rates are tabulated by region in Tables A3.14.2 and A3.14.3.

A special analysis of these data on a quarterly basis, showed a rise in conceptions following the 'pill scare' in 1995.[88] The increase was particularly notable in conceptions leading to abortion among younger women. Another analysis compared conception rates for different types of area and found them highest in Inner London.[89]

Interpreting trends in abortion

The impact on fertility of the legalisation of abortion is difficult to assess. This is because of the problem, to which we referred earlier, of estimating the extent of illegal abortions. Ernest Lewis-Faning tried to collect information about both miscarriage and induced abortion in his survey. He concluded that there was some under-reporting of miscarriages particularly those which had occurred some years earlier, and considerable under-reporting of criminal abortions.[30,39]

In 1947, the Abortion Law Reform Association published an estimate of 100,000 illegal abortions a year in England and Wales.[90] Considerable controversy ensued and estimates ranging from 20,000 to 250,000 were produced and summarised in the Lane Committee's report.[72] An analysis of data from abortion notifications estimated retrospectively that there were about 100,000 a year in the early 1960s, and that illegal abortion declined rapidly after the Act came into force, reaching about 8,000 in 1973.[91] The decline in maternal deaths due to abortion suggested that this was the case.

As we mentioned earlier, only a small proportion of illegal abortions will have come to the attention of the police and been included in the Home Office's *Crime statistics*. As Table A4.19.1 shows, however, the numbers of such cases decreased rapidly as the 1967 Act came into operation. It is less likely that police would be willing to turn a blind eye to illegal abortionists in the 1970s than before the Act was passed, so the crime statistics are likely to mirror the real decline in illegal abortion. The recent rise in offences against children shown in Table A4.19.2 is more likely to be related to domestic violence against live born children than to criminal abortion.

The knowledge that illegal abortion was widely practised before the Abortion Act came into force, coupled with the lack of data about its incidence, has implications for any attempts to assess the impact of legal abortion and free contraception and their possible impact on stillbirth and infant mortality rates. Unwanted pregnancies which were either prevented by birth control or terminated illegally may well have been those which carried a particularly high risk of perinatal death. Thus the mortality rate would be expected to fall once birth control and legal abortion became available. Studies in the United States which compared the introduction of legal abortion in a number of states with the decline in perinatal mortality rates reached conflicting conclusions.[92–97] Such studies should also take into account changes over the same time period in the other factors which are known to be associated with mortality.

Fertility control at the end of the twentieth century

The surveys we have quoted give estimates of time trends in the use of birth control, although there are suggestions that there is some element of under-reporting, especially in the earlier years. In general, the use of birth control increased and the social class differences in usage have disappeared. While middle class women started to use oral contraceptives sooner after their introduction in 1961 than did working class women, they also started to move away from them in the early 1970s.[98] By 1995 women with GCSE grades A–C or a higher qualification were more likely to use the pill in their twenties than women with no qualifications but less likely to do so in their forties.[99]

In 1997, 21 per cent of women aged 16–49 had partners who used condoms while 26 per cent used the pill.[55] Overall, 11 per cent of women had been sterilised and 10 per cent had a partner who had been sterilised, with sterilisation being most common in the oldest age group. The use of emergency contraception increased considerably over the period since it became available. While the availability of contraception and legal abortion may have influenced measures of the outcome of pregnancy by reducing unwanted pregnancies, many other factors are likely to have played a part. These are discussed in the chapters which follow.

References

1   Seven songs recorded by the BBC from Mrs Costello of Birmingham. *Journal of the English Folk Dance and Song Society* 1953; 7: 96–105.

2   Ministry of Health and Home Office. *Report of the interdepartmental committee on abortion*. London: HMSO, 1939.

3   Royal College of Obstetricians and Gynaecologists. *Report of the RCOG working party on unplanned pregnancy*. London: RCOG, 1991.

4   Laslett P. *The world we have lost*. London: Methuen, 1971.

5   Wrigley SA. Family limitation in pre-industrial England. *Economic History Review* 1966; 19: 82–109.

6   Child FJ. *The English and Scottish popular ballads* . Reproduction of 1883–1898 edition. New York: Folklore Press, 1956.

7   Potts M, Diggory P, Peel J. *Abortion*. Cambridge: Cambridge University Press, 1977.

8   Chamberlain M. *Old wives' tales: their history, remedies and spells*. London: Virago, 1981.

9   Potterton D. Culpeper and his cure-alls. *Health and Social Service Journal* 1983; (3rd February): 146.

10   Culpeper N. *The English physician enlarged: with three hundred and sixty-nine medicines, made of English herbs, that were not in any impression until this. Being an astrologo-physical discourse of the vulgar herbs of this nation ...* London: E Ballard, 1770.

11   Spenser E. *The faerie queene*. 1590; Vol. III (ii): 49.

12   Dryden J. *Juvenal*. 1693; Vol. vi: 755.

13   Burstow H. *Folk Song Journal* 1903; 1: 210–211.

14   Damme C. Infanticide: the worth of an infant under law. *Medical History* 1978; 22(1): 1–24.

15   Sauer R. Infanticide and abortion in nineteenth century Britain. *Population Studies* 1978; 32: 81–93.

16   Rose L. *Massacre of the innocents: infanticide in Great Britain, 1800–1939*. London: Routledge and Kegan Paul, 1986.

17   Keown J. *Abortion, doctors and the law: some aspects of the legal regulation of abortion in England from 1803 to 1982*. Cambridge: Cambridge University Press, 1988.

18   Smith FB. *The people's health, 1830–1910*. London: Croom Helm, 1979.

19   Newsholme A. *The elements of vital statistics*. 3rd edition. London: S Sonnenschein and Co, 1899.

20   Jones HR. The perils and protection of infant life. *Journal of the Royal Statistical Society* 1894; 69: 1–103.

21   Brookes B. *Abortion in England, 1900–1967*. London: Croom Helm, 1988.

22   Himes N. *Medical history of contraception*. New York: Gamut Press, 1963.

23   Draper E. *Birth control in the modern world*. London: Allen and Unwin, 1965.

24   Peel J, Potts M. *Textbook of contraceptive practice*. Cambridge: Cambridge University Press, 1969.

25   McLaren A. *Birth control in nineteenth century England*. London: Croom Helm, 1978.

26   Soloway RA. *Birth control and the population question in England, 1877–1930*. Chapel Hill: University of North Carolina Press, 1990.

27   Leathard A. *The fight for family planning*. London: Macmillan, 1980.

28   Grier J. Eugenics and birth control: contraceptive provision in North Wales, 1918–1939. *Social History of Medicine* 1998; 11(8): 443–458.

29   Williams AS. *Women and childbirth in the twentieth century: a history of the National Birthday Trust Fund, 1928–93*. Stroud: Sutton, 1997.

30   Szreter S. *Fertility, class and gender in Britain, 1860–1940*. Cambridge Studies in Population, Economy and Society in Past Time No. 27. Cambridge: Cambridge University Press, 1996.

31   Clay C. Statistics and observations on liability to abortion. *Glasgow Medical Journal* 1935; 1859(6): 408–410.

32   Local Government Board. *Third report by the Medical Officer on infant mortality in Lancashire. Supplement to the forty-third annual report of the Local Government Board, 1913–14*. Cd 7511. London: HMSO, 1914.

33   Ministry of Health. *Report on an investigation into maternal mortality*. Cmd 5422. London: HMSO, 1937.

34   Committee on Medical Aspects of Abortion. Report. *British Medical Journal* 1936; 2(Supplement): 230–238.

35   Whitehouse B. Abortion: its frequency and importance. *British Medical Journal* 1929; 2: 1095–1099.

36   Parish TN. A thousand cases of abortion. *Journal of Obstetrics and Gynaecology of the British Empire* 1935; 42: 1107–1121.

37   Simms M. Abortion: the myth of the golden age. In: Hutter B, Williams G, eds. *Controlling women: the normal and the deviant*. London: Croom Helm, 1981.

38   Lewis J. Mothers and maternity policies in the twentieth century. In: Garcia J, Kilpatrick R, Richards M, eds. *The politics of maternity care*. Oxford: Clarendon Press, 1990.

39   Lewis-Faning, E. Report of an enquiry into family limitation and its influence on human fertility during the past fifty years. In: Royal Commission on Population. *Papers*. Vol. 1. London: HMSO, 1949.

40   Woolf M. *Family intentions. An enquiry undertaken for the General Register Office*. Social Survey Report SS 408. London: HMSO, 1971.

41   Woolf M, Pegden S. *Families five years on. A survey carried out on behalf of the Population Statistics Division of the Office of Population Censuses and Surveys*. Social Survey Report SS 499. London: HMSO, 1976.

42   Dunnell, K. *Family formation, 1976. A survey carried out on behalf of Population Statistics Division I of the Office of Population Censuses and*

Surveys on a sample of women (both single and ever married) aged 16–49 in Great Britain. Social Survey Report SS 1080. London: HMSO, 1979.

43   United Nations Economic Commission for Europe. *Questionnaire and code book: fertility and family surveys in countries of the ECE region.* New York: UN, 1992.

44   Wellings K. *Sexual behaviour in Britain: the national survey of sexual attitudes and lifestyles.* Harmondsworth: Penguin, 1994.

45   Johnson AM, Wadsworth J, Wellings K, Field J, Bradshaw S. *Sexual attitudes and lifestyles.* Oxford: Blackwell Scientific Publications, 1994.

46   Tanner L. The IPD. Sung by Judy Small on *One voice in the crowd.* Greentrax, Scotland.

47   Outcome Magazine: the East Bay Men's Center Newsletter. The intrapenile device being fitted. In: Oakley A. *Subject women.* Oxford: Martin Robertson, 1981.

48   Monopolies and Mergers Commission. *Contraceptive sheaths: a report on the supply in the United Kingdom of contraceptive sheaths.* Cmnd 8689. London: HMSO, 1982.

49   Goodrich J, Wellings K, McVey D. Using condom data to assess the impact of HIV/AIDS preventive interventions. *Health Education Research* 1998; 13(2): 267–274.

50   Allen I. *Family planning, sterilisation and abortion services.* London: Policy Studies Institute, 1981.

51   Department of Health. *NHS contraceptive services, England: 1997–98.* Statistical Bulletin 1999/5 London: Department of Health, 1999.

52   Bone M. *Family planning services in England and Wales. An enquiry carried out by the Social Survey Division of OPCS on behalf of the Department of Health and Social Security.* Social Survey Report SS 467. London: HMSO, 1973.

53   Bone M. *The family planning services: changes and effects. A survey carried out on behalf of the Department of Health and Social Security.* Social Survey Report SS 1055. London: HMSO, 1978.

54   Bone M. *Family planning in Scotland in 1982.* London: HMSO, 1985.

55   Dodd T, Freeth S. *Contraception and sexual health, 1997.* Series OS11. London: Office for National Statistics, 1999.

56   Office for National Statistics. *Health in England 1995: What people know, what people think, what people do.* London:HMSO, 1996.

57   Office for National Statistics. *All change? The Health Education Monitoring Survey one year on.* London: The Stationery Office, 1998.

58   Raleigh VS, Almond C, Kiri V. Fertility and contraception among ethnic minority women in Great Britain. *Health Trends* 1997; 29(4): 109–113.

59   Wiseman RA, MacRae KD. Oral contraceptives and the decline in mortality from circulatory disease. *Fertility and Sterility* 1981; 35(3): 277–283.

60   Bone M. The 'pill scare' and fertility in England and Wales. *IPPF Medical Bulletin* 1982; 16(4): 24.

61   Wood R. Trends in conceptions before and after the 1995 pill scare. *Population Trends* 1997; 89: 5–12.

62   Bone M. Recent trends in sterilisation. *Population Trends* 1978; 13: 13–15.

63   Bledin KD, Beral V, Ashley JSA. Recent trends in sterilisation in women. *Health Trends* 1978; 10: 84–87.

64   Office of Population Censuses and Surveys. *Day case statistics, 1975–1978*. OPCS Monitor MB4 82/1. London: OPCS, 1982.

65   Williams BT, Nicholl JP, Thomas KJ, Knowelden J. Analysis of the work of independent acute hospitals in England and Wales, 1981. *British Medical Journal* 1984; 289(6442): 446–448.

66   Nicholl JP, Beeby NR, Williams BT. Role of the private sector in elective surgery in England and Wales, 1986. *BMJ* 1989; 298(6668): 243–247.

67   Williams BT, Nicholl JP. Patient characteristics and clinical caseload of short stay independent hospitals in England and Wales, 1992–3. *BMJ* 1994; 308(6945): 1699–1701.

68   Williams B. Utilisation of National Health Service hospitals in England by private patients, 1989–95. *Health Trends* 1997; 29: 21–25.

69   Kuh D. The MRC National Survey of Health and Development. *Journal of the British Menopause Society* 1997; (December): 6–7.

70   Hardy R, Kuh D. Reproductive characteristics and the age at inception of perimenopause in a British national cohort. *American Journal of Epidemiology* 1999; 149(7): 1–9.

71   Kuh DL, Wadsworth M, Hardy R. Women's health in midlife: the influence of the menopause, social factors and health in earlier life. *British Journal of Obstetrics and Gynaecology* 1997; 104: 923–933.

72   Committee on the Working of the Abortion Act. *Report*. [Chair: Mrs Justice Lane]. Cmnd 5579. Vol. 1. London: HMSO, 1974.

73   Lewis TL. Legal abortion in England and Wales 1968–78. *British Medical Journal* 1980; 280(6210): 295–296.

74   Fowkes FG, Catford JC, Logan RF. Abortion and the NHS: the first decade. *British Medical Journal* 1979; 1(6158): 217–219.

75   NHS General Medical Services. *Statement of fees and allowances payable to general medical practitioners in England and Wales (The Red Book)*. Updated to June 1998. London: Department of Health/Welsh Office, 1996.

76   Filakti H. Trends in abortion, 1990–1995. *Population Trends* 1997; 87: 11–19.

77   Raleigh VS. Abortion rates in England in 1995: comparative study of data from district health authorities. *BMJ* 1998; 316(7146): 1711–1712.

78 Ashton JR, Dennis KJ, Rowe RG, Waters WE, Wheeler MJ. The Wessex abortion studies: I. Interdistrict variation in provision of abortion services. *Lancet* 1980; i(8159): 82–85.

79 Ashton JR. Methodological kit: monitoring statistics relating to the control of fertility and the provision of abortion. *Community Medicine* 1981; 3(1): 44–54.

80 Ubido J, Ashton J. Small area analysis: abortion statistics. *Journal of Public Health Medicine* 1993; 15(2): 137–143.

81 Everett C. Incidence and outcome of bleeding before the 20th week of pregnancy: Prospective study from general practice. *BMJ* 1997; 315(7099): 32–34.

82 Kline J, Shrout P, Susser M, Warburton D. Environmental influences on early reproductive loss in a current New York City study. In: Porter IH, Hook EB. *Human embryonic and fetal death*. New York: Academic Press, 1980: 225–240.

83 Miller JF, Williamson E, Glue J, Gordon YB, Grudzinskas JG, Sykes A. Fetal loss after implantation. A prospective study. *Lancet* 1980; ii(8194): 554–556.

84 Warburton D, Strobino B. Recurrent spontaneous abortion. In: Bennett MJ, Edmonds DK, eds. *Spontaneous and recurrent abortion*. Oxford: Blackwell Scientific, 1987.

85 Regan L. Recurrent miscarriage. *BMJ* 1991; 302(6776): 543–544.

86 Susser E. Spontaneous abortion and induced abortion: an adjustment for the presence of induced abortion when estimating the rate of spontaneous abortion from cross-sectional studies. *American Journal of Epidemiology* 1983; 117(3): 305–308.

87 Ashton JR, Machin D, Osmond C, Balarajan R, Adam SA, Donnan SP. Trends in induced abortion in England and Wales. *Journal of Epidemiology and Community Health* 1983; 37(2): 105–110.

88 McNeil N. *Sexually transmitted disease: a summary of new cases, 1968–1973*. Glasgow: Communicable Diseases (Scotland) Unit, 1975.

89 Wood R. Subnational variations in conceptions. *Population Trends* 1996; 84: 21–27.

90 Chance J, Edge M, Ryan M. *Back street surgery*. London: Abortion Law Reform Association, 1947.

91 Francome C. Estimating the number of illegal abortions. *Journal of Biosocial Science* 1977; 9(4): 467–479.

92 Bauman KE, Anderson AE. Legal abortions and trends in fetal and infant mortality rates in the United States. *American Journal of Obstetrics and Gynecology* 1980; 136(2): 194–202.

93 Quick JD. Liberalized abortion in Oregon: effects on fertility, prematurity, fetal death, and infant death. *American Journal of Public Health* 1978; 68(10): 1003–1008.

94 Pakter J, O'Hare D, Nelson F, Svigir M. Two years experience in New York City with the liberalized abortion law – progress and problems. *American Journal of Public Health* 1973; 63(6): 524–535.

95 Garfinkel J, Chabot MJ, Pratt MW. *Infant, maternal and childhood mortality in the United States, 1968–1973*. Rockville, Md: US Department of Health Education and Welfare, 1975.

96 Wallace CF. The modernisation of United States contraceptive practice. *Family Planning Perspectives* 1972; 4: 9–12.

97 Grossman M, Jacobowitz S. Variations in infant mortality rates among counties of the United States: the roles of public policies and programs. *Demography* 1981; 18(4): 695–713.

98 Cartwright A. *Recent trends in family building and contraception*. Studies on Medical and Population Subjects No. 34. London: HMSO, 1978.

99 Office for National Statistics. *Living in Britain: results from the 1995 General Household Survey*. London: The Stationery Office, 1997.

5 Inequalities in the social background of parents and the circumstances in which they live

> ' ... comparisons which are really comparisons between two social classes with different standards of nutrition and education are palmed off as comparisons between the results of a certain medical treatment and its neglect. Thus it is easy to prove that the wearing of tall hats and the carrying of umbrellas enlarges the chest, prolongs life and confers comparative immunity from disease; for the statistics show that the classes which use these articles are bigger, healthier, and live longer than the class which never dreams of possessing such things.'
>
> Bernard Shaw. Preface to *The doctor's dilemma*.[1]

> 'I'm not suggesting any sort of plot,
> Everyone knows there's not,
> But you unborn millions might like to be warned
> That if you don't want to be buried alive by slagheaps,
> Pit falls and damp walls and rat traps and dead streets,
> Arrange to be democratically born
> The son of a company director,
> Or a judge's fine and private daughter.'
>
> Leon Rosselson. *Palaces of gold*.[2]

In his study *Birth, poverty and wealth*[3] published in 1943, Richard Titmuss commented on past trends in infant mortality:

> 'The termination of an individual life is the product of an enormous number of complex and inter-related forces ... . Reducing this diversity to identify, to find the causation of infant mortality, we can distinguish two main factors operating in the past to produce a high death rate. One can be summed up in the word poverty; the other is unsanitary urbanisation ... . Thus in Farr's day the public health administrator was faced with two main problems, poverty and drains. But though both were indubitably present only one was recognised as a problem – poverty was part of the natural order of things – and all the emphasis was concentrated on drains.'[3]

It was perhaps for this reason that, as we described in Chapter 3, considerable effort was devoted to comparing the mortality experience of people living in different types of area. After a long series of battles, fought throughout the nineteenth century, brought about improved sanitation, interest turned to the problem of poverty. This in its turn gave rise to considerable debate about how to classify the social position of individuals and to measure the differences between them. There is still a live issue at the end of the twentieth century. Issues include whether to compare geographical populations or individuals grouped according to particular characteristics or circumstances.

In the first section of this chapter we assess the extent to which classification of occupations into groups measures people's position in society and how the social classes it defines are associated with the outcome of pregnancy. Later in the chapter we discuss the extent to which differences in other characteristics of parents or their socio-economic circumstances can be measured in statistics. This includes their age and marital status, factors associated with ethnic origin, and parents' employment and unemployment.

Social class based on occupation

The origins of the Registrar General's classification

Starting in 1851, the *Registrar General's decennial supplement* included comparative analyses of men's mortality according to their occupations.[4-6] In addition, occupations involving the use of similar materials or having other features in common were grouped together. For the analysis of the 1911 census, this process was formalised by constructing 'social classes' based on groups of occupations.[7] One of the criteria for doing this was to classify people according to their social position. The primary reason for doing this was to investigate the decline in fertility.[8,9] In the 1911 census, women were asked for information about the births of their children and whether they had died. The fathers' occupations were grouped into classes in order to investigate differences in fertility rates and also in childhood mortality.[10,11] Despite the emphasis on fertility, the first published analyses which used the classes were of infant mortality.[12]

In this section we assess the extent to which this classification measures people's position in society and how the social classes it defines are associated with the outcome of pregnancy. Later in the chapter we discuss the extent to which differences in this outcome for people in different specific occupations can be measured in official statistics.

In a paper given to the Royal Statistical Society in 1928, THC Stevenson, Superintendent of Statistics at the General Register Office, explained the reasons for basing the classification on occupation. He first pointed to the reason for classifying individuals instead of comparing affluent and deprived areas:

> 'There is a large admixture of poverty in the wealthiest and most fashionable areas, if only in the shape of domestic servants and others employed in ministering to the ease and the comfort of the rich; and the poorest quarters are not without their comparatively wealthy classes such as the publicans and pawnbrokers who abound in such neighbourhoods. The ideal method would classify individuals and not whole populations, by their degree of prosperity, but in most parts of the world the necessary data are lacking.'[7]

Information about parents' income had been collected in small scale studies, such as an investigation of associations between the birthweight of babies born during the first world war at St Thomas' Hospital, London, and their parents' circumstances. The study, published in 1924, classified employed fathers according to whether their net incomes were above or below the average. Those who were 'not in receipt of any discoverable income at all' were classified as 'in bad health', 'enemy aliens', 'deserters', 'out of work' or 'thoroughly unsatisfactory'.[13] Not surprisingly, however, parents' incomes were not recorded at birth registration or in population censuses.

Stevenson suggested that the lack of data about the income of individuals was perhaps not as important as it might appear at first sight. He cited the low mortality of the clergy as evidence that low mortality rates were less closely associated with wealth than with what he described as 'culture'.

In the discussion which followed Stevenson's presentation, Major Greenwood said, 'I think Dr Stevenson means by 'wealth' the purchasing power of the family unit and by 'culture', not an acquaintance with differential equations or the minor poems of Horace, but a combination of knowledge and skill which enables a person to use his purchasing power wisely.'[14] He went on to add that 'In any community such as ours there does exist a group of persons whose purchasing power is so small that no amount of culture in Dr Stevenson's sense could possibly enable them to provide adequately for the family unit.'[14]

Although the Registrar General's social classes were put forward as a measure of 'culture' or 'way of life', the different but not unrelated concept of 'occupational status' was used to define them. After revising the classification for the 1921 census,[15] 'five social grades are used as follows: 1 upper and middle classes; 2 intermediate between 1 and 3; 3 skilled workmen; 4 intermediate between 3 and 5; and 5, unskilled labourers.'[7] The occupations were grouped into the classes in a way which agreed with Stevenson's preconceptions of their status, rather than according to any coherent scheme or philosophy.[9] He justified this on the grounds that 'The scheme under discussion has yielded natality (1921) and mortality (1921–23) rates varying regularly with social status, from a minimum for the highest class (1) to a maximum for the lowest (5).'[7]

Status and skill have continued to be the stated basis of the Registrar General's social classes defined in Table 2.10 although the way occupations have been classified continues to be arbitrary and subjective. The classification has changed both as new occupations, such as those associated with computers, appeared on the scene and as the status of occupations changed, but the overall structure remains remarkably similar to that used in 1921. Thus, although information about whether a person is an employee, an employer or self employed is taken into account as well as his or her occupation, and some account is taken of whether an employee is a manager, supervisor or foreman, the classes do not directly reflect her or his relationship to the means of production.[16,17] Furthermore it is impossible for the classes to represent social groups of which people perceive themselves to be members, as perceptions of these will differ from person to person.

Criticisms of the Registrar General's social classification

From the 1930s onwards, people began to question the validity and usefulness of the occupationally based social class classification. An analysis of births in 1939 used the new data about mother's age and parity collected under the Population Statistics Acts to look back critically at the analyses of fertility in the 1921 and 1931 Decennial Supplements.[15,18-20] It included an appendix by the demographer David Glass, who pointed out that there had never been an independent assessment of the grading of occupations in the Registrar General's classification. In the early 1990s, a historian, Simon Szreter, made a detailed re-analysis of the fertility rates for each individual occupation from which data were published in the *Fertility report* of the 1911 census. He showed that the way the classification was constructed obscured major differences between groups of occupations.[9]

Criticism of a different sort came in 1984 from two epidemiologists, Ian Jones and Donald Cameron. They argued that the Registrar General's social class classification should be abandoned as 'an embarrassment to epidemiology'. Their grounds were that it is 'an empiricist methodology which has been engineered to conform to the prejudices of narrow minded professionals and blatantly manipulated to produce smooth mortality gradients.'[21] This article was cited in support of the decision to restrict severely the analysis by social class in the *Registrar General's decennial supplement* relating to the 1981 census.[22]

Development and use of data from decennial supplements

In the late 1970s, the Labour administration set up the *Working party on inequalities in health* chaired by Sir Douglas Black.[23] Based on data from the *Decennial supplement* on *Occupational mortality, 1970–72*[24] and other sources, its report recommended action to reverse the social class differences observed in the data. A small number of typescript copies of the report were 'made available for discussion . . . without any commitment by the government to its proposals' but a revised paperback version was widely read.[25]

A decade later, closer inspection of the social class analyses of mortality among adults, most of which were published on microfiche,[22] showed widening differentials between 1970–72 and the years around 1981.[26] These were summarised and discussed by Margaret Whitehead in a report, *The health divide*.[27] Together with the 'Black' report, it was reissued in paperback and contains a useful summary of the problems involved in interpreting the data.[28]

OPCS subsequently published a separate *Childhood supplement* on social class differences on infant and childhood mortality.[29] This was the first occasion on which jointly registered births outside marriage were analysed by the babies' fathers' social class, in combination with births within marriage.

This report showed the usual gradient in mortality but did not look at trends over time.

At the end of the 1980s, OPCS changed its publication policy and decennial supplements are now much more broadly based documents. The traditional analyses of death and census data are set alongside analyses of relevant data from other sources, notably the Longitudinal Study. These are listed in Appendix 2. For the 1991 census, there were two separate publications. One dealt with *Occupational mortality* and *Health inequalities* focused on social class analyses.[30,31]

Health inequalities returned to the public agenda in 1990. In his last annual report before retiring as Chief Medical Officer of the Department of Health, Sir Donald Acheson drew attention to the social class differentials in health and mortality.[32] These were allowed back on the policy agenda, in a muted form, labelled as 'health variations'. After the change of government in 1997, the Department of Health reinstated the term 'health inequalities' and called Sir Donald Acheson out of retirement to head an independent inquiry into ways of reducing them. This drew considerably on the class analyses in the *Health inequalities* decennial supplement.[31]

The need for better data and the health of women and children both came high on the list of recommendations in the inquiry's report.

'1.2 We recommend a review of data needs to improve the capacity to monitor inequalities in health and the determinants at national and local level.

2. We recommend a high priority is given to policies aimed at improving health and reducing health inequalities in women of childbearing age, expectant mothers and young children.'[33]

Developing a new social classification for official statistics

Although data based on the Registrar General's social classes had underpinned the published analyses and public activity, scepticism about basing social classifications on occupation persisted. In response to this, OPCS commissioned a review in 1994. The review team's first brief was to consider whether a social classification based on factors other than occupation should be devised for the 2001 census. It was decided that this was needed but so also was a new classification based on occupation.[34]

The result is called the National Statistics socio-economic classification.[35-37] In constructing it, David Rose and Karen O'Reilly were able to draw on a large body of work which had been done to construct classifications which, unlike the Registrar General's classes, were based on identifiable and explicitly stated social theories.[38-40] As well as being used in academic research, some of these classifications have come into use alongside social class in government datasets, notably in the Longitudinal Study and in the Health Survey for England.[41,42]

The new classification is based on employment conditions and relations rather than skill or status. It is very similar to the 'CASMIN' scheme developed by John Goldthorpe and Robert Erikson for use in research.[38]

The primary classification is into employers, own account, self-employed and employees. In its longest version, the classification has 30 subdivisions. These can be progressively collapsed down to the seven shown in Table 2.12. It is due to be introduced in 2001 for coding the census and other official data, including those collected at birth and death registration. Pilot studies have been undertaken on a number of official datasets.[43] One of these analysed infant mortality by the babies' fathers' classes and found the same pattern seen in mortality among adults.[44] This is discussed later.

Meanwhile, despite the limitations of the Registrar General's social classes, they point to considerable inequalities with the lowest rates of mortality and morbidity in the most privileged groups and the highest rates among the least privileged babies and their parents. This is perhaps not surprising given that infant mortality was used to test and calibrate the classification but it also applies to most, although not all of a wide range of health indicators. In what follows, we describe how social class is used on a wide range of records, making it potentially possible to compare data from different sources, provided that they are interpreted with caution.

Interpreting trends in births

Throughout the twentieth century, analyses using Registrar General's classes suggested a tendency for women married to manual workers to have more children than women married to non-manual workers. In THC Stevenson's retrospective analyses of the fertility data collected in the 1911 census, professional workers had the lowest fertility during the latter part of the nineteenth century, while unskilled labourers, miners and agricultural workers had the highest fertility.[8] Similar differences were seen in data collected in 1921 and 1931 and the Family Census of 1946 showed marked differences in fertility in the early part of the twentieth century.[45] Table 5.1 shows a picture of declining average family size. While the differential was maintained at this period, a more complex picture emerged later in the century.[46-48] In 1971, but not in subsequent censuses, more detailed questions were asked about fertility, enabling comparisons to be made with the position in 1911. These analyses were published in the *Fertility report from the 1971 census*.[47] Because of the absence of corresponding data fom the 1981 and 1991 censuses, analyses of fertility by social class at this level of detail are not available for more recent years.

As a result of the changes in the labour market and in the type of work people did, the tendency from the 1970s onwards was for the numbers of babies born to women with husbands in professional occupations to account for an increasing proportion of all births. This is illustrated in Figure 5.1 and Tables A5.1.1 and A5.1.2. As well as being derived from data which have been published annually in *Birth statistics, Series FM1* since 1970, these tables also include data from special studies done in 1950[49] and 1964[50] for comparison. The data for 1950 and 1964 should be interpreted with care as they are based on different versions of the *Classification of occupations*.

Table 5.1

Family size and men's occupation in the early and mid twentieth century

(a) Estimated average size of completed family according to period of marriage.

Date of marriage	Women married to non-manual workers	Women married to manual workers	Ratio
1900–09	2.79	3.94	1.41
1910–14	2.34	3.35	1.43
1915–19	2.05	2.91	1.42
1920–24	1.89	2.73	1.44
1925–29	1.73	2.49	1.44

Source: *Family census of Great Britain, 1946.*[45]

(b) Average family size for women married once only* by social class of husband and selected durations of marriage, 1971.

Marriage duration, completed years	Approximate period of marriage	Social class of husband						
		All classes	I	II	IIIn	IIIm	IV	V
10–14	1956–61	2.24	2.23	2.12	1.99	2.28	2.30	2.56
15–19	1951–56	2.29	2.25	2.17	2.00	2.34	2.37	2.66

*Married before the age of 45.
Source: *1971 census.*[46]

(c) Mean number of live births to women first married between 1956 and 1965, after ten years of marriage.

	Social class of husband†				All
	I and II Professional and intermediate	III Skilled non-manual	III Skilled manual	IV and V Partly skilled and unskilled	
Mean number of live births	2.0	2.2	2.1	2.3	2.1
Percentage with 3 or more live births	28	36	31	40	32

†Based on social class of husband at the time of interview. Women who had no husband or whose husband's occupation was not coded are included in the total column.
Source: *Family formation, 1976. (Table 4.8)*

Figure 5.1

Numbers of live births by social class of father, England and Wales, 1970–97

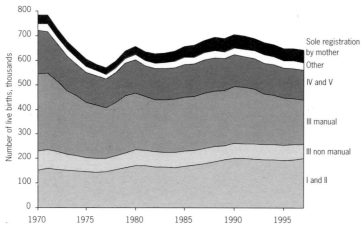

Source: Office for National Statistics *Birth statistics, Series FM1*

The 1970 classification of occupations was used from 1970 to 1979

The 1980 classification was used from 1980 to 1990.

The 1990 classification was used from 1991 onwards

Low birthweight

The marked social class differences in low birthweight in England and Wales are illustrated in Figure 5.2. The data for 1982–96 are given in Table A5.2.1 with data for stillbirths in Table A5.2.2. Rather than a uniform gradient, the data show a high proportion of low birthweights among babies whose fathers were in partly skilled and unskilled manual jobs or who were registered by their mother alone, but much smaller differences between the other groups. Combining singleton and multiple births tends to diminish social class differences in the incidence of birthweights under 1,500g and differences are more visible in Tables A5.3.1 and A5.3.2 in which singleton and multiple births are shown separately.

Data for Scotland, in Tables A5.3.3 and A5.3.4, show a more complex pattern. Gestational age and birthweight are collected in the SMR2 system, but are not passed on to the registration system as in England and Wales. The SMR2 system no longer collects the information used to derive social class, as it was found to be incomplete. Instead, social class is added to datasets when required, by linkage with birth registration. In Scotland the father's occupation is recorded for births inside marriage and the mother's for births outside marriage. Birthweight and the percentage of low weight births are tabulated in this way in Table A5.3.3 and gestational age in A5.3.4. In both cases, data are tabulated for singleton and multiple births separately.

Tables A5.1.1 to A5.3.4 are based on special analyses for this book, but tabulations of births and infant deaths by birthweight and the babies' father's social class are published annually in *Mortality statistics, Series DH3*. Taken together, the overall picture in England and Wales, and also in

Figure 5.2

Low birthweight by social class of father, births within marriage and jointly registered outside marriage, England and Wales, 1997

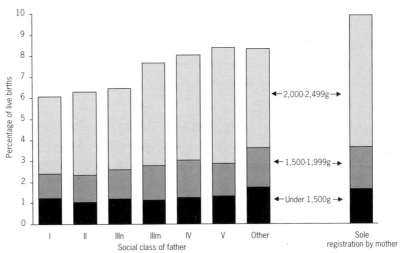

Source: Office for National Statistics, *Mortality statistics, Series DH3*

Scotland, is of inequalities in low birthweight, with the most marked differences being at the bottom of the social scale.

Patterns of low birthweight in Scotland in Table A5.3.3 relate to a single year, 1995, so the number of births is small. Although differences can be seen it would be inappropriate to draw detailed conclusions without subjecting the data to formal statistical tests.

Preterm birth

Table A5.3.4 contains data about gestational age at which babies were born in Scotland for the years 1990–95 combined. The percentage of preterm births was lower among women married to men in professional and executive groups than among those married to other men. Within these, the percentage is higher in the manual groups. Outside marriage, preterm births are much more common, particularly among women with no stated occupation. There are some signs of differences in gradient between occupational classes, but the numbers of events are small in some groups.

Stillbirths and deaths in infancy

Stillbirth and infant mortality rates tabulated by the father's social class are shown in Figures 5.3 and 5.4. In these deaths among babies born within marriage are combined with those among babies born outside marriage and jointly registered by both parents. Deaths among babies registered by mothers alone are also shown. Mortality shows its usual gradient with the highest rates among the babies with fathers in manual occupations and those registered solely by their mothers. The gradient is wider for postneonatal mortality than for neonatal mortality. In contrast to this,

Figures 5.5 and 5.6 show stillbirth and infant mortality rates for the new National Statistics socio-economic classes defined in Table 2.12.[35-37] The data come from the pilot study mentioned earlier.[44] It found that stillbirth and infant mortality rates were lowest among babies with fathers in higher managerial and professional occupations and also among babies with fathers who were small employers or worked on their own account.

Evidence of a widening in social class differences in mortality among adults during the 1980s[31] raises questions about stillbirth and infant mortality rates. These are difficult to answer for a number of reasons. First, concerns about the way the Registrar General's classification was constructed initially and modified for each census make it difficult to interpret long term trends, but social class differences in postneonatal mortality appear to have widened slightly between 1911 and 1931[3] and between 1921 and 1971.[51] Up to 1970–72, social class differences in postneonatal mortality were always much wider than the corresponding differences in neonatal mortality.[3,24,50]

Secondly, stillbirth and infant mortality rates were not routinely tabulated by social class of father for births outside marriage before 1993. This may have been reasonable up to the late 1970s when under ten per cent of births took place outside marriage. Data from the 1980s, when the percentage of live births outside marriage rose from 11.8 per cent in 1980 to 28.3 per cent in 1990, are difficult to interpret, however.

To fill this gap Tables A5.4.1 to A5.4.6 contain the results of special analyses in which data about births within marriage and infant deaths among these babies were combined with the corresponding data for jointly registered

Figure 5.3

Stillbirth rates for births inside marriage and jointly registered births outside marriage, by social class of father, England and Wales, 1997

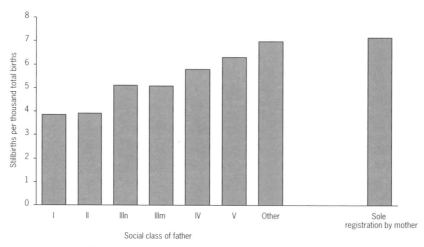

Source: Office for National Statistics, *Mortality statistics, Series DH3*

Figure 5.4

Infant mortality rates for births inside marriage and jointly registered births outside marriage, by social class of father, England and Wales, 1997

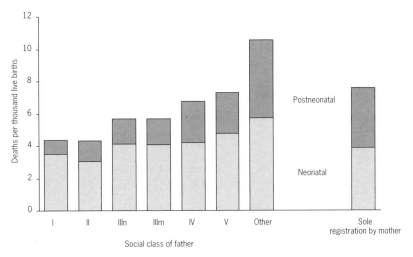

Source: Office for National Statistics, *Mortality statistics, Series DH3*

Figure 5.5

Infant mortality rates for births inside marriage and jointly registered births outside marriage, by National Statistics socio-economic class of father, England and Wales, 1996

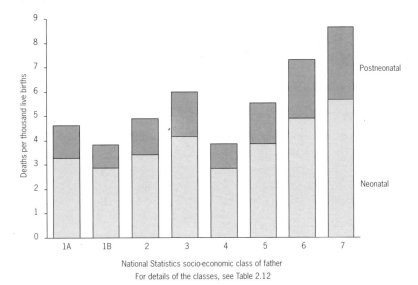

Source: Office for National Statistics, special analysis

Figure 5.6

Stillbirth rates for births inside marriage and jointly registered births outside marriage, by National Statistics socio-economic class of father, England and Wales, 1996

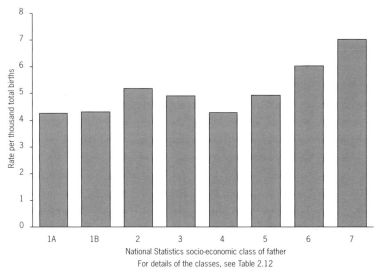

National Statistics socio-economic class of father
For details of the classes, see Table 2.12

Source: Office for National Statistics, special analysis[44]

births outside marriage. These are 'birth cohort' analyses, in which deaths are tabulated according to the year in which the baby was born.

The traditional analyses of stillbirth and mortality rates within marriage are shown in Tables A5.5.1 to A5.5.6. These incorporate data from special linkage studies done in 1949/50 and 1964 and unpublished tabulations prepared for the *Registrar General's decennial supplement* for 1971.[24,49,50]

The 1991 *decennial supplement* showed a narrowing between 1980 and 1995 of the difference between infant mortality rates for babies born within marriage with fathers in social class I and those in social class V. The gap narrowed considerably between 1991 and 1992, coinciding with the later stages in decline in mortality attributed to cot deaths.[52] In contrast, there was a slight widening of mortality rates for children aged 1 to 14 years. Figure 5.7 shows a similar analysis, but done on a 'birth cohort' basis. It groups together by their fathers' social class deaths among all babies born inside marriage and those jointly registered outside marriage. Figure 5.8 shows a similar analysis of stillbirth rates. These show broadly similar trends to an analysis which, like the *decennial supplement* analyses, was done on a death cohort basis.[53] Both sets of analyses show that the social class differentials in infant mortality still exist, but that the gap between sole registrations and couple registrations appeared to narrow in the neonatal period betwen the mid 1970s and the mid 1990s. Thus the narrowing may be more a consequence of changes in factors associated with health care than of lone mothers' social and economic circumstances.[53]

Figure 5.7

Infant mortality by social class of father and year of birth, England and Wales, 1979–95

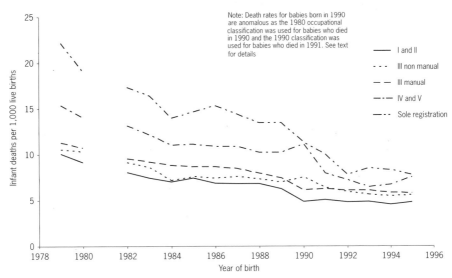

Note: Death rates for babies born in 1990 are anomalous as the 1980 occupational classification was used for babies who died in 1990 and the 1990 classification was used for babies who died in 1991. See text for details

Source: Authors' analysis of ONS data, Table A5.4.5

Figure 5.8

Stillbirth rates by social class of father and year of birth, England and Wales, 1979–96

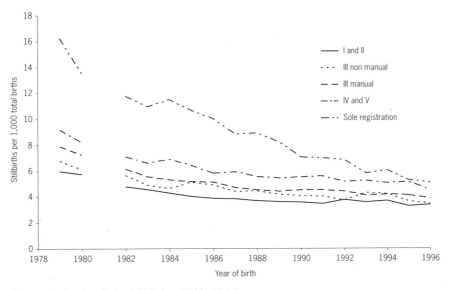

Source: Authors' analysis of ONS data, Table A5.4.1

In interpreting the trends shown in Tables A5.5.1 to A5.5.6, account also has to be taken of changes made in each census in the ways occupations are classified. As was mentioned in Chapter 2, social class data for England and Wales for the years 1979 to 1990 were derived from the 1980 *Classification of occupations* and thus cannot be directly compared with the data for 1970 to 1978 for which the 1970 classification was used. To provide a measure of the differences involved, a sample of 1979 births and deaths was also classified according to the 1970 classification. The method and results were described in OPCS publications[54,55] and in Table A5.6.1. It found that there were differences between the two classifications, but they were not large.

Ten years later, a similar exercise, comparing the way a sample of men's occupations were classified using the 1980 classification and the classification used for the 1991 census, showed that the changes were much less radical than those a decade earlier.[56] No comparison was made of the coding of parents' occupations on registrations of live births and infant deaths, as it was assumed that the differences would be correspondingly small and that any discontinuities between data for 1990 and those for 1991 would be negligible.

Data in Tables A5.4.4 and A5.4.5 cast doubt on this assumption as they show an anomaly in the postneonatal mortality data for 1990. This could result from the fact that for babies who were born in 1990 and died in 1991, their parents' occupations at birth would be coded according to the 1980 classification and the occupations at death would be coded according to the 1990 classification. This anomaly in data for postneonatal deaths of babies born in 1990 has affected the infant mortality rates for 1990 shown in Figure 5.7. Nevertheless, the overall picture suggests that it is unlikely that the persisting inequalities shown in Figure 5.7 and 5.8 were affected in one way or another by the change in classification.

Using the extended linkage in operation since 1993, ONS now analyses deaths of children over the age of one year in relation to their parents' characteristics at their birth. Tables A5.8.1 and A5.8.2 show that the same class differences seen in deaths in babies aged under one year persist among one, two and three year olds.[57] Inequalities are therefore not restricted to the first year of life.

In Scotland, tabulations by social class have fallen into disfavour and, for reasons explained earlier, do not appear in the *Stillbirth and infant death report* or other published analyses of SMR2 data.[58,59] Instead, they are analysed by the 'deprivation categories' discussed later in the chapter. Stillbirths and infant deaths are tabulated by social class in the *Annual report of the Registrar General for Scotland*.

The lack of linkage between birth and death registration means that no similar data are available for Northern Ireland, although a tabulation of stillbirths by social class is included in the *Registrar General's Annual Report for Northern Ireland*.

Social class differences at regional and district level

In response to the considerable political attention focused in the late 1970s and early 1980s on the differences between the perinatal mortality rates for individual regions and districts, OPCS published more detailed analysis for local areas, including analyses by class.[60,61] These showed social class differences in mortality within districts and regions. Because of the small numbers of events involved, data for several years were aggregated. Regular production of such tables ceased after the 1981 reorganisation, but special analyses of data for district health authorities for 1983–5 were published in OPCS' *Mortality and geography* supplement.[62] These showed, amongst other things, that districts with the highest proportion of fathers in partly or unskilled manual occupations tended to have the highest percentages of low weight births and, in consequence, the highest infant mortality rates. At the time of writing, work on a new 'geography' decennial supplement, based on data for the 1990s, is under way.

Classifying women and children

There are considerable problems in the way that the social class of a woman or a child has been determined in official statistics. At the registration of a live or stillbirth, in England and Wales, the baby's father's occupation, including his status within it, is recorded for births within marriage and for births outside marriage which are jointly registered by both parents. If a birth outside marriage is registered by the mother on her own, her occupation is recorded.

Since 1986, all mothers have had the option of recording their own occupation when registering babies' births.[63,64] Not all have chosen to do so, although the proportion of mothers recording an occupation which could be coded by social class rose from 31 per cent in 1986 to 57 per cent in 1995.[52] There were many biases in the extent to which occupations were recorded.[63,64]

Before April 1982, if a baby or a child up to the age of 16 died, her or his father's occupation was recorded, if known. Otherwise, the mother's occupation was recorded. Published tabulations of mortality rates in infancy and childhood did not indicate which parent's occupation was used to derive the social class. Since April 1982 both parents' occupations have been recorded, and since January 1983 both have been coded for analysis.

Poor quality and gaps in information about women's occupations is a long standing problem.[65] The dilemmas this poses for analyses of women's mortality as well as that of their children has been acknowledged for many years.[66] John Tatham wrote in the *Decennial supplement* for 1901:

> ' … so great has been the advance of public interest concerning the female occupation, especially in relation to the closely allied question of excessive mortality among infants, that in making preparation for the present supplement it was decided to submit the question of female occupational mortality to a test more exhaustive than any that had been previously applied.'[67]

The decennial supplement, *Occupational mortality, 1970–72* compared married women's own occupations recorded on census schedules with those of their husbands. About half the married women did not state an occupation. Of those who did, 34 per cent of women aged 15–44 were coded to a 'higher' class than their husband, 39 per cent to a 'lower' class, and only 26 per cent to the same class.[24] This suggested there was a need to collect and analyse information about both parents in connection with live births and stillbirths and deaths in infancy. The 1991 decennial supplement *Health inequalities* was the first to include mortality rates tabulated according to the baby's mother's social class as well as the father's.[52]

Aggregated stillbirth and infant mortality rates among babies born in the years 1986–90 and 1991–95 are tabulated by social class of mother in Table A5.9.1 and infant mortality rates for 1991–95 are shown in Figure 5.9. They differ slightly from published data as these deaths are related to the year of birth.[52] In 1986–90, infant mortality was highest among babies whose mothers were in unskilled occupations or who gave no occupation. Rates for the other classes were lower but differences between them were small. By 1991–95, when ascertainment was fuller, there were more signs of a gradient.

These analyses raise questions of how occupations should be recorded and how they should be classified. Many women with young children take up jobs which may be lower in status than those they did before the birth of their first child. Any analysis of associations between conditions of work during pregnancy and its outcome needs information about the woman's employment during that pregnancy.[68,69] On the other hand, if the occupation is being used as a proxy measure of social position, the occupation she pursued before the birth of her first child may be more relevant. In either case other questions may be more important, notably whether she has a partner and, if so, what his occupation is.

Figure 5.9

Infant mortality by mother's social class, England and Wales, 1991–95

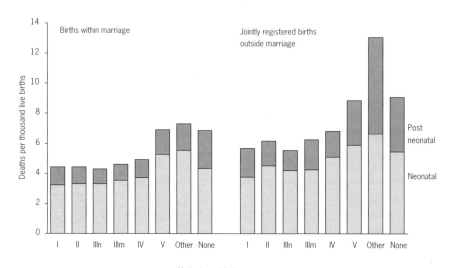

Source: Authors' analysis of ONS data, Table A5.9.1

If occupations are used, questions arise about how class statistics are constructed. The Registrar General's *Classification of occupations* is based largely on the values which those who compiled it felt that society placed on jobs done by men, rather than any explicit social theory.[70] Thus, as Table 3.17 of *Occupational mortality, 1970–72*[24] shows, 'women's work' tends to be coded to social classes III non-manual or IV, while 'men's work' is clustered in social class III manual. Furthermore, in this *Decennial supplement* and in early work on the OPCS Longitudinal Study, when women were classified by their own occupations, there was no sign of the distinct social class gradient seen in mortality among men.[24,71] This suggested that there is no relation between women's work and their mortality, but the assumption was questioned. It was suggested that the classification was not appropriate for classifying the work women do, and different classifications were developed for women's occupations.[72] The suggestion was also made that where pregnancy is concerned, classifications based on both parents' occupations were needed.

There are also problems in trying to fit unemployed people into a classification based on occupations. Unemployed men usually give their last job when registering children's births or deaths. This may happen with unemployed women, but they are probably more often assumed to have no occupation. This assumption became increasingly likely during the 1980s and the early 1990s. As unemployment rose, young women started having children without ever having been in paid employment. At this period, the extent to which rising unemployment might have affected the health of the people concerned was being researched but there was little information about its impact on the outcome of pregnancy.[73]

The lack of data about employment status means that data derived from birth and death registration alone cannot be used to monitor the mortality of unemployed people and their children, let alone whether being unemployed brings forward or postpones people's decisions to have children. This deficiency might be alleviated if, as happens in the census, people were asked separately about whether they were in employment, seeking employment or retired but even this would not tell us about the employment statistics at conception. This suggests that other measures, such as income or education should be used.

Another approach is to group people into their stage in life, as was done in a study of women's health in 1984 and 1993. This grouped women into professional single women, married women with children, never married lone mothers, women with non-employed partners and previously married 'empty-nesters'.[74] It found that the relative differences in the health of women in these groups changed between 1984 and 1993. This could well have implications for the health of children.

There may still be a need to consider whether there is a more sensitive way of classifying parents' occupations, for example by making use of information about both mothers' and fathers' occupations, but there are many alternative measures based on other information about the circumstances of parents, families and their environment. As the way most of the data in this section are collected depends to some extent on the relationship between the parents and its legal status, we start by discussing information which is collected about people's marital and family status.

Marital and family status

'So don't get married,
It'll drive you round the bend,
It's the lane without a turning,
It's the end without an end.

Change your lover every Friday,
Take up tennis, be a nurse.
But don't get married, girls,
For marriage is a curse.'

Leon Rosselson. *Don't get married girls.*[75]

These words, from a song written in the 1970s, reflect changes which were already under way at that time and have accelerated since then. In England and Wales, the proportion of births outside marriage increased steadily from the end of the 1950s onwards, and much more dramatically during the 1980s and 1990s as Figure 5.10 shows.

Figure 5.10

Live births outside marriage, England and Wales, 1900–97

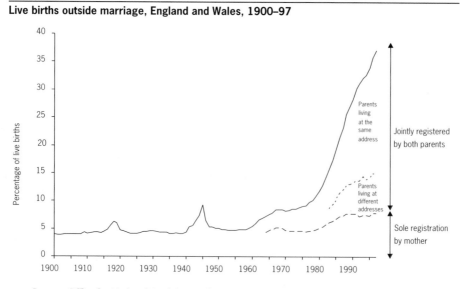

Source: Office for National Statistics, *Birth statistics*, Series *FM1*

Nevertheless, lone parenthood has been perceived as a problem over a much longer period, even though it was less common.[76] The proportion of live births which were registered as 'illegitimate' declined from between six and seven per cent in the 1850s to around four per cent in the early years of the twentieth century.[77] As these babies were particularly at risk of dying and escaping registration in the mid-nineteenth century, the decline may well have been greater than registration records suggest. The percentage of live births registered as 'illegitimate' increased only marginally to between four and five per cent in the 1950s, apart from sharp peaks at the end of the first and second world wars.

The trends since the 1950s have to be interpreted in the light of other changes, notably in attitudes to marriage, which have occurred over the same period. The terms 'legitimate' and 'illegitimate' simply described the legal status of the baby at birth and should no longer be used since the status of 'illegitimacy' was abolished in 1986. Now births are simply categorised in statistics derived from birth registration as inside or outside marriage. Each can, in practice, cover a wide range of circumstances, but as a birth certificate is a legal document it has to record the relationship in law of the baby's parents.

The proportion of births outside marriage which are registered by the mother on her own has always been relatively small, rising from around four per cent of live births in the 1960s to just under eight per cent in the 1990s, as Table A5.10.1 shows. There has been a much larger increase in births outside marriage registered jointly by both parents. These accounted for only around three per cent of live births in the early 1960s but over a quarter in the late 1990s. Nearly three quarters of couples registering births jointly gave the same address when doing so. In contrast, the traditional 'shotgun marriage' is in decline. Births within marriage, but likely to have been conceived before the wedding, accounted for around six per cent of births in the late 1970s, but just over three per cent in the mid 1990s.

Although these statistics, based on the legal process of birth registration, provide useful signposts, they may or may not represent parents' actual circumstances. It does not follow that putting the father's name on the birth certificate means that he intends to contribute financially or otherwise to the care of the baby. The same point might also be made of married couples who separate during the woman's pregnancy or while the baby is still young. Similarly, it can not be assumed that all women who register their babies on their own necessarily lack financial and emotional support. It is possible that they could be receiving financial or social support from their own parents, or in a relationship with a man other than the baby's father or with another woman, for example.

In interpreting data about marital status it also has to be borne in mind that marriage patterns vary from culture to culture. In 1997, only 0.9 per cent of births to women born in Bangladesh were outside marriage, compared with 48.6 per cent of births to women born in the 'Caribbean commonwealth'.[78]

Stillbirth and infant mortality rates differ quite markedly according to the babies' legal status at birth registration as Figure 5.11 and Tables A5.4.1 to A5.4.5 show. To a considerable extent, this reflects differences in their social class distribution. As Figure 5.12 shows, the percentage of births outside marriage but jointly registered by both parents varies strongly by the social class of the baby's father. Figure 5.11 shows social class gradients in infant mortality, both in births within marriage and in jointly registered births outside marriage, with a tendency for mortality to be lower within marriage. Apart from the miscellaneous groups labelled 'other', mortality is highest for mothers registering births on their own.

Thus while mortality rates outside marriage tend to be higher than those within, marital status is increasingly unreliable as a way of identifying women who are necessarily 'at risk' and require special care. This could be wasteful in that it can divert resources from identifying the individual women who really have serious social, financial and other problems and need appropriate help.

Data about the changing numbers of divorces and remarriages shown in Tables A5.12.2 to A5.13.1 in England and Wales are published in the annual volumes of *Marriage and divorce statistics* in the FM2 Series, as are data about adoptions shown in Table A5.12.1. Data about divorces are also published in *Population trends*. Figure 5.13 shows that after increasing in the 1950s and 1960s, the number of children being adopted as babies decreased from the 1970s onwards. In a considerable proportion of adoptions, one of the adoptive parents was the child's natural parent. Similar data for Scotland and Northern Ireland are published in the Registrar General's *Annual reports* for the country concerned.

Figure 5.11

Infant mortality by social class of father and marital status, England and Wales, 1997

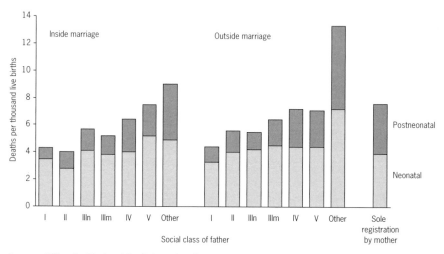

Source: Office for National Statistics, *Mortality statistics, Series DH3*

Figure 5.12

Percentage of live births registered by both parents which were outside marriage, by social class of father, England and Wales, 1997

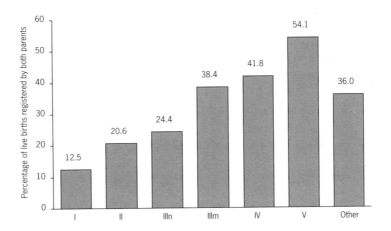

Source: Office for National Statistics, *Mortality statistics, Series DH3*

Figure 5.13

Adoptions of children aged under one year, England and Wales, 1960–97

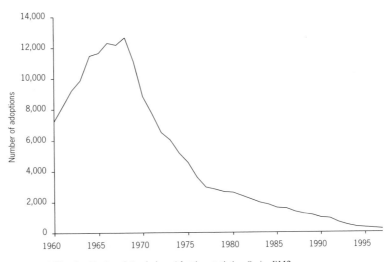

Source: Office for National Statistics, *Adoption statistics, Series FM2*

Figure 5.14

Families with lone parents, Great Britain, 1971–96

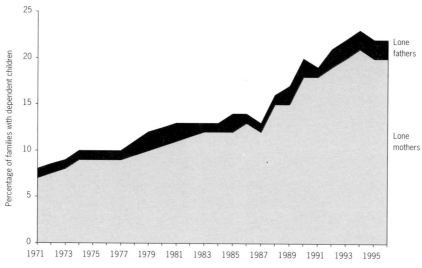

Source: Office for National Statistics, General Household Survey

Like birth and death registration data, marriage, divorce and adoption statistics are records of legal events. Censuses and surveys give a different type of picture of families with young children and their household structure. The rise in lone parent families, from eight per cent of households in Great Britain with dependent children in 1971 to over 20 per cent in the mid 1990s is charted in Table A5.14.1 and Figure 5.14. The steep rise during the 1980s appeared to have levelled off in the mid 1990s. A particular feature, shown in Table A5.14.2 is the decline in the percentage of families with married parents and two or more children and the corresponding increase in the percentage of lone parent families with more than one child. These data are from the General Household Survey, further analyses of which show that many women living as lone mothers are disadvantaged and have poor health.[79]

In the General Household Survey, cohabiting couples are grouped with married couples, irrespective of their legal marital status. In the mid 1990s, it started to record whether children were step children. As Table A5.14.3 shows, in 1996, an estimated eight per cent of families with dependent children and the head of household aged under 59 included a child or children from either the mother's or father's previous marriage. A more detailed tabulation of the family status of children aged 0 to 4 years in Great Britain and its constituent countries is given in Table A5.15.1.

Data from all these sources are frequently combined in more detailed analyses of household and family structure and published in *Population trends* and elsewhere.[80–88] With a continuing fall predicted in the proportion of the population who are married,[89] it is unlikely that interest in the subject will wane.

Ethnic origin

Data collection about ethnic origin is much less developed in the United Kingdom than data collection about social class. This reflects the lack of consensus about definitions, what questions should be asked, how data should be analysed and interpreted and, more fundamentally, whether they should be collected at all.[90] A related question is whether the differences observed relate to cultural or socio-economic differences between minority ethnic groups.

Discussion of ethnic origin tends to be focused on those people who are noticeable because of their skin colour. Any attempt to represent both race and culture within a statistical classification raises innumerable problems. In addition, other groups, such as people of Irish or Italian origin, immigrants from Eastern Europe and refugees from former Yugoslavia may also feel themselves to be different from the majority population.[91] Data currently collected about the outcome of pregnancy fail to take most of these considerations into account, but nevertheless reveal marked differences.

Country of birth

At birth registration, countries of birth of the babies' parents are recorded. These have been used as a proxy measure of ethnic origin although they are more a measure of immigrant status. Analyses of fathers' and mothers' countries of birth are published annually in *Birth statistics, Series FM1*. Trends since 1973 are shown in Tables A5.16.1 to A5.16.2. They show that the percentage of all live births in England and Wales which were to women born outside the United Kingdom increased during the 1970s, declined during the 1980s and increased again during the 1990s. While the increasing numbers of births to women from countries of the 'New commonwealth' rose during the 1970s the increase during the 1990s was in births to women from other parts of the world.

The tabulations by mother's country of birth published in *Birth statistics, Series FM1* include a table for local authority districts with a high percentage of births to women born outside the United Kingdom. Table A5.17.1 shows patterns in the old standard regions and the new government office regions. It can be seen that, as would be expected, births to women from the 'New commonwealth' are more prominent in inner city districts in London, Greater Manchester, the West Midlands and West Yorkshire.

These tabulations are restricted to live births, as is Table A5.18.1 which tabulates babies' birthweights by their mothers' countries of birth. These are published in the volumes of *Mortality statistics, Series DH3*, together with stillbirth and infant mortality rates based on mothers' countries of birth which can be found in Table A5.18.2.

Crude though it is as an indicator, tabulating birthweight and infant deaths by mother's country of birth brings out some marked differences, which can be seen in Figure 5.15. Table A5.18.2 shows that babies of women born in the United Kingdom tend to have lower crude mortality rates than babies whose mothers were born in the countries of the 'New Commonwealth'. Babies of women born in Pakistan have exceptionally high mortality rates. This is perhaps not surprising, as Table A5.18.1 shows a higher incidence of low birthweight among babies of women born in these countries compared with other groups of babies. On the other hand, the association between birthweight and mortality varies between the groups shown. These differences have been explored in greater depth in detailed analyses of death registration data and data from other sources.[52,92–96] Patterns of maternal mortality by country of birth are discussed in Chapter 10.

Problems in classifying ethnic origin

Parents' countries of birth have long been recognised as unsatisfactory measures of ethnic origin. In the past, some white people whose parents were employed in colonial administrations were born in countries of Africa and the Indian subcontinent but there must be relatively few women in this position in the childbearing population today. A more recent source of discrepancy is that increasing numbers of minority ethnic women having babies in England and Wales today, notably those whose own parents arrived from the West Indies in the 1950s and early 1960s, were born here themselves.[97] In addition, some women born in East Africa were born there to parents who moved there from the Indian subcontinent. In the 1970s, OPCS was actively pursuing ways of classifying ethnic origin in official statistics,[98] but a proposed census question on the subject was dropped from the 1981 census.[99] A major reason was the high level of non-response in a

Figure 5.15

Infant mortality by mother's country of birth and ONS cause group, England and Wales, 1993–97

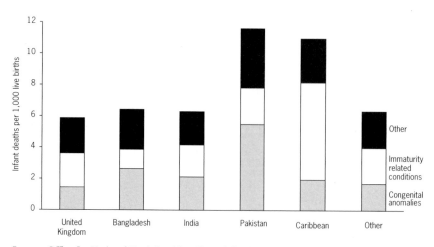

Source: Office for National Statistics, *Mortality statistics, Series DH3*

test census in Haringey.[100] This arose from concerns about how the information might be used.[97]

Routinely collected statistics about ethnic origin, which did exist from sources such as the Labour Force Survey, had already been used to highlight such problems.[97,101] During the 1980s, the view that such work was of value became more widespread. By the end of the decade it was found acceptable to ask people to give their own perception as to which of the categories in Table 2.13 they felt fitted them best. Most people replied to the census question, although it may have deterred some from completing the census form.[102] The replies to the question were analysed in detail in a series of four books.[103-106]

Although the 'ethnic' question from the 1991 census is now widely used in surveys and on NHS records, it has been criticised from a variety of perspectives.[90,107-110] The concept of ethnicity should relate to people's cultural background, but the categories used relate more to skin colour and assumed countries of origin. Thus the Irish population, which sees itself as a distinct cultural group, was not classified separately, although some census tables showed people born in Ireland as a separate category.[111] Even if measures of ethnic origin were more accurate, they would conceal variation within groups. There are vast differences in the social circumstances, custom, religion and diet between and within the populations from different parts of the Indian subcontinent.

As a result, the broad nature of the categories limits the extent to which they can be used for monitoring services. Better data about the ethnic origins of the population would be helpful in the planning of maternity services, particularly screening and diagnostic facilities for inherited disorders which are more common in some racial groups than others. They would also be extremely relevant to the interpretation of trends in mortality and the incidence of low birthweight. Mothers' ethnic origins have been recorded in the Maternity Hospital Episode Statistics since 1995, but analyses by ethnic origin have yet to be published as, up to the time of writing, these data are still incomplete.

The ethnic question in the 1991 census was devised at a time when reminders of social class differences were unwelcome in official circles. As a result, the interface between ethnic and class differences has tended to be ignored.[112] One exception is an analysis in *Health inequalities*, which shows class differences in infant mortality within births to mothers born in the 'New Commonwealth' as well as within births to mothers born in the United Kingdom.[52]

The data about mothers' countries of birth need to be viewed alongside the census data in Tables A5.19.1 and A5.19.2. The first of these shows considerable differences both between ethnic groups and age groups in the childbearing range in the extent to which women from minority ethnic groups were born outside the United Kingdom and gives an impression of the extent to which 'immigrant' mothers may be unrepresentative. Table A5.19.2 shows the differences in family types by ethnic origin, with lone parent families being much more common among the black groups than among the groups associated with the Indian subcontinent.

In response to some of these criticisms and to problems which arose when using the 1991 census classification, a revised question, shown in Table 2.14, will be used in the 2001 census in England and Wales.[113] It includes Irish people as a specific category and introduces categories of mixed ethnic origin in response to the extent to which people have intermarried.

In the hopes of enabling a clearer distinction to be made within ethnic groups, a question on religion, shown in Table 5.2, was proposed in the census white paper.[113] A change to census legislation is needed in England and Wales and in Scotland if questions on religion are to be asked in 2001. The government's intention is particularly aimed at identifying subgroups whose origins are from the Indian subcontinent.[113] On the other hand, the question has been criticised on the grounds that 'belonging' is not sufficiently well defined and that it is unclear what needs the question will fulfil.[114] In Northern Ireland the question on religion will be broadly similar to that used in previous censuses.

Table 5.2

Proposed question on religion for the 2001 census in England and Wales

What is your religion?

Tick one box only

☐ None
☐ Christian (including Church of England, Catholic, Protestant and all other Christian denominations)
☐ Buddhist
☐ Hindu
☐ Muslim
☐ Sikh
☐ Jewish
☐ Any other religion, *please write below*

Source: Office for National Statistics, *The 2001 census of population*.[113]

Ages of parents

The Population Statistics Act, which came into effect in 1938, was passed to monitor the falling birth rate in the late 1930s. Under its terms, additional items of data began to be collected at birth registration. These items included the mother's date of birth. Births in England and Wales are tabulated by age of the mother in *Birth statistics, Series FM1* and stillbirths and infant mortality rates are tabulated by age of the mother in *Mortality statistics, Series DH3*. Live and stillbirths are tabulated by age of mother in the *Annual reports* of the Registrars General for Scotland and Northern

Ireland. Although information about fathers' dates of birth has been collected since 1961, and births are tabulated by the age of the babies' fathers in *Birth statistics, Series FM1*, this variable does not seem to have been used in analyses of stillbirths and infant mortality.

Most published data about stillbirths and infant mortality rates of babies born to women in different age groups show, as do Tables A5.20.1 to A5.21.1, that mortality is high when the mother is under 20, and then relatively low for women in their twenties. The rates then increase with age for women over 30. This pattern is commonly interpreted as meaning that stillbirth and infant mortality rates are necessarily lowest when women are in their twenties, but this can be an oversimplification.

The age at which women have children is influenced by their background including the opportunities they have to gain access to further and higher education and training in their employment. The women who have these levels of education and training are more likely than others to marry men who do professional jobs. Thus relatively few women with partners in social classes I and II have babies before they reach the age of twenty, as Table A5.22.6 shows. At the other end of the age range, some women having babies in their thirties will have long histories of miscarriage and perinatal deaths, while others will have a number of children already and yet others will have only recently decided to start a family. It is unreasonable to consider these as a homogeneous group, all members of which are at equally high risk. Tables A5.22.1 to A5.22.5 show social class differences within age groups. A longitudinal approach, which can relate the outcome of a woman's successive pregnancies to her age, takes some account of this and is discussed in the next section.

Teenage pregnancy

'O daughter, O daughter, how can you say so?
For young men are false as you very well know.
They'll tell you fine things and the devil and all,
And leave you big-bellied with their long peggin' awl.

O mother, O mother, now do not say so.
Before you were sixteen, you very well know,
There was father and mother and baby and all.
You followed my dad for his long peggin' awl.'

Traditional, from the singing of Harry Cox[115]

Rising political concern about teenage pregnancy has increased the extent to which data on the subject are compiled and published. Tables A5.24.1 to A5.24.5 show trends in births, induced abortions and conceptions leading to registrable births or induced abortions among teenagers. Conception rates are calculated in the way described in Chapter 4. Data for England and Wales are published in *Birth statistics, Series FM1*, and in a *Monitor* which was replaced in 1999 by a report in *Population trends*. They suggest that, after declining in the early 1990s, teenage conception rates rose in 1995 and 1996. Data for Scotland are compiled on a slightly different basis and include miscarriages leading to a hospital stay. They are published in the Registrar General's *Annual report* and a special *Health briefing*. Those covering the years 1983–97 show a similar pattern.[116] It is likely some of the rise may be a consequence of the 'pill scare' in October 1995 but other factors may have been involved.[117,118]

A wide ranging review of data about teenage pregnancy showed that, compared with all births, babies born to teenagers had high rates of mortality and percentages of low birthweight.[119] An exception was that, compared with other births in this age group, the percentage of low birthweights was not particularly high among births registered by the mother on her own. In addition, special analyses of data from the Longitudinal Study found higher than average rates of teenage pregnancy among girls who lived in local authority housing or whose fathers were absent from the household or who had three or more siblings.

Parity

In Chapter 2 we explained how the two definitions of parity used in the analysis of fertility and of stillbirth and infant mortality rates in England and Wales are restricted by the Population Statistics Act and differ from those used in clinical practice, and no data are collected when birth takes place outside marriage. As a result, these data which have been collected since 1938, are of decreasing value in the light of the rise in births outside marriage. The White Paper, *Registration: proposals for change*, published in 1990, proposed that all previous live and stillbirths should be recorded for all births irrespective of whether they occurred outside marriage.[120] No time was found for legislation on this White Paper under the last government. In 1999 ONS started to make plans for legislation on registration in the foreseeable future and it is to be hoped that changes will be made to the way data are collected about parity.

Although birth and infant mortality data for England and Wales are tabulated by ONS' existing definitions of parity in *Birth statistics*, *Series FM1* and *Mortality statistics, Series DH3*, we have not considered them worth including in *Birth counts*. ONS produces better estimates of births by parity by combining data from birth registration with data from the General Household Survey, the Longitudinal Study and other sources.[121]

Definitions of parity, based on previous pregnancies, are used in systems based on hospital discharge data such as the Maternity Hospital Episode Statistics in England, and the SMR2 system in Scotland. As mentioned in Chapter 2, HES counts pregnancies leading to a registrable birth, while SMR2 counts pregnancies leading to births, miscarriages or legal abortions.

Even when complete parity data are available, the meaning of the variable is far from clear. Mortality rates for different parities show a similar U-shaped pattern to those for maternal age, probably for some of the same reasons. When it is possible to link data about the outcomes of successive pregnancies in the same women the rate of death tends to decrease with successive pregnancies.[122,123] This is despite the fact women who have a low weight baby in one pregnancy have a much greater than average chance of having a small baby in succeeding pregnancies.[124,125] The ONS Longitudinal Study has been used for analyses of mortality and birthweight in successive pregnancies. The numbers of deaths in its one per cent sample are too small to draw meaningful conclusions. Analyses of birthweight are discussed in Chapter 6.

Women from minority ethnic groups are likely to have more high parity pregnancies than the white population, but this differs between groups and over time.[92] If such comparisons are based on live birth registrations published in *Birth statistics, Series FM1*, they can only be made for the groups among whom all but a few births take place inside marriage. Among women having live births in England and Wales in 1997, 13.0 per cent of women born in Bangladesh, 13.2 per cent of those born in Pakistan, but only 3.2 per cent of those born in India were of parity 4 or more. This showed a considerable decrease since the mid 1980s. In 1986, 35.5 per cent of births to women born in Bangladesh, 23.9 per cent of births to women born in Pakistan and 5.2 per cent of births to women born in India were to women of parity 4 or more.[78] Table A5.16.3 shows differences in total period fertility rates, which declined over this period among women born in India and Bangladesh although not among women born in Pakistan.

Parents' stature

Although usually recorded in hospital notes, data about mothers' heights are not included in any national data collection system in England and Wales. In Scotland, this item is included in the SMR2 system, from which the data in Tables A5.25.1 and A5.26.1 are taken. They show a positive association between babies' birthweights and their mothers' heights and that mothers' heights, like birthweight, tend to be greater in the more advantaged social classes. No data are routinely collected about fathers' heights. The record linkage available in Scotland would make it possible to do more complex analyses over a longer time period. On the other hand, questions about associations between parents' heights and their children's health are better pursued in the much fuller datasets collected in special follow-up studies of cohorts of births.[126]

Housing

In his discussion of possible measures of social position, THC Stevenson commented in 1928:

> 'The method of grading by size of tenement occupied (number of rooms) is also open to much objection. The wealthy bachelor may occupy no more rooms than the cab-driver with six children. The

rooms, indeed, are of different type, but the only feature of rooms ordinarily available for statistical treatment is their number ... .'[7]

Despite this, and probably because of contemporary views about the importance of housing conditions as an influence on mortality, he presented several analyses of infant and child mortality according to size of tenement, an example of which is reproduced in Figure 5.16.

THC Stevenson was able to do these analyses because, in the 1911 census, data were collected not only about housing and the numbers of children born to each woman, but also about their mortality. The possibility of using routine statistics to relate mortality to housing data collected in the census did not arise again until the OPCS Longitudinal Study was set up. Early analyses found that for adults, mortality analysed by housing tenure at the 1971 census showed wider differences than analyses by social class.[71] In addition, infant mortality was lower among babies of women who lived in owner occupied households at the census than when the household had other forms of tenure.

Table A5.26.1 contains a special analysis of infant deaths among babies born to women in the Longitudinal Study sample over the years 1981–94. It shows that mortality was much more strongly associated with low birthweight than with housing tenure, but that among low birthweight babies, those whose mothers lived in privately rented accommodation at the 1981 census were slightly less likely to die than those whose mothers lived in local authority or owner occupied housing. This is an example of the type of analysis which can be done with these data and they need to be explored more fully.

Changes in the housing circumstances of lone parent and other families with young children over the years 1975–96 are shown in Table A5.27.1. These data, from the General Household Survey, show that the move to owner occupation was considerable among married couple families and negligible among lone parent families. Lone parent families were more likely to live in under-occupied accommodation but less likely to have central heating.

Routine statistics tell us little about the quality of housing of pregnant women and new babies and there are no statistics about the numbers of homeless women who are pregnant or have new babies. Although detailed surveys of housing conditions are undertaken for government, they are not related to the outcome of pregnancy. Nevertheless poor housing may carry risks to babies. For example, a study of sudden unexpected infant deaths undertaken as part of the Confidential Enquiry into Stillbirths and Deaths in Infancy found damp or mould in the bedrooms of 13.5 per cent of babies who died, but only 7.2 per cent of the comparison group of living children.[127]

Figure 5.16

Child mortality in relation to size of tenement, 1911

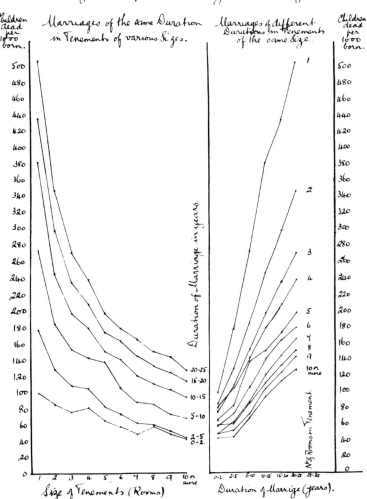

This diagram was based on data collected in the 1911 census. It was drawn by THC Stevenson in about 1920 and was also reproduced in *Longitudinal Study: socio-economic mortality differentials 1971–75, Series LS no. 1* [71]

Exposure to toxic substances and other occupational and environmental hazards

Exposure to toxic substances, either in the workplace or in the wider environment, may affect people's children and their ability to have them. People's risk of exposure can vary according to where they live, the work they do and their personal habits, such as smoking. These, in turn, can be associated with their social, educational and other circumstances. There may be unusually high rates of miscarriage, congenital anomalies and childhood cancer in the offspring of men exposed to some substances. For women, some substances may be more hazardous to the mother during pregnancy than at other times as well as carrying risks to the fetus. They may affect fertility and pregnancy, and may be associated with congenital anomalies, stillbirths, and abnormal postnatal development.

Routinely collected statistics can help identify such hazards in a number of ways. The most direct way is in monitoring the outcome of pregnancy of people in different occupational groups but this can only be done if the data are available. The decision to collect information at birth registration about the occupations of mothers is a positive step forward in this activity.

By 1981, tabulations of stillbirths and infant deaths by parents' occupations revealed relatively small numbers of deaths in each occupational group.[29] This means that indicators other than mortality must be sought for looking at differences between parents' occupations. A series of studies of data for the period 1980–82 attempted to identify hazardous occupations by looking at fertility rates and the birthweight, sex ratios and incidence of congenital anomalies among babies born to people in different occupations. It identified many problems in the recording of fathers' occupation and was hampered by the fact that mothers' occupations were not yet recorded at birth registration.[128]

Ten years later the subject was revisited in the *Occupational health* decennial supplement to the 1991 census.[69] Fathers' occupations were given in terms of job titles and did not clearly reflect exposure to hazards. Mothers' occupations were still not recorded for half the live births and two thirds of stillbirths and infant deaths by 1990. An attempt was made to identify occupations with low fertility rates, although these could be occupations in which few women work.

The lack of data about mothers' occupations is a major gap. An analysis of live births in Scotland for the years 1981–84, when both parents' occupations were recorded in the SMR2 system, found that there were few associations between preterm labour or low birthweights and occupations of parents. Where these did exist they were more likely to be associated with the mother's occupation.[129]

Fertility has also been analysed according to the parents' occupations in past decades. This was done directly using the fertility data collected in the 1911 census.[8,11] Subsequent analyses were done by comparing the occupations of men enumerated in the 1921 and 1931 censuses and the

1939 registration of the population with those of the fathers of babies registered around these years.[15,130] The purpose of these analyses was to assess the relative contribution of different occupational groups to the fertility of the population as a whole, although it was criticised as being inadequate for this purpose.[18,19] Although fertility data were collected in the 1951, 1961 and 1971 censuses, they were not analysed by occupational group.

Since 1974, information about both parents' occupations has been collected on congenital anomaly notifications in England and Wales, but many are missing. In 1997, just 54 per cent per cent of the notifications contained information about fathers' occupations and 62 per cent included the mothers' occupations. The fathers' occupations are analysed in ONS' *Congenital anomaly statistics, Series MB3.*

When it comes to assessing whether individual substances used in a particular process carry a hazard to reproduction, routinely collected statistics on broad occupational groups are not sufficiently specific. Other methods need to be used, for example, case control studies. Often the National Health Service Central Register and routine data collection systems such as congenital anomaly notifications can be used in the selection of samples for these studies.

The Health and Safety Executive carries out epidemiological studies to assess the hazards associated with particular occupations or substances to which people working in them are exposed. Occasionally these relate to reproductive hazards. In the mid 1990s, it investigated miscarriages among women in the semiconductor industry.[131] It also commissioned research on miscarriages in dry cleaning workers and in the health of children born to medical radiographers.[132,133]

The workplace is not, of course, the only place where people may be exposed to reproductive hazards. Perhaps the biggest hazard is smoking. Smoking before and during pregnancy has been monitored in the five yearly infant feeding surveys done by OPCS. Table A5.31.1 shows that in 1995 women with partners in non-manual occupations were less likely to smoke than those with partners in manual occupations or without a partner.[134] For drinking alcohol, the opposite was the case. Women who had a partner in a non-manual occupation and those who had continued in full time education beyond the age of 16 were less likely to have given up drinking but the amounts of alcohol drunk were small.[134]

There are few data about other hazardous substances to which people may be exposed, including drugs taken before or during pregnancy, pesticides to which people may be exposed directly or indirectly through the food chain, and other substances in food and water supplies. While these cannot be monitored directly in official statistics, the National Health Service Central Register and the congenital anomaly notification system can be used to select samples for case control studies in the same way as for investigating specific toxic substances in the workplace.

Parents' education

Information about the level of education of a baby's parents is not routinely collected at birth registration in the countries of the United Kingdom, although it is recorded in the United States and a number of European countries.[135,136]

In the past, the level of education has not proved to be a useful criterion for dividing the population of the United Kingdom into groups, because such a high proportion of the people left school at the minimum age. In addition, census questions asked on the subject have aimed to identify people with higher qualifications, rather than monitor the educational level of the population at large. The 1971 census asked about qualification at GCE Advanced Level and above. Only 9 per cent of men and 6 per cent of women aged 18–74 included in the Longitudinal Study sample in 1971 recorded qualifications at A-level or above. In the 18–44 age group, however, 19 per cent of men and 14 per cent of women recorded such qualifications. This made it feasible to analyse fertility and perinatal mortality by parents' educational qualifications in the *Fertility report from the 1971 census* and in the Longitudinal Study.[47,71]

Table 5.3, taken from the first report of the Longitudinal Study, shows that the perinatal mortality rate among babies born in 1971–75 to women with qualifications in 1971 was considerably lower than that of babies born to women without them.[71] The group whose qualifications were not stated had the highest perinatal mortality but included a significant proportion of women who were under 15 when the census was taken and were not asked to state their qualifications. They were too young to have gained any of the qualifications recorded in the census and it is their age which suggests a higher risk of perinatal loss. The same could be true of women aged 16–18 at the time of the census. The question about qualifications in the 1981 and 1991 censuses was designed to ascertain numbers of people with higher qualifications and asked respondents not to give qualifications normally obtained at school. This means it has not been possible to repeat these analyses.[41]

Table 5.3

Perinatal mortality by mother's education, Longitudinal Study 1971–75

Educational qualifications	Perinatal deaths	Live and still births	Perinatal mortality rate
Higher qualifications	28	2,207	12.7
A-levels only	24	1,645	14.6
No qualifications	405	23,461	17.3
Qualifications not stated	28	1,206	23.2
All women	485	28,518	17.0

Source: *OPCS Longitudinal Study 1971–75, Series LS, No. 1.*[71] (Table 7.7)

There are good arguments for using educational level as a social indicator. If it is to be used then data should be collected in a way which reflects the spectrum of education experienced by members of the population.

Paid employment in pregnancy and after childbirth

The employment of married women outside the home was repeatedly cited in the 1890s and early 1900s as a cause of infant mortality.[137] For example, a paper read to the Royal Statistical Society in 1894 reached the conclusion that:

> 'The children of women engaged in industrial occupations suffer from the effects of maternal neglect. They are handicapped from the moment of birth in their struggle for existence, and have to contend not only against the inevitable perils of infancy but also against perils due to their neglect by their mothers and to the ignorance of those to whose care they are entrusted.'[138]

In the ensuing discussion, Noel Humphreys said that he thought the question had been prejudged without sufficient evidence.[138] Four years later a more detailed attack was launched on the paper by Clara Collett, who had served as Assistant Commissioner to the Royal Commission on Labour.[139]

The argument continued for a number of years, but in April 1910 the journal *Public health* commented:

> 'The importance of the industrial employment of married women as a factor in the causation of infant mortality is a subject upon which the current opinion has been gradually changing in recent years. Formerly it was almost universally held to be an aetiological factor of preponderating importance, but the application of more precise methods of investigation has cast grave doubts on this view, and has called for a restatement of the whole question.'[140]

In the same year, THC Stevenson expressed a different view when outlining plans for the 1911 census:

> 'The census can be made to supplement the results of the recent Home Office enquiry into the industrial employment of married women in its relation to infantile mortality. For this purpose, it is proposed to record on the card used the wife's occupation as well as the husband's. The occupations of wives would be roughly grouped under a small number of comprehensive headings, which will suffice for the purpose, as after all the main point is to know whether the wife is or is not engaged in gainful occupation. It will also be important to differentiate gainful employments pursued at home.'[5]

The analysis outlined here was eventually published after the first world war, in 1923.[11] It showed a higher death rate under two years in the children of women gainfully employed outside the home than in those women gainfully employed at home, but did not speculate whether it was factors which brought about the need for paid employment, the arrangements made for child care or the work itself which caused the excess mortality.

As with housing, the next chance to do an analysis using routine data did not arise until the Longitudinal Study was set up. The analysis compared the mortality of babies born in 1971 between April, when the census was taken, and the end of the year, according to whether the mothers had stated in their census return that they either were or were not in paid employment.[141] There were some ambiguities in this question and coding instructions were unclear about treatment of maternity leave, but the effect of these ambiguities is not obvious. The infant mortality rates of babies whose mothers were in employment on census night were found to be higher than those whose mothers were not in paid employment but the analysis could not take into account the gestational ages or the birthweights of the babies in the two groups as these data were not available. Because it contained only 75 deaths and 4,574 live births, it was not possible to subdivide the data by more than one variable at a time and this made it impossible to investigate differences within groups.

The limitations of this analysis were acknowledged by the authors.[141] Like Stevenson's earlier analysis, however, it emerged at a time of rising unemployment when there was a prevailing desire to get women out of the labour force. As a result, the article received wide publicity and was reported in a way which did not reflect its authors' reservations.[142] Although the Longitudinal Study has been used extensively to examine associations between people's employment status and their own health, no further attempts have been made to analyse associations with the health of babies.

Tables A5.29.1 and A5.29.2 show the employment status of women with dependent children and Table A5.30.1 shows that in the mid 1980s lower income was associated with having a disabled child. Data from routine systems and surveys tell us very little about women's employment and unemployment during pregnancy, however. A survey by the Policy Studies Institute of women who had babies in 1988 found that seventy eight per cent of first time mothers were in work twelve months before the birth, compared with just over a third of women having their second or subsequent child.[143] Surveys of employers and mothers in the mid 1990s investigated the impact of changes made in 1994 in the system of maternity rights and benefits.[144] These surveys are discussed more fully in Chapter 11.

Income of parents and households

In the 1990s as in the 1920s, there was little information about parents' income in routine data collection systems. It is likely that people would consider it strange to be asked their income when registering a birth or a death. People have not so far been asked about their income in censuses in the United Kingdom.[145]

As users of census data have asked for data about people's gross income, the government proposed a question on the subject in its white paper on the

2001 census.[113] The proposed format is shown in Table 5.4. ONS was concerned that including such a question would lower the response rate to the census. In a test in 1997, it included the question in questionnaires sent to half the sample and this lowered the response rates by 3 per cent overall. In the light of the census rehearsal in April 1999, in which the income question was included, it was decided to drop the income question.[145]

Data about the income of parents of dependent children are collected in the General Household Survey and their spending is investigated in the Family Expenditure Survey. Table 5.5 shows huge disparities between the income distributions of one and two parent households.[146] Although two parent households tend to have more children as well as more adults, the income differences are far larger than differences in their needs. Figure 5.17, taken from the Family Expenditure Survey, shows the average weekly expenditure per head in one and two adult families with children.[147] In each case, the income distribution is divided into quintiles. Although the difference in average weekly spending of the two groups differed relatively little at the bottom of the income distribution, the gap was very wide in the top quintile.

Concern about the extent to which babies are born into poverty raises questions about how it can be measured. There is no consensus about how this should be done but there are two different approaches which can be taken.

One of these is to use the concept of absolute poverty to define a 'poverty line'. Although this has a long history in determining eligibility for poor

Table 5.4

Income question proposed for the 2001 census

What is your total current gross income from all sources?

- ◆ *Do not deduct* tax, national insurance, superannuation or health insurance payments

- ◆ Tick the box that covers your income
  Count all income, including
  Earnings
  Pensions
  Benefits
  Interest from savings or investments
  Rent from property
  Other (for example maintenance payments, grants)

Per week	*or*	Per year (approximately)
Nil	☐	Nil
Less than £60	☐	Less than £3,000
£60 to £119	☐	£3,000 to £5,999
£120 to £199	☐	£6,000 to £9,999
£200 to £299	☐	£10,000 to £14,999
£300 to £479	☐	£15,000 to £24,999
£480 or more	☐	£25,000 or more

Source: Office for National Statistics. *The 2001 census of population.*[113]

Figure 5.17

Average weekly expenditure per person in one and two adult households with children, by gross income quintile group, Great Britain, 1997/98

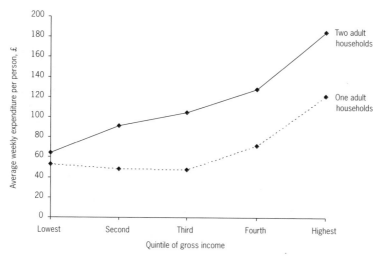

Source: Office for National Statistics, *Family expenditure survey, 1997/98*

Table 5.5

Income of families with dependent children by family type, Great Britain, 1996

Family type	Usual gross weekly household income						
	£0.01–100.00	£100.01–£150.00	£150.01–£200.00	£200.01–£300.00	£300.01–£400.00	£400.01–£500.00	£500.01 and over
	Percentage of households of each type						
Married couple	3	4	5	11	15	15	48
Cohabiting couple	6	12	10	15	13	13	31
Lone mother	33	27	12	13	7	3	5
Lone father	27	15	6	14	14	6	19
All lone parents	33	26	11	13	7	4	6

Source: ONS, *General Household Survey, 1996*[146]

relief, the term was coined by Seebohm Rowntree in the 1890s for some minimum standard of economic welfare based on primary needs for food, clothing and warmth. This approach has been used throughout the twentieth century, both for means testing and in social surveys of poverty.

In contrast, relative poverty is based on an individual's or household's position within the income distribution for a given population. The definition adopted in the United Kingdom in the 1980s is based on a household's total income and assumes, questionably, that income is equally distributed within every household. Statistics are then produced which relate members of households to the household's position in the income distribution. People in households whose total income falls below half the

Figure 5.18

Numbers of people in households with children below half average income before housing costs, Great Britain, 1961–93

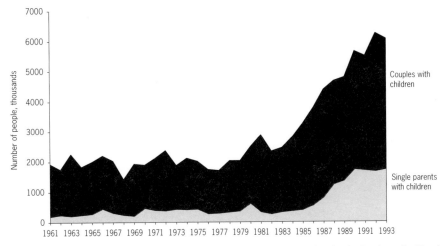

Source: Analysis of Office for National Statistics, *Family expenditure survey* data by the Institute for Fiscal Studies

average are considered to be in poverty. As Figure 5.18 shows, the numbers of people in households with children, especially those with a single parent, whose income fell below this level increased considerably from the mid 1980s onwards in Great Britain.[148] This trend slowed down in the mid 1990s.[149] There are no data which relate these trends directly to the outcome of pregnancy.

Social circumstances of young children and their parents

The 1911 census was unique in including data about mortality in childhood and relating them to the circumstances of young children and their parents. Other censuses, while lacking data about the outcome of pregnancy, are sources of data about the circumstances of young children and their parents. The 1991 census was no exception, and the range of data available are described in *The 1991 census user's guide*.[150] Between censuses, data on the circumstances of households containing young children can be obtained from the General Household Survey.

The regional variations in perinatal and infant mortality have a broadly similar pattern to regional variations in mortality in adults. All these are statistically associated with measures of characteristics of the regions such as the state of the housing stock and consumption of food, alcohol and tobacco. Data about these are collected in the General Household Survey, the Family Expenditure Survey, the Family Resources Survey and the National Food Survey. All these surveys are based on the use of the new Government Office regions rather than NHS regions. Regional data derived from them are shown in Table A5.32.1.

A series of studies done in the 1970s compared data collected at successive censuses about conditions in different regions and smaller geographical areas.[151-153] They showed a strong statistical association between adverse conditions and measures of the outcome of pregnancy. As these were based on the variables which were chosen for inclusion in the census, they could not be used to identify the individual factors which may have caused a given woman to have a baby who was born small, was stillborn or who died in infancy, but did show that the chances of these events happening were greater in the less privileged parts of the country. Other past research reached similar conclusions,[73] as did analyses in OPCS' *Mortality and geography decennial supplement*.[62]

In more recent years analyses have been done using much smaller geographical areas, down to the level of wards and enumeration districts. Methods have been developed to group together similar areas for statistical analysis by using items of census data to construct 'deprivation indices'. Four of these deprivation indices are commonly used, the Jarman Index,[154,155] the Townsend index,[156] the 'Depcat' or Carstairs index[157] commonly used in Scotland and the Department of the Environment index of local deprivation.[158,159] As was mentioned in Chapter 3, ONS developed its own categories and these were being revised in 1999.

In Scotland, in particular, the geographical deprivation categories are used in preference to individual people's social class in documents on health inequalities.[160] In *Births in Scotland, 1976–1995* low birthweight is tabulated by deprivation category and is lowest in the least deprived groups of areas.[58]

It is often implied that a choice has to be made between individual and area measures. Yet an analysis which used both and tabulated low birthweight rates for enumeration districts in England and Wales grouped using the Carstairs index and by fathers' social classes suggested that both were needed.[161] It found that within each social class there was a gradient in low birthweight by deprivation score and also that there were gradients by social class within areas grouped by deprivation score. For sole registrations, no clear gradient was seen by social class. The authors found that over half the births registered by the mother alone and nearly two thirds of those where the father was in social classes IV or V took place outside the areas in the most deprived quintile.

Monitoring inequalities in the 1990s and 2000s

The data reviewed in this chapter reveal consistent inequalities in mortality and low birthweight in relation to a number of classifications, with the poorest outcomes in the least privileged groups. They also suggest that other factors on which data are not collected routinely, such as the mother's educational level might have associations with adverse outcome, and that key data needed to monitor inequalities in health may be lacking. The view that a unidimensional approach is inadequate is becoming more widespread. In particular, groupings which take account of both the circumstances of individuals and the areas where they live may offer a way forward for the future.

This reinforces the view that both the analyses based on individuals, and those based on geographical areas show a strong association between the outcome of pregnancy and the parents' social and economic circumstances. Before discussing data which can be used to assess the extent to which these differences can be mitigated by the care given to pregnant women and newborn babies, we outline, in the next chapter, the data which are collected about the characteristics of babies.

References

1   Shaw B. Preface to The doctors' dilemma. In: Shaw B, *Prefaces by Bernard Shaw*. London: Constable and Company, 1934.

2   Rosselson L. Palaces of gold. In: Rosselson L, *Look here*. London: Harmony Music, 1968.

3   Titmuss RM. *Birth, poverty and wealth*. London: Hamish Hamilton, 1943.

4   General Register Office. *Fourteenth annual report of the Registrar General of births, deaths and marriages in England*. London: HMSO, 1855.

5   Stevenson THC. Suggested lines of advance in English vital statistics. *Journal of the Royal Statistical Society* 1910; 73: 685–702.

6   McDowall M. William Farr and the study of occupational mortality. *Population Trends* 1983; 31: 12–14.

7   Stevenson THC. The vital statistics of wealth and poverty. *Journal of the Royal Statistical Society* 1928; 91: 207–230.

8   Stevenson THC. The fertility of various social classes in England and Wales from the middle of the nineteenth century to 1911. *Journal of the Royal Statistical Society* 1920; 83: 401–432.

9   Szreter S. *Fertility, class and gender in Britain, 1860–1940*. Cambridge Studies in Population, Economy and Society in Past Time No. 27. Cambridge: Cambridge University Press, 1996.

10   General Register Office. *Census of England and Wales, 1911*. Cd 8678. Vol. XIII: Fertility of marriage. Part I. London: HMSO, 1917.

11   General Register Office. *Census of England and Wales, 1911*. Vol. XIII: Fertility of marriage. Part II. London: HMSO, 1923.

12   Local Government Board. *Second report by the Medical Officer on infant and child mortality. Supplement to the forty-second annual report of the Local Government Board, 1912–1913*. Cd 6909. London: HMSO, 1913.

13   Bruce Murray M. *The effect of maternal social conditions and nutrition upon birthweight and birth length*. Medical Research Council Report No. 81. London: HMSO, 1924.

14   Discussion on Dr. Stevenson's paper. *Journal of the Royal Statistical Society* 1928; 91: 221–230.

15   General Register Office. *The Registrar General's decennial supplement for England and Wales, 1921*. Vol. II: Occupational mortality, fertility and infant mortality. London: HMSO, 1927.

16   Nichols T. Social class: official, sociological and marxist. In: Irvine J, Miles I, Evans J, eds. *Demystifying social statistics*. London: Pluto Press, 1979.

17   Dorling D, Simpson S, eds. *Statistics in society: the arithmetic of politics*. London: Edwin Arnold, 1998.

18   Hopkin WAB, Hajnal J. Analysis of birth in England and Wales by father's occupation. Part I. *Population Studies* 1947; 1: 187–203.

19   Hopkin WAB, Hajnal J. Analysis of birth in England and Wales by father's occupation. Part II. *Population Studies* 1947; 1: 275–300.

20   General Register Office. *The Registrar General's decennial supplement for England and Wales, 1931*. Vol. IIa: Occupational mortality. London: HMSO, 1938.

21   Jones IG, Cameron D. Social class analysis: an embarrassment to epidemiology. *Community Medicine* 1984; 6: 37–46.

22   Office of Population Censuses and Surveys. *Occupational mortality: decennial supplement 1979–80, 1982–83. Part 1: Commentary*. OPCS Decennial Supplement Series DS No. 6. London: HMSO, 1986.

23   Working Group on Inequalities in Health. *Inequalities in health: report of a research working group [Chair: D Black]*. London: Department of Health and Social Security, 1980.

24   Office of Population Censuses and Surveys. *Occupational mortality: decennial supplement 1970–1972, England and Wales*. OPCS Decennial Supplement Series DS No. 1. London: HMSO, 1978.

25   Townsend P, Davidson N. *Inequalities in health: the Black report*. Harmondsworth: Penguin, 1982.

26   Marmot MG, McDowall ME. Mortality decline and widening social inequalities. *Lancet* 1986; ii(8501): 274–276.

27   Whitehead M. *The health divide: inequalities in health in the 1980s*. London: Health Education Council, 1987.

28   Townsend P, Davidson N, Whitehead M. *Inequalities in health: the Black report and the health divide*. Harmondsworth: Penguin, 1992.

29   Office of Population Censuses and Surveys. *Occupational mortality 1979–80, 1982–83, England and Wales. Childhood supplement*. OPCS Decennial Supplement Series DS No. 8. London: HMSO, 1988.

30   Drever F, ed. *Occupational health*. OPCS Decennial Supplement Series DS No.10. London: HMSO, 1995.

31   Drever F, Whitehead M, eds. *Health inequalities*. ONS Decennial Supplement Series DS No. 15. London: The Stationery Office, 1997.

32   Acheson ED. Introduction. In: *On the state of the public health. The annual report of the Chief Medical Officer of the Department of Health for the year 1990*. London: HMSO, 1991.

33   Independent Enquiry into Inequalities in Health. *Report. [Chair: Sir Donald Acheson]*. London: The Stationery Office, 1998.

34   Rose D. *A report on phase 1 of the ESRC review of OPCS classifications.* Swindon: Economic and Social Research Council, 1995.

35   Rose D, O'Reilly K. *Constructing classes: towards a new social classification for the UK.* Swindon: Economic and Social Research Council and the Office for National Statistics, 1997.

36   Rose D, O'Reilly K, Martin J. The ESRC review of government social classifications. *Population Trends* 1997; 89: 49–89.

37   Rose D, O'Reilly K. *The ESRC review of government social classifications.* London: Office for National Statistics and the Economic and Social Research Council, 1998.

38   Erikson R, Goldthorpe JH. *The constant flux.* Oxford: Clarendon Press, 1993.

39   Wright EO. *Classes.* London: Verso, 1985.

40   Stewart A, Prandy K, Blackburn RM. Measuring the class structure. *Nature* 1973; 245: 415–417.

41   Hattersley L, Creeser R. *Longitudinal study 1971–1991: history, organisation and quality of data.* OPCS Longitudinal Study Series LS No.7. London: HMSO, 1995.

42   Smith J, Harding S. Mortality of women and men using alternative social classifications. In: Drever F, Whitehead M, eds. *Health inequalities.* ONS Decennial Supplement Series DS No. 15. London: The Stationery Office, 1997.

43   Rose D, O'Reilly K, eds. *ESRC review of government social classifications. Workshop on validation studies,* Wivenhoe House Conference Centre, Essex, 3–4 December 1998.

44   Dollamore G, Fitzpatrick J. Examining mortality rates by NS-SEC using death registration data and the 1991 census. In: Rose D, O'Reilly K, eds. *ESRC review of government social classifications. Workshop on validation studies,* Wivenhoe House Conference Centre, Essex, 3–4 December 1998.

45   Glass DV, Grebenik E. *The trend and pattern of fertility in Great Britain: a report on the family census of 1946.* Vol. I: Report. Vol. II: Tables. London: HMSO, 1954.

46   Pearce D, Britton M. The decline in births: some socio-economic aspects. *Population Trends* 1977; 7: 9–14.

47   Office of Population Censuses and Surveys. *Fertility report from the 1971 census.* OPCS Decennial Supplement Series DS No. 5. London: HMSO, 1983.

48   Cartwright A. *Recent trends in family building and contraception.* Studies on Medical and Population Subjects No. 34. London: HMSO, 1978.

49   Heady JA, Heasman MA. *Social and biological factors in infant mortality.* Studies on Medical and Population Subjects No. 15. London: HMSO, 1959.

50   Spicer CC, Lipworth R. *Regional and social factors in infant mortality*. Studies on Medical and Population Subjects No. 19. London: HMSO, 1969.

51   Pharoah POD, Macfarlane AJ. Recent trends in postneonatal mortality. In: Office of Population Censuses and Surveys, London School of Hygiene and Tropical Medicine. *Studies in sudden infant deaths*. Studies on Medical and Population Subjects No. 45. London: HMSO, 1982:1–8.

52   Botting B. Mortality in childhood. In: Drever F, Whitehead M, eds. *Health inequalities*. ONS Decennial Supplement Series DS No. 15. London: The Stationery Office, 1997.

53   Whitehead M, Drever F. Narrowing social inequalities in health? Analysis of trends in mortality among babies of lone mothers (Abridged). *BMJ* 1999; 318: 908–912.

54   Office of Population Censuses and Surveys. *Infant and perinatal mortality, 1980*. OPCS Monitor DH3 82/3. London: OPCS, 1982.

55   Office of Population Censuses and Surveys. *Infant and perinatal mortality, 1979: social class bridge-coding*. OPCS Monitor DH3 82/5. London: OPCS, 1982.

56   Drever F. How were census-based mortality rates calculated? In: Drever F, Whitehead M, eds. *Health inequalities*. Appendix B. ONS Decennial Supplement Series DS No. 15. London: The Stationery Office, 1997.

57   Da Hani N. Mortality in children under 4. *Health Statistics Quarterly* 1999; 2: 41–49.

58   Information and Statistics Division. *Births in Scotland 1976–1995*. Edinburgh: ISD, 1997.

59   Information and Statistics Division, Scottish Programme for Clinical Effectiveness in Reproductive Health. *Small babies in Scotland: a ten year overview, 1987–1996*. Births in Scotland Publication Series. Edinburgh: ISD, 1998.

60   Office of Population Censuses and Surveys. *Infant and perinatal mortality*. OPCS Monitor DH1 79/1. London: OPCS, 1979.

61   Office of Population Censuses and Surveys. *Infant and perinatal mortality*. OPCS Monitor DH1 79/2. London: OPCS, 1979.

62   Botting BJ, Macfarlane AJ. Geographic variation in infant mortality in relation to birthweight 1983–85. In: Britton M. *Mortality and geography: a review in the mid 1980s, England and Wales*. OPCS Decennial Supplement Series DS No. 9. London: HMSO, 1990:48–57.

63   Cooper J, Botting B. Analysing fertility and infant mortality by mother's social class as defined by occupation. *Population Trends* 1992; 70: 15–21.

64   Botting BJ, Cooper J. Analysing fertility and infant mortality by mother's social class as defined by occupation – Part II. *Population Trends* 1993; 74: 27–33.

65   Higgs E. Women, occupations and work in the nineteenth century censuses. *History Workshop Journal* 1987; 23: 59–80.

66   Macfarlane AJ. Official statistics and women's health and illness. In: Roberts H, ed. *Women's health counts.* London: Routledge, 1990.

67   Tatham J. Letter to the Registrar General on mortality in certain occupations in the three years 1900, 1901, 1902. In: *Supplement to the 65th annual report of the Registrar General.* Vol. III. London: HMSO, 1908.

68   Office of Population Censuses and Surveys. *Congenital malformations and parents' occupations.* OPCS Monitor MB3 82/1. London: OPCS, 1982.

69   Babb P. Occupation and fertility. In: Drever F, ed. *Occupational health.* OPCS Decennial Supplement Series DS No.10. London: HMSO, 1995.

70   Bartley M, Blane D, Davey Smith G. Making sense of health inequalities. In: Dorling D, Simpson S, eds. *Statistics in society: the arithmetic of politics.* London: Edwin Arnold, 1998.

71   Fox AJ, Goldblatt PO. *Longitudinal study: socio-demographic mortality differentials, 1971–1975.* OPCS Longitudinal Study Series LS No. 1. London: HMSO, 1982.

72   Martin J, Roberts C. *Women and employment: a lifetime perspective.* London: HMSO, 1984.

73   Macfarlane AJ, Cole TJ. From depression to recession: evidence about the effects of unemployment on mothers' and babies' health, 1930s to 1980s. In: *Born unequal: perspectives on pregnancy and childbearing in unemployed families.* London: Maternity Alliance, 1985:38–57.

74   Bartley M, Sacker A, Firth D, Fitzpatrick R. Social position, social roles and women's health in England: changing relationships, 1984–1993. *Social Science and Medicine* 1999; 48: 99–115.

75   Rosselson L. Don't get married girls. In: *Bringing the news from nowhere: 125 songs by Leon Rosselson.* Wembley Park: Fuse Records, 1992.

76   Lewis J, Welshman J. The issue of never-married motherhood in Britain. *Social History of Medicine* 1997; 10(3): 401–418.

77   Pearce D, Farid S. Illegitimate births: changing patterns. *Population Trends* 1977; 9: 20–23.

78   Office for National Statistics. *Birth statistics.* Series FM1 No.26. London: The Stationery Office, 1998.

79   Shouls S, Whitehead M, Burström B, Diderichsen F. The health and social circumstances of British lone mothers over the last two decades. *Population Trends* 1999; 95: 41–46.

80   Ni Bhrolcháin M. *New perspectives on fertility in Britain*. Studies on Medical and Population Subjects No. 55. London: HMSO, 1993.

81   Haskey J. Birth cohort analyses of dependent children and lone mothers living in one parent families in Great Britain. *Population Trends* 1998; 92: 15–22.

82   Babb P, Bethune A. Trends in births outside marriage. *Population Trends* 1995; 81: 17–22.

83   Haskey J. One-parent families and their dependent children in Great Britain. *Population Trends* 1998; 91: 5–14.

84   Haskey J. Divorce and children: fact proven and interval between petition and decree. *Population Trends* 1996; 84: 28–31.

85   Haskey J. Children who experience divorce in their family. *Population Trends* 1997; 87: 5–10.

86   *Private lives and public responses: lone parenthood and future policy in the UK*. London: Policy Studies Institute and the University of Bath, 1998.

87   Ford R, Marsh A, Finlayson L. *What happens to lone parents: a cohort study, 1991–1995*. London: The Stationery Office, 1998.

88   Haskey J. Divorce and remarriage in England and Wales. *Population Trends* 1999; 95: 18–22.

89   Government Actuary's Department. *Marital status projections for England and Wales*. London: The Stationery Office, 1999.

90   Ahmad WIU. Ethnic statistics – better than nothing or worse than nothing? In: Dorling D, Simpson S, eds. *Statistics in society: the arithmetic of politics*. London: Edwin Arnold, 1998.

91   Aspinall PJ. Describing the 'white' ethnic group and its composition in medical research. *Social Science and Medicine* 1998; 47(11): 1797–1808.

92   Parsons L, Macfarlane AJ, Golding J. Pregnancy, birth and maternity care. In: Ahmad W, ed. *Race and health in contemporary Britain*. Milton Keynes: Open University Press, 1993.

93   Balarajan R, Raleigh VS. The ethnic populations of England and Wales: the 1991 census. *Health Trends* 1993; 24: 113–116.

94   Balarajan R, Raleigh VS. Variations in perinatal, neonatal and postneonatal and infant mortality by mother's country of birth, 1982–85. In: Britton M, ed. *Mortality and geography: a review in the mid-1980s England and Wales*. OPCS Decennial Supplement Series DS No.9. London: HMSO, 1990.

95   Balarajan R, Soni Raleigh V, Botting B. Mortality from congenital malformations in England and Wales: variations by mother's country of birth. *Archives of Disease In Childhood* 1989; 64(10): 1457–1462.

96   Raleigh VS, Balarajan R. The health of infants and children among ethnic minorities. In: Botting B, ed. *The health of our children*. OPCS Decennial Supplement Series DS No.11. London: HMSO, 1995.

97   Runnymede Trust, Radical Statistics Race Group. *Britain's black population*. London: Heinemann Educational Books, 1980.

98   Sources of statistics on ethnic minorities [editorial]. *Population Trends* 1982; 28: 1–6.

99   Office of Population Censuses and Surveys. *The government's decision on an ethnic question in the 1981 census*. OPCS Monitor CEN 80/3. London: OPCS, 1980.

100   Office of Population Censuses and Surveys. *Tests on an ethnic question*. OPCS Monitor CEN 80/2. London: OPCS, 1980.

101   Hollis J, Myers M. Ethnic minorities and social needs. In: *Papers presented at the British Society for Population Studies conference on the implications of current demographic trends in the UK for social and economic policy*. OPCS Occasional Paper No. 19. London: OPCS, 1980.

102   Simpson S. Non response to the 1991 census: its impact on the enumeration of ethnic groups. In: Coleman D, Salt J, eds. *Ethnicity in the 1991 census*. Vol. 1: Demographic characteristics of ethnic minority populations. London: HMSO, 1996.

103   Coleman D, Salt J, eds. *Ethnicity in the 1991 census*. Vol. 1: Demographic characteristics of ethnic minority populations. London: HMSO, 1996.

104   Peach C, ed. *Ethnicity in the 1991 census*. Vol. 2: The ethnic minority populations of Great Britain. London: HMSO, 1996.

105   Radcliffe P, ed. *Ethnicity in the 1991 census*. Vol. 3: Social geography and ethnicity in Britain: geographical spread, spatial concentration and internal migration. London: HMSO, 1996.

106   Karn V, ed. *Ethnicity in the 1991 census*. Vol. 4: Employment, education and housing among the ethnic minority population of Great Britain. London: HMSO, 1997.

107   Sheldon TA, Parker H. Race and ethnicity in health research. *Journal of Public Health Medicine* 1992; 14(2): 104–110.

108   Bradby H. Ethnicity: not a black and white issue. *Sociology of Health and Illness* 1995; 17: 405–417.

109   McKenzie KJ, Crowcroft NS. Race, ethnicity, culture, and science [editorial]. *BMJ* 1994; 309(6950): 286–287.

110   Senior PA, Bhopal R. Ethnicity as a variable in epidemiological research. *BMJ* 1994; 309: 327–330.

111   Aspinall PJ. *The health of the Irish in Britain: an annotated bibliography*. Bibliographies in Ethnic Relations. London: Centre for Research on Ethnic Relations, 1999.

112 Nazroo J. The racialisation of inequalities in health. In: Dorling D, Simpson S, eds. *Statistics in society: the arithmetic of politics*. London: Edwin Arnold, 1998.

113 Office for National Statistics. *The 2001 census of population*. London: The Stationery Office, 1999.

114 Southworth J. The religious question: representing reality or compounding confusion? In: Dorling D, Simpson S, eds. *Statistics in society: the arithmetic of politics*. London: Edwin Arnold, 1998.

115 Traditional song sung by Harry Cox on *Songs of seduction* (Caedmon TC 1143). Cited in: Lloyd AL, *Folksong in England*. London: Lawrence and Wishart, 1967.

116 Information and Statistics Division. *Teenage pregnancy in Scotland: a fifteen year review, 1983–1997*. Health Briefing 98/04. Edinburgh: ISD, 1998.

117 Ruddock V, Wood R, Quinn M. Birth statistics: recent trends in England and Wales. *Population Trends* 1998; 94: 12–18.

118 Wood R, Botting B, Dunnell K. Trends in conceptions before and after the 1995 pill scare. *Population Trends* 1997; 89: 5–12.

119 Botting B, Rosato M, Wood R. Teenage mothers and the health of their children. *Population Trends* 1998; 93: 19–28.

120 Office of Population Censuses and Surveys. *Registration: proposals for change*. Cm 939. London: HMSO, 1990.

121 Cooper J, Jones C. Estimates of the numbers of first, second, third, and higher order births. *Population Trends* 1992; 70: 8–14.

122 Bakketeig LS, Hoffman HJ. Perinatal mortality by birth order within cohorts based on sibship size. *British Medical Journal* 1979; 2(6192): 693–696.

123 Adams MM, Herman AA, Notzon FC. International symposium on maternally-linked pregnancy outcomes, Atlanta, Georgia, September 1995. Proceedings and abstracts. *Paediatric and Perinatal Epidemiology* 1997; 11 (Suppl 1): 1–150.

124 Bakketeig LS. The risk of repeated preterm or low birthweight delivery. In: Reed DM, Stanley FJ, eds. *The epidemiology of prematurity*. Baltimore, Munich: Urban and Schwarzenberg, 1977.

125 Macran S, Leon DA. *Patterns and determinants of birth weight in consecutive live births: results from the OPCS Longitudinal Study, 1980–88*. Series LS Working Paper No.74. London: City University, 1995.

126 Kuh D, Ben-Shlomo Y, eds. *A life course approach to chronic disease epidemiology*. Oxford: Oxford University Press, 1997.

127 Confidential Enquiry into Stillbirths and Deaths in Infancy. *4th annual report for 1 January to 31 December 1995*. London: Maternal and Child Health Consortium, 1997.

128 McDowall M. *Occupational reproductive epidemiology: the use of routinely collected statistics in England and Wales, 1980–82*. Studies on Medical and Population Subjects No. 50. London: HMSO, 1985.

129 Sanjose S, Roman E, Beral V. Low birthweight and preterm delivery, Scotland, 1981–84: effect of parents' occupation. *Lancet* 1991; 338(8764): 428–431.

130 General Register Office. *The Registrar General's decennial supplement for England and Wales, 1931 and 1939*. Vol. IIb: Occupational fertility. London: HMSO, 1953.

131 Elliott R, Jones J, McElvenny D, Pennington J, Northage C, Clegg T, Clarke S, Hodgson J, Osman J. *Spontaneous abortion in the UK semiconductor industry: an HSE investigation*. London: The Stationery Office, 1998.

132 Doyle P, Roman E, Beral V, Brookes M. Spontaneous abortion in dry cleaning workers potentially exposed to perchlorethylene. *Occupational and Environmental Medicine* 1997; 54: 848–853.

133 Roman E, Doyle P, Ansell P, Bull D, Beral V. Health of children born to medical radiographers. *Occupational and Environmental Medicine* 1997; 33: 73–79.

134 Foster K, Lader D, Cheesbrough S. *Infant feeding, 1995. Results from a survey carried out by the Social Survey Division of ONS on behalf of the UK health departments*. Social Survey Report SS 1387. London: The Stationery Office, 1997.

135 Masuy-Stroobant G, Gourbin C. Infant health and mortality indicators. *European Journal of Population* 1995; 11: 63–84.

136 Macfarlane AJ. Revised US certificate of birth: a view from England. *Birth* 1989; 16(4): 193–195.

137 Dyhouse C. Working-class mothers and infant mortality in England, 1895–1914. *Journal of Social History* 1978; 12(2): 248–267.

138 Jones HR. The perils and protection of infant life. *Journal of the Royal Statistical Society* 1894; 69: 1–103.

139 Collett CE. The collection and utilization of official statistics bearing on the extent and effects of the industrial employment of women. *Journal of the Royal Statistical Society* 1898; 61: 219–261.

140 The industrial employment of women and infantile mortality [editorial]. *Public Health* 1910; 23: 229.

141 McDowall M, Goldblatt P, Fox J. Employment during pregnancy and infant mortality. *Population Trends* 1981; 26: 12–15.

142 Rodmell S, Smart L. *Pregnant at work*. Open University and Kensington, Chelsea and Westminster Area Health Authority, 1982.

143 McRae S. *Maternity rights in Britain: the experience of women and employers*. London: Policy Studies Institute, 1991.

144 Callender C, Millward N, Lissenburgh S, Forth J. *Maternity rights and benefits in Britain 1996*. DSS Research Report No. 67. London: The Stationery Office, 1997.

145 Office for National Statistics, General Register Office for Scotland, Northern Ireland Statistics and Research Agency. *Census news*, No. 4. London: Government Statistical Service, 2000.

146 Office for National Statistics. *Living in Britain: results from the 1996 General Household Survey*. London: The Stationery Office, 1998.

147 Office for National Statistics. *Family spending: a report on the 1997–98 Family Expenditure Survey*. London: The Stationery Office, 1998.

148 Goodman A, Webb S. *For richer, for poorer, the changing distribution of income in the United Kingdom 1961–1991*. London: Institute for Fiscal Studies, 1994.

149 Goodman A, Johnson P, Webb S. *Inequality in the UK*. Oxford: Oxford University Press, 1997.

150 Dale A, Marsh C. eds. *The 1991 census user's guide*. London: HMSO, 1993.

151 Ashford JR, Read KL, Riley VC. An analysis of variations in perinatal mortality amongst local authorities in England and Wales. *International Journal of Epidemiology* 1973; 2(1): 31–46.

152 Fryer JG, Harding RA, Macdonald MD, Read KLQ, Abernathy JR. Comparing the early mortality rates of the local authorities of England and Wales. *Journal of the Royal Statistical Society* 1979; 142A: 181–198.

153 Ashford JR. Perinatal mortality as an indicator of the effectiveness of medical care. *Evaluation and the Health Professions* 1981; 4: 235–258.

154 Jarman B. Identification of underprivileged areas. *British Medical Journal* 1983; 286: 1705–1709.

155 Jarman B. Underprivileged areas: validation and distribution of scores. *British Medical Journal* 1984; 289: 1587–1592.

156 Phillimore P, Beattie A, Townsend P. Widening inequality of health in Northern England, 1981–91. *BMJ* 1994; 308: 1125–1128.

157 Carstairs V, Morris R. *Deprivation and health in Scotland*. Aberdeen: Aberdeen University Press, 1991.

158 Department of the Environment. *1991 deprivation index: a review of approaches and a matrix of results*. London: HMSO, 1995.

159 Department of Environment, Transport and the Regions. *1998 index of local deprivation*. London: DETR, 1998. On the Internet at http://www.regeneration.detr.gov.uk/98ild/intro.htm.

160 McClaren GL, Bain MRS. *Deprivation and health in Scotland: insights from NHS data*. Edinburgh: ISD Scotland Publications, 1998.

161 Pattenden S, Dolk H, Vrijheid M. Inequalities in low birthweight: parental social class, area deprivation and 'lone mother' status. *Journal of Epidemiology and Community Health* 1999; 53: 355–358.

6 Characteristics of babies

'Some say to live single it is the best plan
But I was ne'er happy till I got a man,
When I got a man, I soon got a wain
A wee little totum to toddle its lane.

It gangs toddlin' but, and gangs toddlin' ben
The wee little totum gangs toddlin' its lane.'

The wee totum, 'bothy ballad' from north east Scotland.[1]

This chapter describes the characteristics of new babies which feature most commonly in routine statistics. It opens by describing how birthweight is measured and classified, including its relationship to gestational age. It continues with a brief discussion of other characteristics before going on to explore differences between boys and girls and trends in multiple birth and its outcome.

Birthweight and gestational age at birth

'It is unlucky to weigh them. If you do, they will probably die, and at any rate, will not thrive. I have caused great concern in the mind of a worthy old monthly nurse by insisting on weighing mine. They have, however, all done very well, with the exception of one, the weighing of whom was accidentally forgotten to be performed.
The nurse always protested against the weighing in a timorous sort of a way; saying that, no doubt it was all nonsense, but still it had better not be done ... .'

Superstitions about new-born children. *The book of days, a miscellany of popular antiquities*, 1866.[2]

Even if the views of this Suffolk 'monthly nurse' were unusual, birthweight was not yet considered an important enough item of information to be included in vital statistics in the latter part of the nineteenth century or the early twentieth century. For example, Florence Nightingale did not include it in her list of items to be recorded in midwifery statistics.[3] Interest in the measurement of birthweight developed amongst obstetricians from the late seventeenth century onwards, although it may not have been widespread.[4]

The idea of weighing babies regularly to monitor growth developed in the latter half of the nineteenth century.[4] Adolphe Quetelet was the first person to make a series of measurements from birth onwards. At this period, 'prematurity' was often certified as a cause of death. Concern about its contribution to infant mortality was expressed early in the twentieth century in the reports of the Local Government Board,[5-7] but it was not defined in terms of gestational age or of birthweight.

Some attempt at definition was made by George Newman in his book *Infant mortality*, published in 1906 and mentioned in Chapter 3.[8] He divided the 'antenatal influences' on infant mortality into four types, 'infections, toxaemia, prematurity and immaturity'. Of 'prematurity', he said:

> 'The following somewhat mechanical definitions of terms may be convenient:
>
> Abortion – Expulsion of ovum before the end of the fourth month of uterogestation
>
> Miscarriage – Expulsion from end of fourth to end of sixth month
>
> Premature birth – End of sixth month to end of pregnancy but on the whole it is better to consider births as 'abortions' if under a viable age, and if over that age as 'prematurity'. All these hard and fast terms, however, have considerable disadvantage, and can only be used as general indications.'[8]

George Newman also quoted the possibility of defining babies weighing less than 2,500g or less than 3,000g as 'premature'. He suggested a number of adverse circumstances could lead to 'prematurity', including infections, poor housing and nutrition and 'the activities and pleasures of society'. Of 'immaturity', he said:

> 'This term is used to include all those conditions of congenital disability other than prematurity... Atrophy, debility, some forms of 'wasting' disease, congenital defects, non-expansion of the lungs (atelectasis) and general frailty are conditions of this kind. Infants thus heavily handicapped may yet survive for some weeks and even grow up to adult life. But the mark of death is upon them.'[8]

George Newman went on to cite data which suggested that poor nutrition and heavy work in late pregnancy could lower the birthweight of a woman's baby.

A paper by the statistician John Brownlee in the Medical Research Committee's report *Mortalities of birth, infancy and childhood*, published in 1917, included some birthweight data, but only as part of the overall pattern of growth from conception to adulthood.[9] A series of pathological studies of stillbirths and infant deaths published between 1922 and 1930[10-13] included birthweight data, but did not analyse them. Weights of individual organs were analysed in considerable detail, however. The first of these studies, Eardley Holland's report, *The causation of foetal death*, confined itself to 'viable' fetuses. It defined these as 'foetuses ... whose length measured from the crown of the head to the heel equalled or exceeded 35 cms or whose period of intra-uterine life, as calculated from the date of the last menstrual period, equalled or exceeded 28 weeks.'[10] Birthweight was not mentioned as a criterion.

A number of studies done after the first world war in Germany and Austria to investigate the effects of food shortages on the weights of babies born during the war led to questions about whether there had been any adverse effects in this country. In response to these, a study was done of women who had their first babies at St Thomas' Hospital, London in 1914, 1915 and 1918.[14] The birthweight and length at birth of the babies was related to their mothers' economic circumstances during pregnancy, and St Thomas' Hospital was chosen because these data had been recorded about women who delivered there. No association was found between birthweight and the mother's circumstances. As babies described as 'premature', a term which was admittedly not defined, were excluded from the analysis, the lack of association is hardly surprising.

An enquiry into infant mortality by Janet Campbell was published by the Ministry of Health in 1929. It included an analysis by a statistician, Peter McKinlay, of the average birthweights of babies born into different social circumstances and housing conditions.[15] His sample was confined to babies who were born alive and died after surviving the first day of life but under the age of one year. It is hardly surprising that he did not find the average birthweights of these babies to be affected by social circumstances. Had he included those who died in the first day of life, his results might well have been different.

Definitions

Definitions were discussed when the analyses of birthweights done on the continent were reviewed and extended by Arvo Ylppo, a Finnish doctor working in Germany. In his classic article *On the physiology, care and fate of premature babies*, published in 1919, he pointed out that babies born at the same gestational age can vary in their degree of physiological maturity and outlined the problems of measuring this.[16] Having suggested that premature birth should be defined as weighing 2,500g or less at birth, he acknowledged that the term 'premature birth' (*fruhgeburt*) was inappropriate and suggested the term 'immature child' (*unreifes kind*) instead. He admitted that the cut off point of 2,500g was arbitrary and was not necessarily related to other indicators of immaturity, for example having a birth length less than 45 cm.

Ylppo's definition was widely adopted and his work was cited in the section headed 'A definition of prematurity' in the *Annual report of the Chief Medical Officer for England and Wales* for 1937. Having referred to the unreliability of data about gestational age, the report said:

> 'Recently the Royal College of Physicians of London has issued a more exact definition of a standard in the following terms:
> "That in conformity with the standard in international use, an infant whose birthweight is 5$\frac{1}{2}$ lb (approximately 2,500 grammes) or less, shall be considered, for the purpose of comparison of records, as either immature or prematurely born, according as the estimated period of gestation is full time or less".'[17]

Despite the distinction made here, all babies with birthweights below this arbitrary cut off point continued to be referred to as 'premature'. Indeed, the term did not disappear from the *Chief Medical Officer's annual report* for

England and Wales until 1973 or from *Scottish health statistics* until 1979. It was still in common parlance in the late 1990s.

The *Chief Medical Officer's annual report* for 1970, referred to the distinction between short gestation and slow fetal growth, and remarked that 'The international definition of prematurity is thus seen to have certain limitations and the expression "low birthweight" is now being used more commonly.'[18] This was happening in response to suggestions from an international group of obstetricians that all words incorporating 'maturity' should be dropped. Instead they suggested defining 'low birthweight' as 2,500g or less. They also suggested classifying gestational ages under 259 days as 'pre-term', those from 259 to 293 days as 'term', and those of 294 days or more as 'post-term'.[19] They did not specify whether gestational age was to be estimated from the date of the mother's last menstrual period or from a paediatric assessment.

Definitions of 'low birthweight', 'gestational age' and 'pre-term' did not appear in the *International classification of diseases* until the ninth revision was published in 1977.[20] These definitions are given in Chapter 2 of this book and the same birthweight data are tabulated using both old and new definitions in Table 2.5. As we mentioned there, the definition of low birthweight was changed to 'less than 2,500g' and this definition became widely adopted by the early 1980s. The definition of gestational age in the ninth revision of the ICD states that 'the duration of gestation is measured from the first day of the last normal menstrual period',[20] and this same definition is given in the tenth revision.[21]

Collection of data

Over the first half of the twentieth century, it became increasingly common to record babies' birthweights in hospital and local authority records. In some areas, such as the county of Hertfordshire, the notifications of birth to medical officers of health under the Notification of Births Act of 1907 and the Notification of Births Extension Act of 1915 contained the baby's birthweight. During the 1990s, a growing interest in studying associations between the health of adults and their birthweight and circumstances at birth has led to a search for these local records.[22–24]

Towards the end of the second world war, concern about 'prematurity' was accompanied by the first attempt to collect data about birthweight on a national scale in England and Wales. The *Chief Medical Officer's annual report* for the years 1939–1945 said:

> 'It has long been known that some 50 per cent of neonatal deaths were due to prematurity, and, as for some years the neonatal mortality rate has not shown the same rate of decrease as the infant mortality rate, the Medical and Professional Sub-Committee of the Minister's Advisory Committee on the Welfare of Mothers and Young Children was asked to advise on the care of premature infants.
>
> Following their Report, Circular 20/44 of March 1944 drew the attention of welfare authorities to the need for improving facilities for the care of premature infants, both in hospital and in the home, and to secure early

information of premature births, asked them to provide notification of birth cards designed to indicate when the birthweight was 5½ lb or less.'[25]

Between 1945 and 1952, different methods were used to collect data for hospital and home births and the totals were inconsistent. In 1953 the system was reorganised, the weight groups changed and a single return, the LHS 27/1, mentioned in Chapters 2 and 3, was used for all live births weighing 5½ lb or less in each local authority area in England and Wales.[26] Stillbirths were included from 1955. The data presented in Tables A3.4.1 and A3.5.1 come from this system. In 1963, births weighing up to 1,500g were subdivided into 'up to 1,000g' and '1,001g to 1,500g' as these groups have very different mortality rates. Deaths from 1 to 27 days were subdivided into deaths from 1 to 6, and from 7 to 27 days after birth. Analyses for England were published each year in the *Chief Medical Officer's annual report* until 1985, after which they were replaced by data from birth registration. Until 1973, LHS 27/1 returns were compiled by local authorities. From 1974 to 1981, data were aggregated by area health authorities and from 1982 until the system was ended in 1988, they were compiled by district health authorities.

Similar data have been published in *Scottish health statistics* since 1972, while data for the years 1963–72 were published retrospectively. Originally the data were derived from birth notifications, as in England and Wales. Since 1975, the data have been derived from the SMR2 maternity discharge system. In Northern Ireland, data are compiled from birth notifications by each of the health and social services boards, but are not published routinely.

Birthweight data were not collected through the registration system until the certificates of stillbirth in use in England, Wales and Scotland were amended under the Population (Statistics) Act of 1960. Tabulations of stillbirths according to their birthweight and gestation have been published since 1961 in *The Annual report of the Registrar General for Scotland*, from 1961–73 in the *Registrar General's statistical review for England and Wales* and subsequently in *Mortality statistics, Series DH3*. Since 1963, similar tables have been included in the *Annual report of the Registrar General for Northern Ireland*. By 1996, only 1.8 per cent of stillbirth registrations in England and Wales did not have birthweight stated on the certificate and gestational age was missing in only 0.4 per cent of cases.

In 1975, OPCS started to include birthweight but not gestational age on registrations of live births. Instead of seeking information about the baby's birthweight from the parent registering the birth, local registrars of births and deaths must obtain the birthweight from the district health authority, which receives it on the birth notification form. Since 1991, notifications are usually passed to community trusts. Originally, many birthweights were missing as the information did not arrive in time to be included on the 'draft entry' of birth registration, which local registrars sent to OPCS. The problem appeared to be largely resolved in 1980 when registrars were allowed to hold back the 'draft entry' for a further week to allow time for the birthweight to be included.[27]

By 1983, only 0.14 per cent of birthweights were missing, as Table A3.4.2 shows. Unfortunately, in mid 1989, financial constraints at OPCS led to a decline in the completeness of birthweight data with nearly four per cent missing from 1990 to 1992, as Table A3.4.2 shows. After considerable effort to investigate and solve the problems, some of which were consequences of the computerisation of birth registration, the situation improved from 1993 onwards and only 0.24 per cent of birthweights were missing in 1996.

Live births, stillbirths and infant deaths in England and Wales, tabulated by birthweight and other factors as shown in Tables A6.1.1 to A6.2.4. Similar data for individual years are published in ONS' *Mortality statistics, Series DH3* and in *Health statistics quarterly*.

From 1967, until 1985 when it ended, birthweight and gestational age were among the data items collected in the Maternity Hospital In-Patient Enquiry. Because of the increase over these years in the proportion of births which took place in hospital, the data from this source cannot be used to monitor trends over time in the population as a whole. Data for the years 1967 to 1971 were used to tabulate birthweight by gestational age for singleton births.[28] The analyses were done separately for male and female babies and for first and subsequent births. They revealed similar patterns to those seen in the data for babies born in Aberdeen from 1948 to 1964, which were commonly used at the time as a reference standard in clinical notes.[29]

Since April 1989, data about birthweight and gestational age of babies born in England have been collected through the Maternity Hospital Episode Statistics. Because of their incompleteness, no data from this source were published until 1997, when the first of a series of *Statistical bulletins* appeared.[30] Tables A6.3.1 and A6.4.1 are taken from this bulletin. The high birthweights recorded at gestational ages of under 20, 20 and 23 weeks in Table A6.4.1 should be treated with extreme caution as they are clearly a reflection of the poor quality of the data in Maternity HES.

Birthweight and gestational age data for births in Scotland are collected through the SMR2 and SMR11 systems. Data from Scotland can be found in Tables A3.4.4, A3.5.3 to A3.5.5 and A6.5.1. Data are published annually in *Scottish health statistics* and the *Scottish stillbirth and infant death report* as well as in many special analyses.[31] Trends over time have been reviewed in the *Births in Scotland* publication series. The first of these gave a general overview while the second focused on small babies.[32,33] At the time of writing, no data are published routinely for Wales and Northern Ireland, but developments are under way in both countries, with data being collected via birth notification and child health computer systems.

Trends and variations in birthweight

The fact that data about the incidence of low birthweight were available for local authority areas in England and Wales made it possible to do a series of analyses of the way it varied from place to place during the 1960s and

1970s.[34-38] These studies showed a high degree of statistical association between infant and perinatal mortality and the incidence of low weight birth. They also showed a much higher degree of correlation between the incidence of low weight birth and indicators of adverse socio-economic conditions in each local authority than with indicators of the quality of the health services provided. Much more recent data for health authorities, discussed in Chapter 3 and Chapter 5, show that local differences in low birthweight persist in the 1990s.

Another study in the 1970s which used data about individual babies, suggested that birthweight alone is a better 'predictor' of perinatal death than either gestational age or birthweight and gestational age used together.[39] It is these considerations, coupled with the lack of data about gestational age at birth, except in Scotland, which led us to use birthweight in *Birth counts* as one of the main measures of the outcome of pregnancy.

Figure 3.9 uses data from LHS 27/1 and birth registration data from Tables A3.4.1 and A3.4.2 to show how the incidence of low birthweight has changed over time.[40-43] A closer look at these tables and Table A6.1.1 which shows birthweights of singleton and multiple births separately, shows that this is not the whole story. The proportion of babies at the upper end of the distribution rose over the period, suggesting that overall the average birthweight of singleton babies has increased.[44,45] This may not be the case for multiple births where the percentage weighing under 2,500g increased.

Tables A6.1.2 to A6.1.5 show a general decline in mortality in each birthweight group, both overall and among singleton and multiple births separately. A particularly striking feature is the fall in mortality among the very smallest babies, shown in Figure 6.1. Stillbirths and infant deaths are tabulated by ONS cause groups in Tables A6.2.1 to A6.2.4.

Figure 6.1

Neonatal mortality among extremely low birthweight babies, England and Wales, 1963–97

Source: LHS 27/1 low birthweight returns and ONS *Mortality statistics, Series DH3*

ONS now links deaths of all children born from 1993 onwards to their birth records. As a result it can now derive mortality rates for one, two and three year olds, and will be able to extend this to older children as time goes on. Deaths of children of these ages are tabulated in Table A6.1.6 by their weight at birth.

In the 1970s, the Medical Birth Registry in Norway started to link successive pregnancies to the same woman, making it possible to do analyses of outcome in terms of birthweight and gestational age. It was found that women who had a low weight or preterm birth in their first pregnancy had an above average risk of repeating this in their second pregnancy.[46] Other countries have since developed the capacity to link data in this way.[47] In the United Kingdom, Scotland has the most developed systems of record linkage, but in England and Wales the OPCS Longitudinal Study, now known as the ONS Longitudinal Study has been used for a study of birthweights of successive births to the same mother.[48] Figure 6.2 comes from this source. Eventually it will be possible to go even further and analyse the outcome of women's pregnancies in relation to their own birthweight, as has already been done in Norway.[49] Meanwhile the studies of cohorts of people born in 1946 and 1958 have been used to study their health as adults and the characteristics of their children in relation to their weight at birth.[23]

Figure 6.2

Distribution of weights of second births conditional upon weights of first birth, live singleton births, 1980–88

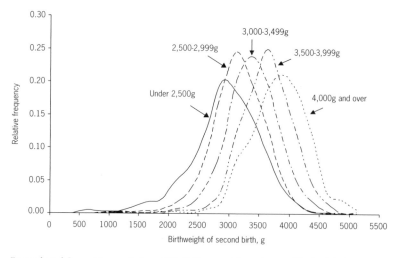

Reproduced from: Macran S, Leon DA. *Patterns and determinants of birthweight in consecutive live births: results from the OPCS Longitudinal Study, 1980–88.*[48]

172

Other characteristics of newborn babies

There is wide variation in the extent to which data about newborn babies are collected locally in England and Wales. In most districts, data collected on birth notification forms are used to initiate records in child health computer systems, maintained by community trusts with contracts for child health services.

Very few data about newborn babies themselves are collected on a national scale. The Hospital In-Patient Enquiry did not include a separate record for a baby delivered in an NHS hospital unless it was admitted to a special or intensive care baby unit. The Hospital Episode Statistics should include records for every baby born, but they are not linked to their mothers' records. Babies who are not admitted are counted separately as 'well babies' but individual data are not collected. The only data included on the mother's record are the number of births, the birthweight and sex of each baby, whether each baby was live or stillborn.

In Scotland, the SMR2 maternity discharge sheet includes, in addition, the baby's Apgar score at five minutes and any operation it may have undergone. Much fuller data are now collected for all births, on the SMR11 neonatal record.[50]

Gender

> 'Now if it's a boy he shall wear a gold ring
> And when he's of age he shall fight for his King
> And his jacket so red and his trousers so blue
> He shall fight for his country like his father used to do.
>
> Now if she's a girl she shall wear a gold brooch
> With silver in her pocket and gold in her purse.
> With silver in her pocket to buy milk and bread
> And you may depend she'll never a trust a soldier in her bed.'[51]

It is well known that differences in attitudes to boys and girls affect their future lives. It is less well known that the risks of dying at or around the time of birth can differ by gender, as can the health of children and adults.[52]

A subject which has frequently fascinated people who analyse vital statistics is the variability of the ratio of the numbers of boys to the numbers of girls born. As William Farr wrote in the Registrar General's Annual Report for 1841:

> 'I showed in the Fourth Annual Report that the proportion of boys to girls born in England was 10,486 to 10,000. The mathematical questions connected with the proportion of the sexes born have been investigated by Laplace, Poisson, Babbage, and other distinguished philosophers; and one of the results which has attracted most attention and created most speculation is, that the proportion of boys is greatest among legitimate children ... the present Return gives a result exactly the reverse; of the legitimate births the boys are to the girls as 105.4 to 100.0; of illegitimate births the boys are 108.1 to 100.0.'[53]

Thirty-five years later, he reported that 'Dr Bertillon and others have collected facts which throw some light on this interesting subject. In the meantime I wish to draw attention to the remarkable fact that this excess in the proportional number of boys born to girls born in England and Wales is less than it was.'[54] It is likely that this trend was a result of improvements in the completeness of birth registration. Evidence from the 1871 census[55] suggested that in a society which valued boy babies more highly than girl babies, the births of girls were more likely to be under-registered than those of boys.[56] In the 1869 edition of his book *Physique sociale*, Adolphe Quetelet discussed variation in the sex ratio while suggesting that the overall rate for Europe was 1.06.[57,58]

William Farr's comments suggest that for him, as well as for other investigators who both preceded him and followed in his footsteps, curiosity was the main motive for analysing the sex ratio. One exception, perhaps, was Wallis Taylor whose stated reason for analysing the sex distribution of children within families in the early 1950s was to inform housing policy-makers of the extent of the need for separate bedrooms.[59] The question is of more than curiosity value when interpreting perinatal statistics, however. This is because the complications arising in pregnancy and the outcome of pregnancy can both vary according to the sex of the fetus.

The 'sex ratio' is defined as the number of males divided by the number of females, and the ratio is sometimes multiplied by a factor of a thousand. An alternative name which has been used for the sex ratio, for example in the Reports of the Registrar General for Scotland in the mid 1940s, is 'masculinity'. Many analyses of the sex ratio seem to imply that a low value is an adverse outcome, but this is, of course, a subjective judgement. More seriously, changes in the sex ratio can be a reflection of environmental factors which may also have harmful effects on some individual fetuses.

The sex ratio at conception is called the 'primary sex ratio' and that at birth the 'secondary sex ratio'. It appears that considerably more females than males are conceived, but miscarriages are more common in female than male fetuses during the first trimester of pregnancy.[60] At the end of this stage, there are more male than female fetuses. After this, more male than female fetuses are miscarried or stillborn.[60]

As Table A6.10.1 shows, the sex ratio is higher for stillbirths than live births. Stillbirth and infant mortality rates have been higher for males than females throughout the twentieth century, as Tables A6.6.1 to A6.6.3 show. Tables A6.8.1 to A6.8.4 show that this is true at all stages of infancy. The differential is narrower for stillbirths than for infant deaths, because central nervous system anomalies, including anencephaly which usually leads to stillbirth, are more common in females than males.[61] As the increasing use of antenatal screening has meant that more anencephalic fetuses are aborted and fewer registered as stillbirths, the differential has been changing.

At first sight, the higher mortality in boys may seem somewhat paradoxical, given that boy babies are on average, heavier than girls, as can be seen in

Tables A6.9.1 and A6.9.2. Tables A6.9.3 to A6.9.5 show that, within birthweight groups, the mortality rates were lower for girls than boys, however. These differences mean that sex-specific birthweight distributions are needed as reference 'standards'.

Changes over time in overall mortality rates can be affected both by changes in the differences between sex-specific mortality rates and changes in the sex ratio.[62] Changes in stillbirth and infant mortality rates are shown in Tables A6.6.1 to A6.6.3 and Figures 6.3 and Figure 6.4 while changes in the sex ratio are shown in Tables A3.1.1 and A3.3.1 and Figure 6.5.

In his extensive review of variations in sex ratio published in 1936, WT Russell commented:

> 'that the number of male births always exceeds that of females is well known to students of vital statistics, but the biological law responsible for the phenomenon has not yet been adequately determined though various theories have been offered in explanation.'[63]

A number of analyses of birth and death registration data were published in the 1940s and 1950s both in the *Registrar General's Statistical Review*[64,65] and elsewhere.[66,67] These suggested that the sex ratio of live births, particularly first births, was lower amongst older mothers while that of stillbirths was higher. Interest in the subject may have been prompted by the marked increase in the sex ratio which occurred during and just after both world wars in all the countries involved.

This, combined with the increase of births after both wars, had implications for the sex ratio of the population as a whole in later years.[68,69] Long-term

Figure 6.3

Stillbirth rates by sex, England and Wales, 1928–97

Source: Office for National Statistics, *Mortality statistics, Series DH3*

Figure 6.4

Infant mortality rates by sex, England and Wales, 1928–97

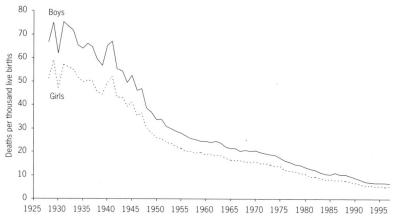

Source: Office for National Statistics, *Mortality statistics, Series DH3*

Figure 6.5

Sex ratio of live births, England and Wales, 1838–1997

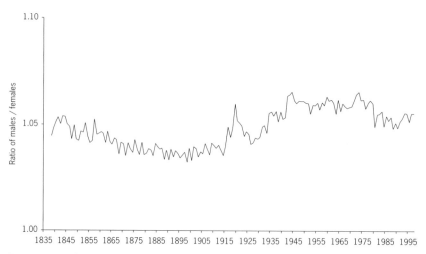

Source: General Register Office, OPCS and ONS *Birth statistics, Series FM1*

trends in the sex ratio of live births in Britain and Ireland are shown in Tables A3.1.1 to A3.1.5 and the sex ratio for England and Wales is plotted in Figure 6.5. In the nineteenth century, the sex ratio in England and Wales was apparently lower than that in Scotland and Ireland. It rose during the first half of the twentieth century then remained virtually constant at about 1.06 until the early 1980s when it began to decline.[70,71] Similar declines were seen in other developed countries.[72] Although it appeared to increase in the early 1990s, analysis of data for 1973–94 did not detect an upward trend at that time.[73,74] As Figure 6.5 shows, the patterns in the 1990s are unclear in England and Wales.

Because of the greater variability, Tables A3.1.2 to A3.1.5 do not give a clear picture of patterns in Scotland and Ireland, with one exception. In 1978 the sex ratio was exceptionally low in Northern Ireland, as Table A3.1.4 shows, and also in the other three counties of Ulster, which lie within the Irish Republic. As Table A3.1.5 shows, the ratio in the Republic fell only slightly, as the sex ratio was not exceptionally low in the rest of Ireland.[75] This phenomenon was not observed in England and Wales or in Scotland. No explanation was found for it.

Despite the lack of explanations for time trends in the sex ratio, there is no shortage of suggestions about why it varies. Exposure to substances at work or in the wider environment was discussed in Chapter 5. It has been observed that sex ratios vary according to the mother's and baby's blood groups.[76] Other studies have suggested that the sex ratio is relatively low amongst children whose fathers fly high performance military aircraft[77] or helicopters[78] and whose fathers spend long periods under water diving for abalone.[79] Disease may also affect the sex ratios in one direction or another.[80]

In the past in England and Wales, the sex ratio of live births was lower in late autumn and winter than during the rest of the year.[81] Apart from a peak in March, this pattern was not very apparent by 1996 as can be seen in Table A6.10.1.

It has been suggested that the sex ratio was lower in births to older women and among babies of higher birth order, although the differences found in an analysis of births from 1968–77 in England and Wales were small.[82,83] An analysis of births in 1988 in England and Wales did not detect such differences, nor did an analysis of data about singleton births in Scotland from 1975 to 1988 in which successive births to the same mother were linked.[84] Neither analysis found differences by social class and the Scottish analysis found no evidence of changes over time or seasonally.

The data for England and Wales showed sex ratios which were much lower in multiple than in singleton births. As the trends in multiple birth rates, described below, are different to those in the sex ratio, they are unlikely to account for the time trends. The conclusion drawn from the analysis of Scottish data was that there was no evidence of gender determination being anything other than a chance process.[84]

It has been argued that the sex ratio varies according to parents' hormonal levels at conception and the time within the menstrual cycle when insemination takes place.[85] The sex ratio at birth reaches a peak when insemination occurs close to ovulation.[86] The reverse occurs when insemination is artificial,[60,86] except when the semen are stored at low temperatures.[60] Sex ratios appear to be lower when assisted conception and ovarian stimulants are used.[72] It may well be that the factors referred to earlier affect the frequency of sexual intercourse and its timing within the menstrual cycle, but the mechanisms are far from clear.[87,88] A further problem is that some of these studies have been done using selected populations, for example, women attending infertility clinics or women using the rhythm method of birth control. This means that they may not apply to the population at large.

Multiple births

In a neat little cottage not far from town
There lived a man called Marcus Brown.
He was well to do, had a neat little wife,
But the want of a family caused them great strife.

Things every day grew worse and worse
He consulted his mother's old family nurse.
'Kind sir, don't fret', was her reply,
'Why don't you the family ointment try?'

Being pleased with the news away he went
And bought a box of the ointment.
Home he goes without delay
His wife took some the very same day.

Next morning to Mr Brown's surprise
His wife was ill, she would not rise.
She lay in bed and the midwife came in
And she threw away two the dead image of him.

'Oh Lord', says he, 'will she have another'
When a drop of the ointment fell on his mother.
'Oh Lord', says he 'will she have more'
In less than an hour, she had twenty four.

The family ointment, Traditional Irish song from the singing of Willy Clancy[89]

After many years of decline, the 1980s and 1990s have seen an overall increase in the percentage of maternities resulting in multiple births in Britain and Ireland as can be seen in Figure 6.6 and Tables A6.11.1 to A6.11.4. Although there was a clear increase in the very small numbers of quadruplets and quintuplets once ovarian stimulants became available in the later 1960s, this was more than offset until the late 1970s by the decline in the numbers of twins and triplets. A particularly dramatic change since the early 1980s has been the quadrupling of the rate of triplet and higher order births in England and Wales, shown in Figure 6.7 and Table A6.11.1. The rates also increased in Scotland and Ireland, as Tables A6.11.2 to A6.11.4 show. Similar increases occurred in other developed countries.[90]

Data about multiple births in England and Wales are published in *Birth statistics, Series FM1* and date back only to mid 1938. Numbers of multiple live births in Scotland have been published in the *Registrar General's annual report* since birth registration began in 1855, but data for stillbirths date back only to the beginning of stillbirth registration in 1939. For the same reason data on multiple births in Northern Ireland date back to 1922 when the first separate *Registrar General's annual report* was published in the province, but stillbirths have been included only since 1961. In the Irish Republic, stillbirth registration did not begin until 1995, so the data in Table A6.11.4 relate only to maternities with multiple live births. Once multiple birth rates which include stillbirths become available, direct comparisons between Ireland and the countries of the United Kingdom will be possible.

These data may all represent an under-enumeration of the numbers of multiple births. If a multiple birth occurs before 24 weeks of gestation and includes both live births and dead fetuses, the fetal deaths are not registrable. On the other hand, as we explained in Chapter 2, the law stipulates that any fetuses which show signs of life should be registered as live births. The extent to which the numbers of multiple maternities are

Figure 6.6

Multiple birth rates, England and Wales, 1938–97

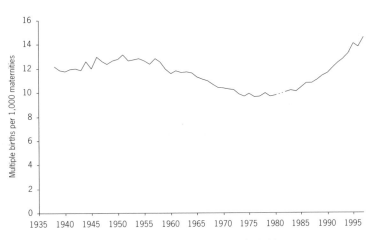

Source: Office for National Statistics, *Birth statistics, Series FM1*

Figure 6.7

Triplet and higher order births, England and Wales, 1938–97

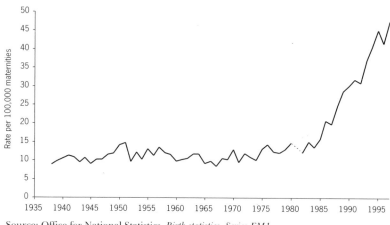

Source: Office for National Statistics, *Birth statistics, Series FM1*

underestimated for these reasons has not been assessed, but should be borne in mind when interpreting the data. The reverse may also occur. If fetuses are born dead together with live births in a multiple birth after 24 or more completed weeks of gestation, they should be registered as stillbirths even if the fetuses had actually died much earlier.

Table A6.12.1, in which multiple maternities are tabulated by the mother's age, shows that maternities with multiple births are more common in older than in younger women. The proportions with multiple births have been increasing in all age groups except for women under 20.[90–92] Following industrial activity by local registrars' of births and deaths, these data could not be compiled for England and Wales for 1981, leaving a gap in the corresponding tables.

It has long been known that stillbirth rates and death rates in infancy are higher among multiple births than among singletons. Before 1975, there were few data on a national scale which could be used to monitor trends. This is because death certificates do not contain data about whether the person who died was part of a multiple birth. Data are available from the first analysis which linked infant deaths to births in 1949/50.[93] Since 1975, data from England and Wales have been available routinely from analyses of infant mortality linked files and published in *Mortality statistics, Series DH3*. Data for Scotland are published in the annual series of *Scottish stillbirth and infant death reports*.

Time trends in crude mortality rates for multiple births in England and Wales are shown in Table A6.13.1, while Tables A6.13.2 and A6.13.3 give rates for twins and triplets separately. These rates are, of course, much higher than those for singleton births. This is largely a consequence of the

Figure 6.8

Birthweight distributions of singleton and multiple births, England and Wales, 1996

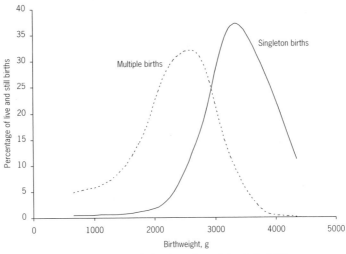

Source: Office for National Statistics, *Mortality statistics, Series DH3*

Table 6.1

Stillbirth and infant mortality rates by birthweight and multiplicity, England and Wales, babies born in 1996

	Birthweight, g						All
		Under 1,000	1,000 – 1,499	1,500 – 1,999	2,000 – 2,499	Under 2,500	
Stillbirth	Singleton	297.1	100.2	49.0	13.7	53.7	5.1
	Multiple	203.5	33.2	9.3	6.1	27.5	17.5
Neonatal	Singleton	386.4	63.1	17.7	6.5	38.8	3.4
	Multiple	481.9	50.4	7.4	2.5	43.9	25.2
Postneonatal	Singleton	51.2	22.4	11.4	6.2	11.6	1.8
	Multiple	40.6	10.4	3.1	4.4	7.4	4.7
Infant	Singleton	437.6	85.5	29.1	12.7	50.5	5.3
	Multiple	522.5	60.8	10.5	6.9	51.3	29.8

Babies born in 1996 may have died in 1996 or 1997

Source: Office for National Statistics, *Mortality statistics, Series DH3*

lower birthweights among babies born in multiple births as shown in Table A6.11.1 and Figure 6.8. Apart from babies weighing under 1,000g, stillbirth and infant mortality rates within each birthweight range are similar or lower for babies born in a multiple birth. This is illustrated in Table 6.1, which summarises data for babies born in 1996 from Tables A6.1.2 to A6.1.5.

Special studies using past data have found mortality rates of second twins born to be higher than those of the first.[94] It is not possible to derive data about the mortality of each in recent years from ONS' birth and death linkage. Although the time of birth of live born multiple births is recorded at birth registration, it is not currently coded for computer analysis in England and Wales. When data for the late 1970s were analysed manually, it was still not possible to derive stillbirth and infant mortality rates for first and second twins, because the time of birth of stillbirths is not recorded.[91] If the time of birth were recorded and coded for all live and stillbirths, it would be possible to calculate separate death rates for first and second twins and to monitor the way these change over time. In addition to helping interpret the outcome of multiple births, data about the time of day of all births could be of use more generally in planning and monitoring maternity services.

While the differences in the mortality rates of singleton and multiple births are far wider than those between the rates of males and females, the differences between the sexes have been analysed far more fully. This may well be because the computational problems involved in the analysis of multiple births are far more complex, rather than because of any inherent lack of interest. The rise in the multiple birth rate in general and in triplet and higher order births in particular, has raised questions about the extent to which it is a consequence of the increasing use of ovarian stimulants and assisted conception, as this information is not routinely linked to birth registration records.[90] This means that special studies are needed to explore questions in greater depth.

The National Study of Triplet and Higher Order Births covered births in England and Wales over the period 1980 to 1985, excluding 1981. It found that the impact of assisted conception was negligible before 1985. In the survey as a whole, 63 per cent of all triplets were conceived spontaneously, 33 per cent after the use of ovarian stimulants and 4 per cent after using assisted conception.[95]

The picture had changed by 1989 when the British Association of Perinatal Medicine found that assisted conception played a major role. In its survey, 33 per cent of sets of triplets were conceived spontaneously, 31 per cent after the use of ovarian stimulants and 35 per cent using other techniques for assisted conception.[96] Using data from the Oxford Record Linkage Study, it was estimated that, in the early 1990s, about 60 per cent of triplet and higher order births and 15 per cent of twin births followed the use of assisted conception.[97] A further national study is needed to produce more reliable and up to date estimates.

The rise in multiple births, especially triplet and higher order births has considerable consequences for health services, families and society. The first national survey found that there were many problems facing parents of triplet and higher order births in the early 1980s and they lacked appropriate support from health and social services.[95] More up to date information can be collected only by doing further surveys.

Newborn babies in the 1990s and 2000s

The routine data in this chapter show increases in the percentages of low birthweight babies during the 1990s. Both the rising rate of multiple births and the increasing tendency to register very low birthweight babies are likely to have contributed to this. Missing birthweight data in the early 1990s in England and Wales made it difficult to interpret trends in low birthweight and birthweight specific mortality. Although survival rates among very tiny babies continued to rise, mortality rates among the low birthweight group as a whole flattened off. Similar trends for preterm births were observed in Scotland. Boys continued to have higher infant mortality rates than girls.

Although there is clearly an association between the rising rate of multiple birth and the use of ovarian stimulants and assisted conception, it is impossible to quantify this using routine statistics. The increasing birth rates among older women are also likely to have reinforced the upward trends.

With increasing numbers of very preterm babies surviving, there are concerns about morbidity in the survivors. These are discussed in Chapters 8 and 9, but before doing so, we consider data about the care provided for mothers and babies.

References

1   The wee totum. In: Ord J, ed. *The bothy songs and ballads of Aberdeen, Banff and Moray, Angus and the Mearns.* Paisley: A. Gardner, 1930.

2   Chambers R, ed. *The book of days: a miscellany of popular antiquities.* Vol. II, p.39. London and Edinburgh: W & R Chambers, 1866.

3   Nightingale F. *Introductory notes on lying-in institutions.* London: Longmans, Green and Co, 1871.

4   Cone TE. The history of weighing the newborn infant. *Pediatrics* 1961; 28: 490–498.

5   Local Government Board. *Report by the Medical Officer on infant and child mortality. Supplement to the thirty-ninth annual report of the Local Government Board, 1909–1910.* Cd 5312. London: HMSO, 1910.

6   Local Government Board. *Second report by the Medical Officer on infant and child mortality. Supplement to the forty-second annual report of the Local Government Board, 1912–1913.* Cd 6909. London: HMSO, 1913.

7   Local Government Board. *Third report by the Medical Officer on infant mortality in Lancashire. Supplement to the forty-third annual report of the Local Government Board, 1913–14.* Cd 7511. London: HMSO, 1914.

8   Newman G. *Infant mortality.* London: Methuen and Co., 1906.

9   Brownlee J. The changes in the physiological processes of the developing child as shown by its response to certain diseases. In: *Mortalities of birth, infancy and childhood.* Medical Research Committee Special Report Series No. 10. London: HMSO, 1917.

10   Holland E. *The causation of fetal deaths*. Reports on Public Health and Medical Subjects No. 5. London: HMSO, 1922.

11   Browne FJ. On the weight and the length of normal fetuses and the weights of fetal organs based on a series of 218 selected cases in Edinburgh. In: *Child life investigations*. Medical Research Council Report No. 86. London: HMSO, 1924.

12   Holland EL, Lane-Claypon JE. *A clinical and pathological study of 1673 cases of dead-births and neonatal deaths*. Medical Research Council Report No. 109. London: HMSO, 1926.

13   Cruickshank J. *The causes of neonatal death*. Medical Research Council Report No. 118. London: HMSO, 1930.

14   Bruce Murray, M. *The effect of maternal social conditions and nutrition upon birthweight and birth length*. Medical Research Council Report No. 81. London: HMSO, 1924.

15   McKinlay PL. Statistical notes. In: Campbell, JM. *Infant mortality with statistical notes by P L McKinlay*. Reports on Public Health and Medical Subjects No. 55. London: HMSO, 1929.

16   Ylppo A. Zur Physiologie, Klinik, und zum Schicksal der Fruhgeborenen. *Zeitschrift Fur Kinderheilkunde* 1919; 24: 1–110.

17   Ministry of Health. *Annual report of the Chief Medical Officer for the year 1937*. London: HMSO, 1938.

18   Department of Health and Social Security. *Annual report of the Chief Medical Officer for the year 1970*. London: HMSO, 1971.

19   Working party to discuss nomenclature based on gestational age and birthweight. *Archives of Disease In Childhood* 1970; 45(243): 730.

20   World Health Organization. *International classification of diseases. Manual of the international statistical classification of diseases, injuries and causes of death. Ninth revision*. Vol. 1. Geneva: WHO, 1977.

21   World Health Organization. *International statistical classification of diseases and related health problems. Tenth revision*. Vol. 1. Geneva: WHO, 1992.

22   Kemp M, Gunnell D, Davey Smith G, Frankel S. Finding and using inter-war maternity records. *Social History of Medicine* 1997; 10(2): 305–329.

23   Kuh D, Ben-Shlomo Y, eds. *A life course approach to chronic disease epidemiology*. Oxford: Oxford University Press, 1997.

24   Barker DJP, Winter PD, Osmond C, Margetts BM, Simmonds SJ. Weight in infancy and death from ischaemic heart disease. In: Barker DJP, ed. *Fetal and infant origins of adult disease*. London: BMJ, 1992.

25   Ministry of Health. *On the state of the public health during six years of war. Report of the Chief Medical Officer, 1939–1945*. London: HMSO, 1946.

26   Ministry of Health. *Annual report of the Chief Medical Officer for the year 1953*. Cmd 9307. London: HMSO, 1954.

27   Lewis AF. Linking birthweight and birth registration data. *Community Medicine* 1980; 2(1): 7–19.

28   Milner RD, Richards B. An analysis of birth weight by gestational age of infants born in England and Wales, 1967 to 1971. *Journal of Obstetrics and Gynaecology of the British Commonwealth* 1974; 81(12): 956–967.

29   Thomson AM, Billewicz WZ, Hytten FE. The assessment of fetal growth. *Journal of Obstetrics and Gynaecology of the British Commonwealth* 1968; 75(9): 903–916.

30   Department of Health. NHS maternity statistics, England: 1989–90 to 1994–95. *Statistical Bulletin* 1997/28: 1–44.

31   Magowan BA, Bain M, Juszczak E, McInnery K. Neonatal mortality among Scottish preterm singleton births (1988–1994). *British Journal of Obstetrics and Gynaecology* 1998; 105: 1003–1010.

32   Information and Statistics Division. *Births in Scotland 1976–1995.* Edinburgh: ISD, 1997.

33   Information and Statistics Division and Scottish Programme for Clinical Effectiveness in Reproductive Health. *Small babies in Scotland: a ten year overview, 1987–1996.* Births in Scotland Publication Series. Edinburgh: ISD, 1998.

34   Fryer JG, Ashford JR. Trends in perinatal and neonatal mortality in England and Wales 1960–69. *British Journal of Preventive and Social Medicine* 1972; 26(1): 1–9.

35   Ashford JR, Read KL, Riley VC. An analysis of variations in perinatal mortality amongst local authorities in England and Wales. *International Journal of Epidemiology* 1973; 2(1): 31–46.

36   Fryer JG, Harding RA, Macdonald MD, Read KLQ, Abernathy JR. Comparing the early mortality rates of the local authorities of England and Wales. *Journal of the Royal Statistical Society* 1979; 142A: 181–198.

37   Pethybridge RJ, Ashford JR, Fryer JG. Some features of the distribution of birthweight of human infants. *British Journal of Preventive and Social Medicine* 1974; 28(1): 10–18.

38   Brimblecombe FS, Ashford JR. Significance of low birth weight in perinatal mortality. A study of variations within England and Wales. *British Journal of Preventive and Social Medicine* 1968; 22(1): 27–35.

39   Hellier JL, Goldstein H. The use of birthweight and gestation to assess perinatal mortality risk. *Journal of Epidemiology and Community Health* 1979; 33(3): 183–185.

40   Alberman E. Stillbirths and neonatal mortality in England and Wales by birthweight, 1953–71. *Health Trends* 1974; 6: 14–17.

41   Pharoah PO, Alberman ED. Mortality of low birthweight infants in England and Wales 1953 to 1979. *Archives of Disease In Childhood* 1981; 56(2): 86–89.

42   Macfarlane AJ, Johnson A, Mugford M. Epidemiology. In: Rennie J, Roberton NR, ed. *A textbook of neonatology.* 3rd edition. Edinburgh: Churchill Livingstone, 1999.

43   Alberman E, Botting B. Trends in prevalence and survival of very low birthweight infants, England and Wales: 1983–7. *Archives of Disease in Childhood* 1991; 66: 1304–1308.

44   Power C. National trends in birth weight: implications for future adult disease. *BMJ* 1994; 308: 1270–1271.

45   Alberman E. Are our babies becoming bigger? *Journal of the Royal Society of Medicine* 1991; 84: 257–260.

46   Bakketeig LS. The risk of repeated preterm or low birthweight delivery. In: Reed DM, Stanley FJ, eds. *The epidemiology of prematurity.* Baltimore, Munich: Urban and Schwarzenberg, 1977.

47   Herman AA, McCarthy BJ, Bakewell JM, Ward RH, Mueller BA, Maconochie NE, Read AW, Zadka P, Skjaerven R. Data linkage methods used in maternally-linked birth and infant death surveillance data sets from the United States (Georgia, Missouri, Utah and Washington State), Israel, Norway, Scotland and Western Australia. *Paediatric and Perinatal Epidemiology* 1997; 11(S1): 15–22.

48   Macran S, Leon DA. *Patterns and determinants of birth weight in consecutive live births: results from the OPCS Longitudinal Study, 1980–88.* Series LS Working Paper No.74. London: City University, 1995.

49   Skjaerven R, Wilcox AJ, Øen N, Magnus P. Mothers' birth weight and survival of their offspring: population based study. *BMJ* 1997; 314(7091): 1376–1380.

50   Cole S. Scottish maternity and neonatal records. In: Chalmers I, McIlwaine G, eds. *Perinatal audit and surveillance.* London: Royal College of Obstetricians and Gynaecologists, 1980.

51   *The oak and the ash.* Version recorded from Florence Chedgy. Cecil Sharp manuscripts, 1909.

52   Macfarlane AJ. Official statistics and women's health and illness. In: Roberts H, ed. *Women's health counts.* London: Routledge, 1990.

53   Farr W. Report to the Registrar General. In: *Fifth report of the Registrar General for the year 1841.* London: Longman, Brown, Green and Longman, 1843.

54   Farr W. Report to the Registrar General. In: *Fortieth report of the Registrar General for the year 1877.* London: HMSO, 1879.

55   General Register Office. *Census of England and Wales, 1871.* Vol. IV: General report. London: HMSO, 1873:55.

56   Glass DV. A note on the under-registration of births in Britain in the nineteenth century. *Population Studies* 1951; 5: 70–88.

57   Quetelet LAJ. *Physique sociale: un essai sur le développement des facultés de l'homme.* Brussels: C. Murquardt, 1869.

58   Diamond M, Stone M. Nightingale on Quetelet II: the marginalia. *Journal of the Royal Statistical Society, Series A* 1981; 144: 176–213.

59   Taylor WA. A note on the sex distribution of sibs. *British Journal of Preventive and Social Medicine* 1954; 8: 178–179.

60   Hytten FE. Boys and girls. *British Journal of Obstetrics and Gynaecology* 1982; 89(2): 97–99.

61   Spina bifida and the sex ratio [editorial]. *British Medical Journal* 1980; 280(6222): 1098.

62   Allan TM. British stillbirths and first week deaths. *British Journal of Preventive and Social Medicine* 1969; 14: 35–38.

63   Russell WT. Statistical study of the sex ratio at birth. *Journal of Hygiene* 1936; 36: 381–401.

64   General Register Office. *The Registrar General's statistical review for England and Wales. Text, Civil, 1940–1945.* London: HMSO, 1951.

65   General Register Office. *The Registrar General's statistical review for England and Wales. Text, Civil, 1946–1950.* London: HMSO, 1954.

66   Martin WJ. The sex ratio. *The Medical Officer* 1948; 79: 153–156.

67   Lowe CR, McKeown T. The sex ratio of human births related to maternal age. *British Journal of Preventive and Social Medicine* 1950; 4: 75–85.

68   Britton M, Edison N. The changing balance of the sexes in England and Wales, 1851–2001. *Population Trends* 1986; 46: 22–25.

69   Craig J. Males and females: some vital differences. *Population Trends* 1995; 80: 26–30.

70   Shaw C. The sex ratio at birth in England and Wales. *Population Trends* 1989; 57: 26–29.

71   Dickinson HO, Parker L. Why is the sex ratio falling in England and Wales? [letter]. *Journal of Epidemiology and Community Health* 1996; 50: 227–230.

72   Davis DL, Gottlieb MB, Stampnitzky JR. Reduced ratio of male to female births in several industrialised countries. *Journal of the American Medical Association* 1998; 279(3): 1018–1023.

73   James WH. The decline in sex ratios at birth in England and Wales, 1973–90. [letter]. *Journal of Epidemiology and Community Health* 1996; 50: 690.

74   Dickinson HO, Parker L. Decline in sex ratios at birth, England and Wales, 1973–90 [letter]. *Journal of Epidemiology and Community Health* 1997; 51(1): 103.

75   Walby AL, Merrett JD, Dean G, Kirke P. Sex ratio of births in Ireland in 1978. *Ulster Medical Journal* 1981; 50(2): 83–87.

76   Allan TM. ABO blood groups and human sex ratio at birth. *Journal of Reproduction and Fertility* 1975; 43(2): 209–219.

77   Snyder RG. The sex ratio of offspring of pilots of high performance military aircraft. *Human Biology* 1961; 33: 1–10.

78   Goerres HP, Gerbert K. Sex ratio in offspring of pilots: a contribution to stress research. *Aviation Space and Environmental Medicine* 1976; 47(8): 889–892.

79   Lyster WR. Altered sex ratio in children of divers [letter]. *Lancet* 1982; ii(8290): 152.

80   Lloyd M, Lloyd O, Lyster W. Slugs and snails against sugar and spice [editorial]. *BMJ* 1988; 297: 1027–1028.

81   James WH. Gonadotrophin and sex ratio [letter]. *Lancet* 1980; ii(8191): 430.

82   James WH. The human sex ratio. Part 1: a review of the literature. *Human Biology* 1987; 59(5): 721–752.

83   James WH, Roston J. Parental age, parity and sex ratio. *Journal of Biosocial Science* 1988; 17: 47–56.

84   Maconochie N, Roman E. Sex ratios: are there natural variations within the human population? *British Journal of Obstetrics and Gynaecology* 1997; 104: 1050–1053.

85   James WH. Sex ratio, coital rate, hormones and time of fertilisation. *Annals of Human Biology* 1997; 24(5): 403–409.

86   Guerrero R. Association of the type and time of insemination within the menstrual cycle with the human sex ratio at birth. *New England Journal of Medicine* 1974; 291(20): 1056–1059.

87   Revelle R. On rhythm and sex ratio [editorial]. *New England Journal of Medicine* 1974; 291(20): 1083.

88   James WH. Time of fertilisation and sex of infants. *Lancet* 1980; i(8178): 1124–1126.

89   *The family ointment.* Traditional Irish song. Sung by Tim Lyons from the singing of Willy Clancy on Easter Snow, Innisfree. SIF 1014. New Canaan, Conn. USA: Green Linnet, 1978.

90   Dunn A, Macfarlane AJ. Recent trends in the incidence of multiple births and associated mortality in England and Wales. *Archives of Disease in Childhood* 1996; 75(1): F10–F19.

91   Botting B, Macdonald Davies I, Macfarlane AJ. Recent trends in multiple births and associated mortality. *Archives of Disease In Childhood* 1987; 66: 941–950.

92   Wood R. Trends in multiple births, 1938–1995. *Population Trends* 1997; 87: 29–35.

93   Heady JA, Heasman MA. *Social and biological factors in infant mortality.* Studies on Medical and Population Subjects No. 15. London: HMSO, 1959.

94 Campbell DM, MacGillivray J. Outcome of twin pregnancies. In: MacGillivray J, Campbell DM, Thompson B, eds. *Twinning and twins*. Chichester: John Wiley, 1988.

95 Botting BJ, Macfarlane AJ, Price FV. *Three, four and more: a national survey of triplet and higher order births*. London: HMSO, 1990.

96 Levene MI, Wild J, Steer P. Higher multiple births and the modern management of infertility in Britain. *British Journal of Obstetrics and Gynaecology* 1992; 99: 607–613.

97 Murphy M, Hey K, Brown J, Willis B, Ellis JD, Barlow D. Infertility treatment and multiple birth rates in Britain, 1938–94. *Journal of Biosocial Science* 1997; 29: 235–243.

7   Care of mothers and babies

'There are several of what may be called secondary influences also, which must affect to a certain extent the results of comparisons of death rates among different groups of lying-in cases... . Such are the general sanitary state of hospitals, wards, houses and rooms where deliveries take place; the management adopted; the classes of patients; their state of health and stamina before delivery; the time they are kept in midwifery wards before and after delivery. These elements are directly connected with the questions at issue, and yet our information regarding them is by no means as full as we could wish – indeed is almost nothing.'

Florence Nightingale, *Introductory notes on lying-in institutions, 1871.*[1]

'Our greatest hope is that, in five years' time, the principles embodied in this report will have become so widely accepted and its practices so commonplace that *Changing childbirth* will have done its work and can take its place on the shelf of history.'

Department of Health, *Changing childbirth, 1993.*[2]

'The purpose of the NHS is "to secure through the resources available the greatest possible improvement in the physical and mental health of the people ... by: promoting health; preventing ill health; diagnosing and treating injury and disease; caring for people with long term illness and disability who need services of the NHS". The NHS executive has identified three key results which it wishes to see achieved by the NHS . . . These are: equity – improving the health of the population as a whole and reducing variations in health status by targeting resources where needs are greatest; efficiency – providing patients with treatment and care which is both effective and good value for money; responsiveness – meeting the needs and wishes of individual patients.'

The new NHS: modern, dependable, 1997.[3]

The first fundamental principle underlying the National Health Service, set out in the Coalition Government's White Paper of 1944 was to 'divorce the care of health from questions of personal means or other factors irrelevant to it.'[4] This objective has been under attack, and may never have been completely achieved.[5,6] As we have shown in Chapter 5, social class differentials in the outcome of pregnancy still persist. The questions of the effectiveness, appropriateness and availability of care and assistance during pregnancy and childbirth have always been, and will probably continue to be the subject of controversy, some of it heated.

In this chapter we try to assess the extent to which routinely collected statistics can describe the resources available, the patterns of care and their relationship with the outcomes of pregnancy. The collection of data has developed as a direct consequence of the way publicly funded maternity services grew up during the twentieth century, so it is relevant to summarise how this came about. We start by giving an overview of this process, before going on to describe and assess the data collected about the resources available for mothers, newborn babies and young children in terms of facilities and staff and the patterns of care provided.

At the beginning of the twentieth century, the most destitute women could receive assistance under the Poor Law or possibly from charities. This could either take the form of 'outdoor relief' to pay a midwife for delivery at home, or admission to workhouse infirmaries for delivery. Starting with its *Annual report* for 1910–11,[7] the Local Government Board published data about women who delivered in some workhouses. In doing so, it repeated its earlier claim that the high rate of infant and maternal mortality was 'due to pre-natal and maternal conditions entirely unconnected with and independent of the character of the administration of the lying-in wards.'[8] On the other hand, the *Minority report of the Poor Laws Commission*[9] published in 1909 suggested there was considerable scope for improving maternity care in workhouses. The *Minority report* is also a source of fuller data about the extent to which workhouses were used as maternity hospitals. The other institutions involved in maternity care were the charities, established from the eighteenth century onwards, to provide maternity care in 'lying-in institutions' and at home.[1,10,11]

The questions about the quality of the care provided at this time and the training of midwives need to be viewed against a background of the controversy about the respective roles of doctors and midwives. In these disputes, assessing the relative merits of the care provided was not a major issue.[12,13] Also, in the first decade of the twentieth century, rising national concern about infant mortality led some local authorities to set up special projects such as 'milk depots', on a model pioneered in France, and 'schools for mothers'.[14-17] Under the Notification of Births Act of 1907, local authorities could set up schemes for notifying births and for providing health visiting and clinics for the babies identified through birth notification. The Women's Co-operative Guild and others campaigned to have this extended to a wider range of maternity services.[18]

The Notification of Births (Extension) Act, passed in 1915, made the notification of births compulsory and extended the role of health visitors. Some local authorities used this information on notification to compile statistics. The Maternity and Child Welfare Act, passed in 1918, gave local authorities powers to provide clinics, home visiting and either maternity homes or maternity beds in existing institutions. Under the Local Government Act of 1929, local authorities were given the option of taking over Poor Law hospitals and were given block grants by central government to provide a range of services. The Midwives Act of 1936 required them to provide a salaried midwifery service, or finance voluntary bodies to do so. Similar legislation had been passed to cover Scotland but the Maternity Services (Scotland) Act, passed in 1937, went further and provided the services of a doctor as well as a midwife for home deliveries. Political and Economic Planning, now known as the Policy Studies Institute, reviewed the extent of the maternity services before and immediately after the second world war.[19,20]

The beginnings of national data collection

The Ministry of Health was set up in 1919 'to promote the health of the people'. One of the four 'immediate and operative factors' which led to this was 'the necessity for taking further measures to secure the health and welfare of child-bearing women and infants, and of reducing the number of authorities concerned with such measures.'[21]

The new ministry had a maternal and child welfare department, headed by Janet Campbell 'assisted by a staff of women doctors, nurses and midwives'.[21] Their task was to co-ordinate and monitor the way local authorities implemented the various Acts of Parliament. As part of this work, the ministry collected statistics from local authorities, which it discussed and summarised in the *Annual report of the Ministry of Health* and the *Annual report of the Chief Medical Officer*. The Welsh Board of Health and the Scottish Board of Health, later the Scottish Department of Health, which were also set up in 1919, did similar work. As had been the case from the end of the nineteenth century, the medical officer of health for each local authority was required to produce an annual report and these reports are a useful source of local data up to 1973.

The number of local authority returns to central government increased over the years. In particular, there was a considerable increase in data collection when the National Health Service came into being in 1948. In 1974, the responsibility for completing many of these returns was passed from local authorities to the newly established health authorities. In the early 1980s, the Steering Group on Health Services Information chaired by Edith Körner recommended major changes to data collection in England, including a change from calendar to financial years for data collection.[22] Most of these were implemented in the financial year 1987/88 but the recommendations about maternity data were implemented some 18 months later.[22,23] Similar changes occurred in Wales and Northern Ireland, but not in Scotland, which had developed a different system of data collection. The changes created discontinuities in the statistical series shown in many of the tables discussed in this chapter. These made it difficult to monitor trends over time.

From 1974 onwards, regional health authorities played a key role in co-ordinating NHS data collection in England. They had information departments which collated data for their regions and many published regional reports. Their abolition in 1996 led to gaps in the data about maternity care, amongst other things.[24] After this, statistical returns were made directly by trusts and health authorities to the Department of Health. Increasingly, they were in electronic form.

Until 1986, data about numbers of beds and patients in each maternity unit were collected in the Hospital Return, SH3. A national summary of these data for England and Wales was first published in the *Annual report of the Chief Medical Officer* for the year ending March 31 1949.[25] Later, these data were published separately for England and Wales. Similar data were published for Scotland and Northern Ireland. In the early 1980s, the Steering Group on Health Services Information set out criteria for a new set of statistical returns which were implemented in England in the financial year 1987/88. Many of these so called 'Körner' returns are also used in Wales and Northern Ireland.

Data from hospitals are usually compiled in medical records departments by staff who spend all their time on this work. Even so, anomalies can arise, particularly if relationships with midwifery and medical staff are not well established. From the early 1980s onwards, maternity units started to develop computerised information systems to collect the data they needed to monitor and audit their work. Unfortunately many of these were stand-alone systems unlinked to their hospital system, so many of the data in them have not ended up in national statistics.[26,27] Since the introduction of the NHS internal market in April 1991, national data have been collected on a trust-wide basis, making no distinction between maternity units within an NHS trust.

In community trusts, there may not be a separate information department, and the work of form filling or data entry into information systems is usually done by the field workers, such as community midwives and health visitors, in addition to their professional activities. The problem is compounded by the fact that the data they are asked to collect may seem to have little direct relevance to the problems they face. The people who complete the forms may receive very little feedback and do not trust the comparative statistics, as they know there are inaccuracies in data they have themselves submitted. A welcome development during the 1990s was the publication of increasing amounts of data about both community and local authority social services, both on paper and in electronic form on diskettes or on the internet.

In addition, as described in Chapter 11, health authorities and trusts submit annual accounts to the financial section of the NHS Executive. Because of the way the data are collected, they cannot be used to identify the resources used in the maternity services.

Towards person-based data

Although these administrative returns can generate some data about the facilities provided, the numbers of staff involved and the numbers of women and babies using the facilities, they do not tell us anything about the state of health of either, or of the type of care women and babies receive. This deficiency was recognised many years ago. For example, the *Registrar General's statistical review* for 1933 commented that:

'Although no national statistics are available of the frequency with which caesarean section is resorted to, this frequency has certainly increased during the past decade and this is reflected in the increasing numbers of deaths with mention of this operation.'[28]

The need for statistics about people admitted to hospital and the outcome of the care they received was already recognised by the mid nineteenth century.[29,30] In a paper written for the International Statistical Congress in London in 1860, Florence Nightingale set out a 'proposal for an uniform plan of hospital statistics'.[31] William Farr, who had attended the congress, commented in the *Twenty-fourth annual report of the Registrar General*:

> 'The Commissioners in Lunacy, the Inspectors of Prisons and the Poor Law Commissioner publish in their annual reports accounts of the respective institutions which come under their cognisance. The statistics of the hospitals of the country are not given at all, or are not given upon a uniform plan. Miss Nightingale, who perceived all the importance of this information, suggested that hospital statistics should be collected in forms of which the members of the statistical congress in London approved. And if the hospital boards carry out the plan, they will place the hospital statistics on a level with those of the other institutions of the country.'[32]

Florence Nightingale's system or something similar was adopted in Army and Navy hospitals in the late 1850s. Nineteenth century annual reports on the health of the Army and the Navy contained detailed analyses of data collected about people admitted to military hospitals. Arthur Newsholme reported that various attempts to set up a similar system in civilian hospitals had not been very successful.[33] He also advocated that: 'every public institution for the treatment of the sick should give to the medical officer of health a weekly statement of the number of new in-patients and out-patients treated during the week, specifying the age, sex and nature of the illness of patients'.[34]

The first attempt to do something along these lines on a national scale was made during the second world war. The Ministry of Pensions set up a central registry of records of patients admitted to Emergency Medical Service Hospitals. These hospitals admitted members of the armed forces, civilians injured in air raids and also some other civilians. The Ministry wanted to use the data to assess applications for war pensions. The cause of admission to hospital was coded according to the Internal Classification of Diseases and data were published in the *Report of the Chief Medical Officer* for 1939–1945.[35] Thus, the Emergency Medical Service set some precedents for the National Health Service, and the data collection system used in it was the forerunner of the Hospital In-patient Enquiry (HIPE).

In 1947, a scheme was set up to obtain minimal data about hospital in-patients to provide a 'comprehensive body of knowledge about the large group of people admitted to hospital for in-patient treatment'.[36] In 1948, Percy Stocks, the Chief Medical Statistician at the General Register Office (GRO), arranged for monthly returns covering 87 selected hospitals, mainly teaching hospitals, to be sent from Regional Hospital Boards to the GRO.

The enquiry was expanded in 1952, when it was decided to take a ten per cent sample of discharges from all NHS non-psychiatric hospitals. As it was apparent that different basic information needed to be collected about maternity care, a special form containing additional items such as mode of delivery, parity and date of delivery, was introduced for maternity patients.[37] In theory, Maternity HIPE was based on a ten per cent sample of all deliveries but there were considerable local variations in the way the sample was selected, the way data were collected, and in their completeness.[38-40]

Its successor, the Maternity Hospital Episode Statistics (HES) came into operation in the financial year 1989/90, two years after the rest of HES, and has always been incomplete. It was intended to contain data about all episodes of in-patient care, but lacks data for about a third of delivery episodes.[41] Like HIPE, there is no linkage about a person's successive spells of in-patient care, although this should be possible in the future once NHS numbers are on all NHS records. In addition to the standard items in the admitted patient record, delivery and birth records have a 'maternity tail' with data about the birth. These include the method of onset of labour and of delivery, the numbers of babies born and their birthweights. The set of data items collected for all in-patients combined with the items in the 'maternity tail' is known as the 'maternity minimum dataset'.

Neonatal care comes under the specialty of paediatrics, so up to 1986 hospital data about admissions to neonatal units were recorded in the main Hospital In-patient Enquiry. As there were relatively small numbers of babies in the sample, and full ward admission procedures were not always carried out when a baby had a very short stay for observation or tests, the data from this source were very variable and unreliable. Neonatal care is still recorded in the main Hospital Episode System, rather than in Maternity HES. Only the general items in the admitted patient record, such as diagnosis, operations and length of time in hospital are recorded. There is currently no linkage with the records of the babies' delivery, although proposals to issue babies NHS numbers at birth should make this possible in the future.[42] Until then it is not possible to analyse data about neonatal care in relation to birth details, except in special studies.

Wales and Northern Ireland have similar systems, but very few of their maternity records have a 'maternity tail' with complete data. In these two countries, alternative ways of collecting maternity data, via child health computer systems, are being explored.

In Scotland, more extensive data about women having babies as hospital in-patients are collected on the SMR2 maternity discharge sheet. It was first introduced in 1969 in a limited set of hospitals. By 1975, some 96 per cent of hospital deliveries were included and since then coverage of hospital deliveries has been virtually complete. Coverage of home births was still not quite complete at the end of the 1990s, however. The SMR11 neonatal record, to which we referred in the previous chapter, had nearly complete coverage by 1981. The system as a whole is now known as the 'Core patient profile information in Scottish hospitals' (COPPISH). As Scotland has a well advanced system of record linkage, data about mothers, babies and neonatal care can be linked.[43-45]

Administrative returns and hospital discharge data are the sources of most of the routinely collected data about the care provided in pregnancy, labour and the puerperium, although there are others, and they are described in what follows. In doing so, we will discuss the extent to which this body of data can provide information about the facilities available, the staff working in them, and the care they provide. Statistical returns in England are listed in an annual Health Service Circular *Central data collections from the NHS*. The Department of Health issues this to health authorities and trusts and places it on its web site, details of which are given in Appendix 1. The National Assembly for Wales, formerly the Welsh Office, publishes a similar list in an appendix to *Health statistics Wales*, while *Scottish health statistics* includes accounts of how data are collected.

This book is going to press at a time when new information strategies have been published, offering a potential for improvement in data collection.[46-48] The chapter therefore closes with a discussion of their implications, in the light of other current changes.

Facilities in the NHS

In the late 1990s, over 99 per cent of births took place within the NHS, and very little neonatal intensive care was done outside the NHS, probably because of the expense involved. There have never been statutory requirements for levels of staffing or items of equipment in NHS maternity and neonatal units. The government has no agreed criteria for assessing the adequacy or otherwise of local services. This is despite the fact that from the 1960s onwards, a succession of reports from parliamentary and professional bodies has called for 'minimum standards', for maternity care.[49-51]

In the mid 1970s, the Committee on Child Health Services demanded more facilities for neonatal special and intensive care.[52] In its wide ranging *Priorities for health and social services in England*, published in 1976, the government expressed the view that 'in general hospital maternity services have attracted too large a share of resources' but that there was 'an urgent need to improve the level of care for low birthweight and sick newborn babies'.[53] This prompted the high profile 'Save a baby' campaign which demanded more facilities and medical staff for maternity and neonatal services.

In response to this, further calls for standards followed in the 1980s, in the House of Commons Social Services Committee's report on *Perinatal and neonatal mortality*[54] and the Maternity Services Advisory Committee's reports on antenatal, intrapartum and postnatal care.[55-57] More specific demands came from professional bodies, in the Royal College of Physicians' report on neonatal care,[58] guidelines from the Royal College of Obstetricians and Gynaecologists on antenatal and intrapartum care[59] and the Obstetric Anaesthetists Association's report on small maternity units.[60]

Neonatal care was a particular issue in the 1980s, as it was developing rapidly and expensive to provide. In 1971, the Expert Group on Special Care for Babies, known as the Sheldon Committee, had recommended a target of six neonatal cots per 1,000 live births.[61] This was based on the assumption that all low birthweight babies and all babies delivered operatively needed special care nursing and other reports in the mid 1970s made similar recommendations.[62,63] The assumption was challenged on the grounds that babies at the upper end of the low birthweight range who were not ill were better off nursed on postnatal wards.[64] This policy was subsequently adopted and became widespread. The need to distinguish between 'special' and 'intensive' care became more apparent in the reports which emerged in the 1980s and early 1990s.[58,65-67] The problems involved in defining these terms are discussed later.

This succession of reports emerged in an era when central government was reluctant to set norms and standards for any of its services. When the House of Commons Health Committee, as it was now called, returned to the subject of maternity care in the early 1990s, its focus was on care for women in normal labour and delivery.[68] Rather than making uncritical demands for the latest technology, as in the past, it asked questions about clinical effectiveness, having been influenced by the publication *Effective care in pregnancy and childbirth*.[69] Both its report, and the Department of Health's response in the Expert Maternity Group's report *Changing childbirth*, concentrated on the co-ordinated organisation and provision of care rather than quantified 'standards'.[2] With establishment of the Cochrane Collaboration, whose activities were originally developed in the perinatal field, clinical effectiveness rose up the agenda.

Reports which emerged subsequently from clinical organisations reflected these concerns while also setting out standards for staffing and facilities. The Clinical Standards Advisory Group published a report on access to neonatal intensive care in 1993.[66] Three years later the British Association of Perinatal Medicine published standards for hospitals providing neonatal intensive care.[67] Minimum standards for care in labour published by the Royal College of Obstetricians and Gynaecologists in 1994 attempted to establish guidelines for staffing, equipment and general facilities on the labour ward.[70] The Obstetric Anaesthetists Association published minimum standards for obstetric anaesthesia services the following year.[71] By the time that the Royal College of Obstetricians and Gynaecologists published a second report, in 1999, this time in conjunction with the Royal College of Midwives, the government agenda had changed.[72]

The change of government in 1997 brought in a new concern for setting national standards for quality in the NHS generally. This was announced in the white paper, *The new NHS: modern and dependable*, and arrangements were set out in greater detail in *A first class service*.[3,73] A National Institute for Clinical Excellence (NICE) was set up to 'provide a focus' for setting clinical standards. Each major care area or disease group will have national service frameworks which lay out what users can expect to receive from the NHS. Arrangements for 'clinical governance' are intended to ensure that standards are met.[74] This includes requiring staff to maintain their professional skills through encouraging 'lifelong learning' and professional self regulation. The Commission for Health Improvement is intended to monitor quality in the NHS through visits to providers, and external audits. Under the *National framework for assessing performance*, clinical indicators have been defined and published for named providers.[75-77] Finally, a new national survey of patient and user experience of the NHS has been commissioned and is under way.

The data collected about care that women receive from the National Health Service during pregnancy, delivery and afterwards relate to the use of primary care and community care services, place of delivery, the attendant at delivery, the clinical activity and the length of hospital stay. We have tried, where possible, to relate the provision of services and activities to the sizes of the groups of women and babies whom they are most likely to serve.

Maternity units

The numbers of births in each hospital each year were recorded on the hospital return SH3, up to 1986. The corresponding Körner return, KH03, was used from 1987/88 onward to record births, along with other activities, by NHS trust rather than by hospital. Since small maternity units are grouped together with other units in trusts, comparison with earlier years would not have been possible using these data. Therefore birth registrations have been tabulated by actual place of birth, to enable comparisons to be made with data from earlier years.

Tables A7.1.1 to A7.1.4 show the numbers of units and of births in them, grouped by size of unit, in the countries of the United Kingdom, for selected years between 1973 and 1996. Changes in the United Kingdom are illustrated in Figures 7.1 and 7.2. Data for England in Table A7.1.1 are also presented for 1973–86 according to whether the 'type' of bed was consultant or general practitioner maternity. After 1986, this statistical breakdown was possible, but the definition of types of bed had changed. The table shows the trend in numbers of units grouped by numbers of births per year. It also shows the trend in numbers of births in units of different size. The overall trend is away from small units towards larger units. Numbers of units with fewer than 200 births per year fell from 85 in 1973 to 45 in 1996. This excludes the 75 hospitals and other locations with under ten births in 1996. By and large these were hospitals in which one or two births took place, presumably unintentionally. Most small maternity units are general practitioner units whose numbers fell from 221 units in 1973 to only 91 in 1986. Meanwhile, the numbers of large units, with more than 3000 births per year, increased from 38 in 1973 to 99 in 1990 and fell slightly to 93 in 1996.

The numbers of maternity units with 4000 or more births per year, increased in England until 1990, and fell slightly by 1996. In Wales and Scotland, however, these units declined in number, while Northern Ireland has never had a unit of this size. Trust mergers, taking place at the time of writing, make it likely that data for the end of the 1990s will show further concentration of births into even larger units.

The reasons for the gradual and continuing shift to larger maternity units is documented in *Where to be born? The debate and the evidence*.[11] Perceptions, whether based on evidence or not, about the safety or otherwise of small

199

Figure 7.1

Numbers of maternity units by numbers of births in units, United Kingdom, 1996

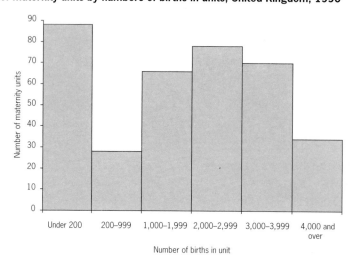

Source: Data in Tables A7.1.1–A7.1.4, excluding units stated to have less than 10 births

Figure 7.2

Distribution of births by numbers of births in units, United Kingdom, 1996

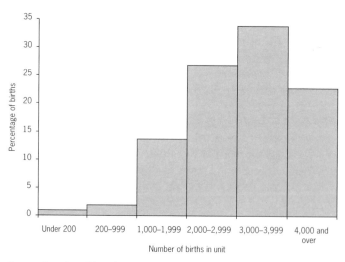

Source: Data in Tables A7.1.1–A7.1.4

units, the availability of around the clock anaesthesia, the problems of transfer to a specialist hospital in the event of problems and pressure from the Royal College of Obstetricians and Gynaecologists all contributed to the closure of small units. Many of these closures, particularly in rural areas, were hotly contested. Changes in specialist medical training, described later, are contributing to changes taking place at the end of the 1990s. This, together with redevelopment of hospitals under the private finance initiative, is leading to pressures to create smaller numbers of larger obstetric units. At the same time, the move to community-based care is leading to moves to set up free standing midwife led units and some have been opened.

Maternity beds

The KH03 return defines a bed slightly more loosely than its predecessor, the SH3 return, as the 'average number of staffed beds available daily during the year, including beds set up temporarily'. The definition of a bed or cot leaves it to local discretion to decide what constitutes adequate staff and facilities to provide treatment. There may well be differences between and within regions. Average daily available beds are calculated by adding the nightly count of available beds over the whole year and dividing it by the number of days in the year.

For the SH3 hospital return, beds were assigned to specialties on the basis of the specialty of the senior clinician supervising the care of the people who occupied them. Local organisation varied so that it was possible that some women, occupying beds normally assigned to consultant obstetricians, may actually have been under the care of general practitioners. The instructions for completing the SH3 return stated that: 'where a general practitioner is acting as a clinical assistant to a specialist the patients and beds should be shown against the appropriate specialist departments'. Where there was regular 'borrowing' of beds between specialties these beds were recorded as available to the borrowing specialty rather than the loaning specialty, but it appears that different conventions may have been adopted for allocating beds to specialties on the SH3 form depending on the arrangements between local general practitioner obstetricians and consultant obstetricians.

In 1987, a new category of 'mixed' maternity beds was introduced in England to deal with this classification problem which reflected a policy change. A joint working party of the Royal College of Obstetricians and Gynaecologists and the Royal College of General Practitioners recommended in 1981 that:

> 'General practitioners with recognised training in obstetrics should be given every assistance to have facilities within or adjacent to consultant units where they can deliver their selected patients. All consultant units should provide such facilities either within their unit or as part of a functionally integrated general practitioner unit.'[78]

This was restated in 1982 by the Working Party on Antenatal and Intrapartum Care.[59]

Routinely published statistics about available maternity beds do not include beds provided for labour and delivery, although they were included in SH3. Published data do not distinguish between beds provided specifically for antenatal care and beds for postnatal care.

Table A7.2.1 shows trends in numbers of available beds by 'type' of bed in England. Data are also shown for Wales, Scotland and Northern Ireland in Tables A7.2.2 to A7.2.4. It is clear that the provision and use of beds has changed dramatically, particularly with the decline in general practitioner maternity beds. In association with the decrease in the number of separate maternity units and shorter lengths of stay in hospital, the overall provision of NHS maternity beds had fallen from 59.3 per 1000 births in 1949, to 20 per 1000 maternities in 1994/95. Thus the total numbers of maternity beds fell by about half between 1975 and the mid 1990s, both in actual numbers and as a rate per 1000 maternities. By 1994/95, numbers of beds assigned specifically to general practitioner maternity care in England had declined to less than 20 per cent of the number in 1975. General practitioner maternity care continued to be provided in 'mixed beds'. A similar trend occurred in Wales and Scotland. In Northern Ireland, the numbers of separate general practitioner maternity beds had fallen to zero by 1996/97.

Trends in available maternity beds between 1981 and 1997/98 in each region in England are shown in Tables A7.2.5 to A7.2.8. Because of the changes in regional boundaries, each table covers the period between each boundary change since 1949. All regions have experienced declines in overall maternity bed availability. Differences between regions have persisted, and in 1997/98, the rate of beds per thousand maternities was lowest in the Anglia and Oxford region and highest in the North West region. These regional differences may reflect a variety of factors, including differences in definition of a bed, the historical legacy of resource allocation in the NHS, and 'local politics', as well as differing regional planning assumptions and financial decisions.

Neonatal cots

Trends in the availability of neonatal cots in each of the four countries of the United Kingdom since the mid 1970s are shown in Table A7.3.1 The overall picture is of a slight decline, both in absolute numbers of cots and in the numbers of cots per thousand live births. The data are difficult to interpret for a number of reasons, however. In each of the four countries data collection methods changed over the time period shown. As methods of data collection and definitions used differed from country to country, it is difficult to assess whether reported differences between rates of provision in the four countries were real.

The most important problem, however, is that none of the countries subdivided the cots into those for special and intensive care until England began to collect data about intensive care cots from 1996/97 onwards. This makes it difficult to interpret trends in provision at a time when the work of neonatal units was moving towards concentration on intensive care for the most preterm or ill babies. Policy changed away from admitting babies with minor illnesses or who simply weighed less than 2,500g at birth, on the grounds that these babies could be cared for more appropriately with their mothers on postnatal wards. Unfortunately routine statistics are inadequate for monitoring the implementation and impact of these changes.

In England, information about cots for special care and neonatal intensive care was collected through the SH3 hospital return up to 1986 and thereafter through the KH03 return. Cots provided for babies in postnatal wards were not recorded in the SH3 return, but were counted separately in the KH03 return from 1987/88 to 1995/96 as 'cots for well babies'. There was no differentiation in the SH3 return between special care and intensive care. In KH03, however, numbers of available and occupied cots were recorded as 'neonatal cots in non-maternity wards' from 1987/88 to 1995/96. Since 1996/97, this return has included numbers of 'neonatal intensive care cots' as a category in section 1 of the form. In addition, the availability and occupancy of cots has also been recorded under 'intensive care for neonates'. Hospital beds used by other sick babies is included in the more general category 'other general and acute: neonates and children'. It is therefore no longer possible to use data from this source to distinguish the bed use by babies from that by older children, and there is no longer a count of cots for 'well babies' in maternity wards on the KH03 return.

This confusion is not surprising, given the lack of consensus about how 'intensive' and 'special' care should be defined. As long ago as 1980, the House of Commons Social Services Committee recognised that intensive care was difficult to define. The most usual definition is that it includes such techniques as 'prolonged mechanical ventilation, total parenteral nutrition and the use of advanced monitoring techniques.' Intensive care also takes the form of very close observation by a highly skilled nurse whether or not any equipment is being used. It is perhaps in the light of this that a joint committee of the British Paediatric Association and the Royal College of Obstetricians and Gynaecologists suggested that one-to-one nursing was a necessary additional criterion for defining intensive care.[65]

Further definitions were proposed by the Steering Group on Health Services Information and in successive reports from professional bodies in the late 1980s and early 1990s.[23,58,66,67] The changes in the agreed definitions over this period reflected a consensus about the equipment and staffing needed for babies with different degrees of dependency. There was inevitable debate about the actual conditions which fell into each category of severity. Because the funding of neonatal units depended on the types of care which they could offer, there may have been some pressure to define care for babies at a higher level than strictly necessary. The first study to be published of actual resources required by babies in neonatal units in one region found that the definitions were unnecessarily complex. The intensity of resources needed for care was determined almost entirely by whether the baby had surgery and the extent of need for oxygen and ventilation.[79] These findings are increasingly being adopted in nationally agreed definitions. Despite this, a study of neonatal units throughout the United Kingdom in 1994 found little consistency between units in their definitions of levels of care.[80]

As was mentioned earlier, the definition adopted in England in 1996/97, aimed to identify how many cots are equipped and staffed for intensive care of babies. On the KH03 return the definition of cots for intensive care was changed to cots which are used 'to provide intensive care for the critically sick, vulnerable newborn babies whose sickness is a consequence of impaired growth and/or premature birth'.[81] When interpreting these data, it cannot be assumed that all hospitals follow the same definition of an intensive care cot.[80] This is reflected in the data for English regions shown in Tables A7.3.2 and A7.3.3. Table A7.3.3 shows that, in 1997/98, the provision of intensive care cots recorded in the KH03 return ranged from 2.9 per 1000 births in Trent NHS region, to 1.6 in the West Midlands.

Equipment

Over the years professional groups have drawn up recommendations about equipment they consider necessary for obstetric and neonatal care.[58,63,65,70,71,82] Neonatal care has attracted particular attention and reports from regional working parties during the 1980s suggested that many neonatal units differed from these recommended levels.[83,84] Other studies of the same era showed that maternity hospitals differed in the equipment available.[85,86] Despite this high level of interest, there are no statistics collected routinely about equipment and the only information available comes from occasional surveys.

The National Birthday Trust carried out a survey of facilities at the place of birth in the United Kingdom in 1984.[87] This investigated the availability of labour ward staff and equipment, and reported differences between regions and between hospitals. At that time, in the 531 maternity units surveyed, there was a real time ultrasound machine in 18 per cent of delivery areas, one or more electronic fetal monitors in 65 per cent, but fetal pH monitors in only 15 per cent. Infusion pumps were available in 66 per cent of delivery areas. In every case, equipment was more likely to be available in large units than in small units, and more likely to be available in units with consultant obstetric cover than in general practitioner units.

There has been no further national survey to monitor changes since 1984, although a more limited survey was done in Wales in the early 1980s.[88] The one exception to this was a national survey of obstetric ultrasound facilities in the early 1990s. It found that ultrasound technology had become widespread for antenatal use, and that most women at that time had at least one scan during pregnancy.[89]

In the past, when obstetric emergencies occurred outside hospital, a team of hospital obstetricians and paediatricians went out as an 'obstetric flying squad'. No national statistics were kept about this activity or the nature of the emergencies. In 1980, the Chief Medical Officer pointed out that obstetric flying squads were not available in some parts of England, while in others the absence of resident staff during a flying squad case effectively withdrew immediate obstetric cover from the hospital maternity unit.[90]

Around this time an RCOG Working Party Report recommended that obstetric and paediatric flying squads should be provided but should not, while on call, reduce staff in maternity units below a safe level.[59] Increasingly, obstetric flying squads were replaced by ambulance paramedics who are trained to care for women and babies on their way to hospital by ambulance. Although statistics are collected about the use made of ambulance services, these activities are not shown separately.

Facilities for social care of babies and young children

Local authority facilities available for care of babies and young children are documented in statistics about residential accommodation, places available for local authority and other nursery day care, and numbers of registered child minders. In addition to the bulletins published by the Department of Health, statistics are also published in *Health and personal social services statistics for England,* and for standard regions in *Regional trends.*

Table A7.4.1 shows the numbers of places in local authority and other types of pre-school provision, such as day nurseries, play groups, and with child minders. The general trend between 1984 and 1997 is of falling direct provision by local authorities and growing provision by registered play groups, day nurseries and child minders. Day nurseries and play groups provided by local authorities have declined by 26 and 39 per cent, respectively, since their high points in the late 1980s. Numbers of places in registered day nurseries have, however, increased sixfold and number of premises sevenfold. Registered play groups were at their most popular in the early 1990s and have since declined in number by 11 per cent. Registered child minders doubled in number between 1984 and 1992 but subsequently declined slightly in number, although the numbers of places with childminders have continued to increase. The reduction in numbers of child minders was because the Children Act of 1989, which came into force in 1991, required them to re-register with their local authority. The continuing increase in numbers of places with child minders arose from the new requirements to register places for 5 to 7 year olds. Numbers of full-time places in nursery schools fell slightly over the period 1984–95 but part-time places more than made up the difference, increasing by 18 per cent.

Similar data about family and child care in Northern Ireland are published in *Community statistics.* Data for Scotland are published by Scottish Executive Social Work Statistics and those for Wales can be obtained from the Welsh Health Statistics Analysis Unit.

Staff in the maternity services

The four central government health departments collect and publish the numbers of staff in the hospital and community health services in post on September 30 of each year. These data are usually described as 'workforce' statistics. Originally the data were collected on paper forms, but they are now derived from computerised payroll information and returned to the relevant department electronically.

In England, the Department of Health publishes annual statistical bulletins containing data from the medical and non-medical workforce census and further data appear in its other statistical publication series. Similar data appear in *Health statistics Wales* and *Scottish health statistics*, while data for Northern Ireland are published in its annual volumes of *Hospital statistics* and *Community statistics*.

Since many staff work less than full-time, numbers of whole-time equivalent staff provide a better basis for comparison. The whole-time equivalent is calculated by expressing the contract hours of staff as a proportion of the full-time contract hours or sessions. Numbers and rates of whole-time equivalent staff are given in Tables A7.5.1 to A7.10.2. When national agreements about full-time hours change, the basis for calculating whole-time equivalent changes, although the actual numbers of hours part-time staff are under contract to work may be unchanged. This in turn affects the numbers given for whole-time equivalent staff.

Health authorities were empowered to reduce nursing and midwifery staff's weekly hours from 40 hours to 37.5 from April 1980 but it was not mandatory until 1981. Therefore regional figures may not be comparable for 1980. The effect of the change was to increase the whole-time equivalent of part-time staff by 6.7 per cent, without any changes in their actual hours worked. In the case of junior doctors, especially at house officer and senior house officer level, part-time working is unusual, and so the changes in contracted hours did not affect the estimated whole-time equivalent numbers of doctors in the same way. Nevertheless, the reduction in contracted hours during the 1990s means that one 'whole-time equivalent' represented a decreasing amount of medical staff time.

Data for 1995 onwards are not directly comparable with those for preceding years. In NHS statistics collected up to 1995, NHS staff were coded according to their pay scale. With the move to local pay bargaining under the NHS internal market, this was no longer possible and since April 1995 NHS staff have been classified according to their occupations. This change created a discontinuity in some time series. In particular it meant that senior midwives and nurses on management pay scales were reclassified as midwives and nurses even though still working as managers.

Midwives

Based on a definition adopted by the International Confederation of Midwives (ICM) and the International Federation of Gynaecologists and Obstetricians (FIGO), the World Health Organisation (WHO) defines a midwife as:

> ' ... a person who having been regularly admitted to a midwifery education programme duly recognised in the country in which it is located, has successfully completed the courses of studies in midwifery and has acquired the requisite qualifications to be registered and or legally licensed to practise midwifery.
>
> She must be able to give the necessary supervision, care and advice to women during pregnancy, labour and the postpartum period, to conduct

deliveries on her own responsibility and to care for the newborn and the infant. This care includes preventative measures, the detection of abnormal conditions in mother and child, the procurement of medical assistance and the execution of emergency measures in the absence of medical help. She has an important task in health counselling and education, not only for the women, but also within the family and the community. The work should involve antenatal education and preparation for parenthood and extends to certain areas of gynaecology, family planning and child care. She may practise in hospitals, clinics, health units, domiciliary conditions or in any other service.'[91]

In the *Midwives' rules* for practising midwives in the United Kingdom, a practising midwife is:

'a midwife who attends professionally upon a woman during the antenatal, intranatal, and/or postnatal period or who holds a post for which a midwifery qualification is essential and who notifies her intention to practise to the local supervisory authority.'[92]

Midwives are obliged to notify the United Kingdom Central Council for Nursing, Midwifery and Health Visiting (UKCC) of their intention to practise in the forthcoming year. Since April 1 1995, the UKCC has required midwives to provide additional information about their practice. UKCC publishes summaries of information from the professional register. In 1998, for example, it published data showing the main areas of practice of registered midwives, and trends in numbers in practice over the last ten years. For the year starting April 1 1998, a total of nearly 94,000 midwives were recorded on the 'effective register' by UKCC. Of these, under 33,000, or 35 per cent, were midwives in practice. Table A7.5.8 shows the trends since 1991 in the ratio of 'effective' and 'practising' midwives on the register.

Regulation of professional standards is maintained by supervisors of midwives. There has been a marked increase in numbers of supervisors, with a decrease from 51 midwives per supervisor in the year ending March 31 1988 to 23 per supervisor in the year ending March 31 1999.[93]

Statistics collected by the Department of Health and given in Tables A7.5.1 to A7.5.4 show that the increase up to 1980 in numbers of whole-time equivalent midwives employed by health authorities in England continued until 1988. After this, the numbers fell every year until 1994/95. In relation to numbers of maternities each year, the numbers of whole-time equivalent midwives in England kept pace with changes in the birth rate over the decade 1984 to 1994. This was despite changes in the way that student midwives, or 'learners' were counted, and also changes in pay scales used for senior midwives who became senior managers in the NHS. As was mentioned earlier, data for 1995 onwards are not directly comparable with those for previous years.

Tables A7.5.6 and A7.5.7 show numbers of midwives in Scotland and Northern Ireland respectively. In Scotland, rates were very much higher than in England with 53 per thousand maternities in 1995, excluding students. In Northern Ireland, the rate fell from 48 per thousand maternities in 1980 to 42 per thousand in 1996. In Wales, statistics did not distinguish midwives separately from 1985 to 1996. Table A7.5.8 shows the numbers of midwifery and nursing staff in the maternity services in Wales in 1997.

Changes introduced in 1990 mean that qualification as a midwife now requires completion of a programme of theoretical and clinical education provided through, and under the direction of, approved educational institutions.[94,95] Midwifery education may be a three year registration course or, for registered nurses, an 18 month course. Students gaining clinical experience are no longer part of the NHS workforce, but are supernumerary when working in clinical practice. They are required to gain clinical experience in one or more periods during their education 'not exceeding a total of 1,000 hours of rostered service contribution for those undertaking pre-registration midwifery programmes'.[95] This amounts to about 6 months full-time work.

Before these changes in student status, pupil midwives were counted as a significant part of the staff of the maternity units in which they trained and they were paid a salary. They were expected to spend a year of their training working in hospital and at least 12 weeks in community midwifery. In 1980, student midwives accounted for 21 per cent of NHS whole-time midwifery staff. The effect of changes in education on trends in numbers of midwives is illustrated in Table A7.5.2 which shows that the number of midwives in training, recorded by the English National Board for Nursing, Midwifery and Health Visiting (ENB) was 2,976 in 1991, and increased to 3,559 in 1999.

The Department of Health's workforce statistics do not provide any information about the setting in which English midwives work. Scottish and Northern Irish data still show community and hospital staff separately in Tables A7.5.6 and A7.5.7. Before the NHS changes in April 1991, an increasing number of districts were organising their midwifery services so that midwives worked in both the hospital and the community services. From 1991 onwards, midwives became employed by NHS trusts. This includes those working wholly in hospital, or wholly as community staff, or, increasingly, as part of a team providing care throughout pregnancy, both in primary care settings and in hospital. A description of midwives' working patterns in different types of practice in the former South East Thames Region was published in 1997.[96]

Postnatal visiting of all women after delivery is regulated through statute in the *Midwives' rules*.[92] These have been updated on a number of occasions since they were first set out in the Midwives' Act, 1902.[97] The way the rules are interpreted is set out in the non-statutory *Midwife's code of practice*. This includes the World Health Organisation's definition of a midwife, which we quoted earlier.[91] The statute has changed relatively little over the years. The current edition defines the postnatal period as:

> 'a period of not less than ten and not more than twenty-eight days after the end of labour during which the continued attendance of a midwife upon the mother and baby is requisite'.[91]

On the other hand, the code of practice has changed considerably, and become much less prescriptive.[97] The current definition was clarified in 1992 as:

> 'each midwife is personally responsible and accountable for the exercise of professional judgement and determining appropriate practice in relation to mother and baby. This naturally includes judgements about the number of visits and any additional visits required in the postnatal period.'[98]

The decreasing lengths of postnatal stay in hospitals, shown in Tables A7.25.1 and A7.25.2 have had implications for the workload of midwives involved in postnatal visiting and the judgements they have needed to make.

Midwives also form part of the staff of neonatal units. From 1981 to 1994, the classification of occupations used for the annual staff census for English health authorities, made it possible to identify staff allocated to neonatal units separately, although the actual deployment of staff may still not be reflected in the statistics. The UKCC also reports the main areas of practice for midwives. Of full-time midwives registering to practise from 1995 to 1998, 56 per cent were in clinical midwifery, 4.9 per cent in special and intensive baby units and 7.0 per cent were in bank nursing and midwifery. The rest were not giving direct care as midwives, with 4.2 per cent in administration, 2.6 per cent in professional teaching and 8.3 per cent in community nursing, gynaecology, paediatrics, family planning and counselling.[93]

Although it is assumed that normal deliveries in hospital are in general attended by a midwife, unit policy may dictate that she may not have complete responsibility for the conduct of labour and diagnosis of warning signs. Since the introduction of the Hospital Episode Statistics, data have been collected about the person conducting the delivery. Data from this source, shown in Table A7.18.2, indicate that between 1989/90 and 1994/95 the proportion of deliveries conducted by a midwife fell from 75.6 per cent to 72.3 per cent.[41] To some extent this reflects an increase in the percentage of deliveries which were by caesarean section.

Nursing staff in hospital maternity departments

Not surprisingly, Tables A7.5.1, A7.6.1 and A7.6.2 show that registered midwives outnumber other nursing staff of all grades employed on maternity wards. In the September 1998 NHS staff census, 7,869 or 30 per cent of whole time equivalent staff in maternity units in England were nurses, compared to 18,479 or 70 per cent who were qualified midwives. National statistics do not record the number of nurses with additional qualifications in nursing sick babies. Only 328 whole time equivalent staff in English maternity services in September 1998 were recorded as registered sick children's nurses.

Health visitors

Table A7.7.1 shows numbers of health visitors employed by health authorities between 1976 and 1997. There were fewer than 9,000 whole-time equivalent health visitors in England in 1981, rising to 10,430 in 1986.

Numbers then declined to 9,290 in 1989 and fluctuated around 10,000 in the mid and late 1990s. The work of health visitors is divided between babies and children on the one hand, and old people on the other, so numbers do not necessarily represent their availability to advise or support pregnant women or new mothers, or to monitor the development of young children. New government initiatives, notably the Home Office's 'sure start' programme, added to their workload at the end of the 1990s.

Hospital medical staff

Statistics collected about doctors show the absolute and whole-time equivalent numbers working in different grades and specialties in NHS hospitals. Data for relevant specialties can be found in Tables A7.8.1 to 7.8.4. In the late 1980s, the Department of Health funded a national enquiry into medical staffing patterns.[99–103] The research done for this enquiry provides information which helps to interpret routine workforce statistics. It shows the way staff worked in the specialties providing maternity and neonatal care at that time. The data should be interpreted in the light of changes which have occurred in policies for employing medical staff in the NHS.

In 1992, the NHS Executive introduced measures to reduce the hours worked by junior doctors. The objective in 1997 was to 'achieve further reductions in juniors' hours and consultant expansion exceeding two per cent in addition to centrally funded posts'.[3]

This change is part of a wider strategy to modify the arrangements for medical training so that more patients will have direct care from qualified specialists. The intention is that the period of training for hospital doctors should be shorter and more clearly defined. These changes were outlined in a report from the Chief Medical Officer, Sir Kenneth Calman, in 1993.[104] All of these policies are still being implemented in the NHS and are included in the NHS Executive's objectives.[3]

Areas of specialism within each broad specialty are reflected in membership of the relevant professional organisation. This is achieved as a postgraduate qualification by examination and practical work. Since 1993, when the Department of Health adopted the recommendations of the report of the Working Group on Specialist Medical Training,[104] the postgraduate specialist training of doctors has changed. Grades of medical staff in training have been redefined, to reduce the overall time in training from an average of 12 years to a minimum 7 years. Previous 'training' grades were replaced with two grades of doctors in basic specialist training and higher specialist training, leading to a Certificate of Completion of Specialist Training and eligibility for consultant posts. The new grades were introduced from April 1 1996 onwards. It was intended that this change would be accompanied by an increase in the numbers of consultants and in the proportion of patients who are cared for with direct consultant input.

Associated with the changes in medical staff structures and hours, there have been corresponding changes in the way contracts of employment are defined. Until 1991, junior doctors were paid by Unit of Medical Time

(UMT). One unit represented a half day, and 10 UMTs were equivalent to full-time. Since 1992, junior doctors have been employed for a number of basic contracted hours. Their whole-time equivalent is calculated by dividing basic contracted hours by 40. Where doctors work longer than basic contracted hours, they can be paid for the extra time, but this is not reflected in the estimated whole-time equivalent workforce. For consultants, 'maximum part-time' contracts are counted as full-time 'to reflect their substantially whole-time commitment'.[105] Where consultants or other medical staff have contracts with more than one NHS trust within a region, the total whole-time equivalent for the region is rounded to one, even if their contracted hours/sessions add up to more than 40 hours or 10 sessions. The Department of Health publishes these data in an annual statistical bulletin about numbers of hospital and community medical and dental staff.

Obstetrics and gynaecology

Overall numbers of whole-time qualified medical staff in obstetrics and gynaecology increased steadily from 1975 onwards, as shown in Table A7.8.1. This reflects a similar growth in numbers of all hospital doctors, but not necessarily a comparable increase in medical staff time available to the NHS. This is partly because of changes in the method of calculating whole-time staff numbers, and partly because of changes in the contractual hours of junior doctors. Most crucially, the statistics do not tell how the doctors divided their time between obstetrics and gynaecology. Hospital practitioners and general practitioners, who also work in hospitals under 'paragraph 94 appointments', are not usually included in statistics about hospital medical staff although they accounted for five per cent of the contract hours of all hospital medical staff in obstetrics and gynaecology in 1980 but well under one per cent in 1996. In addition, the work of staff in the specialty is generally divided about equally between work in obstetrics and gynaecology, although there are a few specialising in either gynaecology or obstetrics alone.

In England, medical staff in obstetrics and gynaecology are unevenly distributed between the NHS regions. Data in Table A7.8.2 show regional differences in whole-time equivalent medical staff in 1996. The Northern and Yorkshire Region had the highest rate at 7.6 obstetricians and gynaecologists per 1000 maternities while the South and West Region had fewer than 5 per 1000 maternities.

The numbers of consultants and senior registrars give a better indication of available specialist skill than total staff numbers do. In spite of the 'Calman' recommendations, the proportion of consultants among hospital medical staff in obstetrics and gynaecology in England did not change between 1980 and 1996, remaining at 26 per cent. Changes in specialist training increased the numbers of staff qualified for consultant posts. The British Medical Association estimated in 1999 that by May 2001 there would be an additional 500 specialists in obstetrics and gynaecology qualified to fill consultant posts but only 50 would become vacant each year.[106]

Paediatrics

The paediatric specialty covers the care of children up to 15 years old. Because of the way their work is organised, the numbers of paediatricians giving neonatal care are not counted separately in administrative returns. To provide fuller information, the Royal College of Paediatrics and Child Health does censuses of paediatric staff. A report based on its 1995 and 1996 censuses showed that 112 of 407 whole-time equivalent tertiary specialists worked in neonatology, along with 36 of 192 whole-time equivalent non-tertiary specialists.[107]

In 1996, the British Association of Perinatal Medicine published recommendations for hospitals providing neonatal intensive care, which were endorsed by the Royal College of Obstetricians and Gynaecologists, the British Paediatric Association and the Neonatal Nurses Association.[67] This called for hospitals with neonatal intensive care units to have at least one consultant paediatrician with neonatal specialist training, and 24 hour cover provided by trained consultants, and resident trained medical staff.

Table A7.8.1 shows that there has been an increase in the number of paediatric medical staff in established posts in hospital departments, rising from 2.5 per thousand births in 1980 to 5.9 in 1996. Numbers of NHS paediatric staff in England rose from 1,736 in 1980 to 4,462 in 1998, and the corresponding whole-time equivalents rose from 1,568.5 to 4,118.7. Hospital practitioners and 'paragraph 94 appointments' in paediatrics form a small proportion of all staff, accounting for only one per cent of all whole-time equivalent paediatric staff in 1996. The absolute numbers have changed little, but the proportion has fallen from nearly 3 per cent in 1980, because of the increase in all other grades of paediatric staff. Numbers of medical staff in paediatric neurology and in paediatric surgery are collected separately, and are also shown in Table A7.8.1. Consultant posts in paediatric surgery in England increased in number from 120 whole time equivalents in 1980 to 258.5 in 1998. In Scotland and Northern Ireland, because of small numbers, paediatric neurology staff numbers are grouped together with paediatric staff.

Numbers of paediatric staff by grade and region in 1996 are shown in Table A7.8.3. Taken together with data from Table A3.13.4, they showed that numbers of whole-time paediatric hospital medical staff varied from over 6.5 per thousand live births in the South Thames region to less than five in the West Midlands and Scotland.

Public health and community health medical staff

Public health medical staff are responsible for a range of functions at health authority level, including needs assessment, health care commissioning and public health. Clinical medical staff in community health services do not provide maternity care, but work together with health visitors and general practitioners to monitor the development of children living in the district. Health authorities vary in the number of developmental tests they offer routinely to children, in addition to the statutory minimum. Since 1991/92, most clinical medical staff previously working as community health staff are employed by NHS community or acute trusts. Table A7.9.1 shows that, in England, all regions have employed an increasing number of public health and community medical staff since 1975. This was not the case for Scotland. It is not possible to estimate from these data the proportion of the time which medical staff in the community health services devote to mother and child health or to commissioning and monitoring maternity and child health services.

General practitioners

Table A7.10.1 shows numbers of general practitioners in England and Wales, those on the 'obstetric list' and those providing contraceptive medical services in 1997. A general practitioner may be included on the obstetric list if she or he has completed six months in a department of obstetrics and gynaecology, or meets other specific criteria detailed in the 'Red book'.[108] In 1997, 91 per cent of general practitioners in England and Wales were on the 'obstetric' list. The number of these general practitioners per thousand maternities ranged from 39.7 in North Thames region to 52.5 in South and West. On the other hand, being on the obstetric list does not necessarily imply involvement in maternity care. This means that Table A7.10.1 cannot be directly compared with data for 1980 which showed that three quarters of general practitioners provided either complete or partial care, irrespective of whether or not they were on the list.

General practitioners are paid fees for the items of maternity care that they provide. Up to 1997, data about general practitioner maternity care could be derived from statistics about their claims for payment, shown in Table A7.10.2. Despite the decline in the quality of the data from this source, they still show the falling numbers of general practitioners' claims for complete maternity care including delivery between 1975 and 1995/96, alongside increasing numbers of claims for antenatal and postnatal care without delivery. The deterioration of the data reflects the lower priority given to them as a consequence of the declining involvement of general practitioners in maternity care. Trends over a much longer period are illustrated in Figure 7.3.

The decrease in available maternity beds which were under the sole responsibility of general practitioners, shown in Table A7.2.1, also reflected the changing role of general practitioners in maternity care. By the early 1990s it was noted that, in some places, hospital maternity care for women with uncomplicated labours and community based maternity care was becoming the primary responsibility of midwives with varying degrees of general practitioner involvement.[2,109]

Other staff of health authorities and trusts

It is often forgotten that the work of staff mentioned so far depends heavily on support provided by others, for example by clerical, technical and other ancillary staff. The numbers of staff in different categories employed by the NHS in England, Scotland and Wales and Northern Ireland are summarised in *Health and personal social services statistics for England, Health*

Figure 7.3

Numbers of claims by general practitioners for providing maternity medical services, England and Wales, 1963–88

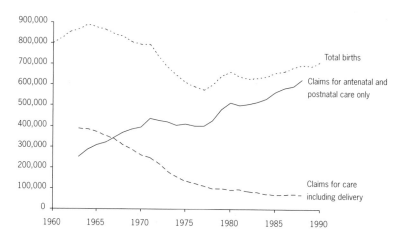

Source: Department of Health and Social Security, FP24 claims

statistics Wales, *Scottish health statistics* and *Hospital statistics* for Northern Ireland. Table A11.4.1 shows their relative levels of pay. The data show declining numbers of ancillary staff employed directly by the NHS, as this work was increasingly contracted out to private companies during the 1980s and 1990s.[110] Interpreters are another and much smaller category of staff who are not visible in statistics. Some of them are employed by the NHS but are not identified separately in published statistics and others are employed by outside organisations under contracts with NHS trusts.[111]

Local authority social services

In the past, women received assistance from home helps after giving birth. By the early 1980s, it was unusual even for families with triplets to have a home help.[112] Following the review of government statistical services by Sir Derek Rayner in 1980, the return from local authorities to DHSS, which gave a breakdown of home helps' work was discontinued.[113] Since 1993, under the NHS and Community Care Act, local authorities have increasingly purchased home help services from private companies rather than employing home helps themselves.[110] This means that data are now collected in terms of contact hours and numbers of households receiving help.

Social workers attached to maternity or neonatal units provide support or advice to families who need it. Because they are paid by local authorities but work with NHS trusts, statistics about their work are complicated to collect. At present, national statistics are not available, although individual local authorities should be able to provide statistics about social workers' activities in their area.

The *Children Act of 1989* redefined the role of social services in child support. Local authorities have a responsibility to arrange for the care of a child where parents are unable to care for him or her. They are therefore involved in cases both of possible neglect or abuse, and also where a child is offered for adoption. The extent to which staff involved in this type of work specifically relate to children under one year of age is not identified in published statistics.

Staff and facilities outside the NHS

Very little information is collected centrally or published about facilities and practice in care, including maternity care, outside the NHS.[110] The percentage of registered maternities in England and Wales which took place in non-NHS hospitals fell from 2.9 per cent in 1964 to 1.0 per cent in 1990, as Table A7.16.1 shows. This was followed by an abrupt fall to 0.4 per cent in the mid 1990s which coincided with the closure of a small number of maternity units in hospitals in the United Kingdom run by the Ministry of Defence for members of the armed forces and their dependents. The Armed Forces Medical Services continues to provide medical services to members and their families posted overseas.

Under Section 23 of the Registered Homes Act 1984, private hospitals and nursing homes were required to register with their local health authority. Health authorities collected a limited amount of data and make an annual return, KO36, to the Department of Health. From 1996 onwards it published summary data in an annual *Statistical bulletin*. In 1997, there were only 67 maternity beds in establishments registered as nursing homes in England, 46 in private hospitals and clinics and 22 in dual registered nursing homes.[114] The numbers of whole-time equivalent midwives in post were correspondingly small, 36 in nursing homes, 90 in private hospitals and clinics and 20 in dual registered homes. Legislation before parliament in 2000 will establish new regulatory authorities in England and in Wales.

Maternity care is not even mentioned in the tables of data about private hospitals and clinics published in *Health Statistics Wales* and *Hospital statistics for Northern Ireland*. No data are published for Scotland. Because maternity care accounts for such a small proportion of the activity of private hospitals and homes, it does not feature explicitly in the results of the series of surveys described in Chapter 4.[115–117]

From 1979 onwards, data about stays by private patients in pay-beds in NHS hospitals were included in the Hospital In-patient Enquiry and they should now be included in the Hospital Episode Statistics.[23,118] In 1980 an estimated 0.5 per cent of deliveries in NHS hospitals were by private patients and the level was similar in 1985.[40] Because of the incompleteness of Maternity HES there are no data from the 1990s.[41,118] Data about pay bed activity published in *Hospital statistics* for Northern Ireland do not identify maternity care separately.

A few women deliver at home with independent midwives. These births cannot be distinguished from home births under the NHS in Tables A7.16.1 and A7.16.2, as they are derived from birth registration. Women who opt for care from independent midwives tend also to book for NHS hospital care. This means they can transfer to hospital if the need arises, but there are no data about the extent to which this occurs. Maternity HES data do not distinguish between these transfers and transfers made by women intending to deliver at home with an NHS midwife.

In general the low level of use of private facilities for childbirth is a consequence of the fact that normal delivery is not covered by private health insurance.

There are many voluntary agencies providing a range of help and support to pregnant women and for new mothers. Many are listed in Appendix 1. The types of help they provide include support and information for parents with children with specific impairments, for families in poverty with young children, for women who wish to prepare for childbirth, for women who wish to breastfeed their baby, or for women who are unsure of their rights with respect to work, benefits or child care. Some of these voluntary groups are national and some work in local areas. While some campaign on particular issues, others provide direct help and yet others do both. The size of the contribution of voluntary sector support for mothers and children is not documented and quantified routinely and there are no statistics on their activities. Information about organisations with charitable status is published by the Charities Aid Foundation. Further information about voluntary organisations in the United Kingdom is available from the National Council for Voluntary Organisations, whose contact details are in Appendix 1.

Care in pregnancy and at birth

'For nine months I've been tired and sick
  Childbirth's no bed of roses – bear down
Swollen up like Moby Dick
  Childbirth's no bed of roses – bear down
Bursting out of all my clotheses
  Childbirth's no bed of roses – bear down.

Just one more push and that'll do
  Childbirth's no bed of roses – bear down
Head and shoulders soon be through
  Childbirth's no bed of roses – bear down
Oh – its feet and toeses!
  Childbirth's no bed of roses – bear down

My baby's born with one last shove
  Childbirth's no bed of roses – bear down
That's what you call a labour of love
  Childbirth's no bed of roses – bear down
I'd do it again though – I supposes
  Childbirth's no bed of roses – bear down'

Sisters unlimited, *Childbirth shanty*.[119]

So far, this chapter has focused on the resources available for maternity care in terms of staff and facilities. Since the early 1990s there has been an increasing emphasis on assessing the clinical effectiveness of the care provided, using randomised trials and other experimental methods and in using this to draw up guidelines for care. To assess the impact of these activities, data are needed to audit and monitor the care actually provided. In what follows, we describe the data collected about maternity care and discuss the extent to which it can be used to monitor changes in the NHS.

For many women, their first contact with NHS maternity services is when they go to have their diagnosis of pregnancy confirmed. A survey in 1981 showed that only about one per cent of the people interviewed were not registered with an NHS general practitioner. It is unlikely that this has changed, although the percentage is likely to be higher in inner city areas. Although a few people opt out of NHS care in favour of private care, it is likely that the people without an NHS general practitioner are amongst the most vulnerable people in society, including travellers and homeless people. For the majority of the population, however, the general practitioner acts as a gatekeeper to other services.

Care before conception

Some health promotion activities aim to improve the outcome of pregnancy for women who are not yet pregnant. For example, most schools are required to give some form of education about sexual and reproductive health and parenthood, but no statistics are explicitly collected about this. The same applies to preconception clinics run in some districts to encourage women to prepare for pregnancy. There are, for example, no statistics about the numbers of women taking folic acid to prevent congenital anomalies.

Couples who experience problems in conceiving may consult a general practitioner, an NHS hospital doctor or a doctor in the private sector. As many health authorities have decided to limit funds for services for management of subfertility, charges may be made to users of services provided on NHS premises or people may seek care in the private sector. This blurring of the margins between NHS and private care and the lack of data about private sector activities means that there are few data on the subject.

Numbers of prescriptions by general practitioners in England and Wales for drugs which can be used in the medical management of subfertility are shown in Table A7.11.1 Similar data are collected about prescriptions in the other countries of the United Kingdom. Some of these prescriptions may be written after consultation with a general practitioner only. In other cases, the general practitioner may write the prescription after the couple receives advice or care from hospital specialists under the NHS or in the private sector. Although the number of prescriptions cannot be directly related to the numbers of people for whom they are prescribed, the general picture in Table A7.11.1 is of an increase up to the mid 1990s, followed by a decrease.

Any NHS or private clinic in the United Kingdom which offers in-vitro fertilisation or donor insemination must register with the Human

Fertilisation and Embryology Authority. It maintains a central database of courses of treatment and, where known, their outcome, and publishes summary data in its annual reports, from which Table A7.12.1 is taken. Not unexpectedly, it shows that the number of cycles of IVF and micromanipulation rose considerably between 1991/92 and 1997/98. Although the percentage of cycles leading to a clinical pregnancy rose over the period, only 14.9 per cent of IVF treatment cycles and 20.7 per cent of micromanipulation cycles led to a live birth in 1997/98.[120]

Antenatal care

Once pregnancy is diagnosed, the form of care which a woman receives will depend on a variety of factors. These include her general practitioner's or midwife's assessment of her need for specialist care, whether the general practitioner is both willing and qualified to be involved in her care, her wishes about where she wants to have her baby, and the organisation and availability of facilities in her district. Through the 1970s and 1980s, most women received antenatal care from a varying combination of general practitioner, community midwife and hospital obstetric staff. During the 1990s, it became more likely that women had midwife led care from a midwifery team, whether based in primary care or in the maternity hospital.[2] Patterns of antenatal care given by these teams vary widely[96,121] and no data on the subject are collected routinely.

Anxiety is frequently expressed about women who do not attend for antenatal care or do so late in pregnancy. There are no national statistics about the numbers of women with no antenatal care. For the majority who do attend, there are no data about the gestational age at first attendance, the numbers of attendances or the differences between attenders and non-attenders. In the 1970 birth survey, the small proportion of women who received little or no antenatal care were largely those from the poorest backgrounds who were also at highest risk of developing problems in pregnancy.[122] No such differences were found in a survey by the Audit Commission in the mid 1990s. The patterns of antenatal care provided have been built up over the twentieth century, often in the absence of any attempt to evaluate what is provided.[14] Reviews of evidence of the effectiveness of care, published since 1980, have been influential in guiding current policy.[123–125]

Because of the way antenatal care is spread across hospital and community services and general practice, routine statistics give a fragmented picture of the care provided to individual women. Data from hospital and community services generally reflected the activities of staff while those from general practice are about claims for fees. Despite their limitations and the discontinuities in methods of data collection in the late 1980s, they point to some broad trends in maternity care.

Numbers of new out-patients and attendances at out-patient clinics in maternity departments in England, shown in Table A7.13.1, fluctuated in the late 1970s and the 1980s, in line with the overall numbers of pregnancies. Numbers of attendances then declined during the 1990s, while attendances at midwife only clinics, collected on return KC54, increased. Data about general practitioners' claims for maternity medical services, shown in Table A7.13.1, declined drastically in quality from the mid 1980s onwards until data collection ended in April 1997. Despite this, they do indicate decreasing involvement in antenatal and postnatal care. Data for Scotland in Table A7.13.2 also show a decline in the use of hospital antenatal clinics in the 1990s. Although numbers of home visits made by domiciliary midwives were higher in the 1990s than in the 1980s, gaps in the data make it difficult to interpret trends in the mid 1990s.

Antenatal preparation for the delivery and advice about caring for a new baby is offered by hospital and community health services. Statistics were collected about relaxation and parent-craft classes in community health clinics in the years up to 1987/88 and published in *Health and personal social services statistics for England*. These did not present a complete picture, as many women attended classes run by voluntary organisations, notably the National Childbirth Trust.

Despite the large number of tests and procedures involved in antenatal care and major developments in antenatal screening, there are no national statistics on the subject. Occasionally surveys are done to fill this gap. The National Study of Triplet and Higher Order Births described care given in the 1980s to women with these pregnancies and comparison groups of women with twin and singleton pregnancies.[112] As was mentioned earlier, in the early 1990s there was a national survey of ultrasound facilities and the use made of them.[89] Reviews have been published of screening for Down's Syndrome[126] and of screening pregnant women for HIV/AIDS which is described in Chapters 9 and 10.[127]

Estimated numbers of antenatal in-patient stays in hospital for England and Wales from 1973 to 1981 and in England from 1980 onwards are shown in Table A7.14.1 Data up to 1985 were collected through the Maternity Hospital In-patient Enquiry.[38,40,128] If a woman was discharged undelivered, there was no link made with the successive re-admissions, including the admission during which the baby was born, so the data cannot tell us how many women were admitted antenatally.

From 1989/90 onwards, data about antenatal in-patient stays have been collected through Maternity HES. At present there is no linkage between successive episodes of care to the same woman, although there are plans to link them in the future using NHS numbers. Because of their quality, the data have yet to be published and are therefore missing from Table A7.14.1.

Numbers of antenatal and in-patient discharges and day cases in Scotland, shown in Table A7.14.5, rose between 1981 and 1996/97. These come from unlinked data and could reflect more re-admissions of the same women for shorter stays. Alternatively, they could result from more day case or in-patient monitoring of women with complicated pregnancies.

Care during delivery

The question of where delivery should take place and the nature of the care which should be provided have both been the subject of much controversy for many years. In both, routinely collected statistics are useful in monitoring trends and geographical variations in the type of care provided. At the same time, attempts to interpret the data raise further questions which can be answered only by doing specific research using other methods, notably surveys and randomised controlled trials.[11]

Place of delivery

'Seeing how destitute of comforts, means and medical appliances some women are, the thought occurred to some benevolent person that they might be received and delivered in hospitals ... Contrary to expectations, the advantages these institutions offered were over-balanced by one drawback; the mortality of mothers was not diminished; nay it became in some instances excessive; in other instances appalling.'

William Farr, *Letter to the Registrar General*, 1872.[129]

'We think that sufficient facilities should be provided to allow for 100 per cent hospital delivery. The greater safety of hospital confinement for mother and child justifies this objective.'

Standing Maternity and Midwifery Advisory Committee,
Domiciliary midwifery and maternity bed needs, 1970.[130]

'There is no evidence to support the claim that the safest policy is for all women to give birth in hospital.'[11]

House of Commons Health Committee, *Maternity services*, 1992.[68]

Numbers of births and maternities in hospital, at home and elsewhere are derived by ONS and the general register offices for Scotland and Northern Ireland from the address of the place of birth. This is recorded by the local registrar when the birth is registered. Data for England and Wales are published annually in *Birth statistics, Series FM1*, while data for local areas are included in the DVS1 tabulations on disk. Numbers of maternities in England and Wales from 1964 onwards and births from 1954 onwards are tabulated by place of delivery in Tables A7.16.1 and A7.16.2. The overall trend is a move from home to hospital birth up to 1987 and a small but steady increase in home births since then, as Figure 7.4 shows.

These tabulations were not done routinely before 1954. Special tabulations by the General Register Office showed that 15 per cent of live births in England and Wales in 1927 took place in institutions which included hospitals, nursing homes, maternity homes and Poor Law institutions.[131] This rose to 24 per cent in 1932 and 34.8 per cent in 1937.[132,133] Of the women sampled in the national survey of a week's births in March 1946, 53.7 per cent delivered in institutions.[134]

Maternities at home in England are tabulated by NHS region in Table A7.15.1, which also contains data for Wales and Scotland. They include all

Figure 7.4

Percentage of registered maternities which occurred at home, England and Wales, 1964–97

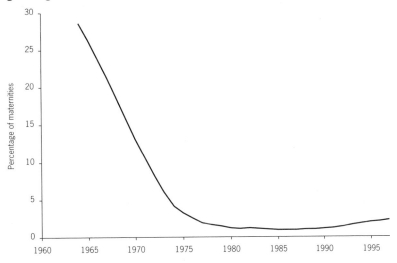

Source: Office for National Statistics, *Birth statistics, Series FM1*

deliveries taking place at the woman's usual address, as stated on the birth registration, irrespective of whether or not she planned to give birth there. These show considerable variations, with a higher percentage of births at home in the South of England and East Anglia than in the North of England and in Scotland.

Until 1992, NHS hospitals in England and Wales were subdivided into two categories. Hospitals with general practitioner maternity beds but no consultant obstetric beds were classified as 'NHS A' and those hospitals with obstetric beds as 'NHS B'. Some hospitals in the 'NHS B' category also had general practitioner maternity beds. Hospitals classified as 'NHS A' were sometimes described as 'isolated general practitioner units'. This could be misleading as they ranged from those which are on an adjoining site or in a nearby but different building from a consultant obstetric unit to those whose nearest consultant unit is 20 or 30 miles away. As Table A7.15.2 shows, the extent to which births took place in 'NHS A' units varied considerably between regions in England.

Births in 'other' hospitals are mainly those outside the NHS, but also include the very occasional births in long stay psychiatric hospitals. As was mentioned earlier, non-NHS hospitals include private, military and charity hospitals and nursing homes. Some private hospitals are constituted as charities. Data for individual districts in ONS' DVS1 tabulations have to be interpreted in the light of local knowledge about maternity facilities outside the NHS. In tabulations of birth registration data, births to women using private pay beds in the NHS are categorised as NHS. Births under the NHS in military hospitals, at the time when they were still offering maternity care, were categorised as non-NHS.

Hospital statistics are a source of data about place of delivery in England, although they do not necessarily cover all births. The Maternity Hospital In-patient Enquiry coded women delivering in NHS hospitals according to whether they were delivered in a consultant obstetric or a general practitioner maternity unit, irrespective of the type of hospital. It should be noted that the HIPE definition, based on department, differed from the one used for classifying beds on the SH3 hospital return. Unlike HES as a whole, Maternity HES should contain a record for every birth in England, including those in non-NHS hospitals or at home. This had yet to be achieved by 1994/95 when there were HES records for only about 3,200 of the approximately 11,300 home deliveries registered in England and fewer than 200 of the 3,500 deliveries in non-NHS hospitals.[41]

The deliveries in NHS hospitals for which data were available in Maternity HES were subdivided into those in consultant wards, general practitioner wards and consultant/general practitioner wards. Table A7.18.1 shows a shift towards the mixed consultant/general practitioner wards during the early 1990s with 58 per cent of births in consultant wards, 3 per cent in general practitioner wards and 39 per cent in consultant/general practitioner wards in 1994/95.[41] A new category for midwifery wards was introduced in 1995/96, but few deliveries were categorised in this way initially. Data about general practitioners' claims for 'item of service' payments for supervising deliveries have been useful in the past, but they do not indicate whether the delivery took place at home or in hospital.

Initially, the SMR2 system was restricted to hospital births in Scotland, although it included data about women who transferred to hospital in labour. From the mid 1990s onwards, ISD attempted to include data about all home births, but had not yet achieved complete coverage by 1999. *Scottish health statistics* tabulates hospital births according to whether they take place in consultant or general practitioner units. This is coded on the SMR2 form and was used for a comparative analysis of mortality in units of different types.[135] As Table A7.14.5 shows, deliveries in general practitioner units declined until they accounted for just over two per cent of deliveries in 1996/97. In that year a new category was added for deliveries in midwifery wards.

These trends are the consequence of a variety of pressures to decrease the practice of home delivery. They culminated in the report of the Standing Maternity and Midwifery Advisory Committee, better known as the Peel Committee, which was published in 1970 and recommended that hospital beds should be available for all births.[130] The Committee did so on the grounds that it believed that hospital delivery was safer for all women, but it produced no evidence from randomised trials or other sources to support its view. Instead, the Committee observed that the increase in the proportion of births taking place in hospital had been accompanied by a decline in perinatal mortality and went on to infer, without justification, that the former had caused the latter.

As was described earlier, there was a tendency from the 1970s onwards for hospital deliveries to be increasingly concentrated in larger units. This trend was compounded by the recommendation in 1976 in *Priorities for health and personal social services in England*[53] that 'isolated' general practitioner units should be phased out. These changes were accompanied by many heated arguments about the relative merits of different places of delivery. In the course of these, people with diametrically opposed views used the same government statistics to reach different conclusions.[54,136]

Most of the problems arose when trying to interpret outcome measures. Up to 1974, only stillbirth rates could be tabulated by place of delivery. From 1975 onwards, OPCS' infant mortality linked files have been used to tabulate stillbirths and infant deaths by place of birth. These are tabulated by birthweight in Table A7.17.1, while perinatal mortality rates for 1975 onwards are plotted in Figure 7.5. In the mid 1990s, perinatal mortality rates for home birth were slightly but consistently below those for hospitals. This was not the case twenty years earlier, when data for the first three years, 1975–77, were published.[137] The House of Commons Social Services Committee interpreted the data as 'conclusive' evidence of the dangers of home birth and recommended that it should be phased out even further.[54]

A later analysis showed that a high proportion of deaths among babies born at home were among babies born outside marriage to women under 20.[138] It was pointed out that not all births occurring at home were planned to occur there.[138,139] A survey of the intended place of delivery of all births at home in 1979 found that two thirds of deaths were among babies whose mothers had booked to deliver in a consultant unit and delivered at home accidentally.[140]

The Steering Group on Health Service Information recognised the need to collect data about any changes in booking as well as where women

Figure 7.5

Perinatal mortality by place of birth, England and Wales, 1975–97

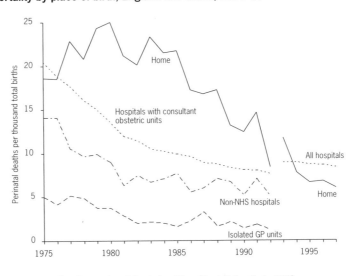

Source: Office for National Statistics, *Mortality statistics, Series DH3*

eventually gave birth.[22] This item is therefore included in the minimum dataset of items collected at delivery in Maternity HES in England. The poor quality of the data has so far limited their use, although data for 1994/95 have been published.[41]

We have concentrated here on data about the place of delivery which can be derived from official statistics. A fuller picture of planned home births in the 1990s can be found in the results of a survey by the National Birthday Trust Fund.[87] Data from other sources were reviewed in *The place of birth*[141] and in 1987 and 1994 in *Where to be born?*.[11] These books also discuss the complex issues involved.

Procedures in labour and delivery

Information about procedures used during labour and delivery in England is collected in the Maternity Hospital Episode System, and similar information for Scotland is collected through the SMR2 system. In Northern Ireland, maternity episodes are included in the Hospital Inpatients System. They are also included in the Patient Episode Database Wales. Although both of these have 'maternity tail', delivery details are missing from most records and no data are published.

Trends in the use of induction, caesarean section, instrumental delivery and episiotomy in England and Wales up to 1980 and England from 1980 onwards can be found in Tables A7.19.1 to A7.21.1. Similar data for Scotland are in Table A7.22.1. Rising trends in operative delivery in England and Wales up to the mid 1980s and in England only from the late 1980s onwards are shown in Figure 7.6. Data for Scotland appear in Figure 7.7.

Figure 7.6

Operative delivery rates, England and Wales, 1955–85, England 1989/90–1994/95

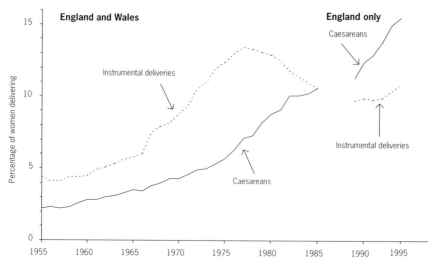

Source: Ministry of Health, Department of Health and Social Security, Welsh Office, Office of Population Censuses and Surveys, *Maternity hospital in-patient enquiry* and Department of Health, *Maternity hospital episode statistics*.

Figure 7.7

Operative delivery rates, Scotland, 1975–97

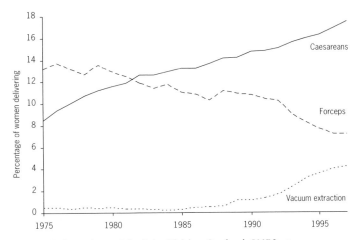

Source: Information and Statistics Division, Scotland, *SMR2 returns.*

The rates for England and Wales for years up to 1985 are expressed as a percentage of total maternities, including deliveries outside NHS hospitals and thus may be a slight underestimate, particularly in the earlier years. It is most unlikely that any caesarean sections would have been done at home, but there may have been a few inductions, some instrumental deliveries and episiotomies in deliveries at home. The 1958 Perinatal Mortality Survey found that forceps were used in 1.0 per cent of home deliveries, 5.5 per cent of deliveries in general practitioner units, and 7.4 per cent of deliveries in consultant units.[142] Eight per cent of all forceps deliveries in the survey were done in home deliveries.

As we mentioned earlier, there are no routinely collected data published about deliveries in non-NHS hospitals and no recent data about deliveries in NHS pay beds. Analyses of Maternity HIPE data for 1980 and 1985 found caesarean section and forceps delivery rates were much higher among private patients than among women having NHS care.[38,143] This is consistent with data from elsewhere which suggest that there were relatively high levels of intervention in private deliveries compared with the NHS.[144–146]

Induction rates for the late 1970s, shown in Table A7.19.1, are probably overestimates. The question about induction on the Maternity HIPE form asked whether the woman had artificial rupture of the membranes, oxytocin or both. Checks on data for 1978 showed that some women whose labours had begun spontaneously but had been accelerated by artificial rupture of membranes or oxytocin, had been wrongly coded as having been induced. Because of this, the category 'admitted to hospital before labour and then discharged delivered' may be a better indicator of the extent of induction at this period, although it includes planned caesarean sections as well. The overall picture is one of increasing rates up to the mid 1970s, followed by a decline up to the mid 1980s in England.

The impact of intervention on the timing of onset of labour can be seen indirectly in the appearance of day of the week variation in numbers of births, shown in Table A3.11.1. This phenomenon appeared and became more marked with the increasing use of induction of labour.[147-149] The day of the week variation was greater in births in 'NHS B' hospitals with consultant obstetric units than in 'NHS A' hospitals without such units.[149]

In Scotland, where the SMR2 form asks simply for the method of onset of labour, induction rates fell between the mid 1970s and late 1980s, as Table A7.22.1 shows. These data are published in *Scottish health statistics*. For England, Figure 7.6 shows all instrumental deliveries combined, but forceps and vacuum extractions are shown separately in Tables A7.20.1 and A7.20.2. For Scotland, they are shown separately in Figure 7.7 and Table A7.22.1. In both countries there was a marked increase in the use of vacuum extraction in the early 1990s. There was considerable variation between NHS regions in England and Wales in the incidence of intervention in labour and delivery, as Table A7.20.4 shows. These data are based on the region where the woman usually lived.

In Table A7.21.1, forceps deliveries, caesarean sections and deliveries in which episiotomies were done are tabulated by maternal age and parity. Episiotomies were most common in first deliveries and they were less frequently done to women having higher parity births. The same was true of forceps deliveries and caesarean sections. Both these procedures were also more common among older women in each parity group than among younger women of the same parity. Use of anaesthetics is recorded in HES. In 1994/95 general anaesthesia was used in 6 per cent of deliveries, an epidural in 20 per cent and a spinal block in 5 per cent.[41] Data for past years suggest that these rates can vary for women in different ethnic groups.[150] Until ethnic origin data in Maternity HES are complete, it will not be possible to monitor this routinely.

In Scotland, more detailed analyses and comparisons between 1975 and 1994 were included in the report of the *National audit of caesarean section in Scotland*.[151,152]

Complications recorded at delivery in England from 1979/80 to 1994/95 are shown in Table A7.23.1. Antenatal complications are likely to be under-recorded on the delivery record and postnatal complications are likely to be restricted to those immediately after giving birth. The proportion of deliveries categorised as normal remained at just under half of all deliveries throughout the period, but the proportion of such deliveries which had some complications rose. For example, there was a rise in the proportion reporting trauma to the perineum and also in postpartum haemorrhage. It is difficult to assess whether this reflects increasing frequency of the conditions or fuller reporting.

Care of mothers and babies after delivery

Postnatal care in hospital

The pattern of postnatal care has changed markedly over the period when most births have occurred in hospital. Data from HIPE and HES in Table A7.26.1 show that the average length of hospital postnatal stay in England fell from 6.3 days in 1970 to 4.1 days in 1985. The proportion of women staying less than three days increased from 18 per cent in 1970 to 60 per cent in 1994/95, when 10 per cent of women left hospital within one day as Figure 7.8 shows. The proportion staying more than 10 days has fallen to only about one per cent of all women delivered in hospital. Similar changes have occurred in Scotland. Table A7.26.2 shows data for specialised units and general practitioner units separately. This decline reflects changes in policy.

As was mentioned earlier, it is a statutory duty of community midwives to care for women up to 28 days after delivery if they deliver at home or return from hospital within this time.[69,92,97] Figure 7.9 and Table A7.29.1 show the changing pattern in their work, up to the late 1980s when the data collected changed. Community midwives' work changed from delivering women to giving postnatal care to women who had delivered in hospital. In 1987/88, the last year for which data were collected, community midwives made postnatal domiciliary visits to about 99 per cent of women who gave birth in England.

Since 1989/90 data for England, shown in Table A7.29.2 have been collected on form KC54 which simply records numbers of antenatal and postnatal face to face contacts in the community by midwives and health visitors. These include clinics held on general practice premises. Over the

Figure 7.8

Length of postnatal stay, England and Wales, 1958–78, England, 1970–1994/95

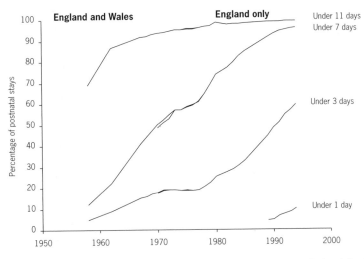

Source: *Maternity hospital in-patient enquiry, Department of Health Maternity hospital episode statistics*

Figure 7.9

Work of community midwives, England and Wales, 1949–87

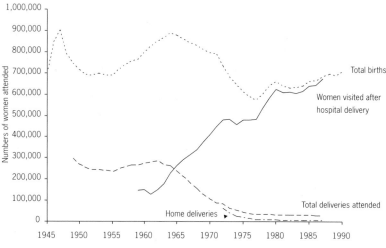

Source: Ministry of Health, Welsh Office, DHSS

period 1988/89 to 1996/97 the numbers of postnatal contacts by midwives declined while those by health visitors rose. In Scotland, numbers of postnatal visits by both midwives and health visitors declined in the early 1990s, as Table A7.13.2 shows.

If need arises, or if they are receiving routine general practitioner maternity care, mothers may also call on the services of their general practitioners. General practitioners claim fees for episodes of postnatal care at standard rates irrespective of the complications that may or may not have arisen. This means that it is not possible to derive much information from this source about the problems which women have after delivery and which lead them to consult their general practitioners and national data collection ended in 1997. Table A7.10.2 shows the numbers of claims made by general practitioners for fees for maternity medical services, including postnatal care, in the years 1978 to 1995/96.

'Well babies'

Most babies are transferred with their mother from the delivery room to the postnatal ward. There are very few routinely collected data in England, Wales and Northern Ireland about either facilities for care given to healthy newborn babies or the nature of the care provided. In England between 1987/88 and 1995/96, numbers of 'well babies' born in NHS hospitals, shown in Tables A7.14.3 and A7.14.4, were counted on form KP70.

Care for sick babies

Babies admitted to a neonatal unit in England are included in non-maternity HES. Maternity HIPE included a question about whether the baby was transferred to a special care baby unit but sometimes these babies

228

were never formally admitted. Maternity HES does not record this explicitly, as the field used to code the baby's destination and discharge does not include a code for neonatal units.

Table A7.26.1 shows numbers of stays in neonatal units in England for 1980 to 1995/96. Average lengths of stay for babies in special care baby units in England were calculated for the SH3 hospital return, until it was discontinued in 1986. The length of stay of babies admitted was also recorded on the HIPE form for those babies in the sample. This is the source of data for England in Table A7.26.1 which shows a declining admission rate and an increasing length of stay. In HES data for 1989/90 onward, episodes of care are subdivided into special and intensive, showing much longer lengths of stay in the very small, but increasing, numbers of episodes of intensive care. Data for the other three countries of the United Kingdom, shown in Tables A7.26.2 to A7.26.4 are not subdivided in this way. Declining admission rates can be seen in Scotland and Wales. In Scotland this is combined with rising lengths of stay.

Except in Scotland, data about episodes of care in hospitals are not routinely linked to data about previous hospital admissions or to details of delivery and neonatal care. This means, for example, that routinely available statistics cannot be used to say whether babies of low birthweight are more likely to be re-admitted to hospital. As mentioned earlier, use of NHS numbers issued at birth may allow such linkages in the future.

In Scotland, information about the care of newborn babies is collected using the SMR11 neonatal record. These can be linked with the SMR2 maternity discharge record to relate aspects of neonatal care to information about the mother and the delivery. This was done, for example, in ISD's report on small babies in Scotland.[153]

Feeding

> 'Well I wasn't exactly looking like "Page three"
> As I unhitched my denim dungarees.
> The baby soon went quiet but the staff began to riot
> At the sight of this working part of me.
>
> Breastfeeding baby in the park
> You'll have to go and do it after dark.
> There are parts of you and me
> That other people don't want to see.
> You can't breastfeed your baby in the park.'

Janet Russell, *Breastfeeding baby in the park.*[154]

Mothers are encouraged to breastfeed their babies and part of a midwife's work is to help the mother and baby to establish successful feeding.[155] Maternity HIPE included information about whether the baby is breast or bottle fed on discharge from hospital, but this is not included in HES. In any case, with babies being discharged at different times, any such data would be difficult to interpret.

Surveys of infant feeding were done by the Social Survey Division of OPCS in 1975, 1980, 1985, 1990 and 1995.[156–160] The surveys were commissioned by DHSS and subsequently by the Department of Health to monitor a recommendation in 1974 that mothers should be encouraged to breastfeed their babies for at least the first two weeks of life and preferably for four to six months.[161] While this was adopted as official policy, it was apparent from other surveys available at that time that the majority of mothers did not breastfeed, and also that they gave solid foods very early. The surveys were done to establish the incidence and prevalence of breastfeeding and to investigate factors which could influence the method of feeding. At the time of the survey, several aspects of maternity care were related to the establishment of breastfeeding. Failure to establish breastfeeding was found to be associated with delays in first suckling. This could arise from the mother's condition after a caesarean section, from admission of the baby to special care or could even result from hospital policies about feeding times.

Table A7.28.2 shows how starting to breastfeed and discontinuing doing so was associated with care given in labour, delivery and the neonatal period. Trends since 1975 are shown in Table A7.28.1, which also shows that breastfeeding rates in England and Wales were higher than those in Scotland while Northern Ireland had the lowest rates. After levelling off during the 1980s, breastfeeding rates increased slightly in the 1990s in each of the countries. Women who had caesarean sections or whose babies were of low birthweight were less likely to continue breastfeeding. Mothers' reasons for stopping are shown in Table A7.28.3.

A strong social gradient is very apparent in Figure 7.10 and Table A7.28.3 where the incidence of breastfeeding both initially and at six weeks is

Figure 7.10

Breastfeeding initially and at six weeks by social class of partner, Great Britain, 1995

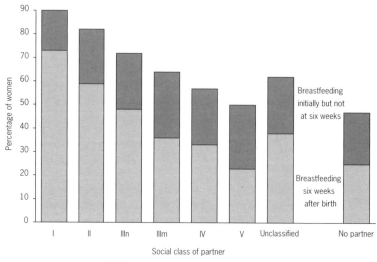

Source: *Infant feeding, 1995*[160]

tabulated by the social class of the women's partner. For both first and subsequent births, women with partners in non-manual occupations were more likely to breastfeed.

A separate survey was done of feeding of a sample of babies born in 1994 to women of Bangladeshi, Indian and Pakistani origin and a sample of white women living in the same areas.[162] As Table A7.28.5 shows, all groups of Asian mothers were more likely to breastfeed than white mothers, with Bangladeshi mothers being most likely and Pakistani mothers least likely to breastfeed.

Mothers, babies and children in the months and year after birth

The only data collected at a national level about care given to babies after they are discharged from hospital are contained in community health returns about domiciliary and clinic visits, and about immunisation and vaccination. Data about children seen at child health clinics and domiciliary visits made by health visitors to children were collected and published by the health departments of England, Wales and Scotland up to the mid 1980s. After this, data were no longer collected about clinic attendances, only about domiciliary visits. Tables A7.30.1 to A7.30.3 show the numbers of children visited at home between 1975 and 1998/99 and in domiciliary face to face contacts in England from 1998/99 onwards.

During the early 1990s, immunisation rates were used as performance indicators for general practitioners. As Tables A7.31.1 to A7.31.4 show, immunisation rates were well over 90 per cent in each of the four countries of the United Kingdom by this time. The exception was whooping cough, where immunisation rates had plummeted at the end of the 1970s, in response to concerns about the safety of the vaccine.

Local authorities have a responsibility to provide services for children in need under the Children Act of 1989. Table A7.32.1 shows the approximate numbers of children in the early years on child protection registers in England, Wales, Scotland and Northern Ireland. Children are put on the register after a social services department has agreed to a child protection conference. Trends in numbers of children under one year on child protection registers in England and Wales and children aged 0 to 4 years in Northern Ireland are shown. Scottish data are not split by age. In England, the numbers of children aged under one year of age on the registers fluctuated between 2,300 and 3,000 during the 1990s. It is not possible to subdivide the numbers by single years of age for Northern Ireland.

Table A7.33.1 shows the numbers of children under one year of age 'looked after' by local authorities. In England, numbers increased from between 1,200 and 1,400 in the early 1980s to 2,200 in 1999 and the rate per thousand live births increased to 2.9 in 1998.

The problems of mothers in prison, particularly those who are pregnant, came into the public eye in the late 1990s, but data are not routinely published on the subject. A survey by the Home Office of women in prison in 1994 found that the numbers of places in mother and baby units was inadequate, even for the women who were aware of them and that many mothers faced housing problems on release.[163]

Monitoring maternity care in the 1990s and 2000s

This chapter has described data which are collected routinely and are relevant to maternity care. Because most were collected originally for purposes other than describing the care given to pregnant women and newborn babies, they neither provide a comprehensive picture of care available, nor is it usually possible to relate the patterns of care provided to the characteristics of the population receiving it. In particular, few data are collected about antenatal and postnatal care. There are few data about newer forms of care. There no data about care given by the voluntary or the private sector and few data about the care given by general practitioners. Data about care in delivery show rising caesarean section rates and a shift from forceps to vacuum extraction for operative vaginal deliveries.

Birth counts goes to press at a time of change in the NHS in general and maternity care in particular. Changes are taking place in the pattern of care, with midwives once again assuming a greater responsibility for caring for women with uncomplicated pregnancies. Although general practitioners' contribution to providing maternity care has diminished, their influence is likely to increase as primary care groups take on the role of commissioning care. The impact of this change on maternity care cannot be predicted, nor do we know how it will affect information systems.

There are considerable differences between the countries of the United Kingdom, with systems for linking and analysing data being much more fully developed in Scotland than elsewhere. In England, the plans set out in the 1980s by the Steering Group on Health Services Information were never fully implemented and are now outdated. Ambitious plans have been published for developing new information systems.[46-48] Providers should maintain electronic patient records which would allow linkages of records of successive episodes of care to the same patient, using their NHS numbers. An electronic health record should summarise information about all the care received by an individual. Proposals have been made to issue babies' NHS numbers at birth, rather than waiting up to six weeks for birth registration, and should be implemented by 2002. This should allow linkages of delivery and neonatal records. The data items to be collected are under review yet again in England.[164] We hope that the resources will be made available to implement these plans and they will improve the quality and range of data which are needed to monitor and audit the care provided to babies and their mothers.

References

1   Nightingale F. *Introductory notes on lying-in institutions*. London: Longmans, Green and Co, 1871.

2   Department of Health. *Changing childbirth*. Part 1: Report of the Expert Maternity Group [Chair: Baroness Cumberlege]. London: HMSO, 1993.

3   Department of Health. *The new NHS, modern, dependable*. Cm 3807. London: The Stationery Office, 1997.

4   *A National Health Service*. Cmd 6502. London: HMSO, 1944.

5   Webster C. *The health services since the War. Vol. I: Problems of health care, the National Health Service before 1957*. London: HMSO, 1988.

6   Webster C. *The health services since the War. Vol. II: Government and health care in the National Health Service, 1958–1979*. London: HMSO, 1996.

7   Local Government Board. *Fortieth annual report of the Local Government Board, 1910–1911*. Cd 5865. Vol. I. London: HMSO, 1911.

8   Local Government Board. *Memorandum by the Local Government Board on deaths among infants in Poor Law institutions*. HC No. 99. London: Local Government Board, 1909.

9   Webb S, Webb B, eds. *The break-up of the Poor Law: being part one of the minority report of the Poor Laws Commission*. London: Longmans, Green and Co, 1909.

10 Loudon I. *Death in childbirth. An international study of maternal care and maternal mortality, 1800–1950*. Oxford: Oxford University Press, 1992.

11 Campbell R, Macfarlane AJ. *Where to be born? The debate and the evidence*. 2nd edition. Oxford: National Perinatal Epidemiology Unit, 1994.

12 Smith FB. *The people's health, 1830–1910*. London: Croom Helm, 1979.

13 Donnison J. *Midwives and medical men*. New York: Schocken Books, 1977.

14 Oakley A. *The captured womb: a history of the medical care of pregnant women*. Oxford: Blackwell, 1984.

15 Newman G. *Infant mortality*. London: Methuen and Co., 1906.

16 Dwork D. *War is good for babies and other young children: a history of the infant and child welfare movement in England, 1898–1918*. London and New York: Tavistock, 1987.

17 Lewis J. Mothers and maternity policies in the twentieth century. In: Garcia J, Kilpatrick R, Richards M, eds. *The politics of maternity care*. Oxford: Clarendon Press, 1990.

18 Davies ML, ed. *Maternity: letters from working women collected by the Women's Co-operative Guild*. London: G. Bell and Sons, 1915.

19   Political and Economic Planning. *Report on the British health services.* London: PEP, 1937.

20   Political and Economic Planning. *A complete maternity service.* London: PEP, 1946.

21   Ministry of Health. *Annual report of the Chief Medical Officer, 1919–1920.* Cmd 978. London: HMSO, 1920.

22   Steering Group on Health Services Information. *First report to the Secretary of State.* London: HMSO, 1982.

23   Steering Group on Health Services Information. *Supplement to the first and fourth Reports to the Secretary of State.* London: HMSO, 1985.

24   Smith L. Problems in retrieving national data on births: questionnaire survey. *BMJ* 1998; 316: 1710–1711.

25   Ministry of Health. *Annual report of the Chief Medical Officer for 1949.* Cmd 8343. London: HMSO, 1951.

26   Kenney N, Macfarlane AJ. Maternity data in England: problems with data collection at a local level. *BMJ* 1999; 319: 619–22.

27   Kenney N, Macfarlane AJ. Are maternity data linked at a local level? Some findings from the 'Changing Childbirth' Information Project. Paper given at the conference on: *Linking data for better health in pregnancy and childhood*, London, January 12–13 1998.

28   General Register Office. *The Registrar General's statistical review, 1933. Text.* London: HMSO, 1935.

29   Macfarlane AJ. Statistical aspects of institutional performance: league tables and their limitations. Discussion of the paper by Goldstein and Spiegelhalter. *Journal of the Royal Statistical Society Series A* 1996; 159(3): 414–415.

30   Spiegelhalter DJ. Surgical audit: statistical lessons from Nightingale and Codman. *Journal of the Royal Statistical Society Series A* 1999; 162A(1): 45–58.

31   Nightingale F. Proposal for an uniform plan of hospital statistics. In: *Programme of the fourth session of the International Statistical Congress.* London: HMSO, 1860.

32   Farr W. Letter to the Registrar General. In: *Twenty-fourth annual report of the Registrar General.* London: HMSO, 1863.

33   Newsholme A. A national system of notification and registration of sickness. *Journal of the Royal Statistical Society* 1896; 59: 1–37.

34   Newsholme A. *The elements of vital statistics.* 3rd edition. London: S Sonnenschein and Co, 1899.

35   Ministry of Health. *On the state of the public health during six years of war. Report of the Chief Medical Officer, 1939–1945.* London: HMSO, 1946.

36   Ministry of Health. *Annual report of the Chief Medical Officer for 1948.* Cmd 7910. London: HMSO, 1950.

37   Ashley JSA. The maternity hospital in-patient enquiry. In: Chalmers I, McIlwaine G, eds. *Perinatal audit and surveillance*. London: Royal College of Obstetricians and Gynaecologists, 1980.

38   Office of Population Censuses and Surveys, Department of Health and Social Security, Welsh Office. *Hospital in-patient enquiry: maternity tables, 1977–1981 England and Wales*. Series MB4 No. 19. London: HMSO, 1986.

39   McIlwaine GM, Dunn FH, Howat RC, Smalls M, Wyllie MM, MacNaughton MC. A routine system for monitoring perinatal deaths in Scotland. *British Journal of Obstetrics and Gynaecology* 1985; 92(1): 9–13.

40   Macfarlane AJ. Trends in maternity care. In: Office of Population Censuses and Surveys, Department of Health and Social Security, Welsh Office. *Hospital in-patient enquiry maternity tables 1977–1981*. Series MB4 No. 19. London: HMSO, 1986:9–25.

41   Department of Health. NHS maternity statistics, England: 1989–90 to 1994–95. *Statistical Bulletin* 1997; 28: 1–44.

42   Department of Health, NHS Executive. *The early issue of NHS numbers to babies*. Leeds: NHS Executive, 1998.

43   Heasman MA, Clarke JA. Medical record linkage in Scotland. *Health Bulletin* 1979; 37(4): 97–103.

44   Cole SK, Smalls M. Trends in infant mortality in Scotland, 1970–1987. *Journal of Public Health Medicine* 1990; 12(1): 73–80.

45   Information and Statistics Division. *Births in Scotland, 1976–1995*. Edinburgh: ISD, 1997.

46   Department of Health, NHS Executive. *Information for health*. Leeds: NHS Executive, 1998.

47   National Information Management and Technology Board. *Strategic programme for modernising information management and technology in the NHS in Scotland*. Edinburgh: Scottish Office, 1998.

48   Welsh Office. *Better information, better health: information management and technology for health care and health improvement in Wales. A strategic framework 1998 to 2005*. Cardiff: Welsh Office, 1998.

49   Royal College of Obstetricians and Gynaecologists. *Report on a national maternity service*. London: RCOG, 1944.

50   Ministry of Health. *Report of the Maternity Services Committee [Chair: Lord Cranbrook]*. London: HMSO, 1959.

51   Ministry of Health. *A hospital plan for England and Wales*. Cmnd 1604. London: HMSO, 1962.

52   Committee on Child Health Services. *Report: fit for the future. [Chair: SDM Court]*. Cmnd 6684. Vol. 1. London: HMSO, 1976.

53   Department of Health and Social Security. *Priorities for health and personal social services in England*. London: HMSO, 1976.

54   House of Commons Social Services Committee. *Second report: perinatal and neonatal mortality. [Chair: R Short]*. Session 1979–1980. HC 663 Vol. I. London: HMSO, 1980.

55   Maternity Services Advisory Committee. *Maternity care in action: Part I. Antenatal care*. London: HMSO, 1982.

56   Maternity Services Advisory Committee. *Maternity care in action: Part II. Care during childbirth (intrapartum care). A guide to good practice and a plan for action*. London: HMSO, 1984.

57   Maternity Services Advisory Committee. *Maternity care in action: Part III. Care during childbirth (postnatal care). A guide to good practice and a plan for action*. London: HMSO, 1984.

58   Royal College of Physicians of London. *Medical care of the newborn in England and Wales*. London: RCP, 1988.

59   Royal College of Obstetricians and Gynaecologists. *Report of the Working Party on antenatal and intrapartum care*. London: RCOG, 1982.

60   Joint Working Party of the Association of Anaesthetists and the Obstetric Anaesthetists Association. *Anaesthetic services in obstetrics – plan for the future*. London: Association of Anaesthetists, 1988.

61   Department of Health and Social Security. *Report of the Expert Group on Special Care for Babies. [Chair: W Sheldon]*. Reports on Public Health and Medical Subjects No. 127. London: HMSO, 1971.

62   Working Party on the Prevention of Early Neonatal Mortality and Morbidity. *Report [Chair: TE Oppé]*. Health Circular HC(76)40. London: DHSS, 1976.

63   Committee on Child Health Services. *Report: fit for the future. [Chair: SDM Court]*. Cmnd 6684. Vol. 2. London: HMSO, 1976.

64   Whitby C, de Cates CR, Roberton NR. Infants weighing 1.8–2.5 kg: should they be cared for in neonatal units or postnatal wards? *Lancet* 1982; i(8267): 322–325.

65   British Paediatric Association, Royal College of Obstetricians and Gynaecologists Liaison Committee. Recommendations for the improvement of infant care during the perinatal period in the UK. In: House of Commons Social Services Committee. *Second report: perinatal and neonatal mortality*. Session 1979–1980. HC 663 Vol. II, pp.166–178. London: HMSO, 1980.

66   Clinical Standards Advisory Group. *Neonatal intensive care: access to and availability of specialist services. Report of a CSAG Working Group [Chair: D Hull]*. London: HMSO, 1993.

67   British Association of Perinatal Medicine. *Standards for hospitals providing neonatal intensive care*. London: BAPM, 1996.

68   House of Commons Health Committee. *Maternity services: second report. [Chair: N Winterton]*. Session 1991–92. HC 29–I Vol. I: Report. London: HMSO, 1991.

69 Chalmers I, Enkin M, Keirse MJNC, eds. *Effective care in pregnancy and childbirth.* 2 vols. Oxford: Oxford University Press, 1989.

70 Royal College of Obstetricians and Gynaecologists. *Report of the Working Party on minimum standards of care in labour.* London: RCOG, 1994.

71 Obstetric Anaesthetists Association. *Recommended minimum standards for obstetric anaesthesia services.* London: OAA, 1995.

72 Royal College of Obstetricians and Gynaecologists, Royal College of Midwives. *Towards safer childbirth: minimum standards for the organisation of labour wards.* London: RCOG Press, 1999.

73 Department of Health. *A first class service: quality in the new NHS.* London: Department of Health, 1998.

74 Department of Health, NHS Executive. *Clinical governance. Quality in the new NHS.* London: Department of Health, 1999.

75 NHS Executive. *Quality and performance in the NHS: High level performance indicators.* Leeds: NHS Executive, 1999.

76 NHS Executive. *Quality and performance in the NHS: Clinical indicators.* Leeds: NHS Executive, 1999.

77 NHS Executive. *Quality and performance in the NHS: Clinical indicators, technical supplement.* Leeds: NHS Executive, 1999.

78 Joint Working Party of the Royal College of Obstetricians and Gynaecologists and the Royal College of General Practitioners. *Report on training for obstetrics and gynaecology for general practitioners.* London: RCOG, 1981.

79 Northern Neonatal Network. Measuring neonatal nursing workload. *Archives of Disease In Childhood* 1993; 68: 539–543.

80 Mugford M, Howard S, O'Neill C, Dunn A, Zelisko M, Normand C, Hey E, Halliday H, Tarnow-Mordi W, The ECSURF (Economic Evaluation of Surfactant) Collaborative Study Group. Limited comparability of classifications of levels of neonatal care in UK units. *Archives of Disease In Childhood* 1998; 78(3): F179–F184.

81 Department of Health, NHS Executive. *Bed availability and occupancy, England, 1996–97.* Leeds: NHS Executive, 1997.

82 Royal College of Obstetricians and Gynaecologists. *Organisational standards for maternity services: the report of a Joint Working Group.* London: RCOG, 1995.

83 Working Party of the Regional Advisory Subcommittee in Paediatrics. *Report on special care baby units of the Trent region.* Trent Regional Health Authority, 1977.

84 South West Thames Regional Health Authority. Second report of the Regional Perinatal Monitoring Group, November 1979. In: House of Commons Social Services Committee. *Second report: perinatal and neonatal mortality.* Session 1979–1980. HC 663 Vol. V: 256–284. London: HMSO, 1980.

85   Gillmer MD, Combe D. Intrapartum fetal monitoring practice in the United Kingdom. *British Journal of Obstetrics and Gynaecology* 1979; 86(10): 753–758.

86   Dunn PM. Newborn care in England, 1978. In: House of Commons Social Services Committee. *Second report: perinatal and neonatal mortality.* Session 1979–1980. HC 663 Vol. V. London: HMSO, 1980.

87   Chamberlain G, Gunn P, eds. *Birthplace: report of the confidential enquiry into facilities available at the place of birth, conducted by the National Birthday Trust.* Chichester: John Wiley, 1987.

88   Rosenblatt RA, Dawson AJ, Larson EH, Tressler CJ, Jones A, Hart LG, Nesbitt TS. A comparison of the investment in hospital-based obstetrical ultrasound in Wales and Washington state. *International Journal of Technology Assessment in Health Care* 1995; 11(3): 571–584.

89   Hay S, McLean E. *The timing and content of routine obstetric ultrasound in the United Kingdom.* London: The College of Radiographers, 1994.

90   Department of Health and Social Security. *On the state of the public health for the year 1980: annual report of the Chief Medical Officer.* London: HMSO, 1981.

91   United Kingdom Central Council for Nursing, Midwifery and Health Visiting. *The midwife's code of practice.* London: UKCC, 1994.

92   United Kingdom Central Council for Nursing, Midwifery and Health Visiting. *Midwives' rules.* London: UKCC, 1993.

93   United Kingdom Central Council for Nursing, Midwifery and Health Visiting. *Statistical analysis of the Council's professional register 1 April 1997 to 31 March 1998 (including midwives intention to practise statistics for the year commencing 1 April 1998).* London: UKCC, 1998.

94   United Kingdom Central Council for Nursing, Midwifery and Health Visiting. *Statement of the Council's requirements concerning European Community amended requirements for practical and clinical aspects of midwifery programmes. UKCC Registrar's letter 2/1990.* London: UKCC, 1990.

95   United Kingdom Central Council for Nursing, Midwifery and Health Visiting. *Midwifery education – amendments to statutory rules and the Council's requirements for the content of pre and post-registration midwifery programmes of education. UKCC Registrar's letter 6/1990.* London: UKCC, 1990.

96   Allen I, Dowling SB, Williams S. *A leading role for midwives? Evaluation of midwifery group practice development projects.* Report No. 832. London: Policy Studies Institute, 1997.

97   Garcia J, Marchant S. The potential of postnatal care. In: Kroll D, ed. *Midwifery care for the future: meeting the challenge.* London: Bailliere Tindall, 1996.

98   United Kingdom Central Council for Nursing, Midwifery and Health Visiting. *Registrar's letter. Community postnatal visiting by midwives.* London: UKCC, 1992.

99   Dowie R. *Paediatrics: patterns of hospital medical staffing*. London: British Postgraduate Medical Foundation and HMSO, 1991.

100   Dowie R. *Obstetrics and gynaecology: patterns of hospital medical staffing*. London: British Postgraduate Medical Foundation and HMSO, 1991.

101   Dowie R. *Anaesthetics: patterns of hospital medical staffing*. London: British Postgraduate Medical Foundation and HMSO, 1991.

102   Dowie R. *Overview: patterns of hospital medical staffing*. London: British Postgraduate Medical Foundation and HMSO, 1991.

103   Dowie R. *Interim report: patterns of hospital medical staffing*. London: British Postgraduate Medical Foundation and HMSO, 1990.

104   Department of Health Working Group on Specialist Medical Training. *Hospital doctors: training for the future [Chair: K Calman]*. Heywood, Lancs: Health Publications Unit, 1993.

105   Department of Health. *Health and personal social service statistics for England, 1996*. London: HMSO, 1996.

106   Beecham L. UK obstetricians face redundancy. *BMJ* 1999; 318: 688.

107   Royal College of Paediatrics and Child Health. *The medical workforce in paediatrics and child health, 1995–1997*. London: RCPCH, 1998.

108   NHS General Medical Services. *Statement of fees and allowances payable to general medical practitioners in England and Wales (The Red Book)*. Updated to June 1998. London: Department of Health/Welsh Office, 1996.

109   House of Commons Health Committee. *Maternity services: second report. [Chair: N Winterton]*. Session 1991–92. HC 29–II Vol. II: Minutes of evidence. London: HMSO, 1991.

110   Macfarlane AJ, Pollock AM. Statistics and the privatisation of the National Health Service and social services. In: Dorling D, Simpson S, eds. *Statistics in society: the arithmetic of politics*. London: Edwin Arnold, 1998.

111   Baxter C, Baylav A, Fuller J, Marr A, Sanders M. *The case for the provision of bilingual services within the NHS*. London: Department of Health and The Bilingual Health Advocacy Project, 1996.

112   Botting BJ, Macfarlane AJ, Price FV. *Three, four and more: a national survey of triplet and higher order births*. London: HMSO, 1990.

113   Department of Health and Social Security Study Team. *Review of the government statistical services: report*. London: DHSS, 1980.

114   Department of Health. Private hospitals, homes and clinics. *Statistical bulletin* 1998/4.

115   Williams BT, Nicholl JP, Thomas KJ, Knowelden J. Analysis of the work of independent acute hospitals in England and Wales, 1981. *British Medical Journal* 1984; 289(6442): 446–448.

116   Nicholl JP, Beeby NR, Williams BT. Role of the private sector in elective surgery in England and Wales, 1986. *BMJ* 1989; 298(6668): 243–247.

117 Williams BT, Nicholl JP. Patient characteristics and clinical caseload of short stay independent hospitals in England and Wales, 1992–3. *BMJ* 1994; 308(6945): 1699–1701.

118 Williams B. Utilisation of National Health Service hospitals in England by private patients, 1989–95. *Health Trends* 1997; 29: 21–25.

119 Sisters Unlimited. Childbirth shanty. Sung on: *No bed of roses.* Workington, Cumbria: Fellside Recordings (FECD104), 1995. Published by Fellsongs Music.

120 Human Fertilisation and Embryology Authority. *Eighth annual report and accounts.* London: The Stationery Office, 1999.

121 Wraight A, Ball J, Seccombe I, Stock J. *Mapping team midwifery: a report to the Department of Health.* IMS Report No. 242. Brighton: Institute of Manpower Studies, 1993.

122 Chamberlain G, Philipp E, Howlett B, Masters K. *British births, 1970.* Vol. 2: Obstetric care. London: Heinemann Medical Books, 1978.

123 Enkin M, Chalmers I, eds. *Effectiveness and satisfaction in antenatal care.* London: Spastics International Medical Publication/William Heinemann Medical Books, 1982.

124 Tucker J, Florey CD, Howie P, McIlwaine G, Hall M. Is antenatal care apportioned according to obstetric risk? The Scottish antenatal care study. *Journal of Public Health Medicine* 1994; 16(1): 60–70.

125 Villar J, Khan-Neelofur D. Patterns of routine antenatal care for low-risk pregnancy (Cochrane review). In: *The Cochrane Library.* Issue 1. Oxford: Update Software, 1999.

126 Mutton D, Ide RG, Alberman E. Trends in prenatal screening for and diagnosis of Down's syndrome: England and Wales, 1989–97. *BMJ* 1998; 317(7163): 922–923.

127 Nicoll A. Antenatal screening for HIV in the UK: what's to be done? *Journal of Medical Screening* 1998; 5: 170–171.

128 Department of Health, Office of Population Censuses and Surveys. *Hospital in-patient enquiry: maternity tables 1982–1985, England and Wales.* Series MB4 No. 28. London: HMSO, 1988.

129 General Register Office. *Thirty-third annual report of the Registrar General for 1870.* London: HMSO, 1872.

130 Department of Health and Social Security, Welsh Office. *Domiciliary midwifery and maternity bed needs. Report of the subcommittee. [Chair: J Peel].* London: HMSO, 1970.

131 General Register Office. *The Registrar General's statistical review for the year 1927.* London: HMSO, 1927.

132 General Register Office. *The Registrar General's statistical review for the year 1932.* London: HMSO, 1935.

133 General Register Office. *The Registrar General's statistical review for the year 1937.* London: HMSO, 1940.

134 Joint Committee of the Royal College of Obstetricians and Gynaecologists and the Population Investigation Committee. *Maternity in Great Britain*. Oxford: Oxford University Press, 1948.

135 Cole SK, Macfarlane AJ. Safety and place of birth in Scotland. *Journal of Public Health Medicine 1995*; 17(1): 17–24.

136 Tew M. Where to be born? *New Society* 1977; 20 January: 120–121.

137 Macdonald Davies I. Perinatal and infant deaths: social and biological factors. *Population Trends* 1980; 19: 19–21.

138 Campbell R, Macdonald Davies I, Macfarlane AJ. Perinatal mortality and place of delivery. *Population Trends* 1982; 28: 9–12.

139 Bull MJV. Perinatal mortality figures distorted. *Pulse* 1980; 3 May.

140 Campbell R, Macdonald Davies I, Macfarlane AJ, Beral V. Home births in England and Wales 1979: perinatal mortality according to intended place of delivery. *British Medical Journal* 1984; 289: 721–724.

141 Kitzinger S, Davis JA, eds. *The place of birth*. Oxford: Oxford University Press, 1978.

142 Butler NR, Bonham DG. *Perinatal mortality. The first report of the British Perinatal Mortality Survey*. Edinburgh and London: E&S Livingstone, 1963.

143 Macfarlane AJ. Holding back the tide of caesareans. [letter]. *BMJ* 1988; 297(6651): 852.

144 Richards M. Perinatal morbidity and mortality in private obstetric practice. *Journal of Maternal and Child Health* 1979; 4: 341–345.

145 Chamberlain G, Chamberlain G, Hewlett B, Claireaux A. *British births, 1970*. Vol. I: The first week of life. London: Heinemann Medical Books, 1975.

146 Cartwright A. *The dignity of labour: a study of childbearing and induction*. London: Tavistock, 1979.

147 Macfarlane AJ, Thew P. Births: the weekly cycle. *Population Trends* 1978; 13: 23–24.

148 Macfarlane AJ. Variations in number of births and perinatal mortality by day of week in England and Wales. *British Medical Journal* 1978; 2(6153): 1670–1673.

149 Macfarlane AJ. Day of the week variations in numbers of births and perinatal mortality rates. *Journal of Maternal and Child Health* 1979; 4(415–416).

150 Parsons L, Macfarlane AJ, Golding J. Pregnancy, birth and maternity care. In: Ahmad W, ed. *Race and health in contemporary Britain*. Milton Keynes: Open University Press, 1993.

151 McIlwaine G, Boulton-Jones C, Cole S, Wilkinson C. *Caesarean section in Scotland 1994/5: a national audit*. Edinburgh: Scottish Programme for Clinical Effectiveness in Reproductive Health, undated.

152 Williamson C, McIlwaine G, Boulton-Jones C, Cole S. Is a rising caesarean section rate inevitable? *British Journal of Obstetrics and Gynaecology* 1998; 105: 45–52.

153 Information and Statistics Division, Scottish Programme for Clinical Effectiveness in Reproductive Health. *Small babies in Scotland: a ten year overview, 1987–1996.* Births in Scotland Publication Series. Edinburgh: ISD, 1998.

154 Russell J. Breastfeeding baby in the park. Sung by Sisters Unlimited on: *No limits.* Manchester: Harbour Town Records (HARC 013), 1991.

155 American Academy of Pediatrics Work Group on Breastfeeding. Breastfeeding and the use of human milk. *Pediatrics* 1997; 100(6): 1035–1039.

156 Martin J. *Infant feeding, 1975: attitudes and practice in England and Wales. A survey carried out on behalf of the Department of Health and Social Security.* Social Survey Report SS 1064. London: HMSO, 1978.

157 Martin J, Monk J. *Infant feeding, 1980.* Social Survey Report SS 1144. London: HMSO, 1982.

158 Martin J, White A. *Infant feeding 1985.* Social Survey Report SS 1233. London: HMSO, 1988.

159 White A, Freeth S, O'Brien M. *Infant feeding 1990. A survey carried out on behalf of the Department of Health, the Scottish Home and Health Department, the Welsh Office and the Department of Health and Social Services in Northern Ireland.* Social Survey Report SS 1299. London: HMSO, 1992.

160 Foster K, Lader D, Cheesbrough S. *Infant feeding, 1995. Results from a survey carried out by the Social Survey Division of ONS on behalf of the UK health departments.* Social Survey Report SS 1387. London: The Stationery Office, 1997.

161 Department of Health and Social Security. *Present day practice in infant feeding. Report of a Working Party of the Panel on Child Nutrition. [Chair: TE Oppé].* Reports on Health and Social Subjects No. 9. London: HMSO, 1974.

162 Thomas M, Avery V. *Infant feeding in Asian families.* London: The Stationery Office, 1997.

163 Caddle D, Crisp D. *Mothers in prison.* Home Office Research and Statistics Directorate, Research Findings No. 38. London: Home Office, 1997.

164 Hartshorn A. *Maternity care data project: overview.* Leeds: NHS Executive, 1999.

8 Measuring disability and impairment in children

'Not withstanding the great interest attached to these classes, both in a social and a physiological point of view, the statistics of blindness and deaf-mutism in this country have not hitherto advanced beyond estimates and conjectures founded chiefly upon returns obtained in foreign states, or the limited experience of a few public institutions. Great disadvantages have resulted from this entire absence of authentic information, not only to society at large, but more especially to those afflicted persons, on whose behalf the appeals and efforts of philanthropy, unsupported by a reference to facts illustrative of their numbers and conditions, have lost much of their intended effect.'

Report of the 1851 census[1]

Most people are surprised to find, 150 years later, that there are still no statistics on disability or impairment collected on a national basis in England, Scotland, Wales or Northern Ireland.

In this chapter, we describe attempts which have been made to collect data on impairment in childhood, focusing particularly on impairments which are either present at birth or have been thought to be associated with events at or around the time of birth. Many of the methodological problems became apparent as long ago as the nineteenth century, when attempts were made to collect these data in the census. Similar problems arose in registers and notification systems developed throughout the twentieth century.

Setting the agenda

In 1980, the back bench House of Commons Social Services Committee's report on *Perinatal and neonatal mortality* drew attention to the lack of data and recommended that 'enquiries should take place into ways of improving the notifications of handicap of perinatal and neonatal origin.'[2] It did so because 'Witnesses were agreed that the provision of proper facilities for the avoidance of intrapartum asphyxia, for swift resuscitation at birth, and for special and intensive care of newborn infants should lead both to an increase in the number of normal children surviving and to a reduction in the proportion of survivors who are handicapped.'[2] This view was accepted at the time, in the absence not only of data but also of agreed definitions.[3]

By the 1990s, the proportion of very low birthweight babies surviving had increased dramatically, as shown in Tables A3.5.1 to A3.5.5 and Figure 6.1. The concern now was that this might have increased the numbers of children with impairments and disabilities. What had not changed was the lack of national statistics on the subject.[4,5]

Any attempt to remedy this situation raises four critical questions. The first is the definition of the conditions to be monitored. The second is the extent to which they can be diagnosed during pregnancy, delivery, the neonatal period or later in childhood. The third question is how to determine whether they have their origins in the periods before, during or soon after birth, and the fourth is how to collect the data.

The World Health Organisation's definitions of impairment, disability and handicap, given in Table 2.8 and the detailed classification set out in the *International classification of impairments, disabilities and handicaps* provoked considerable criticism. In particular, people with disability have criticised it for its medical model and creating an artificial distinction between constraints imposed by their impairments and society's unwillingness to overcome these constraints.

For these reasons, the people working on what is still loosely known as 'ICIDH-2' have based their proposed new classification, on the three dimensions of body functions and structure, activity and participation set out in Table 2.9 and contextual factors consisting of environmental factors and personal factors. At the time of writing the classification has been issued for test purposes and has yet to be adopted officially by the World Health Organisation.

A major use of information about the prevalence of impairment is in planning health and social services. In the 1970s and 1980s, some people took the view that data about the prevalence of impairment could be used as a measure of the outcome of pregnancy in general, and of the quality of perinatal care in particular.[2] It is now agreed that most impairments leading to disability are not caused by events in the perinatal period. Some are genetically determined, some are the consequence of an event in pregnancy while others arise in childhood or later in life as a consequence of illness or injuries. Nevertheless, retinopathy of prematurity, chronic lung disease and some types of deafness and cerebral palsy may be a consequence of events at or around the time of birth.

Early attempts at data collection

The need for statistics on the prevalence of disability had already been recognised by the middle of the nineteenth century.[6] From 1851 to 1911 attempts were made to collect data about certain 'infirmities' in the census.[7] Table 8.1 summarises the questions asked.

The report of the 1851 census suggested that, 'particularly in the case of the deaf and mute there was an under-reporting of the condition in children under 5 years arising from the uncertainty which must exist with respect to infants, and the natural indisposition of parents to form a painful conclusion on the subject while the slightest grounds for doubt exist.'[1]

When the question was repeated in the 1861 census, the report suggested that improved reporting in that year might have masked real changes in the prevalence of the conditions. An attempt was also made in 1861 to distinguish people who were born with visual or hearing impairments from

Table 8.1

Questions asked about 'infirmities' in censuses, 1851–1911

1851	If deaf and dumb or blind	Write 'Deaf and dumb' or 'Blind' opposite the name of the person.
1861	If deaf and dumb or blind	Write 'Deaf and dumb' or 'Blind' opposite the name of the person; and if so from birth, add 'from birth'.
1871	If (1) Deaf and dumb (2) Blind (3) Imbecile or idiot (4) Lunatic	Write the respective infirmities against the name of the afflicted person; and if so from birth, add 'from birth'.
1881	As in 1871	
1891	If (1) Deaf and dumb (2) Blind (3) Lunatic, imbecile or idiot	Write the precise infirmity, if any, opposite the name of the person; and if the infirmity dates from childhood, add 'from childhood'. Do not use such a general term as 'afflicted' or 'infirm'.
1901	If (1) Deaf and dumb (2) Blind (3) Lunatic (4) Imbecile, feeble-minded	Write the precise infirmity, if any, opposite the name of the person; and if the infirmity dates from childhood add 'from childhood'. Do not use such a general term as 'afflicted' or 'infirm'.
1911	If any person included in this schedule is: (1) 'Totally deaf' or 'Deaf and dumb' (2) 'Totally blind' (3) 'Lunatic' (4) 'Imbecile' or 'Feeble-minded'	State the infirmity opposite that person's name and the age at which he or she became afflicted.

Source: General Register Office, *Census of England and Wales, 1911, General Report.*[7]

those who became 'blind' or 'deaf and mute' later in life. The report commented that 'whether the information thus obtained may be regarded as tolerably complete and satisfactory we are not prepared to say. It appears that the term "born blind" is often applied to children losing their sight in the early years of life as well as to those actually blind from birth.'[8] In 1891, the form of the question was changed to ask if the 'infirmity' dated from childhood and in 1911 the date of onset was asked.

The census reports commented frequently on problems of definition. For example, the 1891 report said:

'No person is absolutely blind who can perceive, however faintly, a ray of light, however brilliant; but for practical purposes, anyone may be considered blind who is unable to direct his path by means of sight; and it is probable that much slighter defects in vision than this will have been held sufficient by many sufferers to justify themselves in stating that they were blind. Similarly with deafness; if the standard of absolute deafness, that is the complete inability to perceive sounds, however loud, be once abandoned, no definite line can be insisted upon, on one side of which is deafness, on the other hearing; and each person will draw the line differently.'[9]

The problems were even worse with statistics about 'persons of unsound mind' who were variously returned in the schedules as 'lunatic', 'imbecile' or 'idiot'. As one report for 1881 put it:

'No accurate line of demarcation can be drawn between the several conditions indicated by these terms. Speaking generally, however, the term idiot is applied in popular usage simply to those who suffer from congenital mental deficiency and the term imbecile to persons who have fallen in later life into a state of chronic dementia. But it is certain that neither this nor any other definite distinction between the terms was rigorously observed in the schedules, and consequently no attempt has been made by us to separate imbeciles from idiots. The term lunatic is also used with some vagueness and probably some persons suffering from congenital idiocy and many more suffering from dementia, were returned under this name.'[10]

A second major problem, particularly with mental illness or learning difficulties was under-reporting of children in whom the diagnosis was clear. As the 1891 report put it:

'Rightly or wrongly, parents cannot be induced to write on the schedule "idiot" or "insane from childhood" against the name of their child.'[9]

The 1881 report describes a cross-check which was done:

'We obtained from the managers of a large idiot asylum the addresses of the families of all those idiots who had been admitted into the institution in the year commencing with the day of the census. We then examined the schedules given in by these families and found that in exactly half the cases of such of these indisputable idiots as were 5 but under 15 years of age, no mention whatsoever was made in the schedule as to the existence of any mental incapacity.'[10]

Despite the problems of reporting and definition, the census reports felt that the data shown in Tables 8.2 and 8.3 did point to a decrease in the incidence of blindness and deafness and suggested that the conditions were more common in men than in women. They were less confident in interpreting the finding that incidences of the infirmities appeared to be higher in country districts than in towns as it was felt that the 'infirm' people would be selectively left behind in the immigration to the towns, while the 'persons of unsound mind' would be selectively sent off to institutions. To try to compensate for this, an attempt was made to do an analysis by county of birth rather than county of residence, but information about their place of birth was missing for nearly six per cent of 'deaf-mutes' and 12.7 per cent of 'idiots and imbeciles'.

In the light of these three problems, definition, selective under-reporting, and selective migration, it is not surprising to read in the report of the 1921 census that 'it was decided to omit the enquiry as to infirmities included in previous censuses, in view of the generally recognised fact that reliable information on these subjects cannot be expected in returns made by or on behalf of the individuals afflicted.'[11] The subject was set aside until the 1991 census, when a very different question was used. This is discussed later in this chapter.

Table 8.2

Proportion of 'blind' per million population, England Wales, 1851–1911

Year	'Blind' per million of the population All ages Total	Males	Females	Under 5 years Males	Females
1851	1,021	..	..	..	..
1861	964	..	..	..	..
1871	951	1,029	876	189	180
1881	879	953	809	172	161
1891	809	874	748	168	142
1901	778	835	725	151	108
1911	730	760	702	130	112

It was intended that only those who were totally blind should be included in statistics.

Source: General Register Office. *Census of England and Wales, 1911. General report.*[7]

Table 8.3

Proportion of 'deaf and mute' per million population, England and Wales, 1871–1911

Year	'Deaf and mute' per million of the population at all ages 'Deaf only' Males	Females	'Deaf and mute' Males	Females
1871	..	..	566	451
1881	..	..	563	454
1891	..	..	548	434
1901	..	..	524	417
1911	610	860	468	373

People stated simply to be 'deaf' were not counted before 1891. In 1891 and 1901 they were counted, while in 1911 a special question was asked, which may account for the apparently increased incidence.

Source: General Register Office. *Census of England and Wales, 1911. General report.*[7]

The fact that many potential recruits were unfit for military service in the Boer War from 1898 to 1902 drew particular attention to the conditions in which children were born or grew up. As was mentioned in Chapter 3, a committee was set up to investigate what was described as the 'physical deterioration of the population'. Its report, published in 1904, contained data from a variety of sources, as well as 'evidence' based on hearsay and opinions about the way the conditions in which children grew up affected their health as adults.[12]

It tried to draw on data derived from medical examinations of recruits, at different points in time. While this showed ample evidence of disability and ill health among young men, it was of less value in trying to monitor the extent to which this varied over time, as a witness pointed out to the Committee:

'The class from which recruits are derived varies from time to time with the conditions of the labour market. When trade is good and employment plentiful, it is only from the lowest stratum of the people that the Army receives its supply of men. When on the other hand, trade is bad, a better class of recruit is available. Consequently the records of the recruiting departments of the army do not deal with a homogeneous sample of people taken from one distinct class.'[12]

Even the most cursory examination of the data which are collected today about disability reveal that the problems encountered between 1851 and 1911 have not yet been solved. We return to this theme at the end of the chapter. Meanwhile, we describe the systems in use today and outline how they developed.

Registers of disability

Visual impairment

By the time the attempt to use the population censuses to collect data about numbers of disabled people had been abandoned in 1921, a new attempt to collect data about visual impairments, some of which can originate in the perinatal period, occurred as a by-product of the Blind Persons Act 1920. Under this, people who registered themselves as blind were entitled to a pension at the age of 50 and to domiciliary assistance. The registers set up as a result were, and still are, maintained by local authorities, or by local voluntary organisations acting on their behalf. From the mid 1930s onwards, most local authorities required people registering themselves as blind to complete a special form, numbered BD8.

Data derived from local blind registers were analysed on a national basis in a series of reports by Arnold Sorsby. In a report published in 1950, he reviewed data from 1919 to 1948, and pointed out that the numbers on the registers rose from 25,840 in 1919 to 74,418 in 1940.[13] The numbers then remained almost stationary and rose only slightly between 1940 and 1948 when there were 77,390 people on the registers. He commented:

> 'It may be taken that by 1940 registration had become as fully effective as it can be under conditions in which there is no compulsion on a blind person to seek it, though even now it may be short by as much as 15 to 20 per cent.'[13]

He went on to say that few blind children fail to be registered and that registrations of blindness in children aged 5 to 15 fell from 37.0 per thousand in 1923 to 21.3 per thousand in 1948. He considered this to be a real decrease, rather than an artefact resulting from changes in the definition of blindness.[13]

Despite this overall decrease, the *Annual report of the Chief Medical Officer* of the Ministry of Health for 1950 commented that:

> 'A disturbing new feature first noticed in America in 1942 is the occurrence of what appears to be a new disease which causes blindness in premature babies. This disease retrolental fibroplasia, chiefly affects infants weighing under 3-and-a-half pounds at birth and more recently has been reported as occurring in this country, though the incidence appeared to be much lower than in America.'[14]

In 1952, the Ministry of Health set up an enquiry into the incidence of retrolental fibroplasia, now known as retinopathy of prematurity, in babies born in 1951 who weighed 2,000g or less at birth and survived at least two months. It received information about the eyes of 6,925 babies, a 96 per cent response. Overall there were 127 cases of retrolental fibroplasia, that is, an incidence of 1.8 per cent. There were, however, no cases of retrolental fibroplasia among the 799 babies born and nursed entirely at home.[15] The *Annual report of the Chief Medical Officer* quoted interim findings of an investigation being done by the Medical Research Council. These suggested that retrolental fibroplasia was likely to be the consequence of excessive use of oxygen in therapy for premature babies and suggested that oxygen should only be used in the minimum concentration.

The National Assistance Act of 1948 transferred the duty of providing financial assistance to blind people to the National Assistance Board and extended certain of the welfare services to people with partial sight. As a result, national statistics about numbers of people registering as partially sighted were compiled from 1957 onwards. From 1952 to 1961, statistics about registrations of visual impairment were published in the *Annual reports of the Chief Medical Officer* of the Ministry of Health. Table 8.4 is derived from data published in the report for 1960,[16] and shows how the epidemic of retrolental fibroplasia declined in the mid 1950s. In North America, the retrolental fibroplasia epidemic was even more devastating. It has been described in detail by William Silverman, an American paediatrician.[17]

Arnold Sorsby followed up his first report on blind registration[13] with two further reports, for the years 1948–62[18] and 1963–68.[19] A survey done

Table 8.4

Cases of 'retrolental fibroplasia' recorded in new registrations as blind, England and Wales*, 1951–60

| | Age at examination, years | | | | | | |
	Under 1	1	2	3	4	Total under 5	5 and over
1951	31	12	5	1	0	49	..
1952	25	21	12	1	1	60	..
1953	28	12	8	4	2	54	..
1954	20	7	6	6	4	43	..
1955	10	15	6	6	5	42	1
1956	13	12	3	7	6	41	6
1957	6	4	3	2	1	16	3
1958	3	1	1	2	1	8	6
1959	8	1	3	0	0	12	5
1960	1	3	3	0	2	9	2

* 'The West Country' excluded before January 1955. Wales excluded before April 1955
.. Not known

Source: *Annual report of the Chief Medical Officer for 1960*[16]

between 1968 and 1970 about registration of visual handicap revealed considerable under-registration of affected adults.[20] People were reticent to register because of worries about social stigma. Some of those of working age feared discrimination in employment. The title of the 'Blind register' worried people and was felt by many to be inappropriate, as only about 47 per cent of people registered were totally blind. Others wished they had not delayed so long before registering, however. The report of the survey is also a useful source of information about the process of blind registration, and contains a bibliography of reports on the subject.

It continues to be true that fewer visually impaired children than adults escape registration, because parents are anxious to obtain appropriate educational and other facilities for them. Despite this, the completeness of national statistics declined during the early 1970s. Up to 1970, local authorities sent copies of BD8 forms to regional associations for blind people who collated statistics and sent aggregated data to the Ministry of Health and subsequently to the Department of Health and Social Security (DHSS). These data were virtually complete. In 1970, the system changed and local authorities were asked to send copies of the BD8 forms directly to the DHSS. This had a serious impact on the completeness of the data, with only 65 per cent of the forms being returned in 1976, and falling to 60 per cent in 1983.[21,22] After a review, the system was changed again. A new form was introduced in 1990 with an epidemiological return and data were processed by OPCS.[22] Data for the period April 1990 to March 1991 showed that, for children, the predominant causes of visual impairment were congenital and hereditary conditions.[22–24]

After this, central processing of the forms ceased. A computerised notification system has been developed and is being piloted at the time of writing. As the system is designed to process new applications for registration, it will lack data about past registrations, making estimates of prevalence impossible. For children, there is also no link with their birth details.[25]

The information above about the state of data in 1982 appeared as a footnote to the answer to a parliamentary question about the numbers of children registered as blind or partially sighted as a result of retrolental fibroplasia for each year from 1965 to 1981.[21] The questions were inspired by suspicions of a second epidemic of retinopathy of prematurity.[26–28] The replies showed that the data requested are not analysed centrally in Wales or Northern Ireland, nor has this been done in Scotland since 1972.

Other impairments and disabilities

There was no registration of people with other impairments before the late 1940s. Registration began when welfare payments became available for people disabled as a result of war or industrial injury and for workers defined by the Disabled Persons (Employment) Acts of 1944 and 1958. The National Assistance Act of 1948 gave local authorities powers to provide welfare services to people who registered themselves as deaf or hard of hearing, or who were permanently and substantially disabled in other ways.

Under the Chronically Sick and Disabled Persons Act of 1970, these powers were converted to duties. In 1974, the DHSS wrote to local authorities asking them to keep statistics of the people entitled to these services and suggesting that they did so by keeping registers.[29] The letter pointed out that while there were well-established procedures for assessing visual 'handicap', there were, and still are, no generally agreed criteria for assessing hearing impairment or 'handicapped people in the general classes'. Local authorities were advised to use the categories described in Appendix D of the OPCS survey *Handicapped and impaired in Great Britain.*[30]

Data derived from these registrations in England are published by the Department of Health in a three year cycle in *Registers of people with physical disabilities (general classes), People registered as deaf or hard of hearing* and *Registers of blind and partially sighted people.* Data from these for 1981 onwards are shown in Table A8.1.1. Each of the publications comments on data reliability. In each case the data are likely to be an underestimate as registration is voluntary. There may be a reluctance to register pre-school children as blind, and visually impaired people with an additional disability are likely to be understated, particularly under the age of 16. Otherwise, registration of 'blindness' and 'partial sight' is thought to be relatively complete as payments are involved. Registration of deafness is less complete and that for 'general classes' is almost negligible. In Northern Ireland, similar data are published in *Community statistics.* Data for Scotland are published by the community care statistics branch of the Scottish Executive Health Department and those for Wales are published in *Social services statistics Wales.*

Whatever the merits or otherwise of the registers, children form a very small proportion of the people registered, who are predominantly of pensionable age. Two other sets of registers of disabled people are also concerned mainly with adults. Under the 1944 Employment Act, local offices of the Department for Education and Employment are required to maintain registers of disabled people who are employable or registered for employment. Local Social Security offices maintain registers of people entitled to social security benefits for disabled people and the Department of Social Security compiles statistics about children who have been awarded a mobility allowance or an attendance allowance. There are also regional analyses, but it is not possible to assess whether regional differences in awards arise from variations in the prevalence of disability, or from variability in take up or adjudication as to who should receive the awards.

Specialised local registers

In the early 1960s, a number of people advocated setting up 'at risk' registers of children with disabling conditions or with other problems which may put them at risk of developing such conditions.[31] Mary Sheridan of the Ministry of Health pointed out the problems of trying to screen the whole population of babies and went on to advocate that:

'In order therefore to ensure that infants who have or who are likely subsequently to develop handicapping conditions shall be identified at the earliest possible stage, it is advisable to concentrate on those infants known to be specially "at risk" by reason of unfavourable family history, adverse environmental influences before, during or after birth or who show suspicious presenting symptoms, in the first months of life.'[32]

She went on to advocate that 'at risk' registers should be compiled by Medical Officers of Health and listed recommended criteria for inclusion of babies on registers. The experience of local authorities who already kept 'at risk' registers led her to estimate that they would contain between 10 per cent and 22 per cent of all live births and the number of handicapped children eventually diagnosed would be approximately one per cent of children in the population. Although no pilot studies were done, many local authorities set up 'at risk' registers in the 1960s, but the results were disappointing.[31,33] There was a tendency for a high proportion of children to end up on registers, but often they did not include the very children who had problems.

In the light of this experience it was thus hardly surprising that the Committee on Child Health Services recommended in 1976 that 'at risk' registers be discontinued. Instead, it suggested health authorities should aim to provide health surveillance for all children.[34] Health authorities tended to replace 'at risk' registers by registers of children diagnosed as having impairments. In 1981, OPCS did a survey of the registers kept by health authorities in England and Wales.[35] In the 97 area health authorities which responded, a total of 153 registers were kept. Vast differences were seen between the recorded incidences and recorded prevalences of a number of the conditions for which the registers were kept. It was likely that they arose largely from variations in the completeness of recording. Only 30 per cent of the areas and districts which kept registers mentioned using their registers to provide information to local education authorities. Since that time, the registers of children with disabilities and special needs have been developed to meet a variety of statutory and other requirements.

From the late 1960s onwards, local authorities, and from 1974, health authorities set up child health computer systems to administer immunisation programmes and child development tests. In most, the child's record is initiated by the birth notification. A national child health computer system was established from the late 1970s onwards but not all districts use it and it has not yet proved capable of producing national statistics. Most such systems have a 'special needs' module, for children with impairments. These modules are used for service planning, research, clinical audit, patient care and to help the authority and social service departments to fulfil their duties under the Children Act, 1989.[36] Since April 1991, most child health systems have been run by community trusts.

In the United Kingdom as a whole, the picture is one of diversity. A survey in 1996 found that 60 per cent of districts which replied had a computerised special needs register but their capabilities varied widely. It was concluded that while many could be used successfully for individual care and planning services for the population, many fell short of what was required for research, audit and planning.[36]

For some years, local education authorities in England compiled statistics on educational provision for disabled pupils. These were sent to the Department of Education and Science which produced aggregated statistics in the form shown in Table A8.2.1. There was no breakdown by age or year of birth. This activity stopped as a result of cuts in the Government Statistical Service but under the terms of the Education Act, 1981, it became necessary to start collecting the data again in a slightly different form. In general, Table A8.2.1 shows increasing numbers of children with statements of special educational needs in mainstream schools.

Under the terms of the 1981 Education Act, health authorities are now asked to notify education authorities of pre-school children who have been 'statemented' as having health problems which cause them to have special educational needs. Initially, there were no clear definitions of what constituted 'special educational needs' or guidelines as to how such children should be identified, but these have been developed over the years. Data about these children are published by the Department for Education and Employment in *Education statistics for the United Kingdom* and are shown in Table A8.2.1.

Since the Children Act, 1989 came into force in October 1991, local authority social services departments have been required to keep a register of disabled children and to work with health authority registers, where they exist.[37] The Children Act uses an outmoded definition of disability, similar to that used in the 1948 National Assistance Act. In response to this, the British Association for Community Child Health convened a working party to review alternative definitions and make recommendations.[38]

A problem which often arises when comparing data from different systems is lack of common definitions. In response to this, two working groups convened by the National Perinatal Epidemiology Unit and the former Oxford Regional Health Authority recommended a minimum dataset of items to be collected at the age of two years.[39] In addition, a more rigorous definition of retinopathy of prematurity has been developed.[25]

In the 1980s and 1990s, Scotland, Northern Ireland and a number of NHS regions of England each developed registers to monitor cerebral palsy. Table A8.3.1 gives data from one of these registers, the Oxford Register of Early Childhood Impairment. As well as cerebral palsy, it also monitors visual impairment and hearing problems.[40]

Initially, it was hoped that these registers would exist for a limited time period while child health computer systems developed the capacity to monitor cerebral palsy. Recently, however, comparisons have been made between the registers in Northern Ireland and the four counties of the former Oxford Region and their local child health computer systems. In both cases, the latter under-ascertained cerebral palsy.[41,42] The people responsible for the five remaining cerebral palsy registers in Scotland, Northern Ireland and the Northern, Mersey and Oxford former NHS regions of England are now working together to produce aggregated data on larger numbers of events than are documented in each register on its own.

Congenital anomaly notifications

Notification of what were then described as congenital malformations in England and Wales started in 1964, after a number of women who had taken the drug thalidomide in pregnancy had babies with severely malformed limbs. In some places congenital malformation registers were already in existence. The intention of the notification system was to identify increases in the incidence of anomalies with the aim of going on to investigate possible causes, in the hope of being able to take swift preventive action.

Originally, anomalies apparent in the first seven days of life were to be notified to the local authority and, after 1974, the health authority by the midwife or other birth attendant. Since 1991, they have been notified to the relevant community trust. Notification is voluntary and often the information is included on the birth notification form. Babies with anomalies which are not apparent at birth are unlikely to be included in districts which base the information only on birth notifications. In some districts, the information is passed to the community trust separately, either by individual notification or through a form completed when the baby is discharged from hospital.

The seven day cut off point meant excluding anomalies such as some heart defects, kidney conditions and sight and hearing impairments, which are often not diagnosed until later in life. Following a review of the National Congenital Anomaly System by the Registrar General's Medical Advisory Committee, a number of changes were made in January 1995.[43] Since then, anomalies detected at any age can be reported to the system.

Community trusts in England and Wales pass the information they receive on form SD56 to ONS. If there is a local anomaly register, then the people concerned can offer to send data directly from the register rather than sending individual notifications to ONS for analysis. This includes running monthly analyses of the incidence of babies with anomalies in each district and sending a listing to the community trust. A statistical check is made to see whether any increase or decrease observed in the incidence is larger than would be expected by chance.[43] When such differences do occur, however, the question arises as to how they can be interpreted. Some arise from over-reporting of difficult to diagnose conditions such as congenital dislocation of the hip.

Annual summaries are published by ONS in *Congenital anomaly statistics, Series MB3*. Congenital anomalies are notified separately in Scotland and Northern Ireland. In Scotland, data on congenital anomalies come from three sources, the SMR11 record, SMR1 records of acute hospital in-patient or day care discharges of babies up to one year old and the stillbirth and neonatal death records. The data are published by the Information Statistics Division in *Congenital malformations in Scotland*. In Northern

Ireland, congenital anomalies are monitored by the Regional Medical Genetics Centre at Belfast City Hospital and published in the *Annual report of the Chief Medical Officer for Northern Ireland*. As Table A8.4.1 shows, the overall notification rate in England and Wales rose until 1977 and has fluctuated since then. At the same time there is evidence of local variations in the extent to which individual anomalies are notified, a factor for which the statistical methods used make some allowance.

Local notification rates may vary by condition or fluctuate when staff changes occur. A new midwife may be more or less punctilious about notifying anomalies than her predecessor. Equally, newly appointed and inexperienced junior doctors may be over zealous in diagnosing anomalies, particularly congenital dislocation of the hip, where a special screening test, the Ortolani/Barlow test, is carried out in all newborn babies within 24 hours of birth.

A marked feature in Figure 8.1 is the decline in notification rates for central nervous system anomalies. This probably reflects the increase in antenatal screening and termination of pregnancy but may also reflect uptake of folic acid or a natural decrease in the incidence of these anomalies. Unfortunately, no data are collected routinely about antenatal screening or about the extent to which women take folic acid.

Abortion statistics show an increase in notification of terminations of pregnancy where the fetus is known to have a central nervous system anomaly, as Table A8.6.1 shows. This would appear to be offset by decreases in stillbirths and deaths attributed to central nervous system anomalies. As the overall termination rate has increased it is possible that some

Figure 8.1

Notifications of selected congenital anomalies, England and Wales, 1964–97

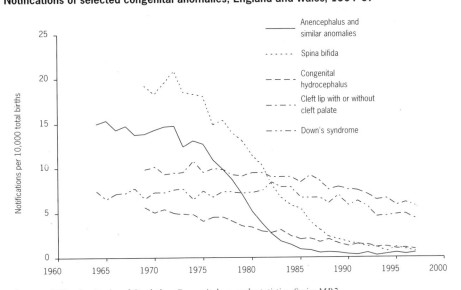

Source: Office for National Statistics, *Congenital anomaly statistics, Series MB3*

terminations of pregnancy done on other grounds, especially those done early in pregnancy, may have involved a fetus with an undiagnosed anomaly.

Congenital anomalies may be caused by exposure to harmful substances used in some work places. These can either act on sperm, on unfertilised ova, or on the fetus. The fetus is thought to be particularly susceptible during the first trimester of pregnancy. Because of this possibility, attempts described in Chapter 5 are made to record parents' occupations on notifications of congenital anomalies, but many are still missing.

Down's syndrome is a condition which often escapes notification to ONS. In 1989, a national register was set up to monitor its prevalence in England and Wales and to monitor the antenatal screening programme.[44] It was estimated that just under half of live births and terminations of pregnancy with Down's syndrome were notified to ONS in the early 1990s.[45]

Another condition known to be under-notified in comparison with regional registers is abdominal wall defects.[46,47] This makes it difficult to monitor trends over time or assess regional differences.[48] ONS is well aware of the deficiencies in its system and is working with regional registers to improve the quality and completeness of data in its system.[49] At present, the network of regional registers does not cover the whole population. To provide more reliable national data resources are needed to ensure complete coverage by a network of local registers collecting data in a consistent way and feeding into a national system. Meanwhile, ONS is working with local registers through the British Isles network of congenital anomaly registers (BINOCAR).

Congenital anomalies can also occur when a woman has a communicable disease during pregnancy. Rubella, formerly known as German measles, is a well known cause of congenital anomalies. Cataracts, deafness, congenital heart disease and microcephaly are the most common consequences. Since May 1971, the National Congenital Rubella Surveillance Programme has been monitoring the incidence of congenital rubella in the United Kingdom.[50] Paediatricians are asked to notify suspected cases of congenital rubella to the British Paediatric Surveillance Unit. Data about notified cases are reproduced in Table A8.7.1. After declining to a very low level they increased slightly in 1996. Although uptake of measles, mumps and rubella vaccine had started to decline from 1995 onwards, this is unlikely to have caused the rise which was associated with an epidemic of rubella among young men who had never been offered vaccination.[51] The decline in uptake of vaccination was greatest in the middle two quarters of 1998, but appeared to have stabilised by the end of the year.[52]

Notifications of congenital rubella are analysed together with data collected routinely about rubella itself. Rubella has been notifiable nationally as a communicable disease since 1988 and it is one of the diseases which selected general practices in the United Kingdom notify to the Royal College of General Practitioners. Laboratories in England, Wales and Northern Ireland and some laboratories in the Republic of Ireland send reports of rubella to the Communicable Disease Surveillance Centre while Scottish laboratories send them to the Scottish Centre for Infection and Environmental Health. Data for England and Wales are published in the *Communicable disease report*. Information about rubella contact or disease or rubella vaccination as grounds for termination of pregnancy should be recorded on abortion notifications in England and Wales. Data published in *Abortion statistics, Series AB*, are reproduced in Table A8.8.1. As with notifications, abortions due to rubella show a marked decline with a slight increase in 1996.

Babies whose mothers have certain sexually transmitted diseases can also be at risk of being born with infections which can result in disability, if left untreated. These diseases are discussed in Chapter 9.

Monitoring disability through censuses and surveys

After a gap of 70 years, an attempt was made to monitor disability in the 1991 census. This time a very general question was used, asking if respondents had 'any long-term illness, health problem or handicap which limits his/her daily activities or the work he/she can do.' Table A8.9.1 gives rates for children aged 0 to 4 years in the countries of the United Kingdom. Rates were higher in Wales than in the other countries and higher among boys than girls. Rates tabulated by the child's ethnic group, in Table A6.14.1, show that they were highest in the black ethnic groups and among children born in Ireland. They were lowest among children in the Chinese group. The question is being asked again in the 2001 census.[53] Once again its main focus is on elderly people and their circumstances. In addition two further questions are proposed, one on general health and one on whether people are providing unpaid personal help.

The General Household Survey asks slightly different questions about whether respondents have a 'long-standing illness, disability or infirmity', and if so whether this limits their activities in any way. As in all other age groups, Table A8.10.1 shows an increase among children aged 0 to 4 years over the years 1972 to 1996. Because General Household Survey data are based on people's subjective assessment of their health, changes over time may reflect changes in people's expectations of their health as well as changes in incidence of ill health.

OPCS was commissioned to do a series of surveys of disability in children and adults in the mid 1980s. A ten point scale was developed to estimate severity of disability. Data for children aged 0 to 4 years are shown in Table A8.11.1.[54] The findings of these surveys have been hotly debated by people with different perspectives on the concepts of disability used.

Collecting and using data in the 1990s and 2000s

The experiences described in this chapter show that the problems involved in trying to collect data about disability and impairment are not new.

Despite all the initiatives which have taken place and the effort which has been expended, routine statistics are still inadequate for the purpose of monitoring impairment in children in relation to events and circumstances at birth.

Much of the effort expended on compiling information about people with disabilities has gone into collecting data which, if it were complete, would enable us to estimate the prevalence of disabilities, or to put it more accurately, the numbers of people living in a given area whose disabilities entitle them to certain benefits or services. The congenital anomaly notifications, on the other hand, are intended to monitor the incidence of the anomalies among babies born in a given time period, although the live born babies may also be recorded in special needs registers.

The concern that neonatal care, which can reduce the death rate among small babies, may also increase the incidence of disability among the survivors is not new. As long ago as 1962, Mary Sheridan postulated that:

> 'During the past 15 or 20 years the infantile mortality rate and the morbidity rate in early childhood have shown steep declines. These have been accompanied by a rising survival rate of immature, malformed, birth injured and weakly babies, so that, although there is no evidence that the actual incidence of abnormal neonates is greater than formerly, there is every indication that larger numbers of them now remain alive.'[32]

As she admitted, she had no data to support her contention and unfortunately this is still the case, at a national level at least. Nevertheless positive steps have been taken in defining common data items and developing local registers, but this needs to be extended further to produce national data.

There are a number of technical problems involved in data collection. Definition has already been mentioned. It is also necessary to create registers which not only contain the information which is needed for planning services for the disabled people in the population but can also provide data about the incidence of disability in babies born at a given time to parents living in a given area. It is not appropriate merely to follow up babies treated in each hospital as patterns of referral may change over time and have spurious influence on the apparent incidence of disability.

A crucial question is whether people are willing to have their names, or their children's names, included on registers of disabled people. There is evidence that people are more willing to do so if it entitles them to some form of benefit. On the other hand, registration still offers some social stigma and lack of self esteem. It is as important to overcome this human problem as it is to resolve the technical problems involved if we want to set up systems to collect reliable and complete data to monitor the incidence and prevalence of disability and impairments. This is needed to assess the extent to which these impairments may be associated with factors at or around the time of birth and to plan services to enable all people with impairments to play a full role in society.

References

1   General Register Office. *Census of Great Britain, 1851. Population tables II*. Vol. I. London: HMSO, 1854.

2   House of Commons Social Services Committee. *Second report: perinatal and neonatal mortality. [Chair: R Short]*. Session 1979–1980. HC 663 Vol. I. London: HMSO, 1980.

3   Ewing H. Reply to parliamentary question. *House of Commons Official Report (Hansard)*. 27th November 1978.

4   House of Commons Health Committee. *Maternity services: second report. [Chair: N Winterton]*. Session 1991–92. HC 29–II Vol. II: Minutes of evidence. London: HMSO, 1991.

5   Johnson A, Mutch LM, Morley R. Memorandum submitted by Ann Johnson, Lesley Mutch and Ruth Morley (MS 176). In: House of Commons Health Committee. *Maternity services: second report. [Chair: N Winterton]*. Session 1991–92 HC 29–III Volume III. Appendices to the minutes of evidence. London: HMSO, 1992:703–709.

6   Higgs E. Disease, febrile poisons and statistics: the census as a medical survey, 1841–1911. *Social History of Medicine* 1991; 4(3): 465–478.

7   General Register Office. *Census of England and Wales, 1911. General report*. London: HMSO, 1917.

8   General Register Office. *Census of England and Wales, 1861. Vol. III: General report*. London: HMSO, 1863.

9   General Register Office. *Census of England and Wales, 1891. Vol. IV: General report*. London: HMSO, 1893.

10   General Register Office. *Census of England and Wales, 1881. Vol. IV: General report*. London: HMSO, 1883.

11   General Register Office. *Census of England and Wales, 1921. Preliminary report*. London: HMSO, 1921.

12   Interdepartmental Committee on Physical Deterioration. *Report*. Cd 2175. London: HMSO, 1904.

13   Sorsby A. *Causes of blindness in England*. MRC Memorandum No. 24. London: HMSO, 1952.

14   Ministry of Health. *Annual report of the Chief Medical Officer for the year 1950*. Cmd 8342. London: HMSO, 1952.

15   Ministry of Health. *Annual report of the Chief Medical Officer for the year 1953*. Cmd 9307. London: HMSO, 1954.

16   Ministry of Health. *Annual report of the Chief Medical Officer for the year 1960*. Cmnd 1418. London: HMSO, 1961.

17   Silverman W. *Retrolental fibroplasia: a modern parable*. New York: Grune and Stratton, 1980.

18   Sorsby A. *The incidence and causes of blindness in England and Wales, 1948–1962*. Reports on Public Health and Medical Subjects No. 114. London: HMSO, 1966.

19   Sorsby A. *The incidence and causes of blindness in England and Wales, 1963–1968*. Reports on Public Health and Medical Subjects No. 128. London: HMSO, 1972.

20   Abel RA. *An investigation into some aspects of visual handicap*. Statistical and Research Reports Series No. 14. London: HMSO, 1976.

21   Retrolental fibroplasia. *House of Commons Official Report (Hansard)*. 2nd February 1982.

22   Evans JR, Wormald RP. Epidemiological function of BD8 certification. *Eye* 1993; 7 (1): 172–179.

23   Evans J, Rooney C, Ashwood F, Dattani N, Wormald R. Blindness and partial sight in England and Wales, April 1990 – March 1991. *Health Trends* 1996; 28(1): 5–12.

24   Evans J. *Causes of blindness and partial sight in England and Wales, 1990–91*. Studies on Medical and Population Subjects No. 57. London: HMSO, 1995.

25   Royal College of Ophthalmologists, British Association of Perinatal Medicine. *Retinopathy of prematurity: guidelines for screening and treatment: the report of a Joint Working Party*. London: RCO and BAPM, 1995.

26   Phelps DL. Vision loss due to retinopathy of prematurity [letter]. *Lancet* 1981; i(8220 Pt 1): 606.

27   Lucey JF. Retrolental fibroplasia may not be preventable [editorial]. *Journal of the Royal Society of Medicine* 1982; 75(7): 496–497.

28   Stark DJ, Manning LM, Lenton L. Retrolental fibroplasia today. *Medical Journal of Australia* 1981; 1(6): 275–280.

29   Bebb GM. *Section 29 of the National Assistance Act, 1948 – registration practice and related statistics*. Letter to Local Authorities. March 18 1974.

30   Harris AI. *Handicapped and impaired in Great Britain*. Social Survey Report SS 418. London: HMSO, 1971.

31   The at-risk register. *Lancet* 1970; ii(673): 595–596.

32   Sheridan MD. Infants at risk of handicapping conditions. *Monthly Bulletin of the Ministry of Health and the Public Health Laboratory Service* 1962; 21: 238–245.

33   Department of Health and Social Security. *Annual report of the Chief Medical Officer for the year 1970*. London: HMSO, 1971.

34   Committee on Child Health Services. *Report: fit for the future. [Chair: Professor S.D.M. Court]*. Cmnd 6684. Vol. 2. London: HMSO, 1976.

35   Balarajan R, Weatherall JA, Ashley JS, Bewley BR. A survey of handicap registers for pre-school children in England and Wales. *Community Medicine* 1982; 4(4): 315–324.

36   Hutchison T, Harpin V. Survey of UK computerised special needs registers. *Archives of Disease In Childhood* 1998; 78(4): 312–315.

37   Miles M. Implications of the Children Act for paediatricians [editorial]. *Archives of Disease In Childhood* 1991; 66(4): 457–458.

38 Working Group on Definitions of Disability in Childhood. *Report. Disability in childhood: towards nationally useful definitions.* Part 1: Language, definitions and recommendations. London: British Association for Community Child Health and Department of Health, 1994.

39 Johnson A. Disability and perinatal care. *Pediatrics* 1995; 95(2): 272–274.

40 Oxford Register of Early Childhood Impairments. *Annual report, 1997.* Oxford: National Perinatal Epidemiology Unit and NHS Executive, Anglia and Oxford, 1998.

41 Parkes J, Dolk H, Hill N. Does the Child Health Computing System adequately identify children with cerebral palsy? *Journal of Public Health Medicine* 1998; 20(1): 102–104.

42 Johnson A, King R. Can routine information systems be used to monitor serious disability? *Archives of Disease In Childhood* 1999; 80: 63–66.

43 Working Group of the Registrar General's Medical Advisory Committee. *The OPCS monitoring system: a review by the Working Group.* OPCS Occasional Paper No. 43. London: OPCS, 1995.

44 Huang T, Watt HC, Wald NJ, Morris JK, Mutton D, Alberman E. Reliability of statistics on Down's syndrome notifications. *Journal of Medical Screening* 1997; 4(2): 95–97.

45 Mutton D, Ide RG, Alberman E. Trends in prenatal screening for and diagnosis of Down's syndrome: England and Wales, 1989–97. *BMJ* 1998; 317(7163): 922–923.

46 Tan KH, Kilby MD, Whittle MJ, Beattie BR, Booth IW, Botting BJ. Congenital anterior abdominal wall defects in England and Wales 1987–93: retrospective analysis of OPCS data. *BMJ* 1996; 313(7062): 903–906.

47 Stone DH, Rimaz S, Gilmour WH. Prevalence of congenital anterior abdominal wall defects in the United Kingdom: comparison of regional registers. *BMJ* 1998; 317(7166): 1118–1119.

48 Clarke S, Dykes E, Chapple J, Abramsky L. Congenital abdominal wall defects in the United Kingdom: sources had different reporting patterns. *BMJ* 1998; 318: 733.

49 Botting B. The impact of more complete data from Wales on the National Congenital Anomaly System. *Health Statistics Quarterly* 2000; 5: 7–9.

50 National congenital rubella surveillance programme. *British Medical Journal* 1979; 2: 396–397.

51 Tookey PA, Peckham CS. Surveillance of congenital rubella in Great Britain, 1971–96. *BMJ* 1999; 318(7186): 769–770.

52 MMR vaccine coverage at 24 months stabilises in the UK. Communicable Disease Report. *CDR Weekly* 1999; 9(13): 113, 116.

53   Office for National Statistics. *The 2001 census of population.* London: The Stationery Office, 1999.

54   Bone M, Meltzer H. *The prevalence of disability among children.* OPCS surveys of disability in Great Britain Report No. 3. London: HMSO, 1989.

9 Illness in babies

'It is unfortunate that in the stress of modern political life the subject of a national system of notification and registration of sickness, except as regards the chief infectious diseases and certain industrial diseases, has been allowed to drop into abeyance.'

Arthur Newsholme, 1899[1]

In the third edition of his book *Vital statistics*, published in 1899 when he was still Medical Officer of Health for Brighton, Arthur Newsholme outlined earlier attempts to compile statistics of diseases. The Metropolitan Association of Health tried in 1857 to set up a system for collecting data about people whose illnesses were treated in hospitals, dispensaries and workhouses. It failed as less than 50 of the 109 hospitals and dispensaries contributed. A system set up in 1860 by the Sanitary Association of Manchester and Salford appears to have been rather more successful.[1]

The General Register Office saw monitoring disease as a key part of its role in promoting public health in the nineteenth century.[2,3] It used data from death certificates to do this, but data were also needed about people whose illnesses were not fatal. In 1875, William Farr set out a plan for the registration of sickness. He suggested that weekly returns of sickness should be compiled in every district and published by 'a staff officer in every county or great city'.[4] He also suggested that the returns should be analysed nationally in London, an arrangement 'that with the present postal arrangements is quite practicable'. Farr optimistically anticipated that with such a system 'Illusion will be dispelled, quackery, as completely as astrology, suppressed, a science of therapeutics created, suffering diminished, life shielded from many dangers.'[4]

It is questionable whether this happy position has been reached by the end of the twentieth century, but we now have a range of statistics about the health of children. These were reviewed in *Children, teenagers and health*, published in 1993 and in an OPCS decennial supplement *The health of our children* published in 1995.[5,6] Inequalities in mortality in childhood and in children's health and lifestyle were discussed in two separate chapters of the ONS' decennial supplement *Health inequalities*.[7,8]

Because of the wealth of material available about health and illness in childhood as a whole in these publications and elsewhere, this chapter outlines briefly data about children's health in their first year of life. It starts by describing the system for notifying communicable disease which developed from the 1890s onwards, before going on to describe systems which were set up in the latter half of the twentieth century. These relate mainly to use of hospital and general practitioner services. The chapter ends by describing data collected through surveys.

Communicable diseases

The importance of communicable diseases as a cause of death and severe illness in the past is reflected in the attempts made to collect statistics about them. In London, this dates back to the plague year of 1563 when numbers of deaths from plague began to be collected in the weekly bills of mortality. Other causes of death were added in 1629, but it was not possible to distinguish deaths of babies and children until 1727 when the recording of age at death began.

The Public Health Act of 1875 enabled local authorities to set up their own notification systems for infectious diseases. These powers were extended in the Infectious Diseases (Notifications) Act of 1889 which made notification of certain diseases compulsory in London from 1891. This was extended to the rest of England and Wales in 1899. In a paper given to the Royal Statistical Society in 1896, Arthur Newsholme set out proposals for a national system.[9] In 1899, by which time over 80 per cent of the population was covered by voluntary systems, a further Act of Parliament made notification compulsory in England and Wales. Further legislation was subsequently introduced to extend the list of notifiable diseases and institute notification systems in Scotland and Northern Ireland. The diseases were notified by doctors to the medical officer of health of the local authority in which the person with the disease lived. The medical officers of health, who were responsible for the health of the local population, then made weekly returns to the appropriate registrar general.

The role of the medical officer of health disappeared in the 1974 reorganisation of local government and the National Health Service. From 1974 onwards, consultants in communicable disease control, employed by the NHS, acted as medical officers of environmental health or 'proper officers' for local authorities. From 1974 onwards they received notifications of communicable diseases. Up to 1981, proper officers provided OPCS with weekly counts of notifications and quarterly statistical returns giving analyses by age and sex. From 1982 onwards, proper officers sent information about the characteristics but not the identity of individual cases, as well as weekly abstracts.[10] OPCS then tabulated individual records centrally until 1997, when responsibility passed to the Communicable Disease Surveillance Centre.[11] From 1922 to 1973, weekly counts were published in the *Registrar General's weekly return*, and from 1974 onwards in an *OPCS monitor, Series WR*. They are now published in *CDR weekly*. Fuller data are published quarterly. Up to 1996, these were published by OPCS in Series MB2. They are now published by the Communicable Disease Surveillance Centre in special quarterly supplements to the *Communicable disease report* and in annual volumes of *Communicable disease statistics*.

In Scotland, communicable diseases are notified to the Information and Statistics Division. Data are published weekly by the Scottish Centre for

Information and Environmental Health and annually in *Scottish health statistics*. Communicable diseases in Northern Ireland are notified to the Department of Health, Social Services and Public Safety. Comparative European data are published monthly in *Eurosurveillance*.

Laboratories in Scotland report isolations of certain organisms to the Scottish Centre for Infection and Environmental Health and data are published weekly. Isolations of these organisms in laboratories in England, Wales, Northern Ireland and some laboratories in the Republic of Ireland are reported to the Communicable Disease Surveillance Centre at Colindale. The data are summarised in the weekly *Communicable disease report* and the annual volume of *Communicable disease statistics, England and Wales* published by the Public Health Laboratory Service.

In addition to the notification system described above, a set of volunteer general practices in the United Kingdom, most of them in England and Wales, notify a wider range of communicable diseases to the Research Unit of the Royal College of General Practitioners. Although derived from a small number of atypical practices, these data are invaluable for charting the course of epidemics of diseases such as influenza which is not statutorily notifiable.

In the past, death registrations were a major source of data about communicable diseases. As the death rates from these diseases in babies and young children are now fortunately very low they are of limited value in monitoring epidemics.

Statutory notifications are far from complete. General practitioners vary in the extent to which they remember to notify the diseases they diagnose. This assumes that the person consults her or his general practitioner in the first place. While it is unlikely that anyone suffering from cholera or Legionnaires' disease would not come into contact with a doctor, this may well not happen, for example, in the event of a mild attack of measles, particularly if another member of the same household has recently contracted the disease and been diagnosed as having it.

Despite these deficiencies, the data prove invaluable in monitoring communicable diseases in the population in general and babies and young children in particular. At the same time, care needs to be taken to ensure that changes in the notification rate do not merely reflect increases or decreases in the extent to which diagnosed cases are being notified instead of the rates of disease.

Rather than attempt to give a comprehensive set of data about communicable diseases we have selected data derived from notifications of diseases which are particularly common in babies. Annual notification rates for whooping cough, measles, meningitis, dysentery and scarlet fever among children aged under one year in England and Wales are shown in Tables A9.1.1 to A9.1.5.

The outbreaks in the late 1970s and early 1980s drew public attention to whooping cough or pertussis. In the 1990s, numbers of notifications fell as uptake of vaccination, shown in Tables A7.31.1 to A7.31.2, rose. Quarterly data shown in Figure 9.1 reveal considerable epidemic fluctuations in the

Figure 9.1

Quarterly notification rates of whooping cough in babies aged under one year, England and Wales, 1944–97

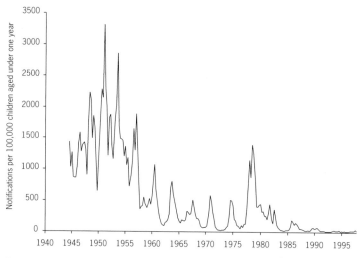

Source: Communicable disease statistics

overall trends. The rise in notifications coincided with a fall in the proportion of babies vaccinated. This resulted from parents' fears about the possibility of vaccine damage.

Although the numbers of notifications of measles have declined since vaccination was introduced in 1968, the considerable numbers of cases still being notified in the 1970s and 1980s reflected a low level of response to the vaccination programme at the time, shown in Tables A7.31.1 to A7.31.4. Combined measles, mumps and rubella (MMR) vaccination was introduced in 1989. In the 1990s, uptake was well over 90 per cent and the numbers of cases notified fell. Quarterly data are shown in Figure 9.2. As can be seen there, before mass immunisation was introduced, notifications of measles had a two year cycle with increases in one year being followed by decreases in succeeding years. This pattern can be seen in seventeenth century bills of mortality.

If a pregnant woman has a sexually transmitted disease, this can result in infection in her newborn baby. For example, babies born to women with gonorrhoea can develop ophthalmia neonatorum, an eye condition which is notifiable as an infectious disease. Notification data for England and Wales are shown in Table A9.1.6. Cases of ophthalmia neonatorum are also included in returns from genitourinary clinics, but the numbers of babies included are much smaller, suggesting that they tend to be treated in paediatric departments rather than clinics. The same is likely to be true of congenital syphilis which is not a notifiable disease. Paediatricians will tend to treat the baby themselves while referring the mother to the clinic, in which case the baby's disease would not be reported. It is suspected that chlamydia trachomatis can cause eye and lung infection and genital herpes occasionally harms babies born to women with the disease.[12,13] Data about sexually transmitted diseases in adults are discussed in Chapter 10.

266

Figure 9.2

Quarterly notification rates of measles in babies aged under one year, England and Wales, 1944–97

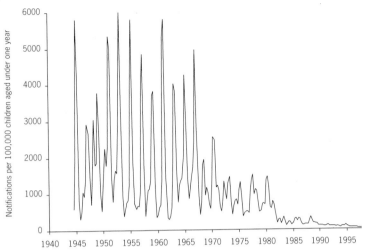

Source: Communicable disease statistics

The reporting system for HIV and AIDS dates back to 1982, when doctors were asked to provide confidential reports to the Communicable Disease Surveillance Centre and its counterparts in the other parts of the United Kingdom. Reports from laboratories began in 1984. Data for the United Kingdom as a whole are collated by the Communicable Disease Surveillance Centre.[14–16] General trends are shown in Table A10.6.1 while Table A9.2.1 shows numbers of children born to HIV infected mothers in two year periods. Both the numbers of children and the numbers reported to be infected increased up to 1992/93. Apparent declines since then probably reflect delays in reporting and resolving whether a child is infected or otherwise.[17] It is known that the numbers of cases are under-reported. Women with HIV infection diagnosed in pregnancy are reported to the Royal College of Obstetricians and Gynaecologists' survey of HIV in pregnancy, coordinated by the Institute of Child Health in London. Children with HIV are reported to the British Paediatric Surveillance Unit.[17]

There is also a comprehensive programme of unlinked anonymous monitoring of levels of HIV infection in specific categories of people, including pregnant women, women having abortions and babies and women attending genitourinary medicine clinics. Since 1988, there has been unlinked anonymous monitoring of prevalence in pregnant women by testing for their antibodies in dried spots of their babies' blood.[18] Using data from these sources, it was estimated that in 1996, 0.19 per cent of pregnant women in London and 0.02 per cent of those elsewhere in the United Kingdom were infected with HIV. This represents a five fold rise in prevalence of infection in women in London since 1988 and a significant rise in prevalence in the rest of England in 1996 compared with earlier years.[19] Despite measures that will substantially reduce the risk of transmission of HIV from mothers to children, such as the use of zidovudine by women during pregnancy, numbers of children were still being born infected by HIV because of low levels of testing and diagnosis in pregnancy.[20]

Other illnesses in babies

Data about the admission of babies to hospital, derived from the Hospital Episode Statistics are shown in Table A9.3.1. It does not include newborn babies in their initial stay in hospital after birth, unless the baby was admitted to a special or intensive care unit. It shows that among children aged under a month most admissions were classified as for 'perinatal conditions' or for 'symptoms, signs and ill-defined conditions'. These, along with respiratory diseases accounted for most of the admissions in the postneonatal period. Boys were more likely to be admitted than girls, especially for respiratory conditions in the postneonatal period.

Data about children's visits to general practitioners have been included in the four surveys of morbidity statistics in general practice.[21-24] These record consultations with a set of volunteer general practitioners. They are not a random sample. General practitioners in inner city areas tend to be under-represented. Consultations by children aged 0–4 years are grouped together in the report of the fourth survey, which took place from September 1991 to August 1992.[24] All children under the age of 16 were grouped together and analysed by ethnic group, housing tenure, social class and employment status of parents. A separate analysis of consultation rates of children aged 0–4 years old found considerable social class differences and highlighted the need for prevention.[25] The survey is therefore a useful source of data about children in general, but published analyses tell very little about babies in the first year of life.

As general practices became computerised, a number of projects were set up to extract data for epidemiological studies. Some of the earliest projects were funded by pharmaceutical companies and were therefore biased towards data about prescriptions issued and linked to particular computer systems. In 1997, the NHS Executive Information Management Group set up the 'MIQUEST' pilot project to develop methods for extracting data from a variety of general practice computer systems. Participating health authorities have used the techniques for a variety of purposes including collecting health promotion data and supporting clinical audit.[26] General practices have used it to inform decisions on clinical priorities and commissioning. Although the results of the pilot are important for meeting the information needs of primary care groups, the data it produced were mainly for local use.

One of the major commercial databases was set up by VAMP Health Ltd in 1987. It aimed to include a good geographical spread of practices. In 1993,

Reuter's took over the company and offered the database to the Department of Health. From 1994 to 1999, ONS ran this database, now known as the General Practice Research Database, on the Department's behalf.[27] In April 1999, ownership was transferred to the Medicines Control Agency, with ONS continuing to operate the database. ONS uses the data to publish an annual volume of *Key health statistics from general practice, Series MB6*.

Tables in this volume do not identify babies separately but a special study of consultations by babies in the first year of life and their mothers is under way in the National Perinatal Epidemiology Unit. Data from this study are shown in Tables A9.4.1 and A9.4.2. They show that in the first 90 days after birth, 87 per cent of babies had been to a general practitioner for immunisation and 45 per cent for a routine check. Some of the other diagnoses recorded in this period may have been related to these checks rather than a specific visit to the doctor. Between ten and twenty per cent of babies had upper respiratory tract infections, conjunctivitis, minor skin problems, diarrhoea and vomiting or thrush.

These same problems were the predominant cause of consultations among older babies. Respiratory problems were particularly common, with over half having consulted at least once for upper respiratory tract infections. Diagnosis of cough, chest infection and snuffles were recorded in between a fifth and just under a third of babies.

Just over a fifth of babies had been seen by general practitioners for ear problems by the end of their first year. Nearly a third had done so for conjunctivitis, about a quarter for a range of skin problems and a third for a range of gastrointestinal tract disorders. Fourteen per cent had consulted for viral illness, three per cent for head injuries and eight per cent as a consequence of other injuries and accidents.

A problem in interpreting these data is variations between practitioners and practices in the ways in which respiratory, skin and gastrointestinal tract conditions are recorded. Further analysis is needed to ascertain the extent to which the same babies may have had more than one diagnosis and assess the overall incidence of such groups of conditions.

As Table A9.2.1 implies, cancer is very rare in children aged under a year. Information about cancer in childhood, which can, in a few rare cases, reflect events during pregnancy, is included in cancer registries. Some regions have specialised children's tumour registries. The National Registry of Childhood Tumours is based in the Childhood Cancer Research Group in Oxford, where data are analysed at a national level. It has shown major increases in survival rates during the last quarter of the twentieth century.[28,29] As well as monitoring trends in childhood cancer, the National Registry of Childhood Tumours can be used for research which examines possible associations between cancers in childhood and events and circumstances at birth, for example the administration of vitamin K.[30]

Taken together, Tables A9.3.1, A9.4.1. and A9.4.2 show that illness in the first year of life is dominated by respiratory and other infections, ear and eye conditions, skin conditions and genitourinary tract disorders. Among babies aged under a month, conditions present at birth play a major role. Most babies are seen in primary care settings for immunisation and, to a considerable though lesser extent, routine checks.

In this age group, accidents and cancer, which are important causes of injury and death in older children, are not common. Thus statistics which group together all children under five, as is done in Table 9.1, do not give a clear picture of the health of babies. This comes from the General Household Survey, which is based on a random sample of households. It includes questions about acute and chronic illness and visits to general practitioners and to out-patient departments. It therefore contains information about people's perceptions or identification of their own ill health or, in the case of children, their parents' perceptions of it. It is difficult to relate this to medically orientated diagnoses, especially as the interviewers are not medically trained. Volumes of data are published annually and some questions change from year to year.

Health in childhood and characteristics at birth

Much more detailed data about health are collected in the series of health surveys for England and Scotland. They do not cover children under the age of two years but there are plans to do so in 2001 and 2002. A special volume bringing together data about young people aged from two to 24 years, collected over the three years 1995 to 1997, was published in 1998.[31] It included an analysis of body mass index of children aged two to 15 years in relation to their birthweight. This showed that 26 per cent of boys and 30 per cent of girls whose birthweight was in the top quintile had body mass indices in the top quintile. By contrast, only 17 per cent of boys and 15 per cent of girls with birthweight in the bottom quintile had body mass indices in the top quintile.[31]

Much more extensive analyses have been done of data from the three national birth cohort surveys. Unfortunately, there is no comparable source of data for children born since the most recent of these cohorts studies was started in 1970.

Table 9.1

Reported illness and use of health services by children aged 0 to 4 years, 1996

Percentage who reported:	Boys	Girls	All
Longstanding illness	14	13	13
Limiting longstanding illness	4	4	4
Restricted activity in the 14 days before interview	12	9	10
Consultation with general practitioner	23	20	22
Attendance at out-patients or casualty in a three month reference period	13	9	11
Hospital treatment in previous 12 months			
As day patient	5	3	4
As in-patient	9	7	8

Source: Office for National Statistics, *General Household Survey, 1996*

In theory, longitudinal data should be available from child health computer systems. Attempts to do this in England have found, however that while birth data are relatively complete, many of the data collected about children around the age of two are missing. In Scotland, the situation is much better. A study in the Grampian Region attempted to link SMR11 records of babies involved in a randomised trial to those records in the community health index, a computer held list of all patients registered with a general practitioner. It was able to match 89.7 per cent of records by computer and the remainder manually.[32]

Monitoring the health of babies in the 1990s and 2000s

The ideas of William Farr and Arthur Newsholme were geared to the monitoring of communicable diseases which have now diminished in their importance. It is perhaps inevitable that it should be easier to collect data about the activities of the hospital and primary health care services than to monitor the course of illness in the population through surveys. Nevertheless, our ability to monitor the health of children grew during the 1990s, with an increase in the number of population surveys and developments in using data from general practice systems. Unfortunately babies are either excluded or not identified separately in the surveys which are undertaken, either because different survey techniques and questions are needed or because larger samples would be required. General practice computer systems offer a potential for deriving fuller information about the health problems of babies in the future, but there are many problems of access and data quality to be tackled before they can do so.

References

1 Newsholme A. *The elements of vital statistics*. 3rd edition. London: S Sonnenschein and Co, 1899.

2 Higgs E. A cuckoo in the nest? The origins of civil registration and state medical statistics in England and Wales. *Continuity and Change* 1996; 11(1): 115–134.

3 Szreter S. The GRO and the public health movement in Britain, 1837–1914. *Social History of Medicine* 1991; 4(3): 435–463.

4 Farr W. Letter to the Registrar General. In: *Supplement to the 35th annual report of the Registrar General on births, deaths and marriages in England, 1861–1870*. London: HMSO, 1875.

5 Woodroffe C, Glickman M, Barker M, Power C. *Children, teenagers and health: the key data*. Buckingham: Open University Press, 1993.

6 Botting B, ed. *The health of our children*. OPCS Decennial Supplement Series DS No. 11. London: HMSO, 1995.

7 Botting B. Mortality in childhood. In: Drever F, Whitehead M, eds. *Health inequalities*. ONS Decennial Supplement Series DS No. 15. London: The Stationery Office, 1997.

8   Botting B, Bunting J. Children's health and lifestyle. In: Drever F, Whitehead M, eds. *Health inequalities*. ONS Decennial Supplement Series DS No. 15. London: The Stationery Office, 1997.

9   Newsholme A. A national system of notification and registration of sickness. *Journal of the Royal Statistical Society* 1896; 59: 1–37.

10   Office of Population Censuses and Surveys. *Infectious diseases, March quarter, 1982*. OPCS Monitor MB2 82/3. London: OPCS, 1982.

11   New arrangements for processing notification of infectious disease returns. *CDR Weekly* 1997; 7(17): 1.

12   Department of Health. *Chlamydia trachomatis. Summary and conclusions of the Chief Medical Officer's Expert Advisory Group*. London: Department of Health, 1998.

13   Tookey P, Peckham CS. Neonatal herpes simplex virus infection in the British Isles. *Paediatric and Perinatal Epidemiology* 1996; 10: 432–442.

14   AIDS and HIV infection in the United Kingdom: monthly report. A new format for data from the United Kingdom. *CDR Weekly* 1999; 9(5): 45–48.

15   Mortimer JY, Evans BG, Goldberg DJ. The surveillance of HIV infection and AIDS in the United Kingdom. *CDR Review* 1997; 7(9): R118–R120.

16   Hughes G. An overview of the HIV and AIDS epidemic in the United Kingdom. *CDR Review* 1997; 7(9): R121–R124.

17   Molesworth A, Tookey P. Paediatric AIDS and HIV infection. *CDR Review* 1997; 7(9): R132–R134.

18   Unlinked Anonymous HIV Surveys Steering Group. *Prevalence of HIV in England and Wales in 1997: report of the unlinked anonymous seroprevalence monitoring programme in England and Wales*. London: Department of Health, PHLS and Institute of Child Health, 1998.

19   Intercollegiate Working Party for Enhancing Voluntary Confidential HIV Testing in Pregnancy. *Reducing mother to child transmission of HIV infection in the United Kingdom: recommendations of the Working Party*. London: Royal College of Paediatrics and Child Health, 1998.

20   Nicoll A. Antenatal screening for HIV in the UK: what's to be done? *Journal of Medical Screening* 1998; 5: 170–171.

21   General Register Office. *Morbidity statistics from general practice, 1955–56*. Studies on Medical and Population Subjects No. 14. London: HMSO, 1958.

22   Royal College of General Practitioners, Office of Population Censuses and Surveys, and Department of Health and Social Security. *Morbidity statistics from general practice, 1971–72: second national study*. Studies on Medical and Population Subjects No. 36. London: HMSO, 1979.

23   Royal College of General Practitioners, Office of Population Censuses and Surveys, and Department of Health and Social Security. *Morbidity statistics from general practice, 1981–82: third national study.* Series MB5 No. 1. London: HMSO, 1986.

24   Royal College of General Practitioners, Office of Population Censuses and Surveys, and Department of Health. *Morbidity statistics from general practice: fourth national study, 1991–1992.* Series MB5 No. 3. London: HMSO, 1995.

25   Saxena S, Majeed A, Jones M. Socio-economic differences in childhood consultation rates in general practice in England and Wales: prospective cohort study. *BMJ* 1999; 318: 642–646.

26   Department of Health, NHS Executive. *Collection of data from general practice: overview.* Leeds: NHS Executive, 1996.

27   Hollowell J. The General Practice Research Database: quality of morbidity data. *Population Trends* 1997; 87: 36–40.

28   Draper GJ. Cancer. In: Botting B, ed. *The health of our children.* OPCS Decennial Supplement Series DS No. 11. London: HMSO, 1995.

29   Draper GJ, Kroll ME, Stiller CA. Childhood cancer. *Cancer Surveys* 1994; 19–20: 493–513.

30   Passmore BJ, Draper G, Brownbill P, Kroll M. Case-control studies of relation between childhood cancer and neonatal vitamin K administration. *BMJ* 1998; 316: 178–184.

31   Prescott-Clarke P, Primatesta P, eds. *Health survey for England. The health of young people, '95–97.* Vol. 1: Findings. London: The Stationery Office, 1998.

32   Ramsay CR, Campbell MK, Glazener CMA. Linking community health index and Scottish morbidity records for neonates: the Grampian experience. *Health Bulletin* 1999; 57(1): 70–75.

10 Maternal mortality and reproductive health

'Queen Jane lay in labour full nine days or more
Till the women were so tired, they could stay no longer there.

"Good women, good women, good women as ye be,
Do open my right side and find my baby."

"Oh no" said the women. "That never may be,
We will send for King Henry, and hear what he do say."

King Henry was sent for, King Henry did come:
"What ails you, my lady, your eyes look so dim?"

"King Henry, King Henry, will you do one thing for me?
That's to open my right side, and find my baby."

"Oh no" said King Henry "That's a thing I'll never do.
If I lose the flower of England, I shall lose the branch too."

King Henry went mourning, and so did his men
And so did the dear baby, for Queen Jane did die then.

And how deep was the mourning, how black were the bands,
How yellow, yellow were the flamboys they carried in their hands.

There was fiddling, aye and dancing on the day the babe was born.
But poor Queen Jane beloved lay cold as a stone.'

The death of Queen Jane[1]

In Britain today, death resulting from pregnancy or childbirth is a relatively rare event, but it has only become so in the latter half of the twentieth century, and is still common in many parts of the world. It would not have appeared as a remote possibility to Mrs Russell, the Dorset woman from whom this version of the ballad of the death of Queen Jane was recorded in 1907.[1] In that year, 3,520 deaths in England and Wales were attributed to the consequences of pregnancy and childbearing, giving a rate of 3.8 per thousand live births. In contrast to this, only 38 direct and indirect maternal deaths were registered in England and Wales in 1997, and the rate was 0.059 per thousand births. Most historians tell us that Jane Seymour died on October 24 1537, twelve days after her son was born naturally, so the ballad account is probably incorrect.[2] Despite this, it reminds us that in the past, not only many ordinary women, but also women from the more privileged social groups, including Mrs Beeton, the writer Mary Wollstonecraft and Princess Charlotte, daughter of the Prince Regent, have died as a consequence of childbearing.[2-4]

The problem of assessing the extent to which women die as a consequence of pregnancy, delivery, miscarriage and induced abortion raises a number of questions. In particular, changes in views about the causes of maternal death influence the way definitions are interpreted. This, in its turn, affects the way death certificates are completed and how the information given on them is classified and analysed.

This chapter starts by discussing the way definitions and classifications of maternal death developed during the twentieth century. It goes on to discuss the extent to which pregnancy is reported on death certificates before describing special enquiries into maternal mortality and how they paved the way for the confidential enquiry system in use today. This is followed by a discussion of trends and variations in maternal mortality.

The second part of the chapter opens by describing data about morbidity directly associated with childbearing. A relatively small number of women experience severe morbidity, but non-life threatening morbidity is much more widespread. The chapter ends with other aspects of reproductive health, notably sexually transmitted diseases and cancer of the reproductive organs.

Measuring maternal mortality

Defining maternal deaths

Traditionally, maternal deaths have been classified as 'true' maternal deaths or deaths from 'puerperal causes' when the pregnancy was directly responsible for the initiation of the sequence of events leading up to the woman's death. Other deaths of pregnant women have been attributed to 'non-puerperal' or 'associated' conditions. In these, the condition which led to death was either unrelated to the pregnancy and therefore coincidental, or existed before and developed during the pregnancy.

The terms 'direct obstetric death' and 'indirect obstetric death', which are defined in Chapter 2, were introduced in the ninth revision of the International Classification of Diseases.[5] It can be seen that to all intents and purposes the definitions of 'true maternal' and 'direct obstetric' deaths are equivalent to each other. Deaths from 'associated conditions' were subdivided in the ninth revision into 'indirect obstetric' deaths, where the existing condition and conditions arising in the pregnancy and puerperium were inter-related, and the remainder, which were defined as 'fortuitous deaths'. This term disappeared in the tenth revision of the ICD. Two new categories, late maternal deaths and pregnancy related deaths were introduced. These are detailed in Table 2.7.

In practice, it has often proved difficult to make these distinctions in individual cases. Furthermore, for women in the early stages of pregnancy, whose pregnancy was not confirmed, or whose pregnancy was concealed, the fact of pregnancy may have been intentionally or inadvertently omitted from their death certificates, particularly in the past. For these reasons, the way maternal deaths have been classified has changed considerably over the years.

Changes in the classification of maternal deaths

Successive revisions of the ICD have included changes both between and within the broad categories of puerperal or 'true maternal' causes and the 'associated' conditions.

The classifications of diseases in use during the nineteenth century divided puerperal causes into two major groups, puerperal sepsis and accidents of childbirth, shown in Table A10.1.1. In 1901, when the first international classification replaced the classification previously in use, 'phlegmasia alba dolens', now usually called puerperal phlebitis and thrombosis was included with puerperal septic diseases among the puerperal causes.

When the classification was revised in 1911, major changes took place. Deaths from puerperal mastitis were transferred from the puerperal sepsis group to deaths from other puerperal causes. Deaths from puerperal nephritis and albuminuria, which were previously classified as diseases of the kidneys, and were therefore grouped with the associated deaths, were now classified as puerperal causes. Until 1939, rates continued to be calculated according to both the pre-1911 and the 1911 classification and these are given in Table A10.1.2 and shown in Figure 10.1.

The changes made in 1921 were fairly minor but those made in 1931 were more extensive. The small numbers of deaths from puerperal tetanus were moved from the 'associated' causes to the deaths from sepsis. Deaths from post abortive sepsis were separated from other deaths from sepsis. In England and Wales, the change had been anticipated and separate totals were produced from 1926 onwards for abortions of known gestation and,

Figure 10.1

Maternal mortality, England and Wales, 1847–1997

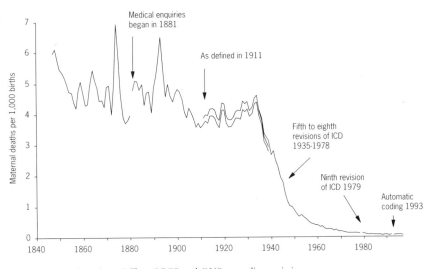

Source: General Register Office, OPCS and ONS mortality statistics

from 1928, for all abortions.[6] Deaths which were known to follow 'criminal abortion' and thus were the subject of coroners' inquests were included in the 'violent deaths' chapter of the ICD. They were given underlying causes of 'suicide', 'homicide', 'manslaughter' and 'open verdict'. These data were moved to the conditions of pregnancy section in the fifth revision which came into use in England and Wales in 1940.

The changes made in the classifications of maternal deaths introduced in 1911, 1921 and 1931 were summarised in a Ministry of Health report on maternal mortality published in 1937.[7] Changes made in the fifth and sixth revisions were summarised in the appendix to an analysis of maternal mortality data between 1921 and 1952 by Wallis Taylor and Marjorie Dauncey.[8] The changes made in the seventh and eighth revisions were not very extensive. This makes it possible to construct a continuous series of cause specific mortality rates for England and Wales from 1940 to 1978, with broader categories going back to 1931. This is given in Table A10.1.3 and mortality rates from all maternal causes are shown in Figure 10.1. Maternal mortality rates for Scotland from 1965–1978 are shown in Table A10.2.5.

In the ninth revision of the ICD, the chapter dealing with conditions of pregnancy, childbirth and the puerperium was revised extensively.[5] Those associated causes which were considered to be 'indirect obstetric' causes, that is 'conditions in the mother classifiable elsewhere but complicating pregnancy, childbirth and the puerperium', ICD 647 and 648, were added to the Chapter of the ICD used to classify deaths from conditions of pregnancy. This marked a change from all previous revisions, in which all 'associated' conditions were given ICD codes outside the chapter. There were a number of changes within the 'direct obstetric' causes. In particular, the section used to classify abortions was widened to 'pregnancies with abortive outcome' and ectopic pregnancies were added to it.

These changes mean that maternal mortality rates derived according to the ninth revision of the ICD in Tables A10.2.1 and A10.2.2 cannot be compared with those based on earlier revisions. In the tenth revision, the codes were rearranged and renumbered and two codes were added for late maternal deaths.[9]

Choice of denominator for maternal mortality rates

Before 1928 in England and Wales, 1939 in Scotland and 1961 in Northern Ireland maternal mortality rates were expressed as deaths per thousand live births. In those years, stillbirth registration started in the countries mentioned and the denominator was changed to total live and stillbirths, although both forms of rate continued to be published to provide continuity. We have used live births as the denominator in Tables A10.1.1 and A10.1.2 and total births in Table A10.1.3.

Although the number of total births is the denominator most commonly used it is probably not the best. This question was discussed in some detail in the report on maternal mortality published by the Ministry of Health in 1937.[7]

There it was pointed out that the number of maternities would be a more appropriate denominator as it represented maternal lives at risk. This is in fact the denominator now used in the *Reports on confidential enquiries into maternal deaths* and in Table A10.1.4.

As maternal deaths include deaths from abortion and ectopic pregnancy it would, theoretically, be more accurate to include these in the denominator as well. This was done for death rates for abortion and ectopic pregnancy in the *Report on confidential enquiries into maternal deaths in England and Wales*, for the three year period 1976–78. In this, the numbers of miscarriages and ectopic pregnancies were estimated from the Hospital In-patient Enquiry, until it was abolished in 1985, as it was unlikely that a woman with an ectopic pregnancy would not be admitted to an NHS hospital. As was pointed out in Chapter 4, however, this method would be likely to underestimate the numbers of miscarriages by an unknown amount. In any case the numbers of induced abortions to residents of England and Wales and Scotland have been known with any accuracy only since the Abortion Act came into force. With the decline in deaths from abortion and the poor quality of data for England in the Maternity Hospital Episode Statistics, abortion statistics are no longer analysed in this amount of detail.

Coverage of maternal deaths in death registration

The first mention of maternal mortality in the Registrar General's annual reports for England and Wales was in the report for 1841.[10] As well as comments from William Farr, this report included a paper by Robert Storrs, a surgeon of Doncaster, about puerperal fever in his private practice. On the subject of puerperal fever in lying-in hospitals, William Farr commented that 'the extent to which these institutions increased the danger of childbirth is now well known.'[10]

He returned to the theme in extended analyses in the *Annual reports* for 1867,[11] 1870[12] and in 1876[13] when he referred to death in childbirth as a 'deep, dark continuous stream of mortality'. Most of the tabulations in the *Annual reports* were of deaths attributed to 'accidents of childbirth' or 'metria', a name for puerperal fever. The rate for both causes combined fluctuated around five per thousand live births. In the mid 1860s, tabulations of 'deaths of women after childbirth' but assigned to other causes and deaths of women 'who were returned as pregnant' were added. In the report for 1870,[12] Farr replied to John Matthews Duncan, an Edinburgh obstetrician, who, in the course of defending lying-in hospitals, had claimed that maternal mortality was vastly under-reported and a more accurate assessment would be about 8 deaths per thousand births.[14]

William Farr also referred to Florence Nightingale's work in *Introductory notes on lying-in institutions*.[15] In this, she had pointed both to the high mortality rates in lying-in institutions and also the difficulty in making comparisons between hospitals because of differences in the ways data were collected.

While John Matthews Duncan's views on hospital births were challenged from a number of directions,[16] it is likely that he was correct in his views about the under-reporting of maternal deaths up to 1880. Evidence for this came in 1881 when the General Register Office started to send out letters of enquiry to medical practitioners who submitted incomplete or ambiguous certificates of cause of death. In 1881, 1,200 letters were sent, resulting in an increase of 330 or 8 per cent in the numbers of deaths attributed to puerperal fever or accidents of childbirth. The *Registrar General's annual report* said of the data for preceding years: 'It need hardly be pointed out that statistics of childbirth mortality such as these, based as they are on such imperfect data, must be used with extreme caution even for the purpose of comparing one year with another and must be entirely rejected as furnishing any sure basis for estimating the actual mortality due to childbirth in any one year.'[17] The 'imperfect data' in question are summarised in the *Registrar General's annual report for 1885*.[18]

The practice of sending out letters of enquiry continued until more extensive enquiries were set up in the 1930s. In 1891, 198 additional maternal deaths were revealed in this way, but by 1911, 12,653 letters of enquiry resulted in the addition of only about 50 maternal deaths. In 1934, about 10,000 enquiries revealed an additional 85 maternal deaths, however.[7]

The criteria for reporting deaths from associated causes in England and Wales changed in 1911. Before this, certifiers were asked to mention childbirth if it occurred within one month before death. From 1911 onwards the time limit was removed, but certifiers were only asked to mention pregnancy or childbirth if it was causally related to the death. It was thought that these changes may have compensated for each other numerically.[7] The major fluctuation in Figure 10.1 was a rise in mortality at the time of the influenza epidemic of 1918.

A new certificate was introduced in 1927, with a revised wording. This asked for mentions of factors 'contributing to death but not related to the immediate cause'. Its effect was to increase the reporting of mortality associated with childbearing.[6] The view was expressed in the *Registrar General's statistical review for 1933* that reporting of associated deaths was relatively complete at the time.[6] It is difficult to assess in retrospect the extent to which this was true, not only of 'associated' deaths but also of deaths from puerperal causes, particularly where illegally induced abortion was concerned. A pathologist's study of deaths in London from 1963 to 1967 in which 'unnatural causes' had been discounted in the coroners' officers' reports revealed deaths from a number of 'unnatural causes' including 'criminal abortion'.[19]

Special enquiries into maternal mortality

In the early years of the twentieth century, it was infant rather than maternal mortality which was considered to be a major problem. The Local Government Board, the forerunner of the Ministry of Health, responded with the series of four reports on infant and child mortality mentioned in previous chapters.[20-23] As part of this enquiry, it also published a report on maternal mortality, focusing particularly on its relationship to infant mortality.[24]

In the years that followed, both infant mortality and overall mortality rates declined. Public attention shifted to the maternal mortality rate which not only failed to fall but actually rose during the 1920s and early 1930s, promoting a series of reports and enquiries on the subject.

Janet Campbell, who was in charge of the division of maternity and child welfare at the Ministry of Health, wrote a number of reports on the organisation of the maternity services. In reviewing the subject of maternal mortality and looking into individual case histories in 1924, she expressed the view that the problem was mainly a result of the inadequacies of the maternity services.[25]

In Scotland, a Scottish departmental committee concluded that 'puerperal mortality is but a section of a much wider group of causes of puerperal morbidity.'[26] It, too, felt that, while environmental factors were important, the solution lay in the improvement and extension of the maternity services and giving particular attention to puerperal sepsis. It suggested the investigation of individual maternal deaths. An enquiry of this sort had been set up in Aberdeen by the Medical Officer of Health, Matthew Hay. His successor, Parlane Kinloch published a report in 1928, based on a detailed analysis of records of 252 maternal deaths between 1918 and 1927.[27]

An enquiry into individual maternal deaths was set up in England and Wales in 1928 as part of the work of a committee appointed by the Ministry of Health 'to advise upon the application to maternal mortality and morbidity of the medical and surgical knowledge at present available, and to enquire into the needs and direction of further research work.' Medical officers of health were invited to obtain information about every maternal death in their area and send confidential reports to the Ministry. Reports on 5,805 deaths, analysed in two series, were included in the Committee's interim and final reports published in 1930[28] and 1932.[29]

The system of scrutiny was continued by the Ministry of Health and summary statements were included in the *Chief Medical Officer's annual reports* from 1932 to 1953. Data from the system were also used in an enquiry into areas with particularly high maternal mortality,[30] in the further reports on maternal mortality in England and Wales published in 1937[7,31] and the report of the Interdepartmental Committee on Abortion published in 1939.[32]

Meanwhile, in Scotland the enquiry method was taken a stage further. Not only were particulars recorded about 2,527 maternal deaths which occurred from 1927 to 1932, data were also collected about all the 39,205 births occurring in a six month period, so that comparisons could be made between the two groups of women.[33] This idea of finding appropriate control groups has yet to be employed in subsequent enquiries into maternal deaths in the United Kingdom.

Confidential enquiries

The system of *Confidential enquiries into maternal deaths*, which is described in Chapter 2, started in England and Wales in 1952. The *Annual report of the Chief Medical Officer* for that year commented that: 'Under the old system the enquiries were often incomplete or had ceased in some areas.'[34] Of the new system, it commented that: 'Its prime purpose was to place the clinical enquiries and assessment of avoidable factors in the hands of practising consultant obstetricians.'[34]

The first report, for the years 1952–54, covered 77 per cent of all the registered 'true maternal deaths'. Unlike the old system, it also included 'associated deaths'. From then onwards, reports were issued triennially until 1982–84.

In Northern Ireland a similar system was set up in 1956 and five reports were published. The first three covered the four-year periods 1956–59, 1960–63 and 1964–67. The fourth, published in 1982, covered the ten-year period 1968–77.[35] Because the population is small and the maternal death rate was low, it was based on only 54 true maternal deaths and 34 deaths from associated conditions. In his introduction, the Chief Medical Officer commented: 'In the period 1978–1981 there have been 15 deaths reported to the Enquiry. It is not expected that another report will be issued for several years.'[35] The last report covered 32 deaths in the years 1978–84.[36]

Similar considerations apply in Scotland where a number of reports have been published. The first dealt with the years 1965–71. The second, for the years 1972–75, covered 50 of the 51 known true maternal deaths in those years and all of the 42 deaths from associated conditions.[37] The next report covered the years 1976–1980.[38] Two further reports covered maternal and perinatal deaths in 1981–85 and 1986–92.[39,40] The Scottish reports subdivided the deaths from associated conditions into 'associated' deaths and 'fortuitous' deaths. The definition of 'associated' deaths given in the Scottish reports is similar to the ninth revision definition of 'indirect' deaths.

From 1985–87 onwards, a single report has been published for the whole United Kingdom. A number of changes were made in the report which covered deaths in the three years 1994–96.[41]

All these enquiries include deaths within one year of delivery or abortion. Thus, in the past, they included deaths which would not be classified as maternal or associated deaths by the ICD, which bases definitions on a period of 6 weeks. As the Northern Ireland report for 1968–77 pointed out, there is a risk that the association with pregnancy in some types of death outside the six week period may be under-reported. It gave as an example women with postnatal depression who commit suicide.[35]

The change in the way death certificates were processed in England and Wales from 1993 onwards led to increased reporting of maternal deaths in the three year period 1994–96. As all the conditions on the death certificates were computerised, from 1993, it became possible to identify certificates where maternal death was not the underlying cause, but pregnancy was an associated factor.[41]

Selected data from the reports are given in Tables A10.4.1 to A10.4.5. The reports have sections devoted to the major groupings of causes of death, but discuss some deaths under more than one heading. For example, if the woman had a caesarean section, her death is likely to be discussed not only in the light of the conditions which led to the caesarean, but also under the headings of deaths associated with caesarean sections and deaths associated with the use of anaesthetics.

Up to the three year period 1976–78, attempts were made to assess whether factors associated with the death were avoidable and to attribute responsibility for these factors. The subjective nature of the process was acknowledged in the report for England and Wales for 1976–78:

> 'Throughout the 27 years of history of these confidential enquiries the presence of avoidable factors has been recorded; there has been a rise in the generally accepted standards of satisfactory care which may have been partly as a consequence of the publication of these reports. It is therefore not surprising to find that the proportion of deaths associated with avoidable factors has not decreased as have the absolute numbers of deaths and the mortality rates. Indeed the entry of new consultant advisers in obstetrics will bring fresh view points and alter standards. In this report most of the avoidable factors concern failure to provide appropriate care.'[42]

In interpreting judgements about avoidability, therefore, it should be borne in mind that there is considerable variation in the views of clinicians as to what constitutes 'appropriate care'. Opinion as to the extent to which a woman who has not availed herself of certain items of care is responsible for 'avoidable' factors related to her own death, beg the question of how much this may have reflected other factors in her life, which she could have explained had she not died. Above all, as the reports acknowledge, even if the 'avoidable' factors had been prevented, it is not possible to state with any certainty that death would not have occurred.

It was for this reason that a different approach was used from 1979–81 onwards. In this report, the term 'avoidable factor' was dropped 'because the term was sometimes misinterpreted to mean that avoiding these factors would have prevented the death.'[43] The focus shifted to identifying 'substandard care'.

Interpreting maternal mortality rates

The earlier analyses of maternal mortality are of more than historical interest. Many of the issues raised are the very ones still being discussed today in relation to stillbirth and infant mortality. They thus provided a useful perspective from which to assess the problems of the 1990s.

Geographical variations

The reported true maternal mortality rates for the counties of England and Wales for four five-year periods between 1880 and 1914 are reproduced in Figure 10.2 from the Ministry of Health's 1937 report on maternal mortality.[7] They do not distinguish between the registration counties used before 1911 for the publication of statistics, and the administrative counties used from 1911 onwards.

These maps illustrate the rise in maternal mortality between the early 1880s and the early 1890s. This is likely to be due in part to the improved reporting which resulted from sending out the letters of enquiry. From 1891 onwards there was a decline in the mortality rate. This continued until about 1910, with a particularly steep decline in deaths from puerperal sepsis.[44]

At first sight, Figure 10.2 shows the usual pattern of raised mortality rates in the north and west compared with the south east which are seen in the maps of infant mortality in Chapter 3, but there are also some differences. As the *Decennial supplement* for 1901–1910 pointed out, there was little relationship between mortality and urbanisation, and the maternal mortality rate unlike other mortality rates, was low in London. In general, the report concluded that: 'puerperal mortality has varied more with geographical situation than with any obvious social and economic circumstance, though the geographical variation presumably has a social basis.'[44]

This observation came at a time when the emphasis was shifting from the social and economic background to mortality to the provision of care for the individual. Although the importance of providing decent housing and sanitary conditions was still acknowledged, attention was moving to setting up services for the supervision of pregnancy and the provision of care during labour. Despite much activity in this direction, the maternal mortality rate fluctuated round a similar level in the early years of the century, and then rose during the late 1920s and early 1930s in England and Wales. In Scotland, and in Northern Ireland the rate rose between 1900 and 1930.

The familiar north-south differences in maternal mortality were still apparent over the years 1924 to 1933, as can be seen in Figure 10.3. It is notable, in passing, that in order to take into account the relatively small numbers of deaths in each county, the authors plotted the extent to which local rates varied from the overall rate for England and Wales. When Figure 10.3 is inspected more closely, it shows some departure from the usual pattern. The reports on maternal mortality mentioned earlier, found that while in some economically deprived areas, such as the textile manufacturing towns of Lancashire, maternal mortality rates were high, the overall statistical association between an area's maternal mortality rate and its economic and housing conditions seemed to have virtually disappeared. Figure 10.3 is not sufficiently detailed to show the extent of local variation. Surprisingly, within London, the maternal mortality rate was higher among women living in Hampstead than in the East End.

Social class

Another finding which contradicts usual experience can be found in the *Registrar General's decennial supplement* for 1931.[45] As can be seen in Table 10.1, the maternal mortality rate was higher among wives of professional men than among wives of men in unskilled occupations. This differential

Figure 10.2

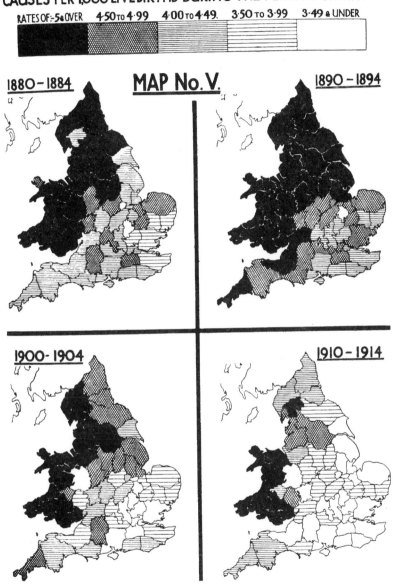

55

COUNTIES OF ENGLAND & WALES (INCLUDING COUNTY BOROUGHS) RANKED ACCORDING TO THEIR MORTALITY FROM ALL PUERPERAL CAUSES PER 1,000 LIVE BIRTHS DURING THE PERIODS SHOWN :—

RATES OF :- 5 & OVER   4·50 to 4·99   4·00 to 4·49.   3·50 to 3·99   3·49 & UNDER

MAP No. V.

1880 – 1884

1890 – 1894

1900 – 1904

1910 – 1914

Reproduced from: Ministry of Health: *Report on an investigation into maternal mortality.*[7]

285

Figure 10.3

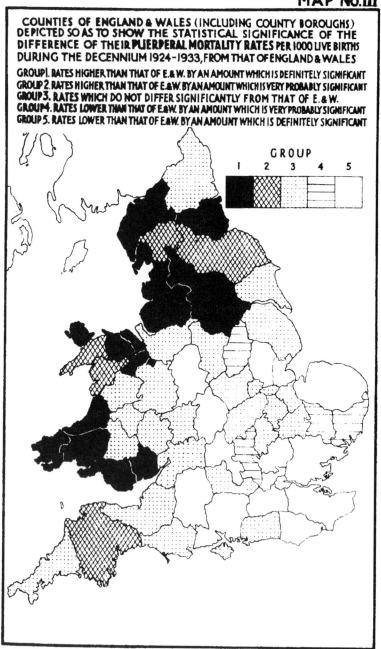

was most evident in deaths from puerperal sepsis and was present for all the tabulated causes of maternal death, except puerperal haemorrhage, for which the rate was highest for women with husbands in social class V.

No obvious interpretation was seen at the time. It was suggested that 'the fact that the average maternal mortality rate is no lower among the better circumstanced classes might possibly be explained by a higher proportion of first births among them counteracting any advantage they enjoy, but it must be remembered that the unskilled class is probably also at a disadvantage owing to a high proportion of births of high order.'[7]

In retrospect, a number of factors which might have played a part both in this social class pattern and in the overall rise in mortality can be identified. Firstly, middle class women may have been more likely to be able to afford to have their babies in nursing homes and other institutions where they were probably at a higher risk of developing puerperal fever than at home.[46,47]

Secondly, the reports on maternal mortality during the 1930s all carried warnings of the dangers of obstetric intervention and the Registrar General's reports pointed to increases in mortality from this cause.[6] Middle class women were more likely to be able to pay to be attended by doctors rather than midwives and thus put themselves at increased risk of unwarranted and sometimes inexpert intervention. Midwives attending difficult births were increasingly likely to send for doctors, who in some cases had inadequate training and experience.[16]

Some light is cast on this by the experience of 'The Rochdale Experiment'. A new medical officer of health appointed in 1930 set to work to try to lower the town's maternal mortality rate, which was one of the highest in

Table 10.1

Mortality from puerperal causes per 1,000 live births, of married women, according to social class of husband, England and Wales, 1930–32.

ICD code	Cause	Class				All married women
		I and II Pro-fessional	III Skilled	IV Semi-skilled	V Unskilled	
140–150	All puerperal causes	4.44	4.11	4.16	3.89	4.13
140–141	Abortion*	0.50	0.56	0.56	0.57	0.55
142–150	Puerperal causes other than abortion	3.94	3.55	3.60	3.32	3.58
145	Puerperal sepsis+	1.45	1.33	1.21	1.16	1.29

*   Excluding abortions certified as 'criminal'.

+   Excluding septic abortions.

Source: *Registrar General's decennial supplement* for 1931.[45]

the country. Campaigns were launched to encourage women to attend antenatal centres for early diagnosis of complications. Conscious efforts were made to disseminate information about pregnancy and childbirth in the community and to bring the dangers of unnecessary use of forceps and other interventions for hastening delivery to the attention of doctors, midwives and expectant mothers. After this the mortality rate fell. One of the major contributory factors was a decrease in deaths from obstetric intervention.[48,49]

Another factor which was not directly related to social class, but was thought to have contributed to the increase in the maternal mortality rate, was mortality from abortion in general and abortion known to be illegally induced in particular. In the absence of any data about the incidence of illegal abortion, various reports referred to impressions that it was on the increase, rising numbers of prosecutions and growing willingness on the part of sellers of substances women bought to induce abortion to pay high prices to advertise them.[6,7,30] On the other hand, the Interdepartmental Committee on Abortion, which reported in 1939, took the view that abortion was no longer becoming more prevalent.[32]

Puerperal sepsis

The maternal mortality rate started to decrease in the early 1930s in Scotland and in the mid 1930s elsewhere in the United Kingdom. This decline is usually attributed to the introduction of sulphonamide drugs as a treatment for puerperal sepsis, followed later by the availability of penicillin and blood transfusion to women who haemorrhaged.[3,8,46,50,51] It has been pointed out, however, that the decrease in the death rate from puerperal sepsis in England and Wales[52] started before 'Prontosil', the first sulphonamide, became generally available in the latter half of 1936. Mortality had also begun to fall in Scotland before this.[33] The same point has been made about blood transfusions.[52] Thus it may be that sulphonamides and blood transfusions, rather than being the sole cause of the decrease, contributed to a fall which had started for other reasons. These could possibly include changes in practice in response to the various government reports on maternal mortality, recovery from the worst aspects of the depression except in Scotland or expansion of antenatal services. A statistical problem involved in interpreting trends is whether the initial declines in mortality were consistent with random variation or were of a magnitude unlikely to occur by chance.[8]

Trends reported in confidential enquiries

Whatever the reason for its decline, puerperal sepsis accounted for only 3.8 per cent of the deaths from 1952 to 1954 covered in the first *Confidential enquiry into maternal deaths in England and Wales*. As a *British Medical Journal* editorial welcoming it pointed out, the four largest groups of causes of deaths were toxaemia, which made up 22 per cent of the total while haemorrhage accounted for 17 per cent, abortion 14 per cent and pulmonary embolus 13 per cent.[53] Trends in mortality from the major groups of causes in the various enquiries are given in Tables A10.4.1 to A10.4.5. In the case of Northern Ireland, rates are not given as these are not calculated in the original report, presumably because of the small numbers of deaths in each category.[35] In interpreting the trends in rates for Scotland, and England and Wales, it must be borne in mind that the rates for earlier years are under-reported to an extent which has decreased over time.

All the reports showed a higher rate of death in women under 20 and in older women, particularly those of high parity, compared with other women. The Scottish report[37] pointed to the high mortality among women with husbands in social classes IV and V, while the report for England and Wales for 1976–1978[42] suggested that there were no social class differences. This contrasts with the social class gradient seen in Table 7.4 of the *Decennial supplement on occupational mortality for 1970–1972*,[54] in which the standardised mortality ratios for maternal deaths among wives of men in social classes IV and V were considerably higher than those in social classes I, II and III. Similar patterns were seen in the report for England and Wales for 1979–81.[43] After this social class analyses were discontinued.[55]

The *Confidential enquiry into maternal deaths in England and Wales* showed that compared with other women, women born in the New Commonwealth had a much higher rate of maternal death in 1982–84, as they had in the three previous triennia.[42,43,55] The rate in 1982–84 for women born in the New Commonwealth was twice that for women born in the United Kingdom.[55] A similar pattern was shown in analyses by country of birth of causes of maternal deaths registered in 1970–78.[56] In a subsequent analysis of deaths registered from 1970–85, women born in West Africa and the Caribbean were shown to be at very high risk.[57] Despite mentioning individual black or 'foreign' women, the confidential enquiry reports did not explicitly return to the issue again until the report for 1994–96.[41]

The reports also discussed mortality associated with caesarean section and anaesthesia.[42,55] Table 10.2 shows trends in mortality associated with these procedures in the 1970s and 1980s. Deaths associated with caesarean section included all women who had caesareans irrespective of whether these were thought to be the cause of death. In contrast to this, the deaths associated with anaesthesia are those directly attributable to the anaesthetic procedures. They do not include all women who had anaesthesia. The report pointed to the increased use of both procedures over the years. Although the caesarean section rate was increasing, mortality associated with it and the overall numbers of deaths declined in the early 1980s. Although mortality associated with anaesthesia declined slightly, the report for 1982–84 pointed to continuing substandard care.[55] The analyses could not be continued in this form after 1982–84 because the end of Maternity HIPE and the poor quality of data in Maternity HES meant that there were no national data about the overall percentage of deliveries by caesarean section or involving use of anaesthesia.

Table 10.2

Estimated death rates associated with caesarean section and the use of anaesthetics, England and Wales, 1970–84

	1970–72	1973–75	1976–78	1979–81	1982–84	Total
Deaths after caesarean sections (Direct maternal and 'associated' deaths from enquiry series)	102	77	80	87	69	415
Estimated fatality rate per thousand caesarean sections	0.99	0.76	0.66	0.52	0.37	0.61
Number of deaths directly associated with anaesthesia	37	27	27	22	18	131
Rate per million pregnancies	12.8	10.5	12.1	8.7	7.2	10.2

Source: *Report on confidential enquiries into maternal deaths in England and Wales 1982-84*[55] (Tables 12.2 and 13.1)

Maternal mortality in the 1990s

The maternal mortality rate for the three year period 1994–96 was 12.2 per 100,000 maternities.[41] This was based on the 268 direct and indirect deaths known to the confidential enquiry. As Table A10.4.3 shows, rates were apparently higher than in 1990–93. This is because, as was mentioned earlier, ONS computer records now include all the causes mentioned on death certificates in England and Wales. This meant that it could give the enquiry details of death registrations where pregnancy was mentioned, but not as the underlying cause. In addition, the increasing age of women at childbirth may have contributed to the rise in mortality.

Although the overall rate was less than a quarter of that in the years 1952–54 covered by the first report and the terminology had changed, three of the four leading causes of death were among those with the higher rates. In 1994–96 the rate for thrombosis and thromboembolism was 21.8 per million maternities and that for hypertensive disorders of pregnancy was 9.1. The mortality rate for antepartum and postpartum haemorrhage, 5.5 per million maternities was lower than that of 7.7 per million maternities for amniotic fluid embolism.[41] Trends from the 1970s to the mid 1990s in these causes of maternal death are shown in Figure 10.4 In contrast, induced abortion, which had been a leading cause of death in the early 1950s, accounted for very few deaths in the 1990s, with a rate of 0.5 per

Figure 10.4

Trends in selected causes of maternal death, England and Wales, 1970–72 to 1982–84, United Kingdom, 1985–87 to 1994–96

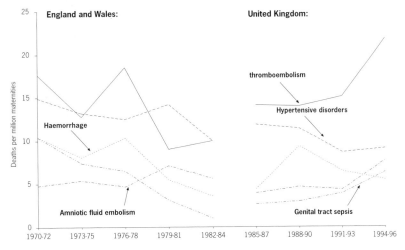

Source: Confidential enquiries into maternal deaths

Figure 10.5

Abortions as a percentage of maternal deaths, England and Wales, 1967–69 to 1982–84, United Kingdom, 1985–87 to 1994–96

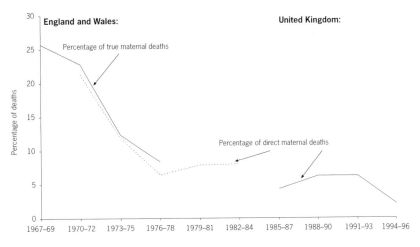

Source: Confidential enquiries into maternal deaths

million maternities. The declining contribution of abortion, including miscarriage to maternal mortality is illustrated in Figure 10.5.

In returning to the question of ethnic origin, the report explored some of the barriers faced by women from minority ethnic groups. While urging caution because of the small numbers involved and the gaps in data about ethnic origin, it found that women from the black ethnic groups appeared to have higher mortality rates than other women.

The 1994–96 report focussed, for the first time, on deaths associated with psychiatric causes and with domestic violence. The report suggested that about ten per cent of maternal deaths were associated with psychiatric conditions. The problems of estimating the proportion of women who experience postnatal depression is discussed later, as are the problems with data about domestic violence and its association with pregnancy.

The concept of reproductive mortality

The report on maternal deaths in England and Wales in 1976–78 expressed the view that the decrease in mortality from abortion was the result of the greater availability of legal abortion and the safer methods of inducing abortion rather than the more effective use of contraception. The report said:

> 'Procedures for sterilisation and termination of pregnancy are not without risk to the patient, and the same is true for the contraceptive pill. However, it should now be regarded as an inherent part of modern practice to ensure that as far as possible, a reliable method of contraception or least hazardous method of sterilisation is available to a woman when a further pregnancy might affect her health or even put her life at risk.'[42]

In an attempt to weigh up the risks of death, Valerie Beral defined what she called 'reproductive mortality'.[58] This estimated deaths from the side effects of various methods of birth control and added them to deaths from complications of abortion, pregnancy, childbirth and the puerperium. The analysis was prompted by her observation that in 21 different countries, the introduction of oral contraceptives was accompanied by increases in mortality among women of childbearing age.[59]

The estimates of reproductive mortality are shown in Table 10.3.[58] They suggest that while reproductive mortality decreased between 1950 and 1975 for women aged 25–34, for women aged 35–44 it decreased from 1950 to 1960 and then rose again as the risks of death from use of oral contraceptives outweighed the decline in mortality from childbearing and abortion. This analysis has yet to be updated. When it is, risks associated with ovarian stimulants and assisted conception should be added.

Table 10.3

Estimated reproductive mortality for women aged 25–34 and 35–44 in England and Wales in 1950, 1960, 1970 and 1975

Cause of death	Numbers of deaths, by age and year							
	Age 25-34				Age 35-44			
	1950	1960	1970	1975	1950	1960	1970	1975
Spontaneous and induced abortion	46	31	13	5	31	15	7	3
Complications of pregnancy, childbirth and the puerperium, other than abortion	235	121	47	35	180	78	29	16
Complications of contraceptive use:								
Oral contraceptives	–	–	21.6	37.0	–	–	68.3	118.5
IUDs	–	–	0.3	0.5	–	–	0.3	0.4
Female sterilisation	..	0.3	1.6	1.4	..	0.3	1.0	0.9
Total reproductive deaths	281	152.3	83.5	78.9	211	93.3	105.6	138.8
Total size of population, 100,000s	32.2	29.1	30.3	33.4	34.3	31.8	28.8	27.8
Reproductive mortality rate per 100,000 women per year	8.7	5.2	2.8	2.4	6.2	2.9	3.7	5.0

Source: Beral V. *Reproductive mortality.*[58]

Pregnancy, childbirth and women's health

> 'Of course, during pregnancy, one never feels well, what with one thing and another. That was my experience; and after confinement I used to be so weak, and by the time I began to regain my strength a little I was in trouble again.'

> *Maternity, letters from working women, 1915.*[60]

> 'I have suffered with the "postnatal blues", even though I have a loving partner and family. At times it is daunting, being responsible for another human being who depends on you so much, so I suppose it takes a while for your emotions to adjust.'

> *Mother Courage, letters from women in poverty at the end of the century, 1997.*[61]

The impact of having a baby on the mother's health are well documented in personal recollections and research.[61-66] Routine statistics on the subject are in much shorter supply. Most of the data which do exist are relatively recent in origin.

The exception to this is the notification of puerperal fever and pyrexia as communicable diseases. They are, however, no longer notifiable in England, Wales or Northern Ireland. In 1967, the last year in which it was notifiable in England and Wales, no deaths occurred among the 4,175 cases of puerperal fever and pyrexia notified,[67] compared with 1,061 deaths from puerperal sepsis and 257 deaths from post abortive sepsis among the 2,094 cases of 'puerperal fever' and 5,806 cases of 'puerperal pyrexia' notified in 1933.[6]

Problems in pregnancy and delivery

If a woman has health problems in pregnancy, her first port of call may be her own general practitioner. Alternatively, the problems may come to light at clinics run by midwives or hospital doctors. If problems are severe, she may be admitted to hospital. This means that she may be recorded in one of a number of information systems. Except possibly in Scotland, these systems are unlikely to be linked to each other so data collection is very fragmented.[68]

In England, episodes of admissions to hospital during pregnancy are recorded in the Hospital Episode Statistics system. Episodes relating to the same woman are not currently linked to each other or to the delivery record, but there are plans to use NHS numbers to do so in the future.[69] Data about complications experienced by women and recorded at delivery over the financial years 1989–90 to 1994–95 are shown in Table A7.23.1 They are taken from the first of a series of Department of Health *Statistical bulletins* based on data from the Hospital Episode Statistics.[70] Although antenatal and postnatal complications are included, they are under-reported, as they include only antenatal conditions recorded on the delivery record and postnatal complications during the episode of care in which birth took place.

In general, the table shows a rising rate of complications over the period, but this may be a consequence of improvements in ascertainment. The data should be interpreted with caution, in the light of the comments made in Chapter 7 about their quality and completeness.

With its system of record linkage, Scotland is better placed to track women's health problems throughout pregnancy and delivery, as it links antenatal admission records to the woman's delivery record. In its publication *Small babies in Scotland*, ISD found that women with a mention of 'pre-eclampsia' of any degree of severity on the SMR2 delivery record were more likely than others to have a preterm birth or a low birthweight baby.[71]

Complications of abortion are included in the Hospital Episode Statistics in England and the principal complication of abortion is coded in the SMR2 system in Scotland. Complications arising at the termination of pregnancy in England and Wales are included on the abortion notification and data are published in *Abortion statistics, Series AB*. These refer only to complications which occur prior to notification and not to any problems either physical or emotional, which may arise subsequently.

These systems may not be adequate for monitoring the relatively rare cases of severe morbidity. Special surveys, such as the survey of eclampsia in 1992 are likely to be needed.[72] A system analogous to that run by the British Paediatric Surveillance Unit may be needed to monitor severe morbidity.

Women's health problems in the postnatal period

In certain senses, the data on episiotomy, induction of labour, instrumental delivery and caesarean section are proxy measures of maternal morbidity as they may lead to problems and complications for the mother afterwards.[63–66,73] Sometimes the morbidity is greater than after a delivery in which these interventions were not used, but on other occasions, for example when a caesarean section is done to avoid prolonged labour and a difficult forceps delivery, intervention may reduce subsequent morbidity for the mother.

Information about the use of these procedures is collected in the Maternity Hospital Episode Statistics in England and SMR2 in Scotland. Data are shown in Tables A7.19.1 to A7.23.1. It is difficult to assess from this source the extent to which, for example, sepsis develops in women who have perineal tears, episiotomies or caesarean sections, even when these occur during the same in-patient episode as delivery. In England, it is currently impossible to link subsequent complications with events during labour or delivery once the woman has left hospital, in national data systems, although there are places where this can be done locally.[68,74]

One of the reasons given for doing episiotomies is to prevent subsequent prolapse of the uterus. Data about colporrhaphy, the operation to correct prolapse of the vaginal walls are collected in the Hospital Episode Statistics and are included in Table A4.1.1. Unfortunately, in England at present, they are not linked routinely with data about whether the women concerned had previous episiotomies or even babies. The same is true of women admitted to hospital for operations to repair a poorly healed perineal tear or episiotomy. Again, there is a potential to make these linkages in Scotland.

Postnatal depression

Women who have postnatal depression may be treated by their general practitioner or, in relatively few cases, admitted to a psychiatric unit. Some women with postnatal depression never seek professional help, so routine data systems can never fully ascertain how many women are affected. This can only be approached via surveys.

Many problems women experience in the first year after giving birth do not lead to re-admission to hospital. The developments in extracting data for general practice computer systems described in Chapter 9 offer the potential to get a picture of the problems for which women consult general practitioners in the postnatal period. Data from the General Practice Research Database are shown in Tables A10.12.1 and A10.12.2. They include data about postnatal checks. The first of these shows, for example, that consultations for postnatal depression are more common in younger age groups. This may or may not be a reflection of true incidence, as younger women may be more likely to seek help from a general practitioner or report depression at a postnatal check. Table A10.12.2 shows consultation by time after birth, but should be interpreted with caution. Conditions noted at 43 days or more after birth include those reported at the postnatal check. Some of these may well have occurred at a much earlier stage but without the woman consulting a general practitioner.

Domestic violence

Rising concern in the late 1990s about domestic violence in general and its association with pregnancy in particular created a demand for statistics. Unfortunately, the data collected routinely are inadequate for the task. The Home Office collects data about violent offences reported to the police and about persons sent for trial. The police do not separately identify the location of the crime or the relationship of the victim to the offender.[75] Even this assumes that the offence is reported, which may not be the case.

To get a better picture, the Home Office carries out surveys in which it asks the police to provide information about the age and sex of the victims and their relationship to the suspect. Two surveys in the early 1990s found that in the case of domestic violence, only a third of the victims were female but nearly half took place at the victim's home.[76] No information was collected about pregnancy.

The British Crime Survey asks samples of the population about crimes they have experienced and so includes offences not recorded by the police. In the 1996 survey, 4.2 per cent of women and 4.2 per cent of men said they had been physically assaulted by a current or former partner in the previous year.[77] The greatest risks of domestic assault were among people under 25 and those in financial difficulties. The sample size is not large enough to assess the extent to which the violence may be associated with pregnancy.

The Home Office has acknowledged that better data are needed to monitor the impact of the policies being implemented to tackle domestic violence.[76-83] The *Confidential enquiry into maternal deaths* cited estimates that about 30 per cent of domestic violence starts during pregnancy and that it can escalate during pregnancy and after birth.[41]

Sexually transmitted diseases

'O mother, dear mother come set you down by me
Come set you down by me and pity my case;
For my wounds are now aching, my poor heart is breaking
And I in a low spirit must die.

So rattle your drums and play your fife over me
So rattle your drums as we march along.
Then return to your home and think on that young girl;
"O there goes a young girl cut down in her prime." '

Traditional, from an unnamed singer, 1909.[84]

The many versions of this song about a young woman, or often a young man, 'cut down in their prime' bear testimony to the virulence of sexually transmitted diseases in the past. It is therefore no surprise to find that they were among the first conditions for which publicly funded treatment became available.

The reporting of sexually transmitted diseases started after free and confidential clinics were set up on lines recommended by the Royal Commission on Venereal Diseases, which reported in 1916. Originally, consultants in charge of the clinics were asked to make quarterly returns of the numbers of new cases of syphilis, gonorrhoea and chancroid. Other diseases were added from the 1950s onwards. In England, the system was extended and modified in 1971, 1988 and 1996.[85,86]

All genitourinary medicine clinics in England are required to complete a KC60 return giving numbers of attendances in the previous quarter. Up to June 1996, these were sent to the Department of Health and they are now sent to the Communicable Disease Surveillance Centre in Colindale. Clinics in Wales send the returns to the Communicable Disease Surveillance Centre in Cardiff.

As these reports are based on diagnoses rather than on individuals, this may result in more than one diagnosis for an individual in the same clinic visit and multiple diagnoses in a reporting year. Data for England and Wales, shown in Tables A10.5.1 and A10.5.2 are now published quarterly in the *Communicable disease report* and a more detailed analysis is published as an annual supplement.[86,87] More limited data are published annually in *Health and personal social services statistics for England* and in *Health statistics Wales*.

In Scotland, where data collection began in 1923, the Information and Statistics Division collects and collates data on sexually transmitted diseases. In April 1995, it moved on to a system based on individuals, allowing much better facilities for analysis.[88] Some regions in England have a similar system.[89] Data shown in Table A10.5.3 are published annually in *Scottish health statistics* and a health briefing, *Cases seen at genitourinary clinics*.

Data on cases seen at genitourinary clinics in Northern Ireland are collected by the Department of Health, Social Services and Public Safety. They are published in its volumes of *Hospital statistics* and are shown in Table A10.5.4. At the time of writing, problems with the computer system in the province's main clinic in the Royal group of hospitals in Belfast means that figures for April 1996 onwards are not yet complete.

When the Public Health Laboratory Service was established in 1939, it set up a system for the voluntary reporting of certain infectious diseases, including sexually transmitted diseases identified in public health laboratories. Reporting through this system is incomplete and will therefore underestimate incidence. The system is useful for monitoring new strains of infection, for example strains of gonorrhoea which are resistant to penicillin. In each country there are general systems covering all laboratory reports and special systems for specific diseases.[86]

The numbers of new cases seen in sexually transmitted diseases clinics shown in Tables A10.5.1 to A10.5.4 are an underestimate of the number of people treated since they do not include people treated in general practice, hospital antenatal and gynaecology clinics and in private practice. They also exclude people who do not seek treatment either because they have no symptoms or because they ignore the symptoms they have. The degree of underestimation varies. For example, for genital chlamydia, it is considered that reports from genitourinary medicine clinics represent 18 per cent of prevalent infections.[90] Data for genital warts and herpes are also thought to be incomplete. On the other hand published reports for syphilis and gonorrhea are much more complete because most people with these conditions are referred to genitourinary medicine clinics. Rises since 1996 in numbers of reports of gonorrhea in England are therefore likely to be of significance.[87]

Data about people admitted to hospital are collected through the Hospital Episode System, the Patient Episode Database Wales and SMR1 in Scotland. Data about illness in newborn babies as a result of sexually transmitted disease in their parents are discussed in Chapter 9.

Data about cases of AIDS/HIV are collected in each of the four countries by the organisations mentioned above. They are collated for the whole of the United Kingdom by the Public Health Laboratory Service, which publishes them in the *Communicable disease reports* and on its web site.[91] Table A10.6.1 shows overall numbers of reports by sex while Table A9.2.1, which shows numbers of children born to HIV infected mothers, is discussed in Chapter 9.

Cancer of the reproductive organs

Diagnoses of cancer should be notified to or collected by the relevant cancer registry. The regional cancer registries in England and the cancer registry in Wales were set up at different stages and there are still differences in the completeness and quality of their data.[92-94] Data from all the registries in England and Wales are collated centrally by ONS and published in the annual volumes of *Cancer statistics, Series MB1* along with a description of the development of the system. Major redevelopment took place from 1990 onwards following a review of the system.[95] ONS' files are now 'live' with late registrations being added retrospectively. Preliminary data published in ONS monitors were transferred to *Health statistics quarterly* in 1999.

Scotland and Ireland have their own registries. Data from the Scottish cancer registry are published in *Scottish health statistics*. The Northern Ireland Cancer Registry was established in 1994 and in 1999 it published its first report, *Cancer incidence in Northern Ireland, 1993–95*.[96] Cancer statistics for the Irish Republic are published by its National Cancer Registry.[97]

Table A10.7.1 gives incidence rates for cancers of men's and women's reproductive organs from 1971–93 in England and Wales. To allow for the changing age structure of the population, the rates have been age standardised using the 'standard European population'. Table A10.7.2

gives provisional estimates of the incidence of new cases of cancer diagnosed in the years 1994 to 1996.[98] These figures are also age-standardised to allow for changing age structures. In Table A10.8.1, crude death rates for cancers of the reproductive organs are given for five year periods from 1971–75 to 1991–95 while standardised rates are shown in Table A10.9.1.

When a person dies in England and Wales, his or her death certificate is linked with the corresponding cancer registration. This enables analyses to be done of the survival rates of people with various forms of cancer. An ONS monitor, *Cancer survival in England and Wales, 1981 and 1989 registrations*, analysed the extent to which people whose cancers were registered in 1981 and 1989 survived for one, and five years after the cancer was registered.[99] Much fuller analyses were published on paper and on a CD-ROM as *Cancer survival trends in England and Wales, 1971–1995: deprivation and NHS region*.[100,101] Data from this publication, shown in Table A10.10.1, suggest survival increased over the period. The report also showed marked regional and social class differences in survival rates. Apart from the question of the effectiveness or otherwise of the various forms of treatment for cancer, the estimated survival times are also affected by the stage the cancer had reached before it was detected and registered. Data on occupational and social class differences in cancer mortality appear in *Registrar General's decennial supplements*.

Pathology laboratories keep records of the numbers of cervical smears they read and the proportions that are positive, suspicious and negative. Summaries of these sent to the Department of Health, the Welsh Office, ISD Scotland and the Department of Health and Social Services in Northern Ireland are shown in Table A10.11.1. Data held in the computer systems used to call and recall women for screening are used to estimate the proportions of women screened. Data for England are published in the statistical bulletin *Cervical screening programme, England*. A similar system was set up to monitor breast cancer screening. The data are also shown in Table A10.11.1. Data for England appears as a statistical bulletin, *Breast screening programme, England*.

Monitoring reproductive health in the 1990s and 2000s

Despite the amount of data collected about the morbidity associated with childbearing, sexual activity and cancers of the reproductive organs, routinely collected statistics give a somewhat patchy picture of their health consequences. Increased use of record linkage could do much to make the data more useful and greater use of data from general practice would lead to a fuller picture. In other cases the deficiencies arise not so much from negligence but from the underlying problems involved collecting data on subjects such as domestic violence. Here routinely collected data still have a role to play in identifying questions to be approached by special studies. The data we have show that maternal mortality and severe morbidity are now very rare, in the United Kingdom at least. On the other hand, non-life threatening morbidity is common but poorly quantified.

References

1   The death of Queen Jane. *Folk Song Journal* 1909; 3: 67.

2   Dewhurst J. *Royal confinements*. London: Weidenfeld and Nicolson, 1980.

3   Loudon I. Deaths in childbed from the eighteenth century to 1935. *Medical History* 1986; 30: 1–41.

4   Loudon I. *Death in childbirth. An international study of maternal care and maternal mortality, 1800–1950*. Oxford: Oxford University Press, 1992.

5   World Health Organization. International classification of diseases. *Manual of the international statistical classification of diseases, injuries and causes of death*. Ninth revision. Vol. 1. Geneva: WHO, 1977.

6   General Register Office. *The Registrar General's statistical review, 1933. Text*. London: HMSO, 1935.

7   Ministry of Health. *Report on an investigation into maternal mortality*. Cmd 5422. London: HMSO, 1937.

8   Taylor W, Dauncey M. Changing patterns of mortality in England and Wales. II: maternal mortality. *British Journal of Preventive and Social Medicine* 1954; 8: 172–175.

9   World Health Organization. *International statistical classification of diseases and related health problems*. Tenth revision. Vol. 1. Geneva: WHO, 1992.

10   General Register Office. *Fifth annual report of the Registrar General for 1841*. London: Longman, Brown, Green and Longman, 1843.

11   General Register Office. *Thirtieth annual report of the Registrar General*. London: HMSO, 1869.

12   General Register Office. *Thirty-third annual report of the Registrar General*. London: HMSO, 1872.

13   General Register Office. *Thirty-ninth annual report of the Registrar General*. London: HMSO, 1878.

14   Duncan JM. *Mortality of childbed and maternity hospitals*. Edinburgh: Adam and Charles Black, 1870.

15   Nightingale F. *Introductory notes on lying-in institutions*. London: Longmans, Green, and Co, 1871.

16   Donnison J. *Midwives and medical men*. New York: Schocken Books, 1977.

17   General Register Office. *Forty-fourth annual report of the Registrar General*. London: HMSO, 1883.

18   General Register Office. *Forty-eighth annual report of the Registrar General*. London: HMSO, 1886.

19   Johnson HMR. The incidence of unnatural deaths which have been presumed to be natural in coroners' autopsies. *Medicine, Science and the Law* 1969; 9: 102–106.

20   Local Government Board. *Report by the Medical Officer on infant and child mortality. Supplement to the thirty-ninth annual report of the Local Government Board, 1909–1910.* Cd 5312. London: HMSO, 1910.

21   Local Government Board. *Second report by the Medical Officer on infant and child mortality. Supplement to the forty-second annual report of the Local Government Board, 1912–1913.* Cd 6909. London: HMSO, 1913.

22   Local Government Board. *Third report by the Medical Officer on infant mortality in Lancashire. Supplement to the forty-third annual report of the Local Government Board, 1913–14.* Cd 7511. London: HMSO, 1914.

23   Local Government Board. *Report on child mortality at ages 0–5. Forty-fifth annual report of the Local Government Board, 1915–16.* Cd 8496. London: HMSO, 1916.

24   Local Government Board. *Report on maternal mortality in connection with childbearing and its relation to infant mortality. Supplement to the forty-fourth report of the Medical Officer, 1914–1915.* Cd 8153. London: HMSO, 1916.

25   Campbell JM. *Maternal mortality.* Reports on Public Health and Medical Subjects No. 25. London: HMSO, 1924.

26   Scottish Departmental Committee on Puerperal Morbidity. *Report.* Edinburgh: HMSO, 1924.

27   Kinloch JP, Steven JA. *Maternal mortality. Report on maternal mortality in Aberdeen, 1918–1927, with special reference to puerperal sepsis.* Edinburgh: Scottish Board of Health, 1928.

28   Ministry of Health. *Interim report of the Departmental Committee on Maternal Mortality and Morbidity.* London: HMSO, 1930.

29   Ministry of Health. *Final report of the Departmental Committee on Maternal Mortality and Morbidity.* London: HMSO, 1932.

30   Campbell J, Cameron ID, Jones DM. *High maternal mortality in certain areas.* Reports on Public Health and Medical Subjects No. 68. London: HMSO, 1932.

31   Ministry of Health. *Report of an investigation into maternal mortality in Wales.* Cmd 5423. London: HMSO, 1937.

32   Ministry of Health and Home Office. *Report of the interdepartmental committee on abortion.* London: HMSO, 1939.

33   Douglas CA, McKinlay PL. *Report on maternal morbidity and mortality in Scotland.* Edinburgh: HMSO, 1935.

34   Ministry of Health. *Annual report of the Chief Medical Officer for 1952.* Cmd 9009. London: HMSO, 1953.

35   Department of Health and Social Services, Northern Ireland. *A report on an enquiry into maternal deaths in Northern Ireland, 1968–1977.* Belfast: HMSO, 1982.

36   Department of Health and Social Services Northern Ireland. *A report on an enquiry into maternal deaths in Northern Ireland, 1978–1984.* Belfast: HMSO, 1988.

37   Scottish Home and Health Department. *A report on an enquiry into maternal deaths in Scotland, 1972–1975.* Edinburgh: HMSO, 1978.

38   Scottish Home and Health Department. *A report on an enquiry into maternal deaths in Scotland, 1976–1980.* Edinburgh: HMSO, 1987.

39   Scottish Home and Health Department. *Report on maternal and perinatal deaths in Scotland, 1981–1985.* Edinburgh: HMSO, 1989.

40   Scottish Office Home and Health Department. *Report on maternal and perinatal deaths in Scotland, 1986–1990.* Edinburgh: HMSO, 1994.

41   Department of Health, Welsh Office, Scottish Office Department of Health, Department of Health and Social Services, Northern Ireland. *Why mothers die. Report on confidential enquiries into maternal deaths in the United Kingdom, 1994–1996.* London: The Stationery Office, 1998.

42   Department of Health and Social Security. *Report on confidential enquiries into maternal deaths in England and Wales, 1976–1978.* Reports on Health and Social Subjects No. 26. London: HMSO, 1982.

43   Department of Health and Social Security. *Report on confidential enquiries into maternal deaths in England and Wales, 1979–81.* Reports on Health and Social Subjects No. 29. London: HMSO, 1986.

44   General Register Office. *Supplement to the seventy-fifth annual report of the Registrar General of births, deaths and marriages in England and Wales.* Vol. III: Registration summary tables, 1901–1910. London: HMSO, 1919.

45   General Register Office. *The Registrar General's decennial supplement for England and Wales, 1931.* Vol. IIa: Occupational mortality. London: HMSO, 1938.

46   Loudon I. Puerperal fever, the streptococcus and sulphonamides 1911–1945. *British Medical Journal* 1987; 295: 485–490.

47   Loudon I. *The tragedy of childbed fever.* Oxford: Oxford University Press, 2000.

48   Topping A. Maternal mortality and public opinion. *Public Health* 1936; 45: 342–349.

49   Oxley WHF, Phillips MH, Young J. Maternal mortality in Rochdale. *British Medical Journal* 1935; 1: 304–307.

50   Winter JM. Infant mortality, maternal mortality and public health in Britain in the 1930s. *Journal of European History* 1979; 8(2): 439–462.

51   Stocks P. Fifty years of progress as shown by vital statistics. *British Medical Journal* 1950; 1: 54–57.

52   Webb J, Weston-Edwards P. Recent trends in maternal mortality. *The Medical Officer* 1951; 86: 201–204.

53   Maternal mortality. *British Medical Journal* 1957; 2: 280–281.

54 Office of Population Censuses and Surveys. *Occupational mortality: decennial supplement, 1970–1972, England and Wales.* OPCS Decennial Supplement Series DS No. 1. London: HMSO, 1978.

55 Department of Health and Social Security. *Report on confidential enquiries into maternal deaths in England and Wales, 1982–84.* Reports on Health and Social Subjects No. 34. London: HMSO, 1989.

56 Marmot MG, Adelstein AM, Bulusu, L. *Immigrant mortality in England and Wales, 1970–1978: causes of death by country of birth.* Studies on Medical and Population Subjects No. 47. London: HMSO, 1984.

57 Ibison JM, Swerdlow AJ, Head JA, Marmot M. Maternal mortality in England and Wales, 1970–1985: an analysis by country of birth. *British Journal of Obstetrics and Gynaecology* 1996; 103(10): 973–980.

58 Beral V. Reproductive mortality. *British Medical Journal* 1979; 2(6191): 632–634.

59 Beral V. Cardiovascular-disease mortality trends and oral-contraceptive use in young women. *Lancet* 1976; ii(7994): 1047–1052.

60 Davies ML, ed. *Maternity: letters from working women collected by the Women's Co-operative Guild.* London: G. Bell and Sons, 1915.

61 Gowdridge C, Williams AS, Wynn M, eds. *Mother courage: letters from mothers in poverty at the end of the century.* London: Penguin Books in association with the Maternity Alliance, 1997.

62 Beral V. Long term effects of childbearing on health. *Journal of Epidemiology and Community Health* 1985; 39: 343–346.

63 Glazener CMA, MacArthur C, Garcia J. Postnatal care: time for a change. *Contemporary Review of Obstetrics and Gynaecology* 1993; 5(July): 130–136.

64 MacArthur A, MacArthur C, Weeks S. Epidural anaesthesia and low back pain after delivery: a prospective cohort study. *BMJ* 1995; 311(7016): 1336–1339.

65 MacArthur C, Lewis M, Knox EG. *Health after childbirth: an investigation of long term health problems beginning after childbirth in 11701 women.* London: HMSO, 1991.

66 Chamberlain G, Wraight A, Steer P, eds. *Pain and its relief in childbirth: the results of a national survey conducted by the National Birthday Trust.* Edinburgh: Churchill Livingstone, 1993.

67 General Register Office. *The Registrar General's statistical review of England and Wales for the year 1967.* Vol. I. London: HMSO, 1968.

68 Kenney N, Macfarlane AJ. Are maternity data linked at a local level? Some findings from the 'Changing Childbirth' Information Project. Paper given at the conference on: *Linking data for better health in pregnancy and childhood,* London, January 12–13 1998.

69 Department of Health, NHS Executive. *The electronic patient record programme.* Leeds: NHS Executive, 1997.

70   Department of Health. NHS maternity statistics, England: 1989–90 to 1994–95. *Statistical bulletin* 1997/28: 1–44.

71   Information and Statistics Division and Scottish Programme for Clinical Effectiveness in Reproductive Health. *Small babies in Scotland: a ten year overview, 1987–1996.* Births in Scotland Publication Series Volume 2. Edinburgh: ISD, 1998.

72   Douglas KA, Redman CW. Eclampsia in the United Kingdom. *BMJ* 1994; 309(6966): 1395–1400.

73   MacArthur C, Lewis M, Knox EG. Finding of relation between epidural anaesthesia and long term backache remains valid. *BMJ* 1997; 315: 679.

74   Henderson J, Goldacre MJ, Fairweather J, Seagroatt V. Time spent in hospital by children as a health care indicator: inter district comparisons. *Journal of Public Health Medicine* 1992; 14(1): 35–38.

75   Povey D, Prime J. *Notifiable offences, England and Wales, April 1997 to March 1998.* Home Office Statistical Bulletin 22/98. London: Home Office, 1998.

76   Watson L. *Victims of violent crime recorded by the police, England and Wales, 1990–1994.* Home Office Statistical Findings 1/96. London: Home Office, 1996.

77   Mirlees-Black C, Byron, C. *Domestic violence: findings from the BCS self completion questionnaire.* Home Office Research, Statistics, Development and Statistics Directorate, Research Findings No. 86. London: Home Office, 1999.

78   Domestic violence. In: Department of Health. *On the state of the public health: the annual report of the Chief Medical Officer of the Department of Health for the year 1996.* London: The Stationery Office, 1997.

79   Henderson S. *Service provision to women experiencing domestic violence in Scotland.* Edinburgh: Scottish Office Central Research Unit, 1997.

80   Scottish Needs Assessment Programme, Women's Health Network. *Domestic violence.* Glasgow: Scottish Forum for Public Health Medicine, 1997.

81   Bewley S, Friend J, Mezey G, eds. *Violence against women.* London: RCOG Press, 1997.

82   Royal College of Midwives. *Domestic abuse in pregnancy.* Position Paper No. 19. London: RCM, 1997.

83   Department of Health, NHS Executive. *Domestic violence.* London: Department of Health, 1997.

84   The young girl cut down in her prime. *Journal of the Folk Song Society* 1913; 4: 325–326.

85   Sexually transmitted disease surveillance 1978. *British Medical Journal* 1979; 2: 1375–1376.

86   Hughes G, Catchpole M. Surveillance of sexually transmitted infections in England and Wales. *Eurosurveillance* 1998; 3(6): 61–65.

87   Hughes G, Simms J, Rogers PA, Swan AV Catchpole, M. New cases seen at genitourinary medical clinics, England, 1997. *Communicable Disease Report, CDR Supplement* 1998; 8(7): S1–11.

88   Noone A, Chalmers J, Young H. Surveillance of sexually transmitted infections in Scotland. *Eurosurveillance* 1998; 3(6): 65–68.

89   Maguire H, Davidson F. Regionwide surveillance of sexually transmitted infections in Scotland. *Irish Journal of Medical Science* 1994; 163(Supplement 13 (Abstract)).

90   Department of Health. *Chlamydia trachomatis. Summary and conclusions of the Chief Medical Officer's Expert Advisory Group.* London: Department of Health, 1998.

91   Mortimer JY, Evans BG, Goldberg DJ. The surveillance of HIV infection and AIDS in the United Kingdom. *CDR Review* 1997; 7(9): R118–R120.

92   Hawkins MM, Swerdlow AJ. Completeness of cancer and death follow-up obtained through the National Health Service Central Register for England and Wales. *British Journal of Cancer* 1992; 66: 408–413.

93   Villard-Mackintosh L, Coleman MP, Vessey MP. The completeness of cancer registration in England: an assessment from the Oxford-FPA contraceptive study. *British Journal of Cancer* 1988; 58: 507–511.

94   Gulliford MC, Bell J, Bourne HM, Petruckevitch A. The reliability of cancer registry records. *British Journal of Cancer* 1993; 67: 819–821.

95   Office of Population Censuses and Surveys. *A review of the National Cancer Registration system in England and Wales.* Series MB1 No. 17. London: HMSO, 1990.

96   Gavin AJ, Reid J. *Cancer incidence in Northern Ireland, 1993–95.* London: The Stationery Office, 1999.

97   *Cancer in Ireland, 1995.* Cork: National Cancer Registry, Ireland, 1998.

98   Quinn MJ, Babb PJ, Jones J, Brock A. Report: Registrations of cancer diagnosed in 1993–1996, England and Wales. *Health statistics quarterly* 1999; 4: 59–70.

99   Office for National Statistics. *Cancer survival in England and Wales: 1981 and 1989 registration.* ONS Monitor MB1 98/1. London: ONS, 1998.

100 Coleman MP, Babb P, Damiecki P, Grosclaude P, Honjo S, Jones J, Knerer G, Pitard A, Quinn MJ, Sloggett A, De Stavola BL. *Cancer survival trends in England and Wales, 1971–1995: deprivation and NHS region.* Studies in Medical and Population Subjects No. 61. London: The Stationery Office, 1999.

101 Coleman MP, Babb P, Mayer D, Quinn MJ, Sloggett A. *Cancer survival trends in England and Wales, 1971–1995: deprivation and NHS region (CD-ROM).* London: Office for National Statistics, 1999.

11   Costs of having a baby

'I remember it was a very big struggle to get all that was quite necessary for ourselves and the expected baby . . . In the first place, I felt a doctor would be too expensive, so only had a midwife. Things were just not right with baby, so I had to call in a doctor and pay £1 5s. My nurse I only engaged for a fortnight then thought I could manage, but I took cold, and had a most awful gathered breast, and had to go back to bed again for another week or two.'

Maternity, letters from working women, 1915.[1]

'The provision of free confinement care under the National Health Service Act is the first step towards the removal of the economic obstacles to child bearing. But a policy designed to reduce childbirth costs substantially would only be successful if it assisted mothers with their non-medical expenditure.'

Maternity in Great Britain, 1948.[2]

'When I first left work, seven weeks prior to my daughter's birth, it was not too bad because I was receiving 90 per cent of my average pay in the first six weeks, but when it was reduced to £50 plus, life became very difficult, and we found it hard to meet the bills.'

Mother Courage: letters from mothers in poverty at the end of the century, 1997.[3]

'If an organisation cannot keep track of its resources it is unlikely to be using them effectively.'

Royal Commission on the National Health Service, 1979.[4]

The value of the birth of a new child to an individual woman, to her family and to society is undeniable, but cannot be measured simply. In providing care and facilities for pregnant women and their babies, however, society makes use of people's time and effort, equipment and consumable materials, buildings and energy. Public debate about priorities for public expenditure highlights the fact that all these resources could be used in other ways to satisfy different needs.

The meaning of cost depends on who defines it. Accountants measure the outlay for their organisation. Families might measure the change in their spending power or standard of living. An overall view of the cost of maternity to society, its social cost, can be measured by the value of the alternative opportunities that are foregone in order to provide for mothers and babies.

Even when consideration is restricted to the cost of maternity care rather than the more general costs of maternity, costs arise outside the NHS. The family gives up time and income. Employers may lose labour temporarily, local authorities finance facilities for mothers and babies, and central government administers the transfer of cash benefits to eligible pregnant women and mothers. When the resources used are reflected in market values, costs can be measured by the money spent by families, government, the NHS or employers. There are also costs that arise from the use of resources which have no explicit market value. For example, even if we ignore the thorny problem of ascribing values to emotional sacrifices, unpaid time devoted to housekeeping and child care can be measured. If time given by parents is not valued in estimates of costs of alternative patterns of care, the implied allocation of resources may not be the best for society as a whole.[5]

The costs of childbearing were brought to public attention early in this century by the Women's Co-operative Guild.[1] The woman we quoted at the beginning of this chapter married in 1884 and had two children before her husband, a policeman, died in 1887. We do not of course know whether having the doctor as well as a midwife present at her delivery would have affected the outcome. The most relevant consideration in her choice of care was that the doctor's fee was equal to her husband's wages for a week.

The National Insurance Acts, the first of which was passed in 1911, included a maternity benefit of 30 shillings paid to the insured person, usually the husband. In addition, only employed people could join the scheme.

The letter we quoted was one of a collection of accounts of childbirth published in 1915 by the Women's Co-operative Guild. It did this as part of its campaign to extend the range of maternity benefits so as to ensure that every woman could have the means to pay for skilled attention at her delivery. Pressure from the Guild and other women's organisations had a considerable influence on the legislation that was passed on the subject over the next twenty-five years.

In 1946, when families still had to meet at least some of the costs of doctors' and midwives' fees, the Royal College of Obstetricians and Gynaecologists and the Population Investigation Committee initiated a survey of social and economic aspects of childbirth in Great Britain. This survey of a week's births in 1946 included a study which considered the costs of childbearing in some detail. It concluded that: 'The costs of childbearing are so high that they may deter many mothers of all classes from having children. Even the new maternity benefit will go only a small way to meet this large expenditure.'[2]

Since then there has not been a further equally comprehensive study of social and economic aspects of maternity. The subsequent birth surveys, undertaken in 1958 and 1970, had a different focus.[6,7] Furthermore, there is very little information available routinely about costs of maternity services in Britain. This chapter discusses the costs of maternity in the light of the available information.

Costs to central government

In the United Kingdom, the government finances most health and social services, which are, in principle, available to the whole resident population. The parliamentary process by which planned public expenditure is debated and approved is thoroughly documented in a series of House of Commons and parliamentary papers, listed on the House of Commons web site, details of which can be found in Appendix 1. The accounts of expenditure in preceding years are presented to parliament by the Government Actuary in *Appropriation accounts*. These show differences between planned expenditure and outturn, which is the cash actually spent. A good explanation of the expenditure plans and accounting system at the end of the 1970s was given in the 'Explanatory and technical notes', Section 5 of *The government's expenditure plans 1981–1982 and 1983–1984*.

Since this was published, the government has changed the way it presents its spending plans, and now only cash amounts are given. Thus it is not possible, without knowledge of changes in prices faced by health authorities, to divide the planned expenditure into 'real' and 'inflationary' components. The Department of Health uses price adjustment to present expenditure data in 'real' terms for various purposes, including the information it gives in evidence to the House of Commons Health Committee and for other purposes.[8,9] A price index indicates changes in the level of prices of goods and services. General price levels in the economy, including overseas trade are reflected in the Gross Domestic Product (GDP) deflator. The Retail Price Index indicates consumer price levels, and the NHS pay and prices index reflects levels of prices and wages in the NHS. Examples of the changes in prices and costs over time, as reflected in these indices, are given in Table A11.1.1. The differences in the rates of change of different price indices, and the faster rate of inflation in health care than in general prices, illustrate the importance of using the appropriate price index to compare changes in expenditure over time.

The accounts for funds voted by parliament to the health and personal social services budget are not presented in a way that makes it possible to identify separately the funds specifically allocated to maternity and child health services. In reply to a question from the House of Commons Social Services Committee in 1980, the Department of Health and Social Security presented estimates[10] for identifiable health service expenditure per birth and per child aged 0–4 years. These estimates are explained more fully later. This information was produced in subsequent years as part of a departmental programme budgeting exercise, which started in 1976. The data are passed to the House of Commons Health Committee which publishes them each year in its annual publication *Public expenditure on health and social services*.

Until 1988, the Department's budget also included the administration of social security payments to pregnant women and their families. Since 1988, this has been included in the budget of the Department of Social Security. Total amounts of benefits of all categories and administrative costs are given in the accounts of government expenditure. More detail is given in *Social security statistics*. Provision of social security benefits does not represent a net use of resources by the government, except in administration, because the funds are not used by the government to purchase goods and services. It is a transfer of purchasing power from taxpayers to people receiving benefits.

Other programmes of government spending also reflect resources used directly or indirectly for maternity care. For example, the defence programme includes the costs of the armed forces medical services which provide obstetric care to United Kingdom services dependants. In 1979, however, deliveries by the armed forces medical services in the United Kingdom accounted for less than one per cent of the total. By 1997, there were no armed forces medical services hospitals offering childbirth services in the United Kingdom. Service families in the United Kingdom now use NHS services, purchased by the Ministry of Defence on their behalf. The education budget includes some health education in schools and university costs related to education of health services staff, in addition to costs covered from NHS funds. Funds for medical and health services research financed by research councils, mainly the Medical Research Council and the Economic and Social Research Council, are now part of the budget of the Office of Science and Technology which is part of the Department of Trade and Industry.

Costs to the National Health Service

The costs of providing maternity care were already an issue in 1879, when Aeneas Munro estimated the costs of setting up a charitably funded lying-in hospital. He found that

> 'the sum given towards our Metropolitan medical relief system was ... one pound for lying-in purposes ... expended for every £74 ... for all other medical purposes; this cannot be described as an adequate or fair proportion, yet the obstetric branch is more than one third of the whole.'[11]

When he set out to estimate the costs, however, he found that

> 'In work of this kind it is impossible to forecast the result exactly, either as to cost or maintenance.'[11]

Accurate identification and prediction of costs is still a problem for the NHS and for maternity services in particular.

Annual costs of the NHS are estimated in the annual public expenditure estimates. In 1997/98 the overall amount was £44 billion in the United Kingdom, or about £750 per person. Of this total, £33.5 billion was allocated to the NHS in England. The largest proportion of this funding, 74 per cent, was spent in the hospital and community health services (HCHS), and 23 per cent was used in family health services provided by general medical practitioners, pharmacists, opticians and dentists. The remaining three per cent was for centrally funded services and Department of Health administration.

Table A11.2.1 reproduces information published in *Health and personal social services statistics for England* which shows that when capital costs and contracted out services are included, the total expenditure of the hospital and community health sector of the NHS was over £25 billion in 1997/98. A high percentage of NHS costs is absorbed by staff pay. Table A11.2.1 shows that, as was the case in 1980, staff costs still accounted for nearly 70 per cent of current HCHS expenditure in the late 1990s. Staff costs were 65 per cent of total expenditure in 1996/97, when capital costs are included in the total, as Figure 11.1 shows.

Figure 11.1

Spending on hospital and community health services, England, 1996/97

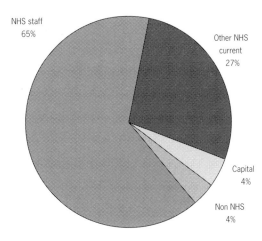

Source: Department of Health, *Health and personal social services statistics for England, 1998*

Data about staff employed in the maternity services are given in Tables A7.5.1 to A7.10.2 and salary scales for 1998 are given in Table A11.4.1. In response to apparent shortages of nursing and midwifery staff, some changes to the career structure were announced by the Department of Health in September 1998. These changes included additional discretionary pay points for staff taking on roles beyond what is expected for their grade, and plans for more senior clinical grades, to allow practising nurses to advance their clinical career without necessarily becoming managers.[12]

Medical consultants in the NHS are eligible for distinction awards in addition to their salary. Table A11.4.2 shows numbers and amounts of distinction award holders in obstetrics and gynaecology, paediatrics and paediatric surgery. Distinction awards are given to consultants in the United Kingdom who are considered to do outstanding professional work. In 1997, consultants in obstetrics and gynaecology and paediatrics had about average numbers of distinction awards, about 12 per cent. Paediatric surgery at 22 per cent, however, had almost twice the average proportion.

There has been concern that consultants from ethnic minorities are discriminated against in making distinction awards. Although they form 13.9 per cent of all consultants, they held only 4.8 per cent of awards in 1996.[13] Table A11.4.2 does not give the breakdown awards by gender, although the data are available, and show that there is an imbalance between numbers of awards to male and female consultants. The purpose of the awards has changed over time. The original awards were to compensate those who worked wholly in the NHS and did not earn high private fees, whereas the awards are now intended to reflect clinical excellence. The process used to allocate the awards was made more transparent in the late 1990s, in response to concerns about the issues mentioned above.

The estimates given to the House of Commons Social Services Committee in 1980 were based on expenditure on client groups, using programme budgets.[10] Although the authors acknowledged the methodology to be crude,[14] the programme budget estimates yielded order of magnitude estimates about the proportion of departmental expenditure which was on maternity and child care. Estimates of hospital and community health services maternity budgets are shown in Table A11.3.1. These figures exclude family practitioner costs, and are dominated by the costs of hospital care, which in 1997/98 constituted 64 per cent of the total programme budget for maternity care. Table A11.3.1 shows the estimated expenditure in relevant categories from 1976/77 to 1997/98, adjusted to 1997/98 price levels.

From 1988/89 the classification and content of the community midwifery and health visiting categories changed, so the figures before and after that year are not exactly comparable. Indeed, the basis for the estimation has been changed every year, and so year on year changes should not be assumed to reflect changes in actual resources for maternity care. The overall total amount identified grew in real terms from 1976/77 until 1980, when inflation was very high. Spending on hospital and community maternity care, adjusted for health pay and price inflation, increased again until 1991/92 but has declined since that date. The programme budget for maternity and early childhood was just over 5.6 per cent of the total of HCHS spending in 1997/98.

Estimates of hospital and community health services maternity budgets, shown in Table A11.3.1, exclude costs of family practitioner services. Much maternity care is provided on general practice premises and some general practitioners provide hospital care. The midwives who provide much of this care are usually employees of NHS trusts, with very few directly employed in general practice,[15] and so their costs are included in HCHS budgets. General practitioners are paid a fee for their maternity services. Table A11.3.2 shows the cash amount paid nationally to general practitioners in England for maternity medical services from 1990/91 to 1996/97. This has increased each year in cash terms, but not in 'real' terms. The fees which general practitioners are paid do not necessarily reflect the true costs of providing maternity care in general practice settings. Rates for 1998/99 are shown in Table A11.4.3. More detail about the numbers and types of claims made by general practitioners for maternity medical services is given in Chapter 7 and Table A7.10.2.

Taken together, the overall identifiable expenditure on NHS maternity care, excluding health visiting costs, in hospital, community and general practice is shown in Table 11.1. In 1996/97 in England, identifiable spending per birth was £1,822. Although the cash amount was growing, the amount expressed at 1996/97 prices, adjusted for health service pay and price inflation, apparently fell over the five year period from 1992/93. This should be interpreted cautiously, given the changing methods for estimating the programme budget. Nevertheless, fewer resources could be identified per birth in the NHS at a time when new initiatives, such as *Changing childbirth*, and the new training arrangements for midwives and for doctors were being implemented. These required investment in training and organisation, and also reduced the extent to which doctors could be present.[16,17]

The early development of accounting systems in the NHS has been described elsewhere.[18] The information system used in the National Health Service was reviewed by the Steering Group on Health Services Information in the early 1980s. As a result of subsequent changes in the NHS, financial information has changed over the intervening years. Before 1980 the health service accounts were not presented by specialty. Under the system of 'functional budgets' within administrative units, information was collected about hospital expenditure by types of service provided, such as 'nursing and staff services', 'medical and paramedical support services' or 'portering'. Because of the way the health services were organised, costs could not easily be ascribed to particular specialties. It was therefore difficult to identify the costs of maternity care within the hospital service. The *Health service costing returns*, which used to be published annually by the Department of Health and Social Security, are no longer published. They contained a national and regional summary of the health service current expenditure, and average costs per patient and per patient day. Much detail was given for hospitals, while community and family practitioner services were presented in less detail.

Table 11.1

Total expenditure on maternity services and average cost per birth, 1992/93 to 1996/97

Financial year	Total expenditure on HCHS maternity services £, thousands	GP maternity payments* £, thousands	All maternity £, thousands	Average cost per birth	
				£, actual prices	£, 1996/97 prices
1992/93	1,011,857	71,243	1,083,100	1,655	1,876
1993/94	1,007,065	72,465	1,079,530	1,687	1,849
1994/95	1,006,546	74,017	1,080,563	1,708	1,826
1995/96	1,012,530	73,148	1,085,678	1,761	1,809
1996/97	1,048,651	76,449	1,125,100	1,822	1,822

* Fees paid to general practitioners for maternity medical services, England

Sources: House of Commons Health Committee. *Public expenditure on health and personal social services*
GP maternity payments: *NHS Executive FIS (FHS)*[4]

In the past, costs of aspects of care within the maternity specialty, such as costs of care for women having operative delivery, or home delivery, were not routinely recorded in the NHS. In 1999, the NHS Executive published a new set of NHS performance indicators, which included the unit cost of maternity, derived from NHS trusts' annual accounts, and general medical services accounts. The unit cost for England in 1996/97 was £1,808.[19] Maternity units may be found in all types of acute hospitals. These show considerable variability in average costs per in-patient per day and week, partly reflecting the differences in 'case mix' in the NHS trusts in which the maternity departments are based. There have been many studies, mostly in the United States, about the costs of providing hospital care both for women and children, and whether reimbursement rates by health funders are adequate to cover these costs.[20]

Increasing concern that it was not possible to link use of NHS resources to particular activities or client groups led to recommendations for patient based, ward based or specialty based costing in the NHS. Several pilot studies were set up both to test feasibility of the new approach, and to look at new methods of financial management.[21,22] These initiatives never progressed to the point of generating routine data about NHS costs, but were overtaken by the reorganisation of the NHS in 1991, and the introduction of the internal market, which radically altered financial responsibilities within the NHS. In the new 'market' for health care following the white paper *Working for patients*,[23] and the ensuing National Health Service and Community Care Act of 1990,[24] most care was commissioned by health authorities from NHS trusts which provided care.[25] Health authorities agreed to pay for the care of a defined range of services for a defined client group. If patients were not covered by the contract, for example, if they lived in other health authority areas or were registered with a fundholding family practitioner, the trust could charge their health authority or fundholding practice for their care. This was known as an extra-contractual referral (ECR).

The NHS Executive set up a Costing and Pricing Working Party to ensure that rules would be laid down for the way NHS trusts should charge for care they provided. Guidance given included that charges should reflect the actual costs of providing the care. While 'income generation' from commercial activities in hospitals was actively being encouraged, trusts were not expected to profit from provision of clinical services to NHS patients. Data about charges for ECRs were circulated within the NHS, but were not published at national level. A change from an emphasis on commercial confidentiality to open publication of data about costs was signalled in *The new NHS: reference costs*. This publication included averages, ranges and variations in costs by diagnostic group, including costs of aspects of hospital maternity care for selected NHS trusts.[26]

In 1995 and 1996, the Audit Commission carried out a study of maternity services, looking at organisation and efficiency. This study found a lack of data within the NHS on the costs of different types of care in maternity and concluded, among other things, that 'it is essential to cost planned changes in the organisation of maternity care so that (purchasers and trusts) can choose between competing priorities.'[27]

On April 1 1999, the system changed and new arrangements were introduced for commissioning NHS services through primary care groups within health authorities. There are several such groups in each health authority and each represents a group of general practices within a particular locality, together with representatives from social services. Principles for commissioning services are still emerging at the time of writing and so it is not possible to say how this will affect information about maternity service costs.[28-30]

If little detail is available about the costs of maternity care in the NHS, even less can be said about the costs of neonatal care. Even if specialty costing were in operation, the inclusion of neonatal special care with the paediatric specialty would make national routine monitoring of neonatal costs difficult. Yet it is precisely this part of perinatal care that aroused most calls for cost benefit analysis in the 1980s[31] and which has been most intensively studied since then.[32] One finding from this review was that NHS ECR charges for neonatal care in 1994 were presented in a different way in each NHS region. This meant that they were very widely variable and were not comparable between regions, and at national level.

Details of capital expenditure by the NHS are summarised in *Health and personal services statistics for England*, and equivalent volumes for Wales and Scotland. They are given in more detail in the *National Health Service accounts*. It is a very difficult exercise to subdivide capital costs between specialties, and this would require special studies. Since 1990, NHS costing rules have required that a capital element is included in cost estimates.[26] Table A11.2.1 includes estimates of capital costs of NHS services.

In recent years, under the Private Finance Initiative (PFI), governments have been initiating new forms of capital finance in which private consortia build and own public facilities such as hospitals, and lease them back to the NHS. The PFI is still new to the NHS and not yet widespread, so it is too early to say how this will affect provision of maternity services, or whether published concerns will be borne out. It is known that the NHS has to include the higher interest rates chargeable in the private sector and payments to leaseholders' shareholders in its payments for leasing facilities. There are also concerns that the new hospitals being built under PFI may not have sufficient capacity to meet the needs for which they are intended.[33]

Costs to local authorities

When the NHS and local government were reorganised in 1974, the community health services took over responsibility for much of the direct health care that was previously provided by local authorities. This NHS responsibility has continued under the 1990 National Health Service and Community Care Act. Social services departments continue to provide some services to families with expectant mothers and with babies. In statistical returns to the Department of Health, local authority social services departments give some information about staff and activities in services provided for families and expectant mothers. For example most local authorities have social workers attached to maternity or neonatal units.

Up to the end of the 1970s, local authorities offered home helps for women during the early postnatal period at home. This was charged on a means tested basis. By 1982, the provision of the service had become very unusual. The statistical return recording numbers of home helps for maternity care was abandoned as part of a general cull of central data collection in the government.[34] This change meant that it was no longer possible to use routine statistics to monitor provision of home help for families with special needs, such as those with a higher order multiple birth. The national study of triplet and higher order births, published in 1990[35] showed that local authority help for this group was very small, and did not meet the families' needs.

Local authorities' expenditure is summarised in their published accounts, but as with health service accounts, it is not possible to isolate the costs of services provided to mothers and babies from published statistics of social services expenditure on family and child care. Some details of costs and usage of social services provided for families with children are given for every local authority in Great Britain, in the personal social services volumes of the *Statistical information series*, published annually by the Chartered Institute of Public Finance and Accountancy (CIPFA).

Costs to families

As has been already mentioned, the Department of Health estimates programme budgets for maternity and child health care and these are shown in Table A11.3.1. Although the costs in a programme budget should, in theory, be the total costs to society and not just to the NHS,[36] the Department used NHS costs as the basis for its calculations. This could reinforce allocation of resources to those services which involve economies to the NHS but relatively high user costs, such as travel to central units, waiting time or home care by members of the family.

When parents choose to have a baby, they can nearly always justify the sacrifices or costs arising from that birth. If, for whatever reason, the family is dependent on state benefits or the pregnancy was unplanned or if a baby has an impairment and special needs, the costs can weigh heavily. Except in special cases, the cost of a baby may be higher if it is the first in a family. To some extent, the costs are offset by provision of benefits and services by the state.

Providing for the baby

The total cost to a family of keeping a child has been considered in some detail by researchers over the last two decades[37-42] and is the subject of claims and counter claims in the debate about the adequacy or otherwise of social security benefits for families with young children. A survey of families with children, sponsored by the Joseph Rowntree Foundation, was published in 1997.[42] It found that the average spending on children up to their seventeenth birthday was £50,000, and that 90 per cent of this came from their parents.

Information about average family expenditures and about prices of goods in general is published annually in *Family spending*, the reports of the Family Expenditure Survey. Regional data, published in *Regional trends*, show the differences between regions both in income and in patterns of expenditure by households. Some of these data are reproduced for standard regions in Table A5.32.1.

In 1979 and 1981 the Child Poverty Action Group sponsored research to find out whether the supplementary benefit scale was sufficient to meet the basic requirements for children. These studies[38,39] specifically excluded the cost of a new baby to a family because this cost varies so much, partly depending on whether or not it is a first child. The studies concluded that at all ages the supplementary benefit level was below the estimated minimum cost of providing for a child. In a survey in the mid 1990s which estimated costs of babies in their first year, families who were receiving income support spent 63 per cent of the allowance for their children on food.[42] The study found that parents do spend more on older children, but that the lower benefit allowances for younger children, leave them 'severely disadvantaged' compared with older children in families with children receiving benefits.

Costs of impairment and its consequences

Sometimes a baby is born with a mental or physical impairment. The costs of a childhood disability were estimated quite crudely[43] in evidence to the House of Commons Social Services Committee in 1980, in an attempt to calculate the savings to society that would follow if it were possible to prevent the occurrence of disability arising before, during or soon after delivery. These exercises did not attempt to evaluate the psychological costs to parents of a baby, or to the surviving disabled child. If the state is not providing adequate resources, the families and communities with disabled members bear the costs directly. Work on costs of disability was done in the mid 1980s[44] but was not translated into information for decision makers, whether they are parents or caregivers. Although research in this field has continued, there has not been a new national survey of disability or its costs since then.

Loss of earnings

There are other costs to the pregnant woman or mother and her family. In addition to meeting the basic living costs for a new baby, most women attend antenatal clinics, and many attend classes. They give up time to do this which might otherwise be used in other ways, and they also bear the costs of getting to and from clinics. Official statistics do not yield much information about waiting times in antenatal clinics or about average distances travelled to clinics, but research has been done which estimated typical waiting times.[45-48] Family expenditure on travel and transport is estimated in the Family Expenditure Survey,[49] but this does not give detail about the purpose of individual journeys. A survey of patients' attitudes to the hospital service, conducted for the Royal Commission on the NHS in

1978[50] gave some information about how patients at that time travelled to hospital and about waiting times. Although they may bear the costs willingly, the costs to women of attending antenatal clinics were shown to be significant in one study in Aberdeenshire. On occasions, costs borne by women outweighed NHS costs, especially in rural areas.[46] Women receiving means tested benefits or on low income can get all or some of the costs of their fares refunded by the Department of Social Security.

Where women leave paid employment to have a baby, they and their families forego income. This may for a short period be offset by Statutory Maternity Pay (SMP) or Maternity Allowance. Some women who are in employment and who are entitled to maternity leave may receive some or all of their pay. Very little information is available about the numbers of women who are both pregnant and in paid employment. Some of it is rather old, but it does illustrate changes which have taken place. The ONS Longitudinal Study, already referred to in Chapter 5, provides some information. In 1971, 29 per cent of 4574 women in the sample who gave birth to live born babies between the census date and the end of the year were employed at the time of the census but only 9 per cent of the women were still in employment during the five months before the birth.[51] This is likely to be an underestimate of the likelihood of women working during pregnancy, because it is possible that there were pregnant women not working at the time of the census who subsequently started working during pregnancy. This analysis has not been repeated for 1981 or 1991.

A survey in 1979 showed that, of a sample of 1,100 women employed outside the home during pregnancy, 23 per cent were in work again eight months after the birth had occurred, and a further 14 per cent were seeking work.[52] Women who did return to work frequently took positions with lower status and income and, in addition, had to meet the costs of child care while they worked. In a survey of nearly 5,000 women who gave birth in December 1987 and January 1988, and over 500 employers, Susan MacRae repeated the 1979 survey.[52,53] She found that in 1988, 55 per cent of women had been in paid work within 12 months before the birth. Of those working when pregnant, 45 per cent had returned to work by nine months after the birth. This survey also showed that job status of women had improved overall since 1979, and, although many women still found themselves demoted, there was less loss of status on return to work than in the 1979 survey.

A survey in 1996 found that the numbers of women in work had increased again. Out of 71 per cent of working women who were entitled to extended maternity leave, two thirds returned before their allowance of leave was used up. Only half of these did so by their own choice.[54]

In addition to the short term costs associated with maternity leave at the time of the birth, family responsibilities have a longer term impact on women's earning power. An analysis of data from the national birth cohort studies of people born in 1946 and 1958 showed that women without children aged 32 in 1978 earned 40 per cent more than mothers of the same age. This was still true for women aged 33 in 1991, but with different related factors.[55]

Although loss of earnings is easier to measure, the time given both antenatally and postnatally by women who were not in employment outside the home also carries a cost. For example, many women find themselves less able to care for elderly dependants or to take their place in play group rotas when pregnant or caring for their young babies. This social resource is documented every 10 years in the census which counts the number of women not actively seeking paid employment, and in the General Household Survey which questions all household members on economic activity. Otherwise it receives little coverage in published statistics. In 1997, ONS added a section on time use by households to the annual Omnibus Survey of individuals. This survey found that 23 per cent of women's time is spent in unpaid work, compared to 16 per cent for men. The percentage of time spent in paid work was 9 per cent for women and 15 per cent for men.[56,57] A separate survey of time use in households was piloted in 1998.

Costs of health care

In the United Kingdom, most medical care is provided free to the user at the time of use, with charges, not directly related to their cost, for prescribed medicines, dental treatment and ophthalmic services. Even these are available without charge to pregnant women, mothers of children aged under one year, and to dependent children. Although the costs of maternity services are provided by the NHS, certain essential items such as nappies, sanitary pads and breast pads are not routinely provided by the health services and represent an additional cost to the family.

Some families choose to be insured privately against medical expenses, or are covered as a benefit provided by their employer. Government policy in the 1980s encouraged private health insurance. Some forms of health insurance can provide cover for costs of private health care while others provide cover for additional family costs arising from illness or stays in hospital. Neither form of insurance usually covers the costs arising from a normal delivery. Insurance cover can be arranged for the medical expenses arising from complications occurring during delivery in the private sector.

Costs to employers

Women aged between 15 and 44 constitute a growing proportion of the employed population. Within that group, an increasing number of women are in paid employment during pregnancy and when their children are young.[58,59]

One study of women in employment[53] suggested that, in 1980, about 3.5 per cent of the female economically active population left work to have a baby in any one year. This figure varied between 1.2 per cent and 7.5 per cent for different companies and different years, depending partly on the age distribution of the workforce. Of these, many were not then entitled to statutory maternity rights. Those who do not return to the same employer may represent a cost to that employer in time given to training, although to society as a whole this may not be a net cost.

Employers are obliged to give paid time off to pregnant workers to attend antenatal clinics, and some pregnant women may need more sick leave than usual. Statistics about women who have claimed social security benefits either for sickness or maternity are given in *Social security statistics*. Figures are given for estimated number of spells of sickness or incapacity arising from conditions of pregnancy or the puerperium. As these figures are estimated from a one per cent sample of claims for sickness benefit, they are likely to be based on very small numbers and therefore may be subject to large chance variation. Even if the figures were correctly estimated, they represent claims for benefit, and so include only the periods of illness where a doctor's certificate was obtained. The requirement for a doctor's certificate for three to six days sickness was removed after 1983, when employers took on responsibility for payment for most sick leave for employees, so such information is no longer available.

Maternity leave and maternity pay

Employers bear some of the costs arising from legislation about maternity leave and pay. A study of maternity rights legislation investigated the impact on employers of legislation about maternity rights.[53] The report concluded that employment rights legislation introduced in the late 1970s, the Employment Protection Act of 1975 and Employment Act of 1980, did not increase the problems employers faced concerning maternity leave and the right to reinstatement for women who qualify. This in part reflects the fact that only a small percentage of the labour force in any single year is likely to consist of women who are both pregnant and eligible for maternity leave. A sample of employers surveyed in 1988 did not identify maternity rights as a problem, although some had concerns about details.[59] This was still true in 1996.[54]

How does the state help to meet the costs?

It is already clear that in the United Kingdom, the state contributes to meeting the costs of maternity in many ways and some of these are summarised in this section.

Health and social services

Although the costs of maternity can be considerable many of these costs are met by the state from taxation, National Insurance contributions, and public borrowing. The National Health Service provides care without charge at the point of use. Where charges are made, pregnant women and mothers of children aged up to one year are exempted.

Local authorities provide some services free at the point of use, but for those who can pay there is usually a charge for nursery care or home help. Certain welfare foods are free to those in need. The uptake of welfare in kind such as milk and vitamins by those eligible is by no means complete. Data published in *Social security statistics* in 1981 suggested that in December 1977, about half of those eligible were not claiming or receiving free milk.

Although the information about uptake of free milk and other benefits in kind is still routinely collected and reported in Department of Social Security quarterly statistics, the information is no longer included in *Social security statistics*.

Financial benefits

Table A11.5.1 shows the numbers of maternity benefit awards made from 1983 until 1996/97. Until 1982, if pregnant women or their husbands had paid National Insurance contributions over a qualifying period they were entitled to claim a Maternity Grant of £25 for each child born. This excluded the small proportion of women who had not paid qualifying contributions but were likely to be most in need of money. From July 1982, the grant was made available to all pregnant women, and not just those who had paid National Insurance contributions. The grant did not increase from 1969, when it was set at £25, until 1986, when the grant was abolished. By 1986, £25 was a very small amount compared with the cost of providing even clothes and bedding for a new baby. From April 1987, maternity payments are paid from the Social Fund on the basis of need.

Maternity Allowance is payable to women who have paid qualifying Class 1 National Insurance contributions, as a regular weekly amount over the statutory period of maternity leave. It is paid for a maximum of 18 weeks, starting 11 weeks before the baby is born, at the earliest. Since April 1987, women in employment paying Class 1 National Insurance contributions and meeting criteria for qualifying length of service and number of hours worked, are entitled to Statutory Maternity Pay from their employers. Statutory Maternity Pay includes an earnings related element and over 90 per cent of this cost is paid by the state. From this time, Table A11.5.1 shows that there was a sharp drop in numbers of awards of Maternity Allowance.

Maternity Allowance is also payable to women who were not employees at the fifteenth week of pregnancy, but at a lower rate. Additions for other dependent children have not been paid as part of the maternity benefit since 1984, but an amount for a dependent adult is paid. Rates of maternity benefit from 1981 to 1997 are shown in Table A11.6.1.

In the budget of March 1999, entitlement to Maternity Allowance was extended, with effect from April 2000, to women with lower earnings and the rates for self employed women were increased to the same amount awarded to employees. Those entitled to the full rate of benefit will be paid at £59.99 per week. Families with low income will be able to apply for up to £200 towards the extra costs of having a new child to the Sure Start Parents' Payment Scheme, which replaces the maternity payments scheme from the Social Fund from April 2000.

Monitoring the costs of childbirth in the 1990s and 2000s

In this chapter we have discussed costs associated with maternity which the different parts of society face. It is clear that it is impossible to derive a figure for the cost of maternity, since this has different meanings for health workers, parents and the Department of Social Security. Reports have highlighted the lack of data about the costs of maternity and maternity care, and people managing maternity services have been advised to consider the cost-effectiveness as well as the effectiveness and acceptability of the services.[16,27] Unless costs beyond those directly falling on the health services are also recognised and taken into account, however, there is little chance the services will be organised in the best way for all concerned.

References

1   Davies ML, ed. *Maternity: letters from working women collected by the Women's Co-operative Guild.* London: G Bell and Sons, 1915.

2   Joint Committee of the Royal College of Obstetricians and Gynaecologists and the Population Investigation Committee. *Maternity in Great Britain.* Oxford: Oxford University Press, 1948.

3   Gowdridge C, Williams AS, Wynn M, eds. *Mother courage: letters from mothers in poverty at the end of the century.* London: Penguin Books in association with the Maternity Alliance, 1997.

4   Royal Commission on the National Health Service. *Report. [Chair: A Merrison].* Cmnd 7615. London: HMSO, 1979.

5   Stacey M. Realities for change in child health care: existing patterns and future possibilities. *British Medical Journal* 1980; 280(6230): 1512–1515.

6   Butler NR, Bonham DG. *Perinatal mortality. The first report of the British Perinatal Mortality Survey.* Edinburgh and London: E&S Livingstone, 1963.

7   Chamberlain G, Philipp E, Howlett B, Masters K. *British births, 1970.* Vol. 2: Obstetric care. London: Heinemann Medical Books, 1978.

8   House of Commons Health Committee. *Public expenditure on health and personal social services. Memorandum received from the Department of Health containing replies to a written questionnaire from the Committee.* Session 1995–1996. HC 698. London: The Stationery Office, 1996.

9   House of Commons Health Committee. *Public expenditure on health and personal social services. Memorandum received from the Department of Health containing replies to a written questionnaire from the Committee.* Session 1997–1998. HC 297. London: The Stationery Office, 1998.

10 House of Commons Social Services Committee. *Second report: perinatal and neonatal mortality. [Chair: R Short].* Session 1979–1980. HC 663 Vol. IV. London: HMSO, 1980:203.

11 Munro AE. *Deaths in childbed.* London: Smith, Elder & Co., 1879.

12 Department of Health. *New £1000 pay boost for nurses, midwives, and professions allied to medicine.* Press release 98/371. London: Department of Health, September 9 1998.

13   Esmail A, Everington S, Doyle H. Racial discrimination in the allocation of distinction awards? Analysis of list of award holders by type of award, specialty and region. *BMJ* 1998; 316(7126): 193–195.

14   House of Commons Social Services Committee. *Second report: public expenditure on the social services. 1982 White Paper*. Cm 306. Session 1981–1982. HC 306 Vol. II. London: HMSO, 1982.

15   United Kingdom Central Council for Nursing, Midwifery and Health Visiting. *Statistical analysis of the Council's professional register 1 April 1997 to 31 March 1998 (including midwives intention to practise statistics for the year commencing 1 April 1998)*. London: UKCC, 1998.

16   Department of Health. *Changing childbirth. Part 1: Report of the Expert Maternity Group [Chair: Baroness Cumberlege]*. London: HMSO, 1993.

17   Department of Health Working Group on Specialist Medical Training. *Hospital doctors: training for the future [Chair: K Calman]*. Heywood, Lancs: Health Publications Unit, 1993.

18   Montacute C. *Costing and efficiency in hospitals*. Oxford: Oxford University Press, 1962.

19   Public Health Development Unit, NHS Executive. *Quality and performance indicators in the NHS: Clinical indicators*. Leeds: NHS Executive, 1999.

20   Mugford M. *How does the method of cost estimation affect the assessment of cost-effectiveness in health care?* D Phil thesis. University of Oxford, 1996.

21   Buxton M, Packwood T, Keen J. *Final report of the Brunel University evaluation of resource management*. HERG Research Reports No. 10. London: Department of Health, 1989.

22   Judge K. Monitoring and evaluating 'Working for patients'. *BMJ* 1989; 299: 1385–1387.

23   Department of Health. *Working for patients*. Cm 555. London: HMSO, 1989.

24   National Health Service and Community Care Act. In: *Public general acts and measures, 1990*. Part II. Chap 19. London: HMSO, 1990: 823–952.

25   McClean K, ed. *Introductory guide to NHS finance in the UK*. 2nd edition. London: HFM/CIPFA, 1993.

26   Department of Health, NHS Executive. *The new NHS – 1998 reference costs*. On the Internet at: http://www.doh.gov.uk/nhsexec/refcosts.htm#down. Leeds: NHS Executive, 1999.

27   Audit Commission. *First class delivery: improving maternity services in England and Wales*. London: Audit Commission, 1997.

28   Smith PC. Setting budgets for general practice in the new NHS. *BMJ* 1999; 318(7186): 776–779.

29 Baker R, Lakhani M, Fraser R, Cheater F. A model for clinical governance in primary care groups. *BMJ* 1999; 318(7186): 779–783.

30 Proctor SR, Campbell JL. Towards primary care groups: managing the future in Bradford. *BMJ* 1999; 318(7186): 783–785.

31 Sinclair JC, Torrance GW, Boyle MH, Horwood SP, Saigal S, Sackett DL. Evaluation of neonatal intensive care programs. *New England Journal of Medicine* 1981; 305(9): 489–494.

32 Mugford M. The cost of neonatal care: reviewing the evidence. *Sozial Und Praventivmedizin* 1995; 40(6): 361–368.

33 Pollock AM, Dunnigan M, Gaffney D, Macfarlane AJ, Majeed FA. What happens when the private sector plans hospital services for the NHS: three case studies under the private finance initiative. *BMJ* 1997; 314(7089): 1266–1271.

34 Department of Health and Social Security Study Team. *Review of the government statistical services: report.* London: DHSS, 1980.

35 Botting BJ, Macfarlane AJ, Price FV. *Three, four and more: a national survey of triplet and higher order births.* London: HMSO, 1990.

36 Culyer AJ. *The political economy of social policy.* Oxford: Martin Robertson, 1980.

37 McClements LD. Equivalence scales for children. *Journal of Public Economics* 1977; 8: 191–210.

38 Piachaud D. *The cost of a child.* London: Child Poverty Action Group, 1979.

39 Piachaud D. *Children and poverty.* London: Child Poverty Action Group, 1981.

40 Consumers' Association. What children cost. *Money which?* 1977; December.

41 Kendall I. *Mothers and babies first?* London: National Maternity Grant Campaign, 1979.

42 Middleton S, Ashworth K, Braithwaite I. *Small fortunes: spending on children, childhood poverty and parental sacrifice.* York: Joseph Rowntree Foundation, 1997.

43 House of Commons Social Services Committee. *Second report: perinatal and neonatal mortality. [Chair: R Short].* Session 1979–1980. HC 663 Vol. I. London: HMSO, 1980.

44 Baldwin S. *The costs of caring: families with disabled children.* London: Routledge & Kegan Paul, 1985.

45 Garcia J. *Findings on antenatal care from Community Health Council studies.* Oxford: National Perinatal Epidemiology Unit, 1981.

46 Meldrum P. *Costing routine ante-natal visits.* University of Aberdeen: Health Economics Research Unit, 1989.

47 Ratcliffe J, Ryan M, Tucker J. The costs of alternative types of routine antenatal care for low-risk women: shared care vs care by general practitioners and community midwives. *Journal of Health Services Research and Policy* 1996; 1(3): 135–140.

48 Young D, Lees A, Twaddle S. The costs to the NHS of maternity care: midwife-managed vs. shared. *British Journal of Midwifery* 1997; 5(8): 465–471.

49 Office for National Statistics. *Family spending: a report on the 1995–96 Family Expenditure Survey.* London: The Stationery Office, 1996.

50 Gregory J. Patients' attitudes to the hospital service. In: Royal Commission on the National Health Service. *Research Papers.* No. 5. London: HMSO, 1978.

51 McDowall M, Goldblatt P, Fox J. Employment during pregnancy and infant mortality. *Population Trends* 1981; 26: 12–15.

52 Daniels WW. *Maternity rights: the experience of women.* London: Policy Studies Institute, 1980.

53 Daniels WW. *Maternity rights: the experience of employers.* London: Policy Studies Institute, 1981.

54 Callender C, Millward N, Lissenburgh S, Forth J. *Maternity rights and benefits in Britain 1996.* DSS Research Report No. 67. London: The Stationery Office, 1997.

55 Joshi H, Paci P, Waldfogel J. *The wages of motherhood: better or worse?* Discussion paper WSP/122. London: Welfare State Programme, Toyota Centre, Suntory and Toyota International Centres for Economics and Related Disciplines, London School of Economics, 1996.

56 Church J, Koudra M, Murgatroyd L. Where has all the time gone? Measuring time in the UK. *Statistical News* 1996; 111: 34–39.

57 Murgatroyd L, Neuberger H. A household satellite account for the UK. *Economic Trends* 1997; 527: 63–69.

58 Moss P, Fonda N, eds. *Work and the family.* London: Temple Smith, 1980.

59 McRae S. *Maternity rights in Britain: the experience of women and employers.* London: Policy Studies Institute, 1991.

12 Statistics from international organisations

'The greatest caution must be exercised in making comparisons between different countries. It is fallacious to compare the maternal mortality rate of England and Wales with that of Holland, Denmark, Sweden or any other country, unless there is the certainty that the basis on which the mortality rate is computed is the same in these countries as in England and Wales.'

Munro Kerr, 1933.[1]

Infant mortality has been used and is still seen[2-5] as an indicator of the socio-economic wellbeing of a country, while deaths of women and babies in the perinatal period are thought to be more closely associated with the quality of care available to mothers and their babies during pregnancy and delivery. So it is not surprising that both infant and maternal mortality have become politically sensitive issues. The result has been that the available mortality data have been compared, ranked and analysed as though they measured the same thing in the same way in every country, although it has been acknowledged for many years that they do not. Differences in legislation and data collection were documented by a Royal Statistical Society working party in 1912.[6] The same point was raised in the context of international comparisons made in the 1930s.[1] All too often, however, attention is focused on the relatively small differences between developed countries, while ignoring the much greater gulf between these and less developed countries, particularly in maternal mortality.[7]

The experience of other countries may provide valuable information about factors affecting infant and maternal mortality in different populations. So rather than dismiss attempts at comparison, this chapter looks at the problems in interpreting and comparing countries' statistics, and gives an overview of the statistics published by international organisations.

Quality and comparability of statistics

In 1969, the United Nations Population Commission estimated that only two per cent of the world's infant deaths were reported completely and accurately.[8] Nearly thirty years later in 1996, when the World Health Organisation (WHO) and UNICEF published revised estimates of maternal mortality rates for 1990, these suggested that there were 585,000 maternal deaths world wide, 99 per cent of them in developing countries and 80,000 more than previously estimated.[9] Not surprisingly, deaths are more accurately recorded in countries with well developed administrative and statistical systems than is the case in economically less developed countries. Surveys in the 1980s and 1990s found that definitions of vital events and completeness of recording still differed even between European countries.[10,11]

Differences in definitions

The definitions of vital events recommended by the World Health Organisation are given in Chapter 2. Because legal and vital statistics systems have often evolved over many years from different cultural roots, countries tend to have legal definitions of events such as live birth, stillbirth or infant death which differ in some way from the recommendations of WHO. A survey conducted by the United Nations (UN) in 1950, asking each member nation to give definitions in use on 1 January 1950, found wide disparity in the definitions used.[12] In the early 1980s, a WHO Study Group conducted an informal survey of the countries of the European Region of WHO.[10] Many European countries which did not use WHO definitions in 1950 had changed their official definitions to conform more closely with them. Out of 23 countries in the European Region, at least 11 had changed their definition of a live birth between 1950 and 1981.

Countries participating in the International Collaborative Effort on Infant and Perinatal Mortality co-ordinated by the United States National Centers for Health Statistics differed in their criteria for registering live and stillbirths and infant deaths.[13] A survey of European countries in 1991 found that they still differed in the criteria for registering births.[11] Although eight countries planned to change over the next three years, they were not moving to identical criteria.

Accuracy and completeness

Statistics published by countries vary in their completeness and accuracy. Where the process of registration of births and deaths is less centralised and where registration or notification of vital events is not required or enforced by law, official statistics frequently underestimate mortality rates. Even in Europe there are differences in the coverage of statistics. For example, in the Irish Republic the law did not require registration of stillbirths before 1995, while in some of the southern countries of Europe there is acknowledged under-reporting of stillbirths and early neonatal deaths where births take place in some remote rural areas. Even in the most economically advanced countries there is some under-reporting and this can affect published statistics significantly. A detailed study of death registration in Georgia, USA in 1973–77 uncovered substantial under-reporting of neonatal deaths, mainly of low birthweight babies from poor families.[14]

In less developed countries such problems are more common. The similarity between the very low infant and maternal mortality rates in nearly all the developed countries of Europe and North America is more striking when compared with rates prevalent in third world countries. This gulf is often overlooked when analyses of differences between rates usually include only developed countries which can provide reliable statistics. In countries where registration is already incomplete or poorly developed, the gap may be understated if political or other pressures compound any tendency to underestimate infant or maternal mortality.

WHO groups countries broadly into:

'1. Countries with no reliable registration system where maternal deaths – like other events – go unrecorded.

2. Countries with relatively complete vital registration in terms of numbers of births and deaths but where cause of death is not adequately classified.

3. Countries with complete vital registration and good cause of death attribution.'[9]

If the process for notifying births and deaths is not very centralised or non-existent, statistics must be based on estimates. Where registration exists but is not well controlled, the figures may be biased by less complete reporting of infant or maternal deaths than of births, thus tending to reduce the calculated mortality rates. As the primary purpose of civil registration of births is to establish identity and nationality, and that of death registration is to allow for legal inheritance of property, it is possible to see how there may be less incentive to register fetal and early infant deaths than to register live births. For countries where there is no registration system or where there is under-registration of deaths, methods for estimating infant and maternal mortality indirectly have been developed.[15,16]

For estimating mortality in childhood, there are 'preceding birth' techniques. This involves collecting data about previous births and their outcome from mothers when they have another baby.[17] The 'sisterhood method' was developed for collecting information about maternal mortality through surveys in which adults are asked about the deaths of their sisters.[18,19] Household surveys can be expensive, however, and the method has been extended to use data collected from women using health care facilities.[19,20] The results compared well with those obtained from household surveys. Induced abortion is an important cause of death in less developed countries and a number of approaches can be taken to investigating it.[21]

When investigating maternal mortality it is important to have a framework for assessing the services available. A set of questions has been proposed for this purpose, starting with an overview of health policy, going on to estimate the level of maternal mortality and relating this to the services available.[22] Concern has been expressed by people who have developed the estimation techniques that international initiatives focus too narrowly on crude measures of childhood and maternal mortality as these are amenable to measurement and ignore broader issues of the health of children and their mothers.[23]

Differences in characteristics of populations

We have pointed out earlier the limitations of using crude mortality rates. It is important to take into account the characteristics of the populations being compared. In particular, more sense can be made of statistics where information is available about birthweight and deaths from congenital anomalies.

Birthweight and gestational age

An increasing number of countries with central vital statistics offices now collect information about birthweight and gestational age for all births.[11] Some countries, including Denmark, Hungary, England, Wales and the United States can link birthweight with infant death registration details.[13,24] Accuracy and completeness of recorded birthweights vary, as do the factors associated with low birthweight.[25]

Although detailed birthweight-specific mortality rates cannot be produced for each country, it is important to take into account the proportion of low weight births.[13] Data are collated from registration and survey sources by the World Health Organisation in its low birthweight database and used to provide estimates of varying accuracy for a large number of countries.

Cause of death

Because it is likely that the way fetal and infant deaths are diagnosed and classified varies from country to country, cause specific infant mortality rates given in the *UN demographic yearbook* and *WHO statistical abstract* should be treated cautiously. Before antenatal screening became widespread, central nervous system anomalies accounted for some of the differences between countries.

Organisations exist to co-ordinate the definition of all anomalies and the collection of data about anomalies in different countries. The International Clearing House for Birth Defects Monitoring Systems collates information from congenital anomaly systems in its member countries. The European Commission sponsors a 'Concerted Action Project in Registration of Congenital Abnormalities and Twins' (EUROCAT), which co-ordinates the activities of such registers in European countries.

When it comes to comparing maternal deaths, problems are even greater. The World Health Organisation and UNICEF have estimated that cause of death is routinely reported in only about 78 countries or areas, covering about 35 per cent of the world's population.[9] Even in countries with complete vital registration systems, maternal deaths can be misclassified for a variety of reasons.[9,26,27]

Causes of the extremely high rates of infant and childhood mortality in many less developed countries are similar to the causes of infant death which were predominant in the late nineteenth and early twentieth century in Europe. They are strongly associated with poverty and malnutrition.[5,7,28] Unfortunately these are not well documented in statistics.

What can international comparisons tell us?

Despite difference in data quality and sources, estimates of maternal and childhood mortality in Tables A12.1.1 and A12.1.2 show a vast difference between the rich and poor countries of the world. The data come from the revised estimates of maternal mortality referred to earlier and from data published by UNICEF in *The state of the world's children*.[29]

Infant mortality rates for developed countries from 1951 to the 1990s in Table A12.2.1 are taken from the World Health Organisation's mortality database containing summary data from member countries. This shows differences in the timing of the decline in mortality in the second half of the twentieth century and in the reported contribution of mortality attributed to congenital anomalies. Infant mortality rates, from the same source, for countries of the former Soviet Union are shown in Table A12.2.2 and reveal rising rates in the 1980s.

Tables A12.3.1 and A12.3.2 come from a study which involved obtaining data directly from individual national statistics offices for the European countries concerned for the whole of the twentieth century.[30-32] Tables A12.5.1 to A12.7.2 come from the same study. They show differences in low birthweight and birthweight specific mortality, while A12.6.1 shows that the triplet rate was beginning to rise in most countries.

Mortality rates at different stages of the first year of life shown in the volume of *Demographic statistics* published by Eurostat, the Statistical Office of the European Communities, are reproduced in Table A12.4.1.[33] Access to Eurostat data can be obtained via the Office for National Statistics Eurostat 'data shop', while university users can obtain them from the Resource centre for access to Europe (r-cade) project. Contact details for both of these can be found in Appendix 1.

With few exceptions, infant mortality rates for countries with developed statistical systems have been falling since the early 1950s. In Europe, the average rate fell from around 34 per thousand live births in 1960 to 12 in 1980 and 5 in 1998. A notable exception is the rise in the rate of infant mortality in the USSR in the 1970s and early 1980s. This and other examples are discussed in more detail elsewhere.[34,35]

Variations in the downward trend are more likely to occur by chance where numbers of births and deaths are relatively small than in countries with larger populations. This is demonstrated in the data for countries such as Malta, and Luxembourg, whereas the values for countries with larger numbers of births such as the United States, Canada, United Kingdom or France show a smoother trend. There is some evidence of a recurring cycle in the rate of decline of mortality in some of the countries for which data are available. Why this should be is difficult to determine. One study has shown correlation, which does not necessarily imply causation, between changes in infant mortality and indicators of economic activity which also follow a cyclical pattern.[36] There have been a number of criticisms of the methodology of this study, however.

A review of health data collected in a range of countries, mainly the more developed countries, is published by the United States National Centers for Health Statistics in its *International health data reference guide*. This is revised every two years or so and details can be found in Appendix 1.

International comparisons in the 1990s and 2000s

Problems in comparing international data have been recognised for a long time, as the opening quotation in this chapter suggests. In 1950, the Chief Medical Statistician at the General Register Office for England and Wales, Percy Stocks, published a paper on trends in mortality[37] including a table of infant mortality rates for various countries between 1900 and 1948. He concluded that over that period 'the ranking of these countries according to their infant mortality has remained remarkably constant', which is still true when today's rates are included. He also pointed out that 'Some rates are not precisely comparable with those in England and Wales owing to exclusion of deaths of infants occurring soon after birth, but in recent years improvements in registration have eliminated many of these faults.'[37]

Since then some progress has been made by international bodies in achieving comparability. Nevertheless it still remains necessary to take account of differences in the populations being compared, rather than assuming that differences in mortality rate reflect only differences in the quality of the medical services in different countries. Controversies surrounding the comparison of infant and perinatal mortality rates echo the debate about maternal mortality rates in the 1930s. A Ministry of Health report on maternal mortality published in 1937 commented that:

> 'The international position of England and Wales is probably neither so completely unsatisfactory as is stated by some observers, nor would its position be 'near the bottom of the list' if a uniform classification were adopted, as others allege.'[38]

This could as easily refer to a range of health indicators at the end of the 1990s, as far as developed countries are concerned. What it ignores is the vast differences between developed and less developed countries in most measures of the health of mothers and babies and in the care provided for them.[39]

References

1   Kerr JMM. *Maternal mortality and morbidity*. Edinburgh: E&S Livingstone, 1933.

2   Committee on Child Health Services. *Report: fit for the future. [Chair: SDM Court]*. Cmnd 6684. Vol. 2. London: HMSO, 1976.

3   Blaxter M. *The health of children: studies in deprivation and disadvantage*. London: Heinemann Educational Books, 1981.

4   World Health Organization. *Manual of mortality analysis*. Geneva: WHO, 1977.

5   Williams CD, Jelliffe DB. *Mother and child health: delivering the services*. Oxford Medical Publications. London: Oxford University Press, 1972.

6   Report of the special committee on infantile mortality. *Journal of the Royal Statistical Society* 1912; 76: 27–87.

7   Mackay J, ed. *The state of health atlas*. London: Pluto, 1993.

8   United Nations Population Commission. *15th session*. C/CN 9/231. Geneva: 1969:82.

9   World Health Organization, United Nations Children's Fund (UNICEF). *Revised 1990 estimates of maternal mortality: a new approach by WHO and UNICEF.* Geneva: WHO, 1996.

10   Mugford M. A comparison of reported differences in definitions of vital events and statistics. *WHO Statistics Quarterly* 1983; 36: 201–212.

11   Gourbin C, Masuy-Stroobant G. Registration of vital data: are live births and stillbirths comparable all over Europe? *Bulletin of the World Health Organization* 1995; 73(4): 449–460.

12   United Nations. *Handbook of vital statistics methods*. New York: Statistical Office of the UN, 1954.

13   *Proceedings of the International Collaborative Effort on Perinatal and Infant Mortality. Papers presented at the Second International Symposium on Perinatal and Infant Mortality*, Bethesda, Maryland, 1990. Vol. III. Hyattsville, Maryland: US Centers for Disease Control / National Center for Health Statistics, 1992.

14   McCarthy BJ, Terry J, Rochat RW, Quave S, Tyler CW. The under-registration of neonatal deaths: Georgia 1974–77. *American Journal of Public Health* 1980; 70(9): 977–982.

15   United Nations. *Indirect techniques for demographic estimation. Manual X.* New York: United Nations, 1983.

16   AbouZahr C. Maternal mortality overview. In: Murray CJL, Lopez A, eds. *Health dimensions of sex and reproduction: the global burden of sexually transmitted diseases, HIV, maternal conditions, perinatal disorders, and congenital anomalies.* Global burden of disease and injury series Vol. 3. Cambridge, Mass.: Harvard School of Public Health on behalf of WHO and the World Bank, 1998.

17   Brass W, Macrae S. Childhood mortality estimated from reports on previous births given by mothers at the time of a maternity. 1: preceding birth technique. *Pacific Forum* 1985; 11: 5–8.

18   Graham W, Brass W, Snow R. Estimating maternal mortality in developing countries [letter]. *Lancet* 1988; i(8582): 416–417.

19   Danel I, Graham W, Stupp P, Castillo P. Applying the sisterhood method for estimating maternal mortality to a health facility based sample: a comparison with results from a household-based sample. *International Journal of Epidemiology* 1996; 25: 1017–22.

20   Danel I, Castillo P, Graham W. Maternal mortality estimation [letter]. *Lancet* 1993; 341(8848): 832.

21   Barreto T, Campbell OM, Davies JL, Fauveau V, Filippi VG, Graham WJ, Mamdani M, Rooney CI, Toubia NF. Investigating induced abortion in developing countries: methods and problems. *Studies in Family Planning* 1992; 23(3): 159–170.

22   Campbell O, Koblinsky M, Taylor P. Off to a rapid start: appraising maternal mortality and services. *International Journal of Gynaecology and Obstetrics* 1995; 48(Suppl): S33–S52.

23   Graham WJ, Campbell OM. Maternal health and the measurement trap. *Social Science and Medicine* 1992; 35(8): 967–977.

24   Adams MM, Herman AA, Nutzon FC. International symposium on maternally-linked pregnancy outcomes, Atlanta, Georgia, September 1995. Proceedings and abstracts. *Paediatric and Perinatal Epidemiology* 1997; 11 (Suppl 1): 1–150.

25   Kramer MS. Determinants of low birth weight: methodological assessment and meta-analysis. *Bulletin of the World Health Organization* 1987; 65(5): 663–737.

26   Salanave B, Bouvier-Colle MH, Varnoux N, Alexander S, Macfarlane AJ, The MOMS Group. Classification differences and maternal mortality: a European study. *International Journal of Epidemiology* 1999; 28: 64–69.

27   Bouvier-Colle MH, Varnoux N, Costes P, Hatton F. Reasons for the underreporting of maternal mortality in France, as indicated by a survey of all deaths among women of childbearing age. *International Journal of Epidemiology* 1991; 20(3): 717–721.

28   Puffer RR, Serrano CV. *Patterns of mortality in childhood: report of the inter-American investigation of mortality in childhood*. Washington, DC: Pan American Health Organization, 1973.

29   United Nations Children's Fund (UNICEF). *The state of the world's children, 1999*. Oxford: Oxford University Press, 1999.

30   Masuy-Stroobant G, Gourbin C. Infant health and mortality indicators. *European Journal of Population* 1995; 11: 63–84.

31   Masuy-Stroobant G. La mortalité infantile en Europe et au Canada: un problème résolu? *Cahiers Québecois De La Démographie* 1996; 23(2): 297–337.

32   Masuy-Stroobant G. Santé et mortalité infantile en Europe: victoires d'hier et enjeux de demain. In: Masuy-Stroobant G, Gourbin C, Buekens P, eds. *Santé et mortalité des enfants en Europe: inégalités sociales d'hier et d'aujourd'hui. Actes de la Chaire Quetelet*, Louvain-la-Neuve, 12–14 Sept 1994. Louvain-la-Neuve: Academia-Bruylant, 1996.

33   European Commission. *Demographic statistics, 1997*. Luxembourg: Office for Official Publications of the European Communities, 1997.

34   Newland K. *Infant mortality and the health of societies*. Washington DC: Worldwatch Institute, 1981.

35   Davis C, Feshbach M. *Rising infant mortality in the USSR in the 1970s*. International Population Reports No. 14. Washington DC: Bureau of the Census, 1980.

36   Brenner MH. Fetal, infant, and maternal mortality during periods of economic instability. *International Journal of Health Services* 1973; 3(2): 145–159.

37   Stocks P. Fifty years of progress as shown by vital statistics. *British Medical Journal* 1950; 1: 54–57.

38   Ministry of Health. *Report on an investigation into maternal mortality.* Cmd 5422. London: HMSO, 1937.

39   Graham W. The scandal of the century. *British Journal of Obstetrics and Gynaecology* 1998; 105(4): 375–376.

13 Conclusions

Looking back

'Now the man in the street knows nothing of "Biometrika": all he knows is that "you can prove anything by figures" though he forgets this the moment figures are used to prove anything he wants to believe.'

'Even trained statisticians often fail to appreciate the extent to which statistics are vitiated by the unrecorded assumptions of their interpreters.'

Bernard Shaw, Preface to *The doctor's dilemma*, 1906.[1]

There are two very common and diametrically opposed views about statistics. One view is that statistics, being just numbers, are neutral, objective 'facts', while the other has it that they are 'damned lies' plucked conveniently out of the blue to support whatever views are being put forward at the time. The statement 'lies, damned lies, and statistics' has been attributed to at least five different nineteenth century politicians, but the riposte 'It isn't that statistics lie, but that liars use statistics' is less well known. In general, we would suggest that viewing statistics as either 'damned lies' on the one hand or 'objective facts' on the other is unhelpful to people who need to interpret and use them.[2]

In this book we have described a vast range of data which are collected by central government and the National Health Service. Relatively few of them are obtained from special enquiries or surveys. The majority are collected as by-products of administrative or legal processes. The nature of these processes, which range from the registration of births, marriages and deaths to the administration of health services inevitably affects the nature of the data which emerge. In addition, it is not uncommon for the people who compile the data to work in a setting which is divorced from the context in which they are used.[3] It would not be surprising, in these circumstances, if people put incorrect information on forms or computers simply because accurate data are not easily accessible. While we are sure some readers may know of instances where people have deliberately falsified data to protect themselves from criticism, we do not think this is the most common source of inaccuracy.

Although the consciousness of the need for data to monitor both people's health and the quality of the care they receive has increased, particularly in the perinatal field, the administrative emphasis in routine data collection still prevails. The Government Statistical Service (GSS), which coordinates national government data collection describes its priorities in these terms:

'To provide Parliament, government and the wider community with the statistical information, analysis and advice needed to improve decision making, stimulate research and inform debate.'[4]

This dual purpose of the systems used to collect government statistics was pointed out nearly 150 years ago by William Farr in his *Letter to the Registrar General* in the first *Annual report*, that for 1837–38:

'The registration of births and deaths proves the connexion of families, facilitates the legal distribution of property, and answers several other public purposes which sufficiently establish its utility; but in the performance of the duty with which you have been pleased to entrust me, I have to examine the registration under a different point of view, and with different objects, which will ultimately prove of not less importance.'[5]

The implication of this is that the data are shaped not only by the views and attitudes of the organisations and individuals who decide which data should be collected and how they should be analysed and presented, but also by the wider assumptions prevailing in society. They are also affected by the other demands made by government and the NHS on the systems through which they are collected. One consequence is that if existing systems do not meet their demands, then new systems are set up, leading to duplication of effort and the complex data flows described in Chapter 2.

The systems which William Farr and his counterparts in Scotland and Ireland established for analysing data from the registration enabled them to produce not only national statistics, but also to do tabulations for local areas and feed them back to medical officers of health. It also provided them with information about individuals, in the form of copies of birth registrations. At the beginning of the twentieth century, medical officers of health, who were setting up schemes for health visitors to visit households with newborn babies shortly after birth, wanted rapid notification at a time when most births took place at home.[6] Parents had and still do have six weeks to register a birth, so the birth notification system was set up to notify medical officers of health within 36 hours of the birth of a new baby.[7]

This system was designed to support the programme of health visiting and, later on the programme of immunisations. It was not designed to produce statistics locally, let alone nationally. Nevertheless, data derived from it appeared in some local public health reports and from the 1950s to the 1980s aggregated data derived locally from birth notification were used to monitor low birthweight on a national level in England and Wales. Since the mid 1970s, birthweight data derived from individual notifications have been passed to local registrars to be added to information collected at birth registration. Other relevant data items, such as gestational age or method of delivery could have been transferred at the same time, but for some now forgotten reason, they were not. Adding them to the system later would have had financial implications, so no change was made.

From the late 1960s onwards, local authorities started to computerise systems for calling parents to bring their babies for immunisation and developmental tests. The responsibility for this passed to health authorities in 1974. In the late 1970s, work began to develop a single national system which could be used in every health authority. The main purpose of the systems was administrative and attempts to use them to monitor child health lagged behind. Not all districts chose to use it and the introduction of the internal market in the early 1990s added to the diversification. The purchaser provider split meant that the systems passed to community trusts, who were responsible for child health surveillance, thus separating them from health authorities who retained responsibility for monitoring child health. As a result, at the end of the 1990s, it was just possible, but still very difficult to extract population-based data for local areas from these systems and impossible to use them as a basis for producing national statistics.

Meanwhile, in the wake of the move to hospital birth, a third stream of data collection was developing and itself becoming increasingly fragmented. In each of the countries, systems such as SMR1 and SMR2 in Scotland and Hospital Activity Analysis and HIPE in England were set up under the National Health Service to collect data about hospital in-patients. They were geared mainly to producing regional and national statistics about the activities of hospitals. Although data were fed back locally, they were not necessarily in the form needed to inform clinical practice within maternity units and provide the data required by professional and regulatory bodies.

The increasing availability and power of personal computers from the early 1980s onwards led many maternity units to set up local systems for collecting clinical data. In some cases, good quality data from these were aggregated at regional level.[8,9] On the other hand, there was duplication of effort as few attempts were made to see that similar data were collected and classified in the same way in different regions or different localities within some regions. As there was usually no linkage between these systems and other computer systems in the same hospital, the information tended not to find its way into datasets contributed by the hospitals to national statistical systems.[10,11]

A further important development in data collection was in general practice systems. Apart from in Scotland, where a system was provided free of charge to encourage all practices to adopt the same system, many different systems came on to the market. Because of their manufacturers' links with pharmaceutical companies, the emphasis in data collection was on prescribing. Nevertheless, they contain a considerable amount of data about minor illnesses in the first year of life, though rather less about pregnancy and childbirth, as a consequence of the diminishing role of general practitioners in this area.

Thus the increasing use of computers did not lead to improvements in national statistics, but it came at a time when national statistics were low on the political agenda. Following the review by Sir Derek Rayner, a white paper published in 1981 set out major cuts in spending on the Government Statistical Service.[12] He established the principle that the government should collect centrally only what it needed for its own purposes, and took a very narrow view of what this should be and the extent to which data should be published. In assessing which data health authorities were to supply to central government, he did not consider whether they collected them for their own purposes anyway. Rayner also failed to take into account the question of whether health authorities had a need for central government to take a role in co-ordinating the way data are collected locally. After the inadequacies of economic statistics led the government to take unwise financial decisions, the 'Rayner principle' was abandoned at the end of the decade. It was replaced by a philosophy that data should be made available more widely, but that costs should be recouped through charges to users.

In the National Health Service, the low priority given to investment in national statistics persisted in the 1990s because of other influences. This came initially from the Steering Group on Health Services Information which reviewed data collection in England in the early 1980s and strongly influenced data collection in Wales and Northern Ireland. The Steering Group saw its main task as specifying data for health service administrators at district level. Based on what it perceived to be administrators' needs, the Steering Group defined a system of central returns and 'minimum datasets' which are still labelled as 'Körner'. It did not see a role for national collation and analysis of clinical data, though it singled out maternity data as an exception to this. Health authorities were asked to implement the new system within their existing budgets. As Maternity HES was last on the list for implementation, there were even fewer resources available for it than for other elements of the Steering Group's proposals.

The emphasis on administrative data was compounded by the introduction of general management into the NHS in the early 1980s and the setting up of the internal market in the early 1990s. Despite the fact that the internal market was financially driven, it did not improve the quality of data on the costs of maternity care or the ability to link data on resources to those about care given and its outcome. In England, data collection was further disrupted by the abolition of regional health authorities, which had always had a key role in data collection, analysis and dissemination. Implicit in the philosophy of the internal market was the idea of a multiplicity of local health services rather than of each being part of a national service, so national statistics were not seen as important or even relevant.

The most recently established data system, the Confidential Enquiry into Stillbirths and Deaths in Infancy was set up in the early 1990s. It decided to set up its own system for 'rapid reporting' of fetal and infant deaths in England, Wales and Northern Ireland. Apart from late fetal losses at 20 to 23 weeks of gestation, the events are also included in the civil registration system, but the Enquiry wanted to collect additional data items. Unfortunately some of the data items collected by CESDI are difficult to interpret, as they are not available for all births in the countries concerned, despite the plethora of data collection just described.

Given their multiple purposes, therefore, it is not surprising that the data in this book do not appear to reflect any conscious attempt to provide a comprehensive set of data for assessing the health of childbearing women and their babies, their social and economic circumstances and for monitoring the performance of the services provided for them. This means that some data which people might expect to find are not collected, and some which are collected do not mean what people expect them to mean.

Moving forward

This second edition of *Birth counts* appears at a time when, potentially, there are opportunities for progress. A much more positive view of national statistics was intially expressed in proposals for an independent national statistical service.[13] Within the NHS, information strategies have set out an ambitious agenda for the National Health Service, although the extent to which adequate resources are available to implement them is perhaps less clear.[14-16] The development of clinical governance means that better data are needed to monitor services.[17] A review of the civil registration service, with some prospect of legislation, offers the hope of making improvements. The need for some of these has been apparent for over twenty years.[18]

The infrastructure, in terms of the vast increase in computing power, provides tools which have the potential for enhancing our analytical capabilities, both through anonymised record linkage and in other ways. The development of the internet allows ever greater communication within the NHS and in the world at large.

Despite these many developments in health care and changes in society, our needs for data today have much in common with those expressed by William Farr in 1839. In suggesting that the analysis of death certificates should be applied to 'the promotion of practical medicine' he commented that:

> 'The extent to which epidemics vary in different localities, seasons and classes of society, will be indicated by the registered diseases; and the experienced practitioner, wherever he may be placed, will learn to administer remedies with discrimination and with due reference to the circumstances of the population.'[5]

To what extent do official statistics as they are collected today enable us to assess the extent to which the outcome of pregnancy reflects inequalities in the 'circumstances of the population' into which babies are born and differences in the ability of the health services to 'administer remedies with discrimination'?

The oldest system in operation and the system which gives the most complete coverage is the civil registration system. Although, as we have suggested in Chapter 3, there may be some local variation in deciding which births are registrable, in general very few events escape it, because it is statutory. Despite the limitations outlined in Chapter 5, the information it contains about parents' social backgrounds reveals marked inequalities in the outcome of pregnancy in different socio-economic and geographical settings.

One way of increasing the potential of registration and other data is through record linkage. Scotland is clearly well ahead of the other countries of the United Kingdom in this. In England and Wales, the ONS, formerly OPCS, Longitudinal Study has proved an invaluable source of data in studying the health of adults, but has yet to be fully exploited in studies of reproductive health. There is also scope for more routine linkage of anonymised records. If the NHS number becomes accurately recorded on all NHS records, it can be used to link registration and NHS data to bring together data about the parents' background and clinical data about pregnancy, delivery and neonatal care.

Although death rates are now a fraction of their former level, data are still needed about why babies die. As Percy Stocks, Chief Medical Statistician of the General Register Office, wrote in 1950:

> 'There is sometimes a tendency to decry the death certificate as an imperfect source of knowledge, and to suggest that in some Utopian future morbidity records will be available of such precision that it will be possible to consign death certificates to the rubbish heap of out-worn instruments. For such an idea there is at present no vestige of probability.'[19]

This is still true at the beginning of the twenty first century, but a variable which has always been difficult to collect accurately and classify appropriately is the cause of death. Reports over the past 160 years have repeatedly revealed inaccuracies, queried the classifications used, and contained exhortations to do better. Some progress has been made in producing material for training the doctors of the future. For the present, it is important that further information, for example the results of post-mortems, are sent in to ONS or the General Register Offices for Scotland or Northern Ireland, so that the conditions initially mentioned on the death or stillbirth certificate can be amended.

The most serious gaps in the available data, except in Scotland, are those about care in pregnancy, labour, delivery and the first year of life. There are also very few data about resources for maternity care. As we have seen, the data are recorded in many systems, but cannot be extracted consistently at national level from any of them. This is a major challenge in the implementation of the NHS information strategies.[14–16]

An increasing gap in our knowledge is in data about the private sector. The only data collection systems with clinical information which cover private practice are the notifications of birth and therapeutic abortion. While relatively few births take place in the private sector, and it is still not very active in the expensive field of neonatal intensive care, it is much more active in other areas, such as abortion, sterilisation and the management of sub-fertility. In the absence of data from the private sector, routine statistics under-estimate the overall numbers of operations and treatments. The process of regulation should be used to obtain fuller data about the activities of the private sector.

While improving the quality of data collected about the services provided and the people who use them would be of undoubted benefit, the problem of assessing the health of the population and the extent of illness and disability still remains. This is particularly important in the context of planning and commissioning services. This book goes to press at a time of change, when it is far from clear what information primary care groups will need or how they will organise information systems.

In the context of this book, our main interest in the prevalence of disability is as a measure of the outcome of pregnancy in women living in a particular geographical area. This contrasts with the problem of measuring the prevalence of disability amongst the residents of an area for which an authority has to provide services. Work is under way in developing ways of extracting data from child heath and general practice systems, but there is a long way to go. Furthermore, experience so far suggests that they are not a good source of data about rare events, notably severe morbidity in mothers and babies. As things stand at present, the best approach would seem to be through dedicated registers and notification systems for specific conditions.

The role of statistics

In encouraging people to make greater use of statistics, we have to admit that it has usually been human experience rather than careful analysis of data which has focused public attention onto the subject of having and bringing up children. Numerous examples can be cited. The unfitness of recruits for the Boer war drew attention to the conditions in which the unfit men were born and brought up. The knowledge that once again many recruits were unfit for the first world war made those in authority more amenable to responding to the campaign waged by women's organisations for a maternity service. The conditions of children evacuated from inner city slums during the second world war brought it home to the people who received these evacuees that poverty and ill health among children had not disappeared.

Many more examples could be given. A strange paradox is that two periods of the twentieth century during which there was particularly great public concern about infant mortality, the first ten years or so of the century and the late 1970s and early 1980s, were periods when mortality was declining rapidly, and yet there seemed to be little public awareness of the decline. In each of these two periods, however, concern gave rise to a spate of data collection and analysis.[20] Analyses of data about infant mortality developed considerably at the beginning of the twentieth century. The attention focused on perinatal mortality in the 1970s and 1980s led to an upsurge of interest in data collection and eventually substantial funding was given to launch the Confidential Enquiry into Stillbirths and Deaths in Infancy.

Meanwhile, other types of data have been collected. The changing agenda means that more weight is given to women's views of their experiences of childbirth and their views about the care they received. Standardised methods have been developed for ascertaining these. On the other hand data are not always made available to service users and this is an area where increased computerisation and use of the internet may exclude people who do not have access to it.

Other equally important questions, notably the effectiveness of innovations in patterns of care, are increasingly investigated using experimental techniques, notably randomised controlled trials. The use of routine statistics to monitor the extent to which the results have been adopted is much less developed. As we have shown, few data are collected about antenatal care in general or antenatal screening in particular. Few data are collected routinely about postnatal care of either healthy or sick babies or about women's health after childbirth. Where data are collected, these tend not to be linked to delivery records. Ensuring that this happens should be a priority for the future. Routinely collected statistics can then be used to establish questions and priorities and then provide a useful backdrop against which such research can be assessed.

A different approach to these problems is to do cohort studies following people not only from birth through into childhood, but also into teenage years and into adult life. The data amassed by following a week's births in 1946, 1958 and 1970 have been used in an extensive range of valuable research. Nevertheless, such studies are expensive and cannot therefore be initiated very often. They therefore complement rather than replace annual statistics collected routinely.

This use of routine data, to prompt further investigation was suggested by Arthur Newsholme in a paper given to the Royal Statistical Society in 1896. Although he was talking specifically about the notification of communicable disease, what he had to say applies to all the data in this book:

> 'Notification is but a means to an end. If the early and authentic information imparted to health officers is simply filed in the office, the course of an epidemic will obviously be undisturbed; but when the notifications are followed by conscientious investigation ... it is evident that the resulting chain of evidence may be, as in many instances it has been, so strong as to lead to immediate preventive measures of a most successful character and in other instances to force the most radical reforms upon even unwilling sanitary authorities.'[21]

In this book we have tried to show that while official statistics have limitations, they also have many strengths. Because of these, they could play a much larger part than they do in monitoring the circumstances faced by childbearing women and the services which exist to help them. We hope that this book will help people to use the data which exist and to take appropriate action to improve them for the benefit of the parents and babies of the future.

References

1   Shaw B. Preface to The doctors' dilemma. In: Shaw B, *Prefaces by Bernard Shaw*. London: Constable and Company, 1934.

2   Dorling D, Simpson S, eds. *Statistics in society: the arithmetic of politics*. London: Edwin Arnold, 1998.

3 Government Statisticians' Collective. How official statistics are produced: views from the inside. In: Irvine J, Miles I, Evans J, eds. *Demystifying social statistics*. London: Pluto Press, 1979.

4 Government Statistical Service. *Annual report, 1997–98*. London: Office for National Statistics, 1998.

5 Farr W. Letter to the Registrar General. In: *First annual report of the Registrar General for the year 1837–1838*. London: Longman, Orme, Brown, Green and Longman, 1839.

6 Pilkington HO. The reduction of infant mortality without municipal milk depots. *Public Health* 1907; 415–416.

7 Dwork D. *War is good for babies and other young children: a history of the infant and child welfare movement in England, 1898–1918*. London and New York: Tavistock, 1987.

8 Paterson CM, Chapple JC, Beard RW, Joffe M, Steer PJ, Wright CS. Evaluating the quality of the maternity services: a discussion paper. *British Journal of Obstetrics and Gynaecology* 1991; 98(11): 1073–1078.

9 Cleary R, Beard RW, Coles J, Devlin HB, Hopkins A, Roberts S, Schumacher D, Wickings HI. The quality of routinely collected maternity data. *British Journal of Obstetrics and Gynaecology* 1994; 101(12): 1042–1047.

10 Kenney N, Macfarlane AJ. Are maternity data linked at a local level? Some findings from the 'Changing Childbirth' Information Project. Paper given at the conference on: *Linking data for better health in pregnancy and childhood*, London, January 12–13 1998.

11 Kenney N, Macfarlane AJ. Maternity data in England: problems with data collection at a local level. *BMJ* 1999; 319: 619–22.

12 Central Statistical Office. *Government statistical services*. Cmnd 8236. London: HMSO, 1981.

13 Office for National Statistics. *Statistics: a matter of trust. A consultation document*. Cm 3882. London: The Stationery Office, 1998.

14 Department of Health, NHS Executive. *Information for health*. Leeds: NHS Executive, 1998.

15 National Information Management and Technology Board. *Strategic programme for modernising information management and technology in the NHS in Scotland*. Edinburgh: Scottish Office, 1998.

16 Welsh Office. *Better information, better health: information management and technology for health care and health improvement in Wales. A strategic framework 1998 to 2005*. Cardiff: Welsh Office, 1998.

17 Department of Health, NHS Executive. *Clinical governance. Quality in the new NHS*. London: Department of Health, 1999.

18 Office for National Statistics, *Registration: modernising a vital service*. London: Office for National Statistics, 1999.

19   Stocks P. Fifty years of progress as shown by vital statistics. *British Medical Journal* 1950; 1: 54–57.

20   General Register Office. *Sixty-seventh annual report of the Registrar General of births, deaths and marriages in England and Wales*. London: HMSO, 1906.

21   Newsholme A. A national system of notification and registration of sickness. *Journal of the Royal Statistical Society* 1896; 59: 1–37.

Appendix 1:
Where to seek further information

Contacts for statistics

The Office for National Statistics (ONS) is the government agency responsible for compiling many of the United Kingdom's economic, social and demographic statistics, but not statistics about health and personal social services. It is responsible for the population census and registration statistics for England and Wales, but not for Scotland and Northern Ireland. ONS also has a co-ordinating role for the Government Statistical Service as a whole. Contacts for population and health statistics in ONS are listed first, followed by other contacts for population, health and health service statistics in each of the countries of the United Kingdom. This is followed by contacts for statistics in other areas which are mentioned in this book in relation to pregnancy and childbirth.

This list was finished in May 1999, and revised in July 1999 and January 2000 when organisations were still changing their names following devolution. Further changes are therefore likely. We will aim to keep an updated version of this appendix on the National Perinatal Epidemiology Unit web site http://www.npeu.ox.ac.uk.

Office for National Statistics
1 Drummond Gate, London SW1V 2QQ

ONS Public Enquiry Service:
General enquiries	020 7533 6262
Copyright enquiries	020 7533 5674
Business statistics	01633 812973
Economic statistics	020 7533 6363/6464
Social statistics	020 7533 6262

Fax: 020 7533 5719
Web site: http://www.statistics.gov.uk/

General information about statistics:
Office for National Statistics. *Guide to official statistics, 2000 edition.*
London: TSO, 2000.
StatBase: UK national statistics online
Web site: http://www.statistics.gov.uk/

Major annual publications:
Annual abstract of statistics
Social trends
Regional trends

Population based statistics for England and Wales

Office for National Statistics

1 Drummond Gate, Pimlico, London SW1V 2QQ

Web site: http://www.statistics.gov.uk

General enquiries

Births and fertility	01329 813758
Cancer	01329 813759
Marriage, divorce and adoption	01329 813620/758
Migration	01329 813889/897
Mortality	01329 813379
Population estimates	01329 813318

Topic enquiries

Abortions	020 7533 5112
Conceptions and fertility	020 7533 5137
Congenital anomalies	020 7533 5641
Infant and perinatal mortality	020 7533 5205
Subnational population projections	01329 813474/865

ONS publication series:

Series	Subject
AB	Abortion statistics
CEN	Census publication
DH1	Mortality statistics, general
DH2	Mortality statistics, cause
DH3	Mortality statistics, childhood, infant and perinatal
DH4	Mortality statistics, injury and poisoning
DH5	Mortality statistics, area, 1974–92 only
DH6	Mortality statistics, childhood, 1986–92 only
EL	Electoral statistics
FM1	Birth statistics

FM2	Marriage and divorce statistics. Adoptions from 1995 FM3 Adoption statistics
LS	Longitudinal study
MB1	Cancer statistics
MB2	Communicable diseases, 1974–95. Now published by Communicable Disease Surveillance Centre, Colindale
MB3	Congenital anomalies
MB4	Hospital In-patient Enquiry. Ended 1985
MB5	Morbidity statistics from general practice
MB6	Key health statistics from general practice
MN	Migration
PP1	Population estimates
PP2	National population projections
PP3	Sub-national population projections
SS	Social survey
VS	Local authority vital statistics

Family research:

Individual copies of birth, marriage and death certificates:

Family Records Centre, run jointly by ONS and the **Public Record Office**

1 Myddelton Street, London EC1R 1UW

Tel: 020 8392 5300

Government Actuary's Department

22 Kingsway, London WC2B 6LE

Tel: 020 7211 2601

Expectation of life and national population projections:

Tel: 020 7211 2622

Public Health Laboratory Service (PHLS) Communicable Disease Surveillance Centre

61 Colindale Avenue, London NW9 5EQ

Tel: 020 8200 6868

Fax: 020 8200 7868

Web site: http://www.phls.co.uk

Health and personal social services statistics for England

Department of Health

Statistical bulletins and most other publications are available from:

Department of Health, PO Box 777, London SE1 6XH

Tel: 0541 555 455

Fax: 01623 724524

Email: doh@prologistics.co.uk

Web site: http://www.doh.gov.uk/

Skipton House, 80 London Road, London SE1 6LW

Branch SD1, Family health services statistics

General Dental and Community Dental Services	020 7972 5392
General Pharmacy Services	020 7972 5504
General Ophthalmic Services	020 7972 5507
Prescription analysis	020 7972 5515

Branch SD2, Hospital and community health services statistics

Maternity statistics	020 7972 5533
Mental illness/handicap	020 7972 5546
Community and cross-sector services	020 7972 5524
Demographic statistics for England	020 7972 5562
Drug misuse	020 7972 5550
Legal status	020 7972 5546
Smoking and alcohol	020 7972 5551
Hospital in-patient activity	020 7972 5529

Branch SD3, Personal social services statistics and surveys

Children's services	020 7972 5581
Adults' services	020 7972 5585
Staffing	020 7972 5595
Financial data	020 7972 5595
Key indicators	020 7972 5599
Health Survey for England and other surveys	020 7972 5560/92

Quarry House, Quarry Hill, Leeds LS2 7UE

Workforce, finance and performance analysis statistics:

NHS medical staff statistics	0113 254 5892
NHS non-medical staff statistics	0113 254 5744
General medical services	0113 254 5911
Performance indicators	0113 254 6425
Waiting lists	0113 254 5555
Hospital activity	0113 254 5522
NHS expenditure	0113 254 5356
Finance statistics	0113 254 5389

Wellington House, 133–155 Waterloo Road, London SE1 8UG
Central Health Monitoring Unit

Our healthier nation	020 7972 4648

Major annual publications:

Health and personal social services statistics for England

On the state of the public health, the annual report of the Chief Medical Officer

Health service circular: *Central data collections from the NHS*, giving details of data requested from the NHS each year. Available on the internet at http://www.doh.gov.uk/

House of Commons Health Committee

Committee Office, House of Commons, London SW1A 0AA

Tel: 020 7219 5466

Web site: http://www.parliament.uk/

Annual publication:

Public expenditure on health and personal social services. Memorandum received from the Department of Health containing replies to a written questionnaire from the Committee.

Health and personal social services statistics for Wales

National Assembly for Wales, formerly the **Welsh Office**
Crown Buildings, Cathays Park, Cardiff CF10 3NQ

Health statistics:
Vivien Trew, Health Statistics Analysis Unit
Tel: 029 2082 5080
Fax: 029 2082 5350
Email: vivien.trew@wales.gov.uk

General contact for publications:
Publications Unit, Statistical Directorate 5, National Assembly for Wales,
Cathays Park, Cardiff CF10 3NQ
Tel: 029 2082 5044/5054
Fax: 029 2082 5350
Email: statswales@gtnet.gov.uk

Annual publications:
Digest of Welsh statistics
Digest of Welsh local authority statistics
Health statistics Wales
Social services statistics Wales

Scotland:

The Scottish Executive Central Statistics Unit
1B–West, 10 Victoria Quay, Edinburgh EH6 6QQ
Tel: 0131 244 0443
Web site: http://www.scotland.gov.uk
Email: statisticsenquiries@scotland.gov.uk

Annual publication:
The Scottish abstract of statistics on the internet at
http://www.scotland.gov.uk/library/sas/sa00–00.htm

General Register Office for Scotland

Ladywell House, Ladywell Road, Edinburgh EH12 7TF

Customer services:

Tel: 0131 314 4254

Fax: 0131 314 4344

Web site: http://www.gro-scotland.gov.uk/

Population statistics:

Email: customer@gro-scotland.gov.uk

Family research:

Individual copies of birth, marriage and death certificates:

New Register House, West Register Street, Edinburgh EH12 7TF

Email: nrh.gros@gtnet.gov.uk

Information and Statistics Division of the Commons Services Agency of the National Health Service in Scotland

Trinity Park House, South Trinity Road, Edinburgh EH5 3SQ

Tel: 0131 551 8899

Fax: 0131 551 1392

Email: cds@isd.csa.scot.nhs.uk

Web site: http://www.show.scot.nhs.uk/isd/index.htm

General information:

ISD Scotland guide: an A–Z of the work of the Information and Statistics Division

Major annual publication:

Scottish health statistics

Scottish Executive Health Department, formerly **Scottish Office Department of Health**

St Andrew's House, Regent Road, Edinburgh EH1 3DG

Web site: http://www.scotland.gov.uk

Economics and information division, health statistics:

Tel: 0131 244 2368

Maternal and child health:

Tel: 0131 244 2289

Community care statistics:

Room 52, James Craig Walk, Edinburgh EH1 3BA

Tel: 0131 244 3777

Annual publications:
Health in Scotland, annual report of the Chief Medical Officer
National Health Service in Scotland annual report

Scottish Centre for Infection and Environmental Health (SCIEH)
Clifton House, Clifton Drive, Glasgow G3 7LN
Tel: 0141 300 1142
Fax: 0141 300 1170
Web site: http://www.show.scot.nhs.uk/ghi/scieh.htm

Scottish Executive Children's Social Work Statistics
1B Victoria Quay, Edinburgh EH6 6QQ
Tel: 0131 244 3745/3607
Web site: http://www.scotland.gov.uk/

Northern Ireland:

Northern Ireland Statistics and Research Agency
Demography and methodology branch
McAuley House, 2–14 Castle Street, Belfast BT1 1SA
Tel: 028 9034 8132
Fax: 028 9034 8134
Web site: http://www.nisra.gov.uk/gro/

General Register Office for Northern Ireland
Oxford House, 49–55 Chichester Street, Belfast BT1 4HL
Tel: 028 9025 2031/2
Fax: 028 9025 2044
Web site: http://www.nisra.gov.uk/gro/

Annual publication:
Annual Report of the Registrar General for Northern Ireland

Northern Ireland Executive Department of Health, Social Services and Public Safety formerly Department of Health and Social Services, Northern Ireland
Regional Information Branch, Annexe 2, Castle Buildings, Stormont, Belfast BT4 3UD
Health and social services statistics
Tel: 028 9052 2800
Email: rib@dhssni.gov.uk
Web site: http://www.dhssni.gov.uk/hpss/statistics/

Major annual publications:
Hospital statistics
Community statistics

Channel Islands

Guernsey
Guernsey Board of Health, John Henry House, Le Vauquiedor, St Martin's, Guernsey GY4 6UU
Tel: 01481 725241
Fax: 01481 35905

Jersey
Department of Public Health and Social Services, Le Bas Centre, St Saviours Road, St Helier, Jersey JE1 4HR
Tel: 01534 789933
Fax: 01534 623720
Email: hsf03@itl.net

Isle of Man

Civil Registry, Registries Building, Deemsters Walk, Bucks Road, Douglas, Isle of Man, IM1 3AR.
Tel: 01624 687038
Fax: 01624 685976

Irish Republic

Central Statistics Office
Skehard Road, Cork, Ireland
Tel: 00 353 21 359000
Fax: 00 353 21 359090
Email: information@cso.ie
Web site: http://www.cso.ie

Major annual publication:
Vital statistics

Department of Health and Children

Hawkins House, Hawkins Street, Dublin 2

Tel: 00 353 1 671 4711

Fax: 00 353 1 671 1947

Web site: http://www.doh.ie

Other Government Statistical Service contacts in the United Kingdom

Department of Social Security

Analytical Services Division, Benton Park Road, Longbenton, Newcastle-upon-Tyne NE98 1YX

General enquiries:

Tel: 0191 225 7373

Web site: http://www.dss.gov.uk/hq/index.htm

Major annual publication:

Social security statistics

Home Office

50 Queen Anne's Gate, London SW1H 9AT

General enquiries about statistics:

Tel: 020 7273 2084

Web site: http://www.homeoffice.gov.uk/rds/index.htm

Health and Safety Executive

Magdalen House, Trinity Road, Bootle, Merseyside L20 3QZ

Health and Safety Statistics   0151 951 4537/4538

Accident and Injury Statistics   0151 951 4865/4842

Web site: http://www.open.gov.uk/hse/hsestats.htm

Information about public expenditure

The Treasury publications in print are all placed on the internet.

Web site: http//www.hm-treasury.gov.uk/pub/html/pip/main.html

Data archives

The Data Archive
University of Essex, Colchester CO4 3SQ
Tel: 01206 872 001
Fax: 01206 872 003
Email: archive@essex.ac.uk
Web site: http://dawww.essex.ac.uk/

Council of European Social Science Data Archives (CESSDA)
Integrated Data Catalogue
Web site: http://www.nsd.uib.no/cessda/idc/

The Database of Irish Historical Statistics
The Centre for Data Digitisation and Analysis, The Queen's University, Belfast BT7 1NN
Tel: 028 9027 3883/3408
Fax: 028 9032 0668
Web site: http://www.qub.ac.uk/cdda/

International organisations

CARE's maternal and child health home page
Web site: http://www.care.org/programs/health/maternal_child.html

Family Care International
Family Care International, 588 Broadway, Suite 503, New York, NY 10012
Tel: 00 1 212 941 5300
Fax: 00 1 212 941 5563
Email: fci@idt.net
Web site: http://www.familycareintl.org/

International Clearinghouse for Birth Defects Monitoring Systems
International Centre for Birth Defects, Via Sabotino 2, 00195 Roma, Italy
Fax: 00 39 6 370 1904
Email: mc2459@mclink.it
Web site: http://www.icbd.org

Marie Stopes International

153–157 Cleveland Street, London W1P 5PG
Tel: 020 7574 7371
Web site: http://www.mariestopes.org.uk/

Population Council

Population Council, Office of Publications, One Dag Hammarskjold Plaza, New York, NY 10017–2201, USA
Tel: 00 1 212 339 0500
Fax: 00 1 212 755 6052
Email: pubinfo@popcouncil.org
Web site: http://www.popcouncil.org/

Safe Motherhood

Division of Family Health, World Health Organisation, 1211 Geneva, Switzerland
Email: info@safemotherhood.org
Web site: http://www.safemotherhood.org/

UNICEF

UNICEF House, 3 United Nations Plaza, New York, NY 10017, USA
Web site: http://www.unicef.org/

United Nations Population Fund (UNFPA)

United Nations Population Fund, 220 East 42nd Street, New York, NY 10017, USA
Web site: http://www.unfpa.org/

World Bank Group

Headquarters, The World Bank, 1818 H Street, N.W., Washington, DC 20433, USA
Tel: 00 1 202 477 1234
Web site: http://www.worldbank.org/

World Health Organisation

Avenue Appia 20, 1211 Geneva 27, Switzerland
Tel: 00 41 22 791 21 11
Fax: 00 41 22 791 07 46
Email: info@who.ch
Web site: http://www.who.int/
WHO reproductive health home page: http://www.who.org/rht

Annual publications:
World health statitics
WHO statistical abstract

Organisation for Economic Co-operation and Development (OECD)

OECD Publications, 2 rue André-Pascal, 75775 Paris CEDEX 16, France

Tel: 00 33 1 45 24 82 67

Fax: 00 33 1 45 24 13 91

Web site: http://www.oecd.org/

United States organisations publishing international data

US Census Bureau

International Programs Center, Bureau of the Census, Washington DC 20233–8860, USA

Web site: http://www.census.gov

National Center for Health Statistics

US Department of Health and Human Services Public Health Service, Centers for disease control and prevention (CDC)/ National Center for Health Statistics, 6525 Belcrest Road, Hyattsville, Maryland 20782, USA.

Tel: 00 1 301 436 7039

Fax: 00 1 301 436 3568

Publication:
International Health Data, Reference Guide

Sources of European data

Eurostat, Statistical Office of the European Communities

Batiment Jean Monnet, Rue Alcide de Gasperi, Luxembourg-Kirchberg, L-2920 Luxembourg

Tel: 00 352 4301 1 (Switchboard) or 00 352 4301 34567

Web site: http://europa.eu.int/en/comm/eurostat/

Annual publication:
Demographic statistics

Resource Centre for Access to Data on Europe (r-cade)

Unit 1L, Mountjoy Research Centre, University of Durham, Durham DH1 3SW

Tel: 0191 374 7350

Fax: 0191 384 4971

Email: r-cade@durham.ac.uk

Web site: http://www-rcade.dur.ac.uk

r-cade disseminates data on behalf of Eurostat, UNESCO, ILO and UNIDO

Eurostat Data Shops network

Eurostat, the statistical office of the European Communities

UNITED KINGDOM, Eurostat Data Shop, Enquiries & advice and publications:

Office for National Statistics, Customers & Electronic Services Unit, 1 Drummond Gate, London SW1V 2QQ

Tel: 020 7533 5676

Fax: 020 7533 5688

Email: gloria.ryan@ons.gov.uk

Web site: http://europa.eu.int/en/comm/eurostat/serven/part8/8c.htm

Concerted Action Project in Registration of Congenital Abnormalities and Twins (EUROCAT)

Eurocat Central Registry, Institute of Hygiene and Epidemiology, 14 rue Juliette Wytsman, B-1050 Bruxelles, Belgium

Tel: 00 32 2 642 5712

Fax: 00 32 2 642 5410

Networked social science tools and resources (NESSTAR)

The Data Archive, University of Essex, Colchester CO4 3SQ

Tel: 01206 872001

Fax: 01206 872003

Email: archive@essex.ac.uk

Web site: http://dawww.essex.ac.uk/projects/nesstar.html

Other organisations concerned with information about health or maternity care

The Cochrane Collaboration
Cochrane Collaboration Secretariat, PO Box 726, Oxford OX2 7UX
Tel: 01865 310138
Fax: 01865 516311
Email: secretariat@cochrane.co.uk
Web sites: http://www.update-software.com/ccweb/cochrane/leaflet.htm
http://www.cochrane.co.uk (The Cochrane Library)
http://www.cochrane.org/
http://www.cochrane.de/

Confidential Enquiries into Maternal Deaths
Room 520, Department of Health, Wellington House, 133–155 Waterloo Road, London SE1 8UG
Tel: 020 7972 4345

Confidential Enquiry into Stillbirths and Deaths in Infancy (CESDI)
Maternal and Child Health Research Consortium, Chiltern Court, 188 Baker Street, London NW1 5SD
Tel: 020 7486 1191
Web site: http://www.cesdi.com

Annual publication:
CESDI annual report

Health Development Agency formerly **Health Education Authority**
Trevelyan House, 30 Great Peter Street, London SW1P 2HW
Tel: 020 7222 5300
Fax: 020 7413 8926
Web site: http://www.hea.org.uk

Health Information Service (Department of Health)
Tel: 0800 665544

Health Service Commissioner
Church House, Great Smith Street, London SW1P 3PW
Tel: 020 7276 2035

National Perinatal Epidemiology Unit

Institute of Health Sciences, Old Road, Headington, Oxford OX3 7LF

Tel: 01865 227000

Fax: 01865 227002

Email: general@perinat.ox.ac.uk

Web site: http://www.npeu.ox.ac.uk/

NHS Confederation formerly the **National Association of Health Authorities and Trusts (NAHAT)**

Birmingham Research Park, Vincent Drive, Birmingham B15 2SQ

Tel: 0121 471 4444

Fax: 0121 414 1120

Web site: http://www.nhsconfed.net/

NHS Direct, where available

Tel: 0845 4647

United Kingdom Public Health Alliance

Membership Department: UKPHA, 138 Digbeth, Birmingham B5 6DR

Tel: 0121 643 7628

Fax: 0121 643 4541

Email: pha@ukonline.co.uk

Web site: http://web.online.co.uk/pht/contents.htm

Regulatory bodies

UK Central Council for Nursing, Midwifery and Health Visiting

23 Portland Place, London W1N 4JT

Tel: 020 7637 7181

Fax: 020 7436 2924

Web site: http://www.ukcc.org.uk

General Medical Council

178–202 Great Portland Street, London W1N 6JE

Tel: 020 7580 7642

Fax: 020 7915 3641

Email: gmc@gmc-uk.org

Web site: http://www.gmc-uk.org

Royal colleges and professional organisations

Chartered Institute of Public Finance and Accountancy
3 Robert Street, London WC2N 6BH
Tel: 020 7543 5600
Fax: 020 7543 5700

Community Practitioners and Health Visitors Association
40 Bermondsey Street, London, SE1 3UD
Tel: 020 7367 6800

Faculty of Public Health Medicine of the Royal College of Physicians of London
11 St Andrew's Place, London NW1 4LE
Tel: 020 7486 8111
Fax: 020 7224 6973
Email: enquiries@fphm.org.uk
Web site: http://www.fphm.org.uk/

Institute of Health Service Management
7–10 Chandos Street, London W1M 9DE
Tel: 020 7460 7654
Fax: 020 7460 7655
Email: mailbox@ihsm.co.uk
Web site: http://www.ihsm.co.uk

Neonatal Nurses Association
Room 7, Third Floor, Milton Chambers, 19 Milton Street, Nottingham NG1 3EN
Tel: 01279 714511
Fax: 01279 714519
Email: nnaoffice@nna.org.uk
Web site: http://www.nna.org.uk/

Royal College of General Practitioners

14 Princes Gate, Hyde Park, London SW7 1PU

Tel: 020 7581 3232
Fax: 020 7225 3047
Email: info@regp.org.uk
Web site: http://www.rcgp.org.uk

Royal College of Midwives

15 Mansfield Street, London W1M 0BE

Tel: 020 7312 3535
Fax: 020 7291 9224

Royal College of Nursing of the United Kingdom

20 Cavendish Square, London W1M 0AB

Tel: 020 7409 3333
Fax: 020 7647 3435
Email: corpaffairs.dept@rcn.org.uk
Web site: http://www.rcn.org.uk

Royal College of Obstetricians and Gynaecologists

27 Sussex Place, Regent's Park, London NW1 4RG

Tel: 020 7772 6200
Fax: 020 7723 0575
Email: coll.sec@rcog.org.uk
Web site: http://www.rcog.org.uk

Royal College of Paediatrics and Child Health

50 Hallam Street, London W1N 6DE

Tel: 020 7307 5600
Fax: 020 7307 5601
Email: enquiries@rcpch.ac.uk
Web site: http://www.rcpch.ac.uk

Royal College of Pathologists

2 Carlton House Terrace, London SW1Y 5AF

Tel: 020 7930 5861
Fax: 020 7321 0523
Email: secretary@rcpath.org
Web site: http://www.rcpath.org

Royal Statistical Society

12 Errol Street, London EC1Y 8LX

Tel: 020 7638 8998

Fax: 020 7256 7598

Email: rss@rss.org.uk

Web site: http://www.rss.org.uk

Trades unions and other organisations representing the interest of health service staff

British Medical Association

BMA House, Tavistock Square, London WC1H 9JP

Tel: 020 7387 4499

Fax: 020 7383 6400

Web site: http://www.bma.org.uk

Community Practitioners and Health Visitors Association

40 Bermondsey Street, London SE1 3UD

Tel: 020 7367 6800

Manufacturing, Science and Finance Union (MSF)

MSF Centre, 33/37 Moreland Street, London EC1V 8BB

Tel: 020 7505 3000

Fax: 020 7505 3014

Web site: http://www.msf.org.uk

Medical Practioners' Union

33/37 Moreland Street, London EC1V 8BB

Tel: 020 7505 3000

Fax: 020 7505 3014

Royal College of Midwives

15 Mansfield Street, London W1M 0BE

Tel: 020 7312 3535

Fax: 020 7291 9224

Royal College of Nursing of the United Kingdom

20 Cavendish Square, London W1M 0AB

Tel: 020 7409 3333

Fax: 020 7647 3435

Email: corpaffairs.dept@rcn.org.uk

Web site: http://www.rcn.org.uk

Unison

Unison, 1 Mabledon Place, London WC1H 9AJ

Tel: 020 7388 2366

Fax: 020 7387 6992

Email: unison-mable@unison.org.uk

Web site: http://www.unison.org.uk

Other national organisations concerned with maternity, child health services and related issues

Action on Pre-Eclampsia (APEC)

31–33 College Road, Harrow, Middlesex HA1 1EJ

Tel: 020 8863 3271

Action for Sick Children

Argyle House, 29–31 Euston Road, London NW1 2SD

Antenatal Results and Choices (ARC)

73 Charlotte Street, London W1P 1LB

Tel: 020 7631 0285

              020 7631 0280 Helpline

Association for Community-based Maternity Care

Newby End Farm, Newby, Penrith, Cumbria CA10 3EX

Tel: 01931 714338

Fax: 01768 361980

Association for Improvements in the Maternity Services (AIMS)

21 Iver Lane, Iver, Bucks SL0 9LH

Tel: 01753 652781 or 020 8723 4356

Fax: 01753 654142

Email: aimsuk@aol.com.

Association for Spina Bifida and Hydrocephalus

ASBAH House, 42 Park Road, Peterborough PE1 2UQ

Tel: 01733 555988

Fax: 01733 555985

Web site: http://www.asbah.demon.co.uk/

Association for Post-Natal Illness

7 Gowan Avenue, Fulham, London SW6 6RH

Association of Community Health Councils for England and Wales

Earlsmead House, 30 Drayton Park, London N5 1PB

Tel: 020 7609 8405

Fax: 020 7700 1152

Web site: http://www.achcew.org.uk/

Association of Radical Midwives

62 Greetby Hill, Ormskirk, Lancashire L39 2DT

Tel: 01695 572776

Fax: 01695 572776

Email: arm@radmid.demon.co.uk

Baby Life Support Systems (BLISS – London)

17–21 Emerald Street, London WC1N 3QL

Tel: 020 7 831 9393

CERES, Consumers for ethics in research

PO Box 1365, London N16 0BW

Caesarean Support Network

2 Hurst Park Drive, Huyton, Liverpool L36 1TF

Tel: 0151 480 1184

Charities Aid Foundation

King's Hill, West Malling, Kent ME19 4TA

Tel: 01732 520000

Web site: http://www.cafonline.org/

Child Bereavement Trust

Harleyford Estate, Henley Road, Marlow, Bucks SL7 2DX

Child and Adolescent Self-Harm in Europe

National Children's Bureau, 8 Wakley Street, London EC1V 7QE

Tel:	020 7843 6008/6000
Fax:	020 7843 6007
Email:	nmadge@ncb.org.uk
Web site:	http://www.ncb.org.uk/

Child Poverty Action Group (CPAG)

94 White Lion Street, London N1 9PF

Tel:	020 7837 7979
Fax:	020 7837 6414
Email:	staff@cpag.demon.co.uk
Web site:	http://www.namss.org.uk/cpag.htm

College of Health

St Margaret House, 21 Old Ford Road, London E2 9PL

Tel:	020 8983 1225

Contact a Family

170 Tottenham Court Road, London W1P 0HA

Down's Syndrome Association, formerly Down's Children's Association

155 Mitcham Road, London SW17 9PG

Tel:	020 8682 4001
Fax:	020 8682 4012

Family Planning Association

2–12 Pentonville Road, London N1 9FP

Tel:	020 7837 4044
Fax:	020 7837 3034
Web site:	http://www.fpa.org.uk/

Foundation for the Study of Infant Deaths

13 Halkin Street, London SW1X 7DP

Tel:	020 7235 0965

Group B Strep Support

PO Box 203, Haywards Heath, West Sussex RH16 1GF

In Touch Trust

19 Norman Road, Sale, Cheshire N33 3DS

Tel: 0161 905 2440

Maternity Alliance

45 Beech Street, London EC2P 2LX

Tel: 020 7588 8583

Fax: 020 7588 8584

Email: info@maternityalliance.org.uk

Miscarriage Association

c/o Clayton Hospital, Wakefield, West Yorkshire WF1 3JS

Tel: 01924 200 795

            01924 200 799 (Helpline)

Multiple Births Foundation

Queen Charlotte's and Chelsea Hospital, Goldhawk Road, London W6 0XG

Tel: 020 8383 3519

Fax: 020 8383 3519

Web site: http://www.multiplebirths.org.uk

National Association of Citizens Advice Bureaux (NACAB)

Central Office, Myddelton House, 115–123 Pentonville Road, London N1 9LZ

Tel: 020 7833 2181

Web site: http://www.nacab.org.uk

Northern Ireland Association of Citizens Advice Bureaux

11 Upper Crescent, Belfast BT7 1NT

Tel: 028 9023 1120

Citizens Advice Scotland

26 George Square, Edinburgh EH8 9LD

Tel: 0131 667 0156

The Scottish association is a separate body from NACAB.

National Childbirth Trust

Alexandra House, Oldham Terrace, Acton, London W3 6NH

Tel: 020 8992 8637

Fax: 020 8992 5929

Web site: http://www.nct-online.org

National Children's Bureau

8 Wakley Street, Islington, London EC1V 7QE

Tel: 020 7843 6008

Fax: 020 7843 6007

Web site: http://www.ncb.org.uk

National Council for One-Parent Families

255 Kentish Town Road, London NW5 2LX

Tel: 020 7267 1361

Fax: 020 7482 4851

Email: ncops@dial.pipex.com

National Council for Voluntary Organisations (NCVO)

Regents Wharf, 8 All Saint's Street, London N1 9RL

Tel: 0800 2 798 798

Web site: http://www.ncvo-vol.org.uk

Parents in Partnership-Parent Infant Network (PIPPIN)

Administration: 2 Middlefield Road, Hoddesdon, Herts EN11 9ED

Tel: 01992 471355

Fax: 01992 444579

The Patients' Association

18 Victoria Park Square, Bethnal Green, London E2 9PF

Tel: 020 8981 5676/5695

PETS, Pre-eclamptic Toxaemia, Society

Rhianfa, Carmel, Caernarfon, LL54 7RL

Radical Statistics

c/o 10 Ruskin Avenue, Heaton, Bradford BD9 6ER

Tel: 01274 482176

Web site: http://www.radstats.org.uk/

Royal Society for Mentally Handicapped Children and Adults (MENCAP)

MENCAP National Centre, 123 Golden Lane, London EC1Y 0RT

Tel:	020 7454 0454
Fax:	020 7608 3254
Email:	info@mencap.org.uk
Web site:	http://www.mencap.org.uk

SCOPE for people with cerebral palsy

12 Park Crescent, London W1N 4EQ

Tel:	020 7619 7100
Fax:	020 7619 7399
Email:	cphelpline@scope.org.uk

STEPS for children who have walking difficulties

Lymm Court, 11 Eagle Brow, Lymm, Cheshire WA13 0LP

Tel:	01925 757 525
Fax:	01925 757 797

Stillbirth and Neonatal Death Society (SANDS)

28 Portland Place, London W1N 4DE

Tel:	020 7436 7940
Fax:	020 7436 3715

Toxoplasmosis Trust

Room 26, 61–71 Collier Street, London N1 9BE

Twins and Multiple Births Association (TAMBA)

Harnott House, 309 Chester Road, Little Sutton, Ellesmere Port CH66 1QQ

Tel:	0870 121 4000 or 0151 348 0020
	01732 868000 TAMBA Twinline
	Weekdays 7pm to 11pm
	Weekends 10am to 11pm
Fax:	0870 121 4001 or 0151 348 0765
Web site:	http://www.surreyweb.org.uk/tamba/

Appendix 2:
Official reports and classifications

Classifications

International classifications of diseases and impairments

World Health Organization. *Manual of the international statistical classification of diseases, injuries and causes of death. Seventh revision.* Volume 1. Geneva: WHO, 1957.

World Health Organization. *International classification of diseases. Manual of the international statistical classification of diseases, injuries and causes of death. Eighth revision.* Volume 1. Geneva: WHO, 1967.

World Health Organization. *International classification of diseases. Manual of the international statistical classification of diseases, injuries and causes of death. Ninth revision.* Volume 1. Geneva: WHO, 1977.

World Health Organization. *International classification of impairments, disabilities and handicaps.* Geneva: WHO, 1980.

International classification of diseases, 9th revision with FIGO definitions. Edinburgh: Information Services Division, 1981

World Health Organization. *International statistical classification of diseases and related health problems. Tenth revision.* Volume 1. Geneva: WHO, 1992.

British Paediatric Association. *Classification of diseases: a paediatric adaptation of ICD-10.* London: Royal College of Paediatrics and Child Health, 1996.

World Health Organization. *International classification of functioning and disability. Beta-2 draft.* On the internet at http://www.who.int/icidh/. Geneva: WHO, 1999.

Classifications of operations and clinical terms

Office of Population Censuses and Surveys. *Classification of surgical operations.* London: OPCS, 1975.

World Health Organisation. *International classification of procedures in medicine.* Two volumes. Geneva: WHO, 1978.

Office of Population Censuses and Surveys. *Tabular list of the classification of surgical operations and procedures.* Fourth revision, consolidated version. London: OPCS, 1990.

NHS Centre for Coding and Classification. *Clinical terms, version 3. (Read codes.) Release overview.* Loughborough: NHSCC, 1994.

Social and occupational classifications

General Register Office. *Census 1951. Classification of occupations.* London: HMSO, 1956.

General Register Office. *Classification of occupations, 1960.* London: HMSO, 1960.

Office of Population Censuses and Surveys. *Classification of occupations 1970.* London: HMSO, 1970.

Office of Population Censuses and Surveys. *Classification of occupations 1980.* London: HMSO, 1980.

Office of Population Censuses and Surveys. *Standard occupational classification. Volume 1. Structure and definitions of major and minor unit groups.* London: HMSO, 1990.

Office of Population Censuses and Surveys. *Standard occupational classification. Volume 2. Coding index.* London: HMSO, 1990.

Office of Population Censuses and Surveys. *Standard occupational classification. Volume 2. Coding index.* Second edition. London: HMSO, 1995.

Office of Population Censuses and Surveys. *Standard occupational classification. Volume 3. Social classifications and coding methodology.* London: HMSO, 1991.

Rose D, O'Reilly K. *Constructing classes: towards a new social classification for the UK.* Swindon: Economic and Social Research Council and the Office for National Statistics, 1997.

Rose D, O'Reilly K. *The ESRC review of government social classifications.* London: Office for National Statistics and the Economic and Social Research Council, 1998.

Area classifications

Webber R, Craig J. *Socio-economic classification of local authority areas.* Studies on Medical and Population Subjects No. 35. London: HMSO, 1978.

Craig J. *A 1981 socio-economic classification of local and health authorities of Great Britain.* Studies on Medical and Population Subjects No. 48. London: HMSO, 1985.

Wallace M, Denham C. *The ONS classification of local and health authorities in Great Britain.* Studies on Medical and Population Subjects No. 59. London: HMSO, 1996.

Office for National Statistics. *Gazetteer of the old and new geographies of the United Kingdom.* London: The Stationery Office, 1999.

Office for National Statistics. *The ONS classification of local and health authorities of Great Britain: revised for authorities in 1999.* Studies on Medical and Population Subjects No. 63. London: ONS, 1999.

Decennial supplements

Reports published in the 1990s

Britton M, ed. *Mortality and geography: a review in the mid-1980s, England and Wales.* OPCS Decennial Supplement Series DS No.9. London: HMSO, 1990.

Drever F, ed. *Occupational health.* OPCS Decennial Supplement Series DS No. 10. London: HMSO, 1995.

Botting B, ed. *The health of our children.* OPCS Decennial Supplement Series DS No. 11. London: HMSO, 1995.

Charlton J, Murphy M, eds. *The health of adult Britain, 1841–1994.* Volumes 1 and 2. ONS Decennial Supplement Series DS Nos. 12 and 13. London: The Stationery Office, 1997.

Drever F, Whitehead M, eds. *Health inequalities.* ONS Decennial Supplement Series DS No. 15. London: The Stationery Office, 1997.

Earlier reports

General Register Office. *Census of England and Wales, 1911.* Cd 8678. Vol. XIII: Fertility of marriage. Part I. London: HMSO, 1917.

General Register Office. *The Registrar General's decennial supplement for the years 1901–1910.* Vol. II. London: HMSO, 1918.

General Register Office. *Census of England and Wales, 1911.* Vol. XIII: Fertility of marriage. Part II. London: HMSO, 1923.

General Register Office. *The Registrar General's decennial supplement for England and Wales, 1921.* Vol. II: Occupational mortality, fertility and infant mortality. London: HMSO, 1927.

General Register Office. *The Registrar General's decennial supplement for England and Wales, 1931.* Part IIa: Occupational mortality. London: HMSO, 1938.

General Register Office. *The Registrar General's decennial supplement for England and Wales, 1931.* Part IIb: Occupational fertility, 1931 and 1939. London: HMSO, 1953.

General Register office. *Decennial supplement, England and Wales, 1951. Occupational mortality, Part II.* London: HMSO, 1958.

General Register Office. *Census 1951, England and Wales. Fertility report.* London: HMSO, 1958

General Register Office. *Registrar General's statistical review. Decennial supplement, England and Wales, 1961. Area mortality tables.* London: HMSO, 1967

Office of Population Censuses and Surveys. *The Registrar-General's decennial supplement for England and Wales, 1961.* Occupational mortality tables. London: HMSO, 1971.

Office of Population Censuses and Surveys. *Occupational mortality: decennial supplement 1970–1972, England and Wales.* OPCS Decennial Supplement Series DS No. 1. London: HMSO, 1978.

Office of Population Censuses and Surveys. *Life tables: decennial supplement 1970–1972, England and Wales.* OPCS Decennial Supplement Series DS No. 2. London: HMSO, 1979.

Office of Population, Censuses, and Surveys. *Area mortality: the Registrar General's decennial supplement for England and Wales, 1969–73.* Series DS No. 4. London: HMSO, 1981.

Office of Population Censuses and Surveys. *Fertility report from the 1971 census.* OPCS Decennial Supplement Series DS No. 5. London: HMSO, 1983.

Office of Population Censuses and Surveys. *Occupational mortality: decennial supplement 1979–80, 1982–83.* Part I: Commentary. OPCS Decennial Supplement Series DS No. 6. London: HMSO, 1986.

Office of Population Censuses and Surveys. *Occupational mortality: decennial supplement 1979–80, 1982–83.* Part II: Microfiche tables. OPCS Decennial Supplement Series DS No. 6. London: HMSO, 1986.

Office of Population Censuses and Surveys. *English life tables: the report prepared by the Government Actuary for the Registrar General for England and Wales.* English life tables No. 14, Series DS No. 7. London: HMSO, 1987.

Office of Population Censuses and Surveys. *Occupational mortality 1979–80, 1982–83, England and Wales. Childhood supplement.* OPCS Decennial Supplement Series DS No. 8. London: HMSO, 1988.

The OPCS/ONS Longitudinal Study

Fox AJ, Goldblatt PO. *Longitudinal Study 1971–1975: socio-demographic mortality differentials.* Series LS No. 1. London: HMSO, 1982.

Fox AJ. *Longitudinal Study 1971–1977: Social class and occupational mortality.* Series LS No. 2. London: HMSO, 1982.

Leon D. *The social distribution of cancer.* Series LS No. 3. London: HMSO, 1988.

Grundy E. *Women's migration: marriage, fertility and divorce.* Series LS No. 4. London: HMSO, 1989.

Kogevinas M. *Longitudinal Study: socio-demographic differences in cancer survival.* Series LS No. 5. London: HMSO, 1990.

Goldblatt P, ed. *Mortality and social organisation.* Series LS No. 6. London: HMSO, 1990.

Hattersley L, Creeser R. *The Longitudinal Study: 1971–1991: history, organisation and quality of data.* Series LS No. 7. London: HMSO, 1995.

Dale A, Williams M, Dodgeon B. *Housing deprivation and social change.* Series LS No. 8. London: HMSO, 1996.

Gleave S, Hattersley L, eds. *Migration analysis using the Office for National Statistics Longitudinal Study*. Series LS No. 9, London: TSO, 2000.

Maternal mortality

Reports published in the 1990s

Department of Health, Welsh Office, Scottish Home and Health Department, and Department of Health and Social Services, Northern Ireland. *Report on confidential enquiries into maternal deaths in the United Kingdom, 1985–87*. London: HMSO, 1991.

Department of Health, Welsh Office, Scottish Home and Health Department, and Department of Health and Social Services, Northern Ireland. *Report on confidential enquiries into maternal deaths in the United Kingdom, 1988–1990*. London: HMSO, 1994.

Scottish Office Home and Health Department. *Report on maternal and perinatal deaths in Scotland, 1986–1990*. Edinburgh: HMSO, 1994.

Department of Health, Welsh Office, Scottish Home and Health Department, and Department of Health and Social Services, Northern Ireland. *Report on confidential enquiries into maternal deaths in the United Kingdom, 1991–1993*. London: HMSO, 1996.

Department of Health, Welsh Office, Scottish Office Department of Health, and Department of Health and Social Services, Northern Ireland. *Why mothers die. Report on confidential enquiries into maternal deaths in the United Kingdom, 1994–1996*. London: The Stationery Office, 1998.

Earlier reports

Local Government Board. *Report on maternal mortality in connection with childbearing and its relation to infant mortality. Supplement to the forty-fourth report of the Medical Officer, 1914–1915*. Cd 8153. London: HMSO, 1916.

Campbell JM. *Maternal mortality*. Reports on Public Health and Medical Subjects No. 25. London: HMSO, 1924.

Campbell JM. *The protection of motherhood*. Reports on Public Health and Medical Subjects No. 48. London: HMSO, 1927.

Kinloch JP, Steven JA. *Maternal mortality. Report on maternal mortality in Aberdeen, 1918–1927, with special reference to puerperal sepsis*. Edinburgh: Scottish Board of Health, 1928.

Ministry of Health. *Interim report of the Departmental Committee on Maternal Mortality and Morbidity*. London: HMSO, 1930.

Ministry of Health. *Final report of the Departmental Committee on Maternal Mortality and Morbidity*. London: HMSO, 1932.

Campbell J, Cameron ID, Jones DM. *High maternal mortality in certain areas*. Reports on Public Health and Medical Subjects No. 68. London: HMSO, 1932.

Colebrook DC. *The source of infection in puerperal fever due to haemolytic streptococci.* Medical Research Committee Special Report Series No. 205. London: HMSO, 1933.

Douglas CA, McKinlay PL. *Report on maternal morbidity and mortality in Scotland.* Edinburgh: HMSO, 1935.

Ministry of Health. *Report of an investigation into maternal mortality in Wales.* Cmd 5423. London: HMSO, 1937.

Ministry of Health. *Report on an investigation into maternal mortality.* Cmd 5422. London: HMSO, 1937.

Ministry of Health. *Report on confidential enquiries into maternal deaths in England and Wales, 1952–54.* Reports on Public Health and Medical Subjects No. 97. London: HMSO, 1957.

Ministry of Health. *Report on confidential enquiries into maternal deaths in England and Wales, 1955–57.* Reports on Public Health and Medical Subjects No. 103. London: HMSO, 1960.

Ministry of Health. *Report on confidential enquiries into maternal deaths in England and Wales, 1958–60.* Reports on Public Health and Medical Subjects No. 108. London: HMSO, 1963.

Ministry of Health. *Report on confidential enquiries into maternal deaths in England and Wales, 1961–1963.* Reports on Public Health and Medical Subjects No. 115. London: HMSO, 1966.

Government of Northern Ireland, Ministry of Health and Social Services. *A report on an enquiry into maternal deaths in Northern Ireland, 1964–1967.* Belfast: HMSO, 1968.

Ministry of Health. *Report on confidential enquiries into maternal deaths in England and Wales, 1964–66.* Reports on Public Health and Medical Subjects No. 119. London: HMSO, 1969.

Department of Health and Social Security. *Report on confidential enquiries into maternal deaths in England and Wales, 1967–69.* Reports on Health and Social Subjects No. 1. London: HMSO, 1972.

Scottish Home and Health Department. *A report on an enquiry into maternal deaths in Scotland, 1965–1971.* Edinburgh: HMSO, 1974.

Department of Health and Social Security. *Report on confidential enquiries into maternal deaths in England and Wales, 1970–72.* Reports on Health and Social Subjects No. 11. London: HMSO, 1975.

Scottish Home and Health Department. *A report on an enquiry into maternal deaths in Scotland, 1972–1975.* Edinburgh: HMSO, 1978.

Department of Health and Social Security. *Report on confidential enquiries into maternal deaths in England and Wales, 1973–1975.* Reports on Health and Social Subjects No. 14. London: HMSO, 1979.

Department of Health and Social Security. *Report on confidential enquiries into maternal deaths in England and Wales, 1976–1978.* Reports on Health and Social Subjects No. 26. London: HMSO, 1982.

Department of Health and Social Services, Northern Ireland. *A report on an enquiry into maternal deaths in Northern Ireland, 1968–1977*. Belfast: HMSO, 1982.

Department of Health and Social Security. *Report on confidential enquiries into maternal deaths in England and Wales, 1979–81*. Reports on Health and Social Subjects No. 29. London: HMSO, 1986.

Scottish Home and Health Department. *A report on an enquiry into maternal deaths in Scotland, 1976–1980*. Edinburgh: HMSO, 1987.

Department of Health and Social Services, Northern Ireland. *A report on an enquiry into maternal deaths in Northern Ireland, 1978–1984*. Belfast: HMSO, 1988.

Department of Health and Social Security. *Report on confidential enquiries into maternal deaths in England and Wales, 1982–84*. Reports on Health and Social Subjects No. 34. London: HMSO, 1989.

Scottish Home and Health Department. *Report on maternal and perinatal deaths in Scotland, 1981–1985*. Edinburgh: HMSO, 1989.

Infant and perinatal mortality

Reports published in the 1990s

Department of Health. *Confidential Enquiry into Stillbirths and Deaths in Infancy: Report of a Working Group set up by the Chief Medical Officer*. London: Department of Health, 1990.

National Advisory Body. *Confidential Enquiry into Stillbirths and Deaths in Infancy: report, March 1992–July 1993*. London: Department of Health, 1994.

Scottish Office Home and Health Department. *Report on maternal and perinatal deaths in Scotland, 1986–1990*. Edinburgh: HMSO, 1994.

Confidential Enquiry into Stillbirths and Deaths in Infancy. *Annual report for 1 January to 31 December 1993*. Part 1: Summary of methods and main results. London: Department of Health, 1995.

Confidential Enquiry into Stillbirths and Deaths in Infancy. *Annual report for 1 January to 31 December 1993*. Part 2: Additional results and tables. London: Department of Health, 1995.

Confidential Enquiry into Stillbirths and Deaths in Infancy. *3rd annual report for 1 January to 31 December 1994*. London: Department of Health, 1996.

Confidential Enquiry into Stillbirths and Deaths in Infancy. *4th annual report for 1 January to 31 December 1995*. London: Maternal and Child Health Consortium, 1997.

Confidential Enquiry into Stillbirths and Deaths in Infancy. *5th annual report*. London: Maternal and Child Health Consortium, 1998.

Confidential Enquiry into Stillbirths and Deaths in Infancy. *6th annual report*. London: Maternal and Child Health Consortium, 1999.

Earlier reports

Local Government Board. *Report by the Medical Officer on infant and child mortality. Supplement to the thirty-ninth annual report of the Local Government Board, 1909–1910.* Cd 5312. London: HMSO, 1910.

Local Government Board. *Second report by the Medical Officer on infant and child mortality. Supplement to the forty-second annual report of the Local Government Board, 1912–1913.* Cd 6909. London: HMSO, 1913.

Local Government Board. *Third report by the Medical Officer on infant mortality in Lancashire. Supplement to the forty-third annual report of the Local Government Board, 1913–14.* Cd 7511. London: HMSO, 1914.

Local Government Board. *Report on maternal mortality in connection with childbearing and its relation to infant mortality. Supplement to the forty-fourth report of the Medical Officer, 1914–1915.* Cd 8153. London: HMSO, 1916.

Chalmers AK, Brend WA, Findlay L, Brownlee J. *Mortalities of birth, infancy and childhood.* National Health Insurance Medical Research Committee Special Report Series No. 10. London: HMSO, 1917.

Holland, E. *The causation of fetal deaths.* Reports on Public Health and Medical Subjects No. 5. London: HMSO, 1922.

Brownlee J. *The use of death rates as a measure of hygienic conditions.* Medical Research Council Special Report Series No. 60. London: HMSO, 1922.

Bruce Murray, M. *The effect of maternal social conditions and nutrition upon birthweight and birth length.* Medical Research Council Report No. 81. London: HMSO, 1924.

Cruickshank JN. *Maternal syphilis as a cause of death of the fetus and of the newborn child.* Medical Research Council Special Report Series No. 82. London: HMSO, 1924.

Child life investigations. The estimation of fetal age and the weight and length of normal fetuses and the weights of fetal organs. Medical Research Council Special Report Series No. 86. London: HMSO, 1924.

Holland EL, Lane-Claypon JE. *A clinical and pathological study of 1673 cases of dead-births and neonatal deaths.* Medical Research Council Report No. 109. London: HMSO, 1926.

Palmer AC. *The cause of fetal death in 144 cases.* Medical Research Council Report No. 118. London: HMSO, 1928.

Campbell, JM. *Infant mortality with statistical notes by P L McKinlay.* Reports on Public Health and Medical Subjects No. 55. London: HMSO, 1929.

Cruickshank JN. *The causes of neonatal death.* Medical Research Council Report No. 118. London: HMSO, 1930.

Joint Committee of the Royal College of Obstetricians and Gynaecologists and the British Paediatric Association. *Neonatal mortality and morbidity.* Reports on Public Health and Medical Subjects No. 94. London: HMSO, 1949.

Heady JA, Heasman MA. *Social and biological factors in infant mortality.* Studies on Medical and Population Subjects No. 15. London: HMSO, 1959.

Ministry of Health. *Enquiry into sudden infant deaths.* Reports on Public Health and Medical Subjects No. 113. London: HMSO, 1965.

Spicer CC, Lipworth R. *Regional and social factors in infant mortality.* Studies on Medical and Population Subjects No. 19. London: HMSO, 1969.

Department of Health and Social Security. *Confidential enquiry into postneonatal deaths, 1964–66.* Reports on Public Health and Medical Subjects No. 125. London: HMSO, 1970.

Adelstein AM, Macdonald Davies I, Weatherall JA. *Perinatal and infant mortality: social and biological factors, 1975–1977.* Studies on Medical and Population Subjects No. 41. London: HMSO, 1980.

House of Commons Social Services Committee. *Second report: perinatal and neonatal mortality. [Chair: R Short].* Session 1979–80. HC 663 Vol. I. London: HMSO, 1980.

House of Commons Social Services Committee. *Second report: perinatal and neonatal mortality. [Chair: R Short].* Session 1979–80. HC 663 Vol. IV. London: HMSO, 1980.

Department of Health and Social Security. *Government's reply to the House of Commons Social Services Committee's second report on perinatal and neonatal mortality.* Cmnd 8084. London: HMSO, 1980.

Office of Population Censuses and Surveys, London School of Hygiene and Tropical Medicine. *Studies in sudden infant deaths.* Studies on Medical and Population Subjects No. 45. London: HMSO, 1982.

House of Commons Social Services Committee. *Third report: perinatal and neonatal mortality - follow-up.* Session 1983–84 HC 308. London: HMSO, 1984.

House of Commons Social Services Committee. *First report: perinatal, neonatal and infant mortality.* Session 1988–89. HC 54. London: HMSO, 1988.

Department of Health. *Government's reply to the House of Commons Social Services Committee's first report on perinatal and neonatal mortality.* Cm 741. Session 1988–89. London: HMSO, 1989.

Scottish Home and Health Department. *Report on maternal and perinatal deaths in Scotland, 1981–1985.* Edinburgh: HMSO, 1989.

Maternity care

Reports published during the 1990s

National Audit Office. *Maternity services: report by the Comptroller and Auditor General.* London: HMSO, 1990.

House of Commons Health Committee. *Maternity services: second report. [Chair: N Winterton].* Session 1991–92. HC 29–I Vol. I: Report. London: HMSO, 1991.

House of Commons Health Committee. *Maternity services: second report. [Chair: N Winterton].* Session 1991–92. HC 29–II Vol. II: Minutes of evidence. London: HMSO, 1991.

Department of Health. *The Government's response to the House of Commons Health Committee's second report on maternity services.* Cm 2018. Session 1991–92. London: HMSO, 1992.

Welsh Health Planning Forum. *Protocol for investment in health gain: maternal and early child health.* Cardiff: NHS Directorate, 1992.

Maternity Unit Study Team. *A study of midwife and GP led maternity units.* London: Department of Health, 1993.

Department of Health. *Changing childbirth. Part I. Report of the Expert Maternity Group.* London: HMSO, 1993.

Department of Health. *Changing childbirth. Part II. Survey of good communications practice in maternity services.* London: HMSO, 1993.

Scottish Home and Health Department. *Provision of maternity services in Scotland. A policy review.* Edinburgh: HMSO, 1993.

Department of Health. *Public health information strategy. Improving information on maternity and child health. Module 8A: mother's and baby's health from pregnancy to one month after birth.* London: Department of Health, June 1994.

NHS. *The patient's charter: maternity services.* Leeds: Department of Health, 1994.

NHS Management Executive. *Woman-centred maternity services.* Executive letter EL(94)9. Leeds: Department of Health, 1994.

Audit Commission. *First class delivery: improving maternity services in England and Wales.* London: Audit Commission, 1997.

Garcia J, Redshaw M, Fitzsimons B, Keene J. *First class delivery. A national survey of women's views of maternity care.* London: Audit Commission, 1998.

Earlier reports

Newsholme A. Memorandum on health visiting and on maternity and child welfare centres. In: *Supplement to the forty-fourth annual report of the Local Government Board, 1914–15.* Cd 8153. London: HMSO, 1916.

Local Government Board. *Maternity and child welfare. Report on the provision made by Local Authorities in England and Wales.* London: HMSO, 1917.

Ministry of Health. *Memorandum with regard to maternity homes and hospitals.* 15/MCW. London: HMSO, 1920.

Ministry of Health. *The selection of maternity cases for admission to hospital.* London: Ministry of Health, 1951.

Ministry of Health. *Report of the Maternity Services Committee [Chair: Lord Cranbrook].* London: HMSO, 1959.

Department of Health and Social Security and Welsh Office. *Domiciliary midwifery and maternity bed needs. Report of the subcommittee. [Chair: J Peel].* London: HMSO, 1970.

Maternity Services Advisory Committee. *Maternity care in action: Part I. Antenatal care.* London: HMSO, 1982.

Maternity Services Advisory Committee. *Maternity care in action: Part II. Care during childbirth (intrapartum care). A guide to good practice and a plan for action.* London: HMSO, 1984.

Maternity Services Advisory Committee. *Maternity care in action: Part III. Care during childbirth (postnatal care). A guide to good practice and a plan for action.* London: HMSO, 1984.

Feeding of babies

Reports published during the 1990s

White A, Freeth S, O'Brien M. *Infant feeding, 1990. A survey carried out on behalf of the Department of Health, the Scottish Home and Health Department, the Welsh Office and the Department of Health and Social Services in Northern Ireland.* OPCS Social Survey Report SS 1299. London: HMSO, 1992.

Department of Health. *Weaning and the weaning diet. Report of the working group on the weaning diet of the Committee on Medical Aspects of Food Policy.* Report on Health and Social Subjects 45. London: HMSO, 1994.

Thomas M, Avery V. *Infant feeding in Asian families.* London: The Stationery Office, 1997.

Foster K, Lader D, Cheesbrough S. *Infant feeding, 1995. Results from a survey carried out by the Social Survey Division of ONS on behalf of the UK health departments.* OPCS Social Survey Report SS 1387. London: The Stationery Office, 1997.

Earlier reports

Report on the breast feeding of infants. Reports on Public Health and Medical Subjects No. 91. London: HMSO, 1944.

Levin B, Mackay HMM, Neill CA, Oberholzer VG, Whitehead TP. *Weight gains, serum protein levels and health of breast fed and articially fed infants.* Medical Research Council Report No. 296. London: HMSO, 1959.

Department of Health and Social Security. *Present day practice in infant feeding. Report of a Working Party of the Panel on Child Nutrition. [Chair: TE Oppé].* Reports on Health and Social Subjects No. 9. London: HMSO, 1974.

Committee on Medical Aspects of Food Policy. *The composition of mature human milk*. Reports on Health and Social Subjects No. 12. London: HMSO, 1977.

Martin J. *Infant feeding, 1975: attitudes and practice in England and Wales. A survey carried out on behalf of the Department of Health and Social Security*. OPCS Social Survey Report SS 1064. London: HMSO, 1978.

Committee on Medical Aspects of Food Policy. *Artificial feeds for the young infant. Report of the Working Party on the Composition of foods for infants and young babies*. Reports on Health and Social Subjects No. 18. London: HMSO, 1980.

Department of Health and Social Security. *Present day practice in infant feeding: 1980*. DHSS Report on Health and Social Subjects No. 20. London: HMSO, 1980.

Department of Health and Social Security. *The collection and storage of human milk*. DHSS Report on Health and Social Subjects No. 22. London: HMSO, 1981.

Martin J, Monk J. *Infant feeding, 1980*. OPCS Social Survey Report SS 1144. London: HMSO, 1982.

Martin J, White A. *Infant feeding, 1985*. OPCS Social Survey Report SS 1233. London: HMSO, 1988.

Department of Health and Social Security. *Present day practice in infant feeding, third report*. Report on Health and Social Subjects No. 32. London: HMSO, 1988.

Costs of maternity care

National Audit Office. *Maternity services: report by the Comptroller and Auditor General*. London: HMSO, 1990.

NHS Management Executive. *Priorities and planning guidance for the NHS for 1992/93*. Executive letter EL(91)103. London: Department of Health, 1991.

Scottish Home and Health Department. *Provision of maternity services in Scotland. A policy review*. Edinburgh: HMSO, 1993.

National Audit Office. *Health of the nation: a progress report. Report by the Comptroller and Auditor General*. London: HMSO, 1996.

Audit Commission. *First class delivery: improving maternity services in England and Wales*. London: Audit Commission, 1997.

Callender C, Millward N, Lissenburgh S, Forth J. *Maternity rights and benefits in Britain 1996*. DSS Research Report No. 67. London: The Stationery Office, 1997.

Department of Social Security, Government Statistical Service, Semmence J, Easto V. *Family resources survey, Great Britain*. London: The Stationery Office, Published annually.

House of Commons Health Committee. *Public expenditure on health and personal social services. Memorandum received from the Department of Health containing replies to a written questionnaire from the Committee.* London: The Stationery Office, Published annually.

Collections of historical statistics

Mitchell BR. *British historical statistics.* Cambridge: Cambridge University Press, 1988.

Williams LJ. Digest of Welsh historical statistics = Crynhoad o ystadegau hanesyddol Cymru. Vol. 1 = Cyfrol 1. Cardiff: Welsh Office, 1985.

Williams LJ. Digest of Welsh historical statistics = Crynhoad o ystadegau hanesyddol Cymru, 1974–1996. Vol. 2 = Cyfrol 2. Cardiff: Welsh Office, 1998.

Wrigley EA, Schofield RS. *The population history of England, 1541–1871: a reconstruction.* With contributions from Ronald Lee and Jim Oeppen. Cambridge: Cambridge University Press, 1989, 1981.

Flinn M, ed. *Scottish population history: from the 17th century to the 1930s.* With contributions from Duncan Adamson and Robin Lobban. Cambridge: Cambridge University Press, 1977.

Vaughan WE, Fitzpatrick AJ, eds. *Irish historical statistics: population, 1821–1971.* Dublin: Royal Irish Academy, 1978.

Appendix 3:
Glossary and acronyms

Glossary of clinical terms

Abortifacient:	a substance which induces abortion
Abortion:	death or expulsion of the fetus either spontaneously or by intention before 24 completed weeks of pregnancy. In addition, a pregnancy deliberately ended on grounds of fetal abnormality at any gestation is classified as an induced abortion
Acceleration of labour:	use of artificial methods to increase strength of contractions and speed delivery
Amniocentesis:	withdrawal of fluid from the amniotic sac surrounding the fetus in the uterus for investigation of genetic constitution of the fetus
Amniotic sac:	a thin membrane which contains the fetus and amniotic fluid
Anaemia:	deficiency of haemoglobin in the red blood cells
Anencephaly:	congenital defective development of the brain. See neural tube defect
Anaesthesia:	a state in which drugs are used to make the whole body, in general anaesthesia, or part of it, in local or regional anaesthesia, insensible to pain
Analgesia:	relief of pain by drugs or other means. May be general or local
Antenatal:	any time in pregnancy before birth
Antepartum:	before the onset of labour
Asphyxia:	lack of air, suffocation
Caesarean section:	delivery of the baby through an incision in the mother's abdominal wall and uterus
Cerebrospinal fluid:	fluid that surrounds the brain and spinal cord
Congenital:	existing at the time of birth

Consultant obstetric maternity unit:	a maternity unit in which women book with a consultant obstetrician to give birth under the supervision of midwives and obstetricians
Down's syndrome:	disorder caused by the presence of an extra chromosome
Eclampsia:	convulsions associated with hypertension in pregnancy
Embryo:	product of conception. Term used in the first 8 weeks from conception. After that it is called a fetus
Electronic fetal monitoring:	use of electronic methods to monitor the pattern of fetal heart beats, either using ultrasound through the mother's abdomen, or from electrodes attached to the baby's head during labour
Epidural:	a local anaesthetic injected into the space around the spinal cord, causing loss of sensation to the lower part of the body
Episiotomy:	surgical cut through the perineum performed at the end of labour immediately before a vaginal birth to facilitate delivery of the baby
Fetal distress:	changes in the condition of the fetus which might indicate a potentially harmful environment in the womb. The most common signs are abnormalities of fetal heart rate and meconium staining of the amniotic fluid
Fetus:	product of conception. Term used from about 8 weeks after conception
Forceps:	instrument applied to the baby's head, used to assist in delivery
General practitioner maternity unit:	a maternity unit in which women book with a general practitioner to deliver under the supervision of midwives and general practitioners
Gestation:	pregnancy. Its duration is usually measured from the first day of the last menstrual period. See Chapter 2 for definition
Gravidity:	the total number of previous pregnancies, including those ending in miscarriage or abortion

Haemorrhage:	bleeding. Loss of blood, either internally into a body cavity, organs or tissues, or externally onto the body surface
Hydrocephaly:	build up of pressure from the cerebro-spinal fluid. In babies this may causeing swelling of the head. See neural tube defect
Hypertension:	raised blood pressure
Hysterectomy:	operation to remove the uterus
Hysterotomy:	operation involving incision of the uterus. A method used for late induced abortion
Iatrogenic:	harm caused by the process of diagnosis or treatment
Induced abortion:	abortion brought on purposefully using drugs or other means
Induction:	of labour or abortion. Process by which contractions of the womb are initiated artificially, either by breaking the membranous sac around the baby, or by drugs, or both
Intracranial haemorrhage:	bleeding within the skull
Intrapartum:	during labour
Intrauterine:	inside the uterus or womb
Intraventricular haemorrhage:	bleeding within the ventricles of the brain
Labour:	the process of delivering a baby. It can be divided into three stages: dilatation of the cervix, delivery of the baby, and delivery of the placenta
Lactation:	production of milk by breasts
Lesion:	medical term for any pathological aspect or loss of function in the body
Live birth:	see Chapter 2 for definition
Midwife:	person qualified to take responsibility for care during uncomplicated pregnancies and deliveries and for care after birth
Midwife-led maternity care:	a scheme or maternity unit in which women book with midwives for delivery under the supervision of midwives
Miscarriage:	the unintentional expulsion of a dead fetus, before the 24th week of completed pregnancy. Also known as spontaneous abortion
Morbidity:	disease, illness or abnormality

Neonatal death:	see Chapter 2 for definition
Neonatology:	the medical speciality concerned with the care of ill newborn babies
Neural tube defect:	a defect of closure of the spinal canal or skull associated with failure of development, or an abnormal protrusion of brain or spinal cord tissue. Includes anencephaly, spina bifida and is often associated with hydrocephaly
Obstetrics:	the medical and surgical specialty concerned with problems arising in pregnancy, delivery and the puerperium
Ophthalmia neonatorum:	eye infection in the newborn baby acquired during delivery. Prophylactic antibiotic eye drops may be used to prevent it
Oxytocin:	hormone drug commonly used in induction and acceleration of labour
Paediatrics:	medical specialty concerned with the care of babies and children
Parity:	total number of previous live births and stillbirths. This does not include abortions or miscarriages
Perinatal:	time period around the birth. See Chapter 2 for definition
Perineum:	a woman's area of pelvic floor between the vagina and the anus
Postnatal:	time after birth, usually taken as a period of six weeks
Postneonatal death:	death after the neonatal period. See Chapter 2 for definition
Post-partum:	after labour and delivery
Pre-eclampsia:	complication of pregnancy including raised blood pressure and protein in urine, also known as toxaemia
Prostaglandin:	hormone used in induction of labour or abortion, among other uses
Psycho-prophylaxis:	preparation for labour involving relaxation and breathing exercises
Puerperium:	time period after delivery during which the mother's body adjusts to the end of pregnancy

Respiratory distress syndrome (RDS):	condition occurring usually in preterm babies: can result from lack of surfactant which is necessary for lung expansion of immature lungs
Retinopathy of prematurity (ROP):	condition affecting eyes. Occurs particularly in preterm babies
Retrolental fibroplasia (RLF):	condition now known as retinopathy of prematurity
Rubella:	German measles
Spina bifida:	Congenital defect of the spinal column. See neural tube defect
Spontaneous abortion:	miscarriage
Stillbirth:	see Chapter 2 for definition
Talipes:	club foot
Termination of pregnancy:	a pregnancy which is deliberately ended, either legally or illegally
Thalassaemia:	a genetic blood disorder
Toxaemia:	see pre-eclampsia
Trauma:	wound or injury
Ultrasound:	high frequency sound waves used in obstetrics. They can be can be of two kinds. Doppler sound is used for measurement of fetal heart patterns. Real time scanning ultrasound gives a picture of the area scanned, allowing assessment of fetal position, size and diagnosis of some malformations or of multiple pregnancy. Also used after birth for assessment of extent of neonatal brain damage caused by intracranial or intraventricular haemorrhage
Uterus:	womb
Vacuum extraction:	method increasingly used as an alternative to forceps to assist delivery. Also known as ventouse delivery. Vacuum extraction may also refer to a method of induced abortion using suction, done early in pregnancy, before 12 weeks of gestation
Ventouse:	equipment used for vacuum extraction

Acronyms used in *Birth counts*

AHAs	Area health authorities
BINOCAR	British Isles network of congenital anomaly registers
CESDI	Confidential Enquiry into Stillbirths and Deaths in Infancy
CHC	Community health council
CIPFA	Chartered Institute of Public Finance and Accountancy
CMO	Chief Medical Officer
COPPISH	Core Patient Profile Information in Scottish Hospitals
DH, DoH	Department of Health
DHAs	District health authorities
DHSS	Department of Health and Social Security, up to 1988 in England, Department of Health and Social Services, in Northern Ireland, up to 1999
ECR	Extra-contractual referral
ENB	English National Board for Nursing, Midwifery and Health Visiting
EUROCAT	European Concerted Action Project on Registration of Congenital Abnormalities and Twins
Eurostat	Statistical Office of the European Communities
FIGO	Fédération Internationale de Gynécologie et d'Obstetrique / International Federation of Gynaecologists and Obstetricians
FPA	Family Planning Association
GDP	Gross Domestic Product
GRO	General Register Office
GSS	Government Statistical Service
HAA	Hospital Activity Analysis
HBGs	Health Benefit Groups
HCHS	Hospital and community health services
HES	Hospital Episode Statistics
HIPE	Hospital In-patient Enquiry
HRGs	Healthcare Resource Groups
ICD	International classification of diseases
ICM	International Confederation of Midwives
ISD	Information and Statistics Division
MMR	Measles, mumps and rubella
NCT	National Childbirth Trust
NHS	National Health Service
NICE	National Institute of Clinical Excellence

NISRA	Northern Ireland Statistics and Research Agency
NPEU	National Perinatal Epidemiology Unit
ONS	Office for National Statistics
OPCS	Office of Population Censuses and Surveys
PEDW	Patient Episode Database Wales
PFI	Private Finance Initiative
r-cade	Resource centre for access to data on Europe
RHAs	Regional health authorities
ROs	Regional offices of the NHS Executive
SCPR	Social and Community Planning Research
SMP	Statutory Maternity Pay
SMR	Scottish Morbidity Records
TPFRs	Total period fertility rates
UKCC	United Kingdom Central Council for Nursing, Midwifery and Health Visiting
UMT	Unit of Medical Time
UN	United Nations
UNICEF	United Nations Children's Fund
WHO	World Health Organisation

Appendix 4:
Chronological table of events and legislation

The table below lists events and legislation relevant to the statistics of population, vital events and health care in general and to the care and health of mothers and babies in particular.

1518	Royal charter granted to College of Physicians.
1538	Thomas Cromwell instructed parish churches in England and Wales to keep a register of every baptism, wedding and burial in the parish.
1540	Incorporation of Barber Surgeons company.
1563	London Bills of Mortality introduced. First regular statistics of mortality. Published during plague years only.
	Birth of mankind. The first English text on midwifery.
1590	Lord Burghley tried unsuccessfully to centralise parish registers for England and Wales.
1590s	Re-introduction of the obstetric forceps by the Chamberlen family, barber surgeons. First recorded use during third century AD.
1597, 1601	Elizabethan *Poor laws* brought together earlier legislation.
1603	Continuous publication of weekly London Bills of Mortality began.
1617	Foundation of the Society of Apothecaries.
1628	William Harvey, *De motu cordis*. Description of circulation of the blood.
1629	London Bills of Mortality recorded cause of death.
1651	William Harvey, *De generatione*. The first modern account of embryology.
1653–1660	During the Commonwealth attempts were made to set up a civil registration system.
1662	John Graunt, *Observations on the bills of mortality*. The first scientific attempt at the analysis of mortality data.
1671	Jane Sharp, *The midwives book*. The first midwifery book in English by a woman.
1727	London Bills of Mortality recorded age at death.
1745	Formation of the Company of Surgeons.
1753	Lord Hardwicke's Act for preventing clandestine marriage. Came into force in 1754.

1795	Alexander Gordon published treatise on puerperal fever.
1795–1796	First board of health set up in Manchester.
1800	Royal charter granted to Company of Surgeons.
1801	First population census of Britain.
1803	Lord Ellenborough's Act revised legal prohibition against abortion.
1831–1832	Cholera outbreaks led to setting up of boards of health in some towns.
1832	*Reform Act*. First of a succession of parliamentary measures towards better electoral representation and social conditions for the working classes.
1834	*Poor Law Reform Act,* intended to stop payments of 'outdoor' relief to poor people from parish rates. Instituted new workhouses for able-bodied paupers from 'unions' of parishes.
	Statistical Society of London, eventually to become Royal Statistical Society, founded.
1836	*Births, Marriages and Deaths Registration Act* (England and Wales). Registration began in July 1837.
1840	Report of the Select Committee on Health in Towns. First such general enquiry by a public body.
	Registrar General's weekly returns for the metropolis introduced.
1841	First population census of Ireland.
1842	Edwin Chadwick's *Report on the sanitary condition of the labouring population of Great Britain* published.
1843	Oliver Wendell Holmes gave a paper on the contagiousness of puerperal fever to the Boston Society for Medical Improvement.
1844	First report of the Royal Commission on the Health of Towns.
1845	Registration of Protestant marriage began in Ireland.
1847	Statistical and Social Enquiry Society of Ireland founded.
1848	An *Act for Promoting Public Health* set up local and national boards of health.
1849	Private enterprise society founded to resist *Public Health Act* of 1848.
1855	Registration of birth, marriages and deaths began in Scotland. General Register Office, Scotland, established.
	Oliver Wendell Holmes published his paper on puerperal fever as a pamphlet.
1857	*Matrimonial Causes Act* allowed civil divorce.

1858	Establishment of General Medical Council as governing body of the medical profession.
1859	First annual report of the Medical Officer to the Privy Council, forerunner of the current Chief Medical Officer's report *On the state of the public health*.
1861	*Offences Against the Person Act* made all abortion a crime.
	Ignaz Semmelweiss published his treatise on puerperal fever.
1864	Registration of births, deaths and Catholic marriages began in Ireland. General Register Office, Ireland, established.
1865	Use of antiseptic methods in medical and nursing practise became accepted after work by Joseph Lister based on findings of Louis Pasteur.
1870	*Education Act* made public elementary education universal.
1872	*An act for the better protection of infant life* made registration of live births compulsory from 1874.
	Public Health Act.
1874	*Births and Deaths Registration Act.*
1875	*Public Health Act* consolidated previous legislation about sanitary measures and administrative procedures.
1880	*Births and Deaths Registration Act (Ireland)* set up procedures for registration.
1880s	Use of sutures in caesarean section operations became accepted practice.
1881	Foundation of Matrons Aid Society, Trained Midwives Registration Society, which became the Royal College of Midwives.
1884	Royal Commission on the housing of the poor.
1887	Royal charter granted to Statistical Society.
1889	*Notification of Diseases Act.*
1893	*Elementary Education (Blind and Deaf Children) Act.*
1895	Publication of disease statistics for London hospitals, notified under the *Notification of Diseases Act*, in the Registrar General's weekly return.
1899	*Elementary Education (Defective and Epileptic Children) Act.*
1902	*Midwives Act.*
1906	*Education (Provision of Meals) Act.*
1907	School Medical Service established by *Education (Administrative Provisions) Act*.
	Notification of Births Act gave local authorities powers to adopt birth notification and set up maternal and child welfare schemes.

1911	*National Insurance Act.* This gave financial aid towards costs of delivery to wives of men qualified for benefit.
1913	National Health Insurance Medical Research Committee set up under the 1911 Act, leading to establishment of the Medical Research Council in 1919.
1915	*Notification of Births (Extension) Act* required local authorities to adopt compulsory birth notification and set up maternal and child welfare schemes.
	First two hospital antenatal clinics opened in Glasgow and Edinburgh.
1916	Treatment for venereal diseases became available free of charge.
1918	*Women's Suffrage Act.*
	Maternity and Child Welfare Act. This gave local authorities powers to provide clinics and maternity homes and to make domiciliary visits.
	World influenza pandemic.
1919	Ministry of Health, Welsh Board of Health and Scottish Board of Health established.
1920	*Census Act* allowed for regular census to be taken at intervals of not less than 5 years without recourse to parliament. Also gave Registrar General the duty to publish population statistics.
	Government of Ireland Act. Establishment of the Irish Free State and Government of Northern Ireland in 1921 meant separation of statistical systems for the two parts of the country.
1921	First family planning clinics opened.
1922	First Registrar General for Northern Ireland appointed.
	Statistics Branch set up in the Department of Industry and Commerce of the Irish Free State.
	Registrar General's weekly returns include vital statistics, as well as statistics of notifiable diseases.
1926	*Births and Deaths Registration Act.* Included the statutory requirement to register stillbirths in England and Wales, taking effect from July 1927.
	Adoption of Children Act.
1928	Foundation of the British Paediatric Association.
1929	*Infant Life (Preservation) Act.*
	Foundation of the College of Obstetricians and Gynaecologists.
1930	Ministry of Health endorsed contraceptive advice on medical grounds at Maternal and Child Welfare clinics. Formation of

the National Birth Control Council, which subsequently became the Family Planning Association (FPA).

1936   *Midwives Act*. This created a salaried midwifery service within local health authorities.

1937   *Public Health Act*.

Factories Act established that it is an offence to employ a woman in a factory during the first four weeks after she has given birth.

Maternity Services (Scotland) Act provided for medical and consultant services at home births in Scotland.

1938   *Population (Statistics) Acts* led to collection of data about parents' age and parity within marriage at birth registration from July 1938 in England and Wales.

late 1930s   Sulphonamides coming into use as a treatment for puerperal fever.

1939   Collection of information about parents' age and parity collected at birth registration started in Scotland and Northern Ireland. Stillbirth registration introduced in Scotland.

National Registration Act created a register of the whole population.

1940   Emergency Medical Services created.

First clinical use of penicillin.

1942   National Blood Transfusion Service set up.

Social Insurance and Allied Services (Beveridge Report) set out scheme for comprehensive welfare state.

1944   *Education Act*.

White Paper proposes introduction of National Health Service.

1945–49   Royal Commission on Population.

1946   *National Health Service Act*.

1947   *National Health Service (Scotland) Act*.

1948   National Health Service established.

1949   Hospital In-patient Enquiry initiated.

Independent Central Statistics Office set up in the Irish Republic.

1951   First analysis of statistics from Hospital In-patient Enquiry published by General Register Office.

Midwives Act set up Central Midwives Board as regulatory body for the profession.

1952   Foundation of College of General Practitioners.

	Confidential enquiries into maternal deaths established in England and Wales.
1954	Introduction of obstetric vacuum extractor (ventouse) by Malmström in Sweden.
mid 1950s	Exchange transfusion became possible for some babies with certain blood disorders.
1956	Formation of Natural Childbirth Trust, which later became the National Childbirth Trust.
1958	Early postnatal discharge for mothers delivered in hospital established in Bradford.
	Royal charter granted to College of Obstetricians.
1960	*Population (Statistics) Act* extended collection of vital statistics, including additional information about stillbirths from 1961.
1961	FPA approved use of oral contraceptives in clinics.
	Association for Improvement in the Maternity Services (AIMS) founded.
	Registration of stillbirths started in Northern Ireland.
1960s	Electronic monitoring of the fetal heart being introduced.
1962	Hospital plan for England published.
	College of Pathologists founded. Granted royal charter in 1970.
1964	Anti-D immunoglobulin introduced for prevention of rhesus haemolytic disease of the newborn.
	Reporting of congenital anomalies started in England and Wales.
1965	FPA approved use of intrauterine devices in family planning clinics.
1966	'Home confinement' grants discontinued.
1967	*Abortion Act.*
	First FPA vasectomy clinics opened.
1969	*Family Law Reform Act.*
late 1960s	Ultrasound being introduced as a diagnostic aid in obstetric practice.
1970	Office of Population Censuses and Surveys (OPCS) formed by merging the General Register Office and the Government Social Survey into a single organisation.
	General Household Survey began.
1971	Royal College of Psychiatrists founded.
1972	*Local Government Act* created new administrative boundaries and responsibilities.

mid 1960s - mid 1970s	Effective respiratory support for immature newborn babies being developed
early 1970s	Prostaglandins being introduced. Used principally in induction of labour and abortion.
mid 1970s	Antenatal diagnosis of chromosomal disorders, neural tube defects and some other disorders being developed and introduced in some centres.
1973	*NHS (Reorganisation) Act.* Three tier system came into effect April 1974. Also made family planning responsibility of NHS.
1974	Reorganisation of NHS and local government took place in April.
1975	*Child Benefit Act* enabled replacement of Family Allowances and income tax allowances for children by Child Benefit. Birthweights of live born babies began to be forwarded to local registrars in England and Wales to be recorded on draft entry to birth registers in England and Wales.
1976	*National Health Service Act 1976* came into force, aimed at reducing numbers of pay beds in NHS hospitals and allowing some private practice by consultants. Royal Commission on the National Health Service established. Royal charter granted to College of General Practitioners.
1977	Birth rate at low point. Social Security benefit payments tied to rate of inflation by amendment to *Finance Act* (Rooker-Wise). *NHS Act.* This act consolidated previous legislation about the NHS and defined the functions of the Secretary of State, CHCs and the Health Service Commissioner.
1978	First baby to be conceived extra-utero delivered by caesarean section.
1979	*Nurses, Midwives and Health Visitors Act.* Health Services workers industrial action. London ambulance strike. *Vaccine Damage Payments Act.* Ruling on Sunday Times publication on thalidomide cases. Tax concessions introduced for private health insurance. Members of Lambeth, Southwark and Lewisham Area Health Authority dismissed for decision to defy cash limits. Royal Commission on NHS report published.
1980	*Inequalities in health.* Report of a working party chaired by Sir Douglas Black published but not implemented. *Coroners Act* abolished requirement for the coroner to view the body.

Employment Protection Act increased the rights of full-time employed women to retain their job after maternity leave.

Abortion (Amendment) Bill talked out in House of Commons.

Nurses and midwives' pay rise of 19.6 per cent. Doctors' and dentists' pay rise of 31.4 per cent.

House of Commons Social Services Committee reports on perinatal and neonatal mortality.

Health Services Act to dissolve the Central Health Services Council, dissolve the Health Services Board which had been formed to phase out private beds in NHS hospitals and to disband area health authorities.

Maternity Alliance formed.

Budget (Finance) Act. Child benefit increased to £4.75 per week, inflation linking for 'short term' benefits dropped.

Maternity Services Advisory Committee established.

1981	White Paper on *Government statistical services*. Set out 25 per cent cut in cost of services.
1981–82	Industrial action by registration officers in England and Wales affected quality and completeness of statistics.
1982	NHS reorganised from 1979 White Paper and 1980 *Health Services Act* on April 1. Area tier abolished and 192 districts became main operational authorities. 'Unit' established as the local management tier and professional consultation and planning procedures pruned.
	First report from the Steering Group on Health Services Information published.
1983	The Griffiths Report on NHS management published. Replaced consensus management with general management in the NHS.
1984	United Kingdom Central Council (UKCC) and National Boards for Nursing, Midwifery and Health Visiting set up. The UKCC is the statutory regulatory body and the National Boards take the responsibility for nurse education.
1986	New forms of certificate introduced for certifying stillbirths and neonatal deaths in England and Wales.
1987	Health Education Council published *The health divide* shortly before being abolished in March.
	Maternity grant abolished in April.
	White paper, *Promoting better health* aimed at introducing more competition into primary care.
1988	The Prime Minister, Margaret Thatcher, announced a fundamental review of the NHS.

	DHSS split into the Department of Health and the Department of Social Security.
1989	Channel four documentary *Cooking the books* prompts Royal Statistical Society enquiry into Government Statistical Services.
	NHS Management Executive, later to become the NHS Executive, established.
	Children Act.
	Caring for people: community care in the next decade and beyond published.
	Working for patients white paper published, proposing introduction of NHS internal market.
1990	*National Health Service and Community Care Act* passed to set up internal market and changes in community care.
	Secretary of State announced phased implementation of *Caring for people*.
	Regional health authorities reconstituted with smaller memberships, excluding representatives of local authorities and trades unions.
	District health authorities and special health authorities reconstituted. Family practitioner committees reconstituted as family health services authorities and made accountable to regional health authorities.
1991	NHS internal market began: first wave trusts and 306 fundholding general practices began to operate.
	Department of Health launched Research and Development strategy.
1992	House of Commons Health Committee published report on *Maternity services*.
	Health of the nation white paper published.
	Patients' charter introduced.
	UN Economic Commission for Europe adopted *Fundamental principles of official statistics*.
1993	Expert Maternity Group's report *Changing childbirth* published.
	Redevelopment of OPCS computer systems. Start of computerisation of registration automatic coding of cause of death.
	Implementation of *National Health Service and Community Care Act*. Funding transferred from Department of Social Security to local authorities for those receiving residential and nursing home care. Clients means tested for care and services contracted to private sector.

Statistics Act in the Irish Republic put National Statistics Board on a statutory basis from 1994.

1994 *Changing childbirth* accepted as government policy.

Maternity services charter published.

Publication of the first NHS comparative performance tables.

1995 Code of practice on openness for NHS published.

Central Statistics Office published *Official statistics code of practice*.

April. First wave of total purchasing fund projects established.

1996 April. Office of Population Censuses and Surveys and Central Statistics Office merged to form the Office for National Statistics. Northern Ireland Statistics and Research Agency formed.

The Carers (Recognition and Services) Act 1995 came into force.

Regional health authorities abolished. Eight regional offices of the NHS Executive established. District health authorities and family health services authorities amalgamated in England and 100 new health authorities set up.

New complaints systems introduced.

The *Community Care (Direct Payments) Act 1996* received Royal Assent.

Publication of white paper, *Primary care: the future choice and opportunity*.

Publication of white paper, *A service with ambitions*.

Publication of second primary care white paper *Primary care: delivering the future*.

1997 White papers, *The new NHS* for England, *Putting patients first* for Wales and *Designed to care: renewing the NHS in Scotland*, published.

1998 Government Statistical Service green paper, S*tatistics: a matter of trust* set out alternatives for an independent statistical service.

Consultation document, *Fit for the future* proposing restructuring of health and social services in Northern Ireland, published.

Public health green papers, *Our healthier nation* for England, *Better health: better Wales*, *Working together for a healthier Scotland* and consultation document *Well into 2000* for Northern Ireland, published.

Information for health and *Strategic programme for modernising information management and technology in Scotland*, information strategies for the NHS in England and Scotland, published.

Report of the *Independent enquiry into inequalities in health*, chaired by Sir Donald Acheson, published.

1999   *Better information - better health*, a strategic framework for information management in Wales, published.

Fit for the future – a new approach, published in Northern Ireland, proposing restructuring of trusts, replacement of health and social services boards with health and social care partnerships and abolition of general practitioner fundholding.

General practitioner fundholding scheme ended on April 1 in England, Wales and Scotland. Establishment of primary care groups in England, local health groups in Wales and primary care trusts and local health care co-operatives in Scotland.

Public health white paper for England, *Saving lives: our healthier nation*, published.

White paper *Building trust in statistics* set out plans for changes in official statistics without legislation and the establishment of an independent statistical commission.

Appendix 5:
NHS and local government regions and districts

During the 1990s, many changes took place in the boundaries of the areas used for the administration of health and local government services in the United Kingdom. The main changes are summarised below and illustrated by maps. The Office for National Statistics has published a gazetteer describing the changes in much greater detail:

Office for National Statistics. *Gazetteer of the old and new geographies of the United Kingdom*. London: The Stationery Office, 1999.

England and Wales

The composition of district health authorities changed considerably in the early 1990s with many mergers. In April 1996, the 14 regional health authorities were abolished and superseded by eight regional offices of the Department of Health. Further changes were made in April 1999 to NHS regions in the south east of England to create a regional office for London.

A different set of regions is used for most other types of government statistics. In April 1997, the standard statistical regions of England were replaced by nine government office regions. The composition of all these regions is summarised below.

NHS regional and district health authorities, 1993–5

In Wales, management units are shown for each district health authority.

Northern

1993	Hartlepool, North Tees, South Tees, East Cumbria, South Cumbria, West Cumbria, Northumberland, Gateshead, Newcastle, North Tyneside, South Tyneside, Sunderland, North Durham, South Durham
1994	Northumberland, Newcastle, North Tyneside, Sunderland, North Durham, South Durham, Tees, South of Tyne, North Cumbria
1995	Northumberland, Newcastle and North Tyneside, Sunderland, North Durham, South Durham, Tees, South of Tyne, North Cumbria

Yorkshire

1993–95   East Riding, Grimsby and Scunthorpe, North Yorkshire, Bradford, West Yorkshire, Leeds, Wakefield

Trent

1993   North Derbyshire, Southern Derbyshire, Leicestershire, North Lincolnshire, South Lincolnshire, Nottingham, Barnsley, Doncaster, Rotherham, Sheffield, North Nottinghamshire

1994–95   North Derbyshire, Southern Derbyshire, Leicestershire, Nottingham, Barnsley, Doncaster, Rotherham, Sheffield, North Nottinghamshire, Lincolnshire

East Anglian

1993   Cambridge, North West Anglia, Norwich, Great Yarmouth and Waveney, Huntingdon, Suffolk

1994–95   Cambridge, North West Anglia, Huntingdon, Suffolk, East Norfolk, Bedfordshire

North West Thames

1993   North Bedfordshire, South Bedfordshire, North West Hertfordshire, South West Hertfordshire, Barnet, Hillingdon, East and North Hertfordshire, Brent and Harrow, Ealing Hammersmith and Hounslow, Kensington Chelsea and Westminster

1994–95   North West Hertfordshire, South West Hertfordshire, Barnet, Hillingdon, East and North Hertfordshire, Brent and Harrow, Ealing Hammersmith and Hounslow, Kensington Chelsea and Westminster

North East Thames

1993–95   North Essex, South Essex, Barking and Havering, Redbridge and Waltham Forest, East London and the City, New River, Camden and Islington

South East Thames

1993   South East Kent, Canterbury and Thanet, Dartford and Gravesham, Maidstone, Medway, Tunbridge Wells, Bexley, Greenwich, Bromley, East Sussex, South East London

1994–95   Bexley and Greenwich, East Kent, West Kent, Bromley, East Sussex, South East London

South West Thames

1993   Mid Surrey, East Surrey, Chichester, Mid Downs, Worthing, Croydon, Wandsworth, Merton and Sutton, North West Surrey, South West Surrey, Kingston and Richmond

1994   East Surrey, Chichester, Mid Downs, Worthing, Croydon, North West Surrey, South West Surrey, Merton Sutton and Wandsworth, Mid Surrey, Kingston and Richmond

| 1995 | Croydon, Merton Sutton and Wandsworth, Kingston and Richmond, Western Surrey, Eastern Surrey, West Sussex |

Wessex

| 1993 | Dorset, Portsmouth and South East Hampshire, Southampton and South West Hampshire, Winchester, Basingstoke and North Hampshire, Salisbury, Swindon, Bath, Isle of Wight |
| 1994–95 | Dorset, Portsmouth and South East Hampshire, Southampton and South West Hampshire, North and Mid Hampshire, Wiltshire and Bath, Isle of Wight |

Oxford

| 1993 | East Berkshire, West Berkshire, Buckinghamshire, Kettering, Northampton, Oxfordshire |
| 1994–95 | Berkshire, Buckinghamshire, Northamptonshire, Oxfordshire |

South Western

| 1993 | Bristol and District, Cornwall and Isles of Scilly, Exeter and North Devon, Plymouth and Torbay, Gloucestershire, Somerset |
| 1994–95 | Bristol, Cornwall and Isles of Scilly, Exeter and North Devon, Plymouth and Torbay, Gloucestershire, Somerset |

West Midlands

| 1993 | Herefordshire, Worcester and District, Shropshire, Mid Staffordshire, North Staffordshire, South East Staffordshire, East Birmingham, North Birmingham, West Birmingham, Coventry, Dudley, Sandwell, Solihull, Walsall, Wolverhampton, South Birmingham, North Worcestershire, Warwickshire |
| 1994–95 | Herefordshire, Worcester, Shropshire, North Staffordshire, Coventry, Dudley, Sandwell, Solihull, Walsall, Wolverhampton, South Birmingham, North Worcestershire, South Staffordshire, Warwickshire, North Birmingham |

Mersey

1993	Chester, Crewe, Halton, Macclesfield, Warrington, Liverpool, St Helens and Knowsley, Southport and Formby, South Sefton, Wirral
1994	Chester, South and East Cheshire, North Cheshire, Liverpool, St Helens and Knowsley, Sefton, Wirral
1995	North Cheshire, South Cheshire, Liverpool, St Helens and Knowsley, Sefton, Wirral

North Western

| 1993 | Lancaster, Blackpool, Wyre and Fylde, Preston, Blackburn Hyndburn and Ribble Valley, Burnley, Pendle and |

	Rossendale, West Lancashire, Chorley and South Ribble, Bolton, Bury, North Manchester, South Manchester, Central Manchester, Oldham, Rochdale, Salford, Stockport, Tameside and Glossop, Trafford, Wigan
1994	Bolton, Stockport, Wigan, North West Lancashire, East Lancashire, South Lancashire, Bury and Rochdale, West Pennine, Manchester, Salford and Trafford, Morecambe Bay
1995	Stockport, North West Lancashire, East Lancashire, South Lancashire, Wigan and Bolton, Bury and Rochdale, West Pennine, Manchester, Salford and Trafford, Morecambe Bay

Wales

District health authorities and management units

Clwyd

| 1993–95 | North Clwyd, South Clwyd |

Gwent

| 1993–95 | North Gwent, South Gwent |

Gwynedd

| 1993–95 | Aberconwy, Arfon, Dwyfor, Meirionydd, Anglesey |

Mid Glamorgan

| 1993–95 | Merthyr Cynon, Ogwr, Rhondda, Rhymney, Taff-Ely |

Powys

| 1993 | Radnor and Montgomery, Brecknock |
| 1994–95 | Brecknock, Montgomery, Radnor |

South Glamorgan

| 1993–95 | South Glamorgan |

West Glamorgan

| 1993–95 | West Glamorgan (East District Hospitals), West Glamorgan (North and West District Hospitals) |

The remainder of Wales was composed of the following health areas over the years 1993–95:

Pembrokeshire

| 1993–94 | Pembrokeshire |

East Dyfed

| 1993–94 | Carmarthen-Dinefwr, Ceredigion, Llanelli-Dinefwr |

Dyfed

| 1995 | Carmarthen-Dinefwr, Ceredigion, Llanelli-Dinefwr, Pembrokeshire |

NHS Executive regional office areas and district health authorities, from 1 April 1996 onwards

April 1996 onwards
Northern and Yorkshire
Bradford, Calderdale and Kirklees, County Durham, East Riding, Gateshead and South Tyneside, Leeds, Newcastle and North Tyneside, North Cumbria, Northumberland, North Yorkshire, Sunderland, Tees, Wakefield

Trent
Barnsley, Doncaster, Leicestershire, Lincolnshire, North Derbyshire, North Nottinghamshire, Nottingham, Rotherham, Sheffield, South Humber, Southern Derbyshire

West Midlands
Birmingham, Coventry, Dudley, Herefordshire, North Staffordshire, Sandwell, Shropshire, Solihull, South Staffordshire, Walsall, Warwickshire, Wolverhampton, Worcestershire

North West
Bury and Rochdale, East Lancashire, Liverpool, Manchester, Morecambe Bay, North Cheshire, North West Lancashire, St Helens and Knowsley, Salford and Trafford, Sefton, South Cheshire, South Lancashire, Stockport, West Pennine, Wigan and Bolton, Wirral

Wales
Bro Taf, Dyfed Powys, Gwent, Morgannwg, North Wales

April 1996 – April 1999
Anglia and Oxford
Bedfordshire, Berkshire, Buckinghamshire, Cambridge and Huntingdon, East Norfolk, Northamptonshire, North West Anglia, Oxfordshire, Suffolk

North Thames
Barking, Barnet, Brent and Harrow, Camden and Islington, Ealing Hammersmith and Hounslow, East and North Hertfordshire, East London and The City, Enfield and Haringey, Hillingdon, Kensington, Chelsea and Westminster, North Essex, Redbridge and Waltham Forest, South Essex, West Hertfordshire

South Thames
Bexley and Greenwich, Bromley, Croydon, East Kent, East Surrey, East Sussex Brighton and Hove, Kingston and Richmond, Lambeth Southwark and Lewisham, Merton Sutton and Wandsworth, West Kent, West Surrey, West Sussex

South and West

Avon, Cornwall and Isles of Scilly, Dorset, Gloucestershire, Isle of Wight, North and East Devon, North and Mid Hampshire, Portsmouth and South East Hampshire, Somerset, Southampton and South West Hampshire, South and West Devon, Wiltshire

April 1999 onwards

The four regions in the south and east of England were reorganised in April 1999 to form a single region for London and three other regions.

London

Barking, Barnet, Brent and Harrow, Camden and Islington, Ealing Hammersmith and Hounslow, East London and The City, Enfield and Haringey, Hillingdon, Kensington, Chelsea and Westminster, Redbridge and Waltham Forest, Bexley and Greenwich, Bromley, Croydon, Kingston and Richmond, Lambeth Southwark and Lewisham, Merton Sutton and Wandsworth

South East

Berkshire, Buckinghamshire, Northamptonshire, Oxfordshire, East Kent, East Surrey, East Sussex, Brighton and Hove, West Kent, West Surrey, West Sussex, Isle of Wight, North and Mid Hampshire, Portsmouth and South East Hampshire, Southampton and South West Hampshire

Eastern

Bedfordshire, Cambridge and Huntingdon, East Norfolk, North West Anglia, Suffolk, East and North Hertfordshire, North Essex, South Essex, West Hertfordshire

South West

Avon, Cornwall and Isles of Scilly, Dorset, Gloucestershire, North and East Devon, Somerset, South and West Devon, Wiltshire

Standard statistical regions 1974–97

These standard statistical regions of England and Wales, were constituted on 1 April 1974 and are used for some tables in Volume 2. They are listed here in terms of counties.

North

Cleveland, Cumbria, Durham, Northumberland, Tyne and Wear

Yorkshire and Humberside

Humberside, North Yorkshire, South Yorkshire, West Yorkshire

East Midlands

Derbyshire, Leicestershire, Lincolnshire, Northamptonshire, Nottinghamshire

East Anglia

Cambridgeshire, Norfolk, Suffolk

South East

Bedfordshire, Berkshire, Buckinghamshire, East Sussex, Greater London, Hampshire, Hertfordshire, Isle of Wight, Kent, Oxfordshire, Surrey, West Sussex

South West

Avon, Cornwall and Isles of Scilly, Devon, Dorset, Gloucestershire, Somerset, Wiltshire

West Midlands

Hereford and Worcester, Shropshire, Staffordshire, Warwickshire, West Midlands

North West

Cheshire, Greater Manchester, Lancashire, Merseyside

Wales

Clwyd, Dyfed, Gwent, Gwynedd, Mid Glamorgan, Powys, South Glamorgan, West Glamorgan

Government office regions, from 1 April 1997

These regions have been used for England since April 1997, and are used in some tables in Volume 2. They are composed of metropolitan and non-metropolitan counties.

North East

Cleveland, Durham, Northumberland, Tyne and Wear

North West and Merseyside

Cheshire, Cumbria, Greater Manchester, Lancashire, Merseyside

Yorkshire and the Humber

Humberside, North Yorkshire, South Yorkshire, West Yorkshire

East Midlands

Derbyshire, Leicestershire, Lincolnshire, Northamptonshire, Nottinghamshire

West Midlands

Hereford and Worcester, Shropshire, Staffordshire, Warwickshire, West Midlands

South West

Avon, Cornwall, Devon, Dorset, Gloucestershire, Somerset, Wiltshire

Eastern

Bedfordshire, Cambridgeshire, Essex, Hertfordshire, Norfolk, Suffolk

London

Greater London

South East

Berkshire, Buckinghamshire, East Sussex, Hampshire, Isle of Wight, Kent, Oxfordshire, Surrey, West Sussex

Scotland

Health board and council areas, from 1 April 1996 onwards

The Local Government etc (Scotland) Act 1994 provided for a new structure of 29 single tier councils to replace the existing 53 District and 9 Regional Councils on 1 April 1996. The 3 Island Councils, Orkney Islands, Shetland Isles and Western Isles, remained unchanged.

Argyll and Clyde

Argyll and Bute, East Renfrewshire (part), Inverclyde, Renfrewshire, West Dunbartonshire (part)

Ayrshire and Arran

East Ayrshire, North Ayrshire, South Ayrshire

Borders

Scottish Borders

Dumfries and Galloway

Dumfries and Galloway

Fife

Fife

Forth Valley

Clackmannanshire, Falkirk, Stirling

Grampian

Aberdeen City, Aberdeenshire, Moray

Greater Glasgow

East Dunbartonshire, East Renfrewshire (part), Glasgow City, North Lanarkshire (part), South Lanarkshire (part), West Dunbartonshire (part)

Highland

Highland

Lanarkshire

North Lanarkshire (part), South Lanarkshire (part)

Lothian

East Lothian, City of Edinburgh, Midlothian, West Lothian

Orkney

Orkney Islands

Shetland

Shetland Islands

Tayside

Angus, Dundee City, Perth and Kinross

Western Isles

Western Isles

Health and social services board areas in Northern Ireland, from April 1974 onwards

At the time of going to press, Northern Ireland has four health and social services boards and 26 local government districts. These are listed below.

In March 1999, the Department of Health and Social Services published a document, *Fit for the future – a new approach,* which proposed abolishing health and social services boards and replacing them with five new health and social care partnerships. It did not set out proposals for the areas which these might cover. Legislation on this will take place in the Northern Ireland Assembly, now that it is established.

Eastern Board

Ards, Belfast, Castlereagh, Down, Lisburn, North Down

Northern Board

Antrim, Ballymena, Ballymoney, Carrickfergus, Coleraine, Cookstown, Larne, Magherafelt, Moyle, Newtownabbey

Southern Board

Armagh, Banbridge, Craigavon, Dungannon, Newry and Mourne

Western Board

Fermanagh, Limavady, Derry, Ormagh, Strabane

Irish Republic

The Irish Republic has eight health boards. The Eastern Board is due to be subdivided at the end of 1999.

North-Eastern

Meath, Cavan, Monaghan, Louth

North-Western

Donegal, Sligo, Leitrim

Eastern

Dublin County Borough, Fingal, Dublin Belgard, Dun Laoghaire Rathdown, Kildare, Wicklow

Midland

Offaly, Laois, Longford, Westmeath

Mid-Western

Limerick County Borough, Limerick, Clare, Tipperary North Riding

South-Eastern

Kilkenny, Wexford, Waterford County Borough, Waterford, Tipperary South Riding, Carlow

Southern

Cork County Borough, Cork, Kerry

West

Galway County Borough, Galway, Mayo, Roscommon

NHS Regional health authorities before 1996

NHS Regional office areas, 1993 to 1996

417

Health board areas in Scotland, 1996 onwards and regional office areas in England, 1999 onwards

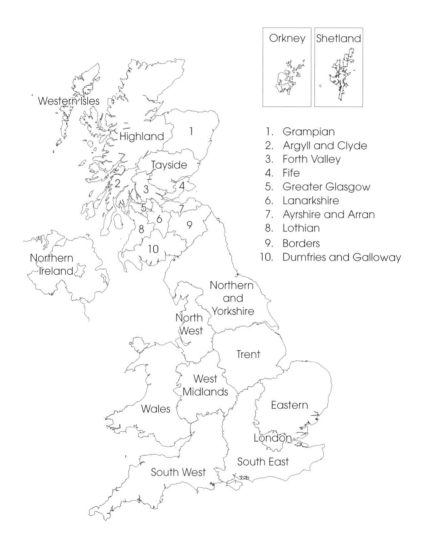

Orkney Shetland

1. Grampian
2. Argyll and Clyde
3. Forth Valley
4. Fife
5. Greater Glasgow
6. Lanarkshire
7. Ayrshire and Arran
8. Lothian
9. Borders
10. Dumfries and Galloway

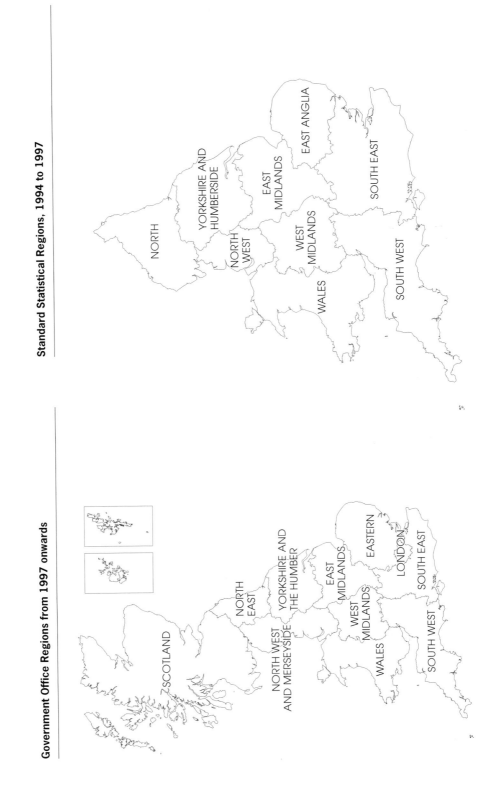

Government Office Regions from 1997 onwards

SCOTLAND

NORTH EAST

NORTH WEST AND MERSEYSIDE

YORKSHIRE AND THE HUMBER

EAST MIDLANDS

WEST MIDLANDS

WALES

EASTERN

LONDON

SOUTH EAST

SOUTH WEST

Standard Statistical Regions, 1994 to 1997

NORTH

YORKSHIRE AND HUMBERSIDE

NORTH WEST

WEST MIDLANDS

EAST MIDLANDS

EAST ANGLIA

WALES

SOUTH WEST

SOUTH EAST

Appendix 6:

Medical certificates of cause of death and stillbirth and 'draft entries' of live birth, stillbirth and death used in England and Wales, 1999

SB 682249

MEDICAL CERTIFICATE OF STILL-BIRTH

(Births and Deaths Registration Act 1953, S 11(1), as amended by the Population (Statistics) Act 1960)
(Form prescribed by the Registration of Births and Deaths Regulations 1987.)

Registered at
Entry No.

To be given only in respect of a child which has issued forth from its mother after the 24th week of pregnancy and which did not at any time after being completely expelled from its mother breathe or show any other signs of life.

*I was present at the still-birth of a *male / *female child born

*I have examined the body of a *male / *female child which I am informed and believe was born

on .... day of .... 19 ...... to .... (NAME OF MOTHER)

at ....
(PLACE OF BIRTH)

{ 1 The certified cause of death has been confirmed by post-mortem.
2 Post-mortem information may be available later.
3 Post-mortem not being held.

*Strike out the words which do not apply.
†Ring appropriate digit.

Weight of fetus .... grams
Estimated duration of pregnancy ....
State (a) the number of weeks of delivery
(b) When the child died
(i) before labour*
(ii) during labour*
(iii) not known*

CAUSE OF DEATH

a. Main diseases or conditions in fetus ....

b. Other diseases or conditions in fetus ....

c. Main maternal diseases or conditions affecting fetus ....

d. Other maternal diseases or conditions affecting fetus ....

e. Other relevant causes ....

I hereby certify that (i) the child was not born alive, and
(ii) to the best of my knowledge and belief the cause of death and the estimated duration of pregnancy of the mother were as stated above.

Signature .... Date ....

Qualification as registered by General Medical Council, or }
Registered No. as Registered Midwife. ....

Address ....

For still-births in hospital: please give the name of the consultant responsible for the care of the mother

THIS IS NOT AN AUTHORITY FOR BURIAL OR CREMATION [SEE OVER]

SB 682249

COUNTERFOIL

For use of Medical Practitioner or Midwife, who should complete in all cases.

Name of mother ....

Date of still-birth ....

Place of still-birth ....

Post mortem† 1 2 3

Weight of fetus .... grams

Duration of pregnancy .... weeks

Death occurred before labour*/during labour*/not known* ....

Cause of death

a ....

b ....

c ....

d ....

e ....

Date of certification ....

Certificate issued to (name) ....

of (address) ....

*Strike out the words which do not apply
†Ring appropriate digit

421

MED B 121434

BIRTHS AND DEATHS REGISTRATION ACT 1953

(Form prescribed by the Registration of Births, Deaths and Marriages (Amendment) (No. 2) Regulations 1985)

MEDICAL CERTIFICATE OF CAUSE OF DEATH OF A LIVE-BORN CHILD DYING WITHIN THE FIRST TWENTY-EIGHT DAYS OF LIFE

For use only by a Registered Medical Practitioner WHO HAS BEEN IN ATTENDANCE during the deceased's last illness, and to be delivered by him forthwith to the Registrar of Births and Deaths.

Registrar to enter
No. of Death Entry

Name of child

Date of death .... day of 19

Age at death .... Sex

Place of death .... days (complete period of 24 hours) .... hours

Place of birth

Last seen alive by me .... day of 19

1 The certified cause of death has been confirmed by post-mortem.
2 Information from post-mortem may be available later.
3 Post-mortem not being held.
4 I have reported this death to the Coroner for further action.
   [See overleaf]

Please ring
appropriate
digit and ...

a Seen after death by me.
b Seen after death by another medical practitioner but not by me.
c Not seen after death by a medical practitioner.

SPECIMEN

CAUSE OF DEATH

a. Main diseases or conditions in infant

b. Other diseases or conditions in infant

c. Main maternal diseases or conditions affecting infant

d. Other maternal diseases or conditions affecting infant

e. Other relevant causes

I hereby certify that I was in medical attendance during the above named deceased's last illness, and that the particulars and cause of death above written are true to the best of my knowledge and belief.

Signature

Address

Qualifications as registered
by General Medical Council

Date

For deaths in hospital: Please give the name of the consultant responsible for the above-named as a patient

MED A 22 482353

BIRTHS AND DEATHS REGISTRATION ACT 1953

(Form prescribed by the Registration of Births and Deaths Regulations 1987)

MEDICAL CERTIFICATE OF CAUSE OF DEATH

For use only by a Registered Medical Practitioner WHO HAS BEEN IN ATTENDANCE during the deceased's last illness,
and to be delivered by him forthwith to the Registrar of Births and Deaths.

Name of deceased ....

Date of death as stated to me .... day of .... Age as stated to me ....

Place of death .... day of ....

Last seen alive by me ....

1 The certified cause of death takes account of information
obtained from post-mortem.

2 Information from post-mortem may be available later.

3 Post-mortem not being held.

4 I have reported this death to the Coroner for further action.

[See overleaf]

*Please ring
appropriate
digit(s) and letter*

a Seen after death by me.

b Seen after death by another medical practitioner
but not by me.

c Not seen after death by a medical practitioner.

CAUSE OF DEATH

*The condition thought to be the 'Underlying Cause of Death' should
appear in the lowest completed line of Part I.*

SPECIMEN

I (a) Disease or condition directly
leading to death†

....

(b) Other disease or condition, if any,
leading to I(a)

....

(c) Other disease or condition, if any,
leading to I(b)

....

II Other significant conditions
CONTRIBUTING TO THE DEATH but
not related to the disease or condition
causing it.

....

*These particulars not to be
entered in death register*

Approximate interval
between onset and death

The death might have been due to or contributed to by the employment followed at some time by the deceased.

Please tick
where applicable

†*This does not mean the mode of dying, such as heart failure, asphyxia, asthenia, etc: it means the disease, injury, or complication which caused death.*

**I hereby certify that I was in medical
attendance during the above named
deceased's last illness, and that the
particulars and cause of death above
written are true to the best of my
knowledge and belief.**

Signature ....

Residence ....

Qualifications as registered
by General Medical Council

Date ....

For deaths in hospital: Please give the name of the consultant responsible for the above-named as a patient ....

423

BIRTH

GRO Reference No.

District & SD Nos.

Register No.

Entry No.

CONFIDENTIAL PARTICULARS

The particulars below, required under the Population (Statistics) Acts, will not be entered in the register. This confidential information will be used only for the preparation and supply of statistical information by the Registrar General.

Date of registration

1. Where the father's name is entered in register:
   Father's date of birth — DAY MONTH YEAR

2. In all cases:
   Mother's date of birth — DAY MONTH YEAR

3. Where the child is born within marriage:
   (i) Date of marriage — MONTH YEAR
   (ii) Has the mother been married more than once? YES NO
   (iii) Mother's previous children (excluding birth or births now being registered) by her present husband and any former husband
   (a) Number born alive (including any who have died)
   (b) Number still-born

X Is this birth one of twins, triplets, etc? YES NO

If YES, complete (a) and (b)
(a) Total number of live and still-births at this maternity*

Live births — (b) Entry No. of births
Still-births — (b) Entry No. of births

Edit Control

*Tick as appropriate

FORM 309 (Rev)

grams

F*

title

(i) (ii) (iii) (iv)

G(a) Father

(va)

H(a)* 1 2 3 4 5

G(b) Mother

(vb)

H(b)* 1 2 3 4 5

POSTCODE

(vi)

BIRTH

Registration district

Register No.

District & S. Dist. Nos.

Administrative area

Entry No.

Sub-district

CHILD

1. Date and place of birth

2. Name and surname

3. Sex

FATHER

4. Name and surname

5. Place of birth

6. Occupation

MOTHER

7. Name and surname

8.(a) Place of birth

8.(b) Occupation

9.(a) Maiden surname

9.(b) Surname at marriage if different from maiden surname

10. Usual address (if different from place of child's birth)

INFORMANT

11. Name and surname (if not the mother or father)

12. Qualification

13. Usual address (if different from that in 10 above)

SPECIMEN

14. I certify that the particulars entered above are true to the best of my knowledge and belief

Signature of informant

15. Date of registration

16. Signature of registrar

NHS Number

OA185 4/94

FORM 309 (Rev)

424

'Draft entry' of stillbirth registration

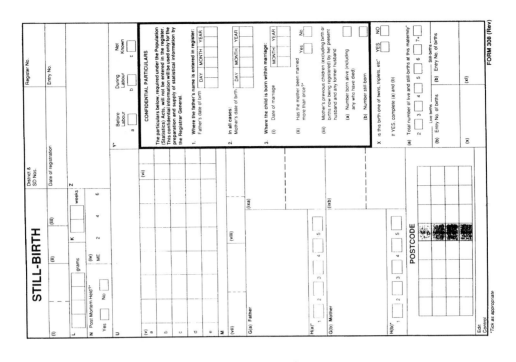

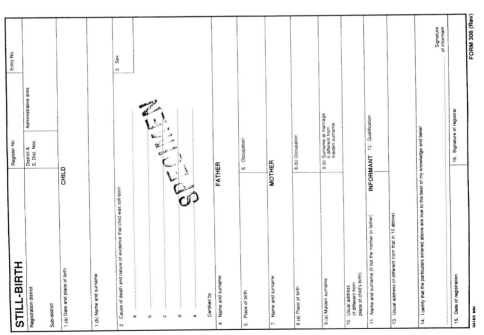

DEATH

Register No.

District & SD Nos

Register No.

Date of registration

D

CONFIDENTIAL PARTICULARS

The particulars below, required under the Population (Statistics) Acts, will not be entered in the register. This confidential information will be used only for the preparation and supply of statistical information by the Registrar General.

At date of death deceased was:

If married insert date of birth of spouse

Day Month Year

Single 1
Married 2
Widowed 3
Divorced 4
Not known 5

E
• 6 months or over
• Under 6 months
(i)
(ii)
(iii)

Z

POSTCODE

G(a) Deceased or †Mother

H(a)* 1 2 3 4 5
G(b) Husband or †Father
H(b)* 1 2 3 4 5

F *
title

(iv)
(v)
(vi)
(vii)
(viii)

J

R Last seen alive
S * Seen or Not Seen after death
a b
T Referred to Coroner by
1 Doctor 2 Registrar

Day Month Year

B SD Enq
Yes 1 No 2
(vii)

1 2 3 4 5 6 ME 2

N • Post Mortem
Yes (ix) a b c
No d e

W • Employment

Edit control

M

† If deceased is under 16 years of age
* Tick as appropriate

Computerised FORM 310(Rev)

DEATH

Register No.

Entry No

Registration district

District & S Dist. Nos

Administrative area

Sub-district

1 Date and place of death

2 Name and surname

3 Sex
4 Maiden surname of woman who has married

5 Date and place of birth

6 Occupation and usual address

7 (a) Name and surname of informant

(b) Qualification

(c) Usual address

8 Cause of death
(a)
(b)
(c)
II

SPECIMEN

Certified by

9 I certify that the particulars given by me above are true to the best of my knowledge and belief

Signature of informant

10 Date of registration

11 Signature of registrar

O NHS No

Q (age)

DA182 1992

Computerised FORM 310(Rev)

Index

eye problems, A9.4.1, A9.4.2
  see also — visual impairment

Faculty of Public Health Medicine, 363
  address, 363
Family census 1946, 48–49, 120–121
Family expenditure survey, 317
Family formation survey, 93, 99, 103, 121
family health services registers, 28
family planning — see birth control
Family Planning Act 1967, 94
Family Planning Association, 95
  address, 368
Family practitioners — see general
  practitioners
Family Record Centre, 349
family size, 48–49, A5.14.1–A5.15.1
  see also — parity
family type, A5.14.1–A5.15.1, A5.19.2,
  A5.27.1, A5.29.2
Farr, William, facing 1, 39, 42–44, 67–70, 115,
  173–174, 195, 220, 263, 271, 279–280,
  338, 341
father:
  age, 24, 140–142
  country of birth, 137–138
  income, 150–153
  occupation, 24, 146–147
  social class, 116–129, A5.1.1–A5.7.1
  stature, 143
  see also — parents
Fédération Internationale de Gynécologie et
  d'Obstétrique, (FIGO), 16, 206
feeding of babies, 229–231, A7.28.1–A7.28.5
fees for medical care:
  contraceptive services, 95
  in 19th century, 308
  private care, 215–216, 319
  to GPs for maternity services, 213, 312–313,
  A11.3.2, A11.4.3
fertility, 47–50, 92–93, 107, 120–121, 143
  age of mother, 47, 49, 140–142,
  A3.2.1–A3.2.5
  decline in 1930s and 1940s, 47–49, 92
  geographical differences, 70–76, A3.14.1
  international differences, A12.1.1
  mother's education, 148–149
  recent trends, 49–50, 107
  reproductive hazards, 146–147
  social class, 116, 118, 120–121
  total period fertility rates, 49, 143
fertility control — see birth control, abortion,
  induced
fetal death,
  WHO definition, 9
  late fetal death — see stillbirth
  see also — stillbirth, abortion, miscarriage
fetal loss — see miscarriage, abortion,
  stillbirth, fetal death
fetal monitors, 204
FIGO — see Fédération Internationale de
  Gynécologie et d'Obstétrique

financial statistics, 307–321, A11.11.1–A11.6.1
  central government, 309–321
  local authorities, 315–316
  NHS, 310–315, A11.2.1–A11.4.3
  capital expenditure, 311, 315, A11.2.1
  maternity services, 313–315
  staff, 311–312, A11.3.2–A11.4.3
finished consultant episodes, 30, A7.14.3,
  A7.14.4
flying squads, 204–205
folic acid, 217, 255
folklore:
  abortifacients, 90
  day of week of birth, 65
  death of Queen Jane Seymour, 275
  gender of baby, 173
  month of birth, 61
  multiple births, 178
  unwanted pregnancy, 89–90
  weighing babies, 165
food:
  consumption and expenditure, 153, A5.32.1
  during second world war, 51–52
  toxic substances in, 148
forceps, 225–226, A7.20.1–A7.22.1
function, definition, 15

gender of baby — see sex of baby
General Household Survey, 32–33, 34, 97, 99,
  102, 136, 142, 144, 151, 153, 257, 270,
  319, A4.6.2–A4.6.7, A4.12.1–A4.12.2,
  A5.14.1–A5.14.3, A5.27.1, A5.29.1,
  A5.29.2
General Practice Research Database, 35,
  268–269, 295–296, A9.4.1, A9.4.2,
  A10.12.1, A10.12.2
general practitioners, 33–35, 95–100, 213,
  264–270, A7.10.1
  antenatal care, 213, 218–219
  care following miscarriage, 106
  care of children, 264–270, A9.4.1, A9.4.2
  computer systems, 35, 268–269, 295–296,
  339, 343
  contraceptive services, 95–99, 213
  delivery, 213, A7.18.2
  fees for maternity care, 213, 314–315,
  A7.10.2, A11.3.2, A11.4.3
  GP maternity units, 199–202, 222–223,
  A7.1.1, A7.2.1–A7.2.4, A7.14.2,
  A7.15.2–A7.17.1, A7.25.2
  hospital appointments, 211–212
  notification of communicable diseases, 33,
  264–265
  postnatal care, 213, 227–228, 295–296,
  A10.12.1, A10.12.2
  subfertility, 217, A7.11.1
  vasectomy done by, 101
  see also — Royal College of General
  Practitioners, National Morbidity Survey,
  General Practice Research Database
General Register Office, England and Wales,
  42, 70, 116, 195, 220, 263, 280, 374, 375, 381

Common Services Agency for the NHS in Scotland (ISD), 16, 24–26, 31, 264–265, 294, 297–298
    formerly Information Services Division
    address, 353
    publications, 353
information strategies, 3, 197, 232, 341
infusion pumps, 204
insemination, timing within menstrual cycle, 178
instrumental delivery, 224–226, A7.20.1–A7.22.1
    forceps, 225–226
    vacuum extraction, or ventouse 225–226
insurance:
    of babies in 19th century, 91
    private health insurance, 319
intensive care:
    cots for, 202–204, A7.3.1–A7.3.3
    definition, 202–204
Interdepartmental Committee on Abortion, Report 1939, 92, 106, 281
Interdepartmental Committee on Physical Deterioration, 45
internal market, 314, 339, 340
International classification of diseases (ICD), 7–13, 15–16, 57–59, 168, 276–278, 373
    bridge coding, 57, 128
    eighth revision, 11, 13, 57–58, 278
    maternal deaths, 276–278
    ninth revision, 7, 11, 13, 16, 57–59, 168, 276, 278
    tenth revision, 7, 9–11, 13, 15, 58–59, 168, 276, 278
International classification of impairments, activities and participation, 15
International classification of impairments, disabilities and handicaps, 14–15, 244
International Clearing House for Birth Defects Monitoring Systems, 330, 357
International collaborating effort on birthweight plurality, perinatal and infant mortality (ICE), 58–59, 328
international comparisons, 327–332, A12.1.1–A12.6.2
    accuracy and completeness of data, 328–329
    birthweight, 330
    congenital anomalies 330
    infant mortality, 327–332, A12.1.2, A12.2.1, A12.2.2, A12.3.2
    maternal mortality, 327–329, A12.1.1
    stillbirths, A12.3.1, A12.4.1
    use of WHO definitions, 328
International confederation of midwives, 206
international organisations, 327–332
    address, 357–360
internet addresses, 347–371
interpreters, 214
intrauterine devices, 95–99, A4.2.1–A4.2.3, A4.6.2, A4.6.3
in-vitro fertilisation — see assisted conception
Ireland, 18–19, 42, 105, 137–140, 177, 265, 298, 357, 420

Northern, 18–19, 105, 177, 196, 297, 298, 354–355, 415
Republic of, 19, 105, 177, 265, 298, 328, 355–356, 415–416
ISD — see Information and Statistics Division
Isle of Man, 19, 105, 355
item of service payments — see fees
IUDs — see intrauterine devices
IVF — see assisted conception

Jarman index, 154
Jersey, States of, 105, 355
Jones, Ian, 118
Joseph Rowntree Foundation, 316

Kerr, Munro, 327
KH03 hospital return, 199–204
Kinloch, Parlane, 281
Körner, Edith, 30, 193
Körner Committee — see Steering Group on Health Services Information
KP70 hospital return, 228

labour, A7.23.1
    beds for, 202
    induction of, 224, 226, A7.19.1, A7.20.4, A7.22.1
        artificial rupture of the membranes, 225
        oxytocin, 225
    procedures during, 224–226
    transfer to hospital during, 223–224
Labour Force Survey, 139
Lancashire:
    abortion in early 20th century, 92
    maternal mortality, 284
Lane Committee, 104, 107, 197
last menstrual period, 10
late neonatal mortality — see mortality, neonatal
learning disabilities, 243–248
legitimacy — see marriage, marital status
letters of enquiry about death certificates, 280, 284
Lewis Faning, Ernest, 93, 98, 102, 107
LHS 27/1 low birthweight return, 55, 169
linkage — see record linkage
Lister, Thomas, 42
live births, 24, 25, 28, A3.1.1–A3.1.8, A3.3.1–A3.3.7, A5.20.6, A5.22.6, A5.23.1, A6.13.1–A6.13.3, A12.1.2
    birthweight, 27, 55–56, 165–172, A3.4.1, A3.4.2, A3.4.4, A5.2.1–A5.3.4, A6.1.1
    burial as stillborn in 19th century, 43–44
    country of birth of mother, 24, 137–138, 143, A5.16.1–A5.18.2
    draft entry, 424
    geographical differences, 128–129, A3.12.1–A3.12.5, A3.13.4, A3.14.1, A3.16.1, A3.16.2
    gestational age, A6.3.1–A6.5.1

multiple cause coding of deaths and stillbirths, 58–59
Munro, Aeneas, 310
mutism, 243–248

National Assembly for Wales, 24, 25, 29, 252
  formerly the Welsh Office, 29, 377, 383
  address, 252
  publications, 252
National Assistance Act 1948, 249, 250, 253
National Audit Office, 384
National Birthday Trust Fund, 224
National Casemix Office, 17
National Centre for Social Research, 32
National Congenital Anomaly Surveillance System, 254–255
National Congenital Rubella Surveillance Programme, 256, A8.7.1
National Council for Voluntary Organisations, 216
  address, 370
National Health Service, 2, 191, 193, 197–213, A11.2.1–A11.4.3
  cost of maternity care to, 310–315
  internal market, 3, 314
  facilities provided in, 197–205
  provision of birth control, 94–95
  provision of sterilisation, 100
  reorganisation, 18, 95, 193, 232, 315, 407–412
  underlying principles, 95, 191
National Health Service Act 1977, 26
National Health Service administrative returns — see administrative returns
National Health Service and Community Care Act 1990, 214, 314, 315
National Health Service Central Register, 27, 28, 147
National Health Service (Family Planning) Amendment Act 1972, 100
National Health Service Information Authority, 17
National Health Service numbers, 27, 28, 31, 196, 219, 232, 294, 342
National Health Service pay and prices index, 309, A11.1.1
National Health Service trusts, 193, 199, 314
National Institute for Clinical Excellence (NICE), 198
National Insurance Act 1911, 308
National Insurance benefits, 33, 34, 308, 320
National Morbidity Survey — see Morbidity Statistics from General Practice
National Perinatal Epidemiology Unit, 253, 269
  address, 362
National Registry of Childhood Tumours, 269
National Statistics socio–economic class, 20–21, 119–120, 124–126, 374
National Study of Triplet and Higher Order Births, 182, 219
neonatal care, 196, 197–199, 212, 229, 316, A7.26.1–A7.26.4
  and impairment, 243–244
  cost of, 315
  cots for, 202–204, A7.3.1–A7.3.3
  definitions, 202–204
  standards, 197–199
  see also — postnatal care, special care baby units
neonatal mortality — see mortality neonatal
Neonatal Nurses Association, 212
  address, 363
neonatal period, definition 9, 11
neonatal record, Scotland, SMR11, 27, 31, 170, 173, 196, 229
neural tube defects, 174, 255, 330, A8.4.1–A8.6.1
  anencephaly, 174, 255, A8.5.1
  hydrocephalus, 255
  spina bifida, 255
'New commonwealth', 137, 289
Newman, George, 44, 46, 74, 166
Newsholme, Arthur, 46, 195, 263, 264, 271, 344
NHS — see National Health Service
NICE — see National Institute for Clinical Excellence
Nightingale, Florence, facing 1, 4, 165, 191, 195, 279–280
nipple problems, A7.23.1, A7.28.3, A10.12.1, A10.12.2
non–NHS care — see private practice, armed forces
'Nordic–Baltic' classification, 59
Northern Ireland Assembly, 18
Northern Ireland Executive, 24
Northern Ireland Statistics and Research Agency (NISRA), 23, 24, 354
  address, 354
Norway, 172
notification of births, 25, 26–27, 34, 55, 168, 170, 338
Notification of Births Act 1907, 168, 192
Notification of Births (Extension) Act 1915, 168, 192
nurseries, 205, 320, A7.4.1
nurses, 311
  in hospital maternity departments, 209, A7.6.1–A7.6.3, A11.4.1
  working hours, 206
  see also — health visitors
nutrition — see food

Obstetric Anaesthetists Association, 197, 198
obstetric units — see maternity units
obstetricians, 201, 211, 311, A7.8.1, A7.8.2, A7.18.2
  consultants, 211, A7.8.2
  paragraph 94 appointments, 211, A7.8.2
  see also — Royal College of Obstetricians and Gynaecologists
obstetrics:
  antenatal care, 218–219, A7.13.1–A7.14.2

442

see also — multiple births
trusts — see National Health Service trusts
twins, 179–182, A6.11.1–A6.11.4, A6.13.2
  see also — multiple births

UKCC — see United Kingdom Central
  Council for Nursing, Midwifery and
  Health Visiting
ultrasound, 204, 219
underlying cause of death, 58
under–reporting,
  birth registration in 19th century, 43–47, 91
  congenital anomalies, 254
  disability, 243–248
  international differences, 328–329
  multiple births, 179
  past use of birth control, 97
  sexually transmitted diseases, 298
unemployment, 150, A5.29.1, A5.29.2, A5.32.1
  social classification of unemployed people,
    131–132
UNICEF, 327–331, 358
  address, 358
unit of medical time (UMT), 210–211
United Kingdom:
  definition, 18
  births to women born in, A5.16.1, A5.16.2
United Kingdom Central Council for Nursing,
  Midwifery and Health Visiting (UKCC),
  207, A7.5.8
  address, 362
United Nations, 328
  Population Commission, 327
  Population Fund, 358
United States, National Centers for Health
  Statistics, 331, 359
  address, 359
uterus:
  cancer of, 298–299, A10.7.1–A10.8.1,
    A10.10.1
  rupture of, A10.4.2

vaccination, 27, 231, 256, 265,
  A7.31.1–A7.31.4
  measles, mumps and rubella (MMR), 266
  rubella, 256
vacuum aspiration, 105, A4.16.1
vacuum extraction, 225–226, A7.20.1, A7.20.3
vagina:
  cancer of, A10.10.1
  infection, A10.12.1, A10.12.2
VAMP database, 268
  see also — General Practice Research
    Database
vasectomy, 100–102, A4.6.2, A4.6.3,
  A4.9.1–A4.9.3, A7.22.1
venereal diseases — see sexually transmitted
  diseases
ventouse — see vacuum extraction
very low birthweight, definition 10
viability, 166

visual impairment, 243–250, 256, A8.1.1,
  A8.1.3
  see also — retinopathy of prematurity
voluntary organisations, 216
  addresses, 366–371

Wales, 196
  see also — National Assembly for Wales
war:
  Boer war, unfitness of recruits for, 45,
    247–248, 343
  first world war:
    decline in early neonatal mortality, 52
    fitness of recruits, 343
    increase in sex ratio after, 175
  second world war:
    conditions of evacuees, 343
    Emergency Medical Services, 195
    increase in sex ratio after, 175
    reasons for decline in stillbirths during,
      50–51
wealth, 117
weather, 64
web sites, 347–371
weddings — see marriage
weekends:
  deficit of births, 65–67
  incidence of low birthweight, 67
  mortality, 66–67
welfare foods, 320
'well babies', 228, A7.14.3, A7.14.4
Welsh Board of Health, 193
Welsh Office — see National Assembly for
  Wales
West Indies — see Caribbean
Whitehead, Margaret, 118
Whitehouse, Beckwith, 92
whooping cough, 231, 265–266, A7.31.1,
  A7.31.4, A9.1.1
whole–time equivalent, 206
Wigglesworth, Jonathan, 16, 58
withdrawal, as a method of contraception,
  A4.6.2, A4.6.3
Wollstonecraft, Mary, 275–276
womb — see uterus
women, 275–299
  cancer of reproductive organs, 298–299,
    A10.7.1–A10.11.1
  employment, 130–131, 149–150
  occupation, 24, 129–132, 146–147, 149
  reproductive hazards, 146–147
  social class, 129–132
  see also — mother
Women's Co–operative Guild, 192, 292, 308
workforce returns — see staff
workhouses, 192
Working Group on Specialist Medical
  Training, 210
Working Party on Antenatal and Intrapartum
  Care, 201
World Fertility Survey, 93
World Health Organisation (WHO), 7–15,

446